MONSTER
THEORY

MONSTER THEORY

Reading Culture

Jeffrey Jerome Cohen, editor

University of Minnesota Press
Minneapolis
London

An earlier version of Chapter 2 was first published in *In Geardagum* (June 1992), reprinted by permission. Chapter 3 originally appeared in Daniel Fischlin, ed., *Negation, Critical Theory, and Postmodern Textuality,* copyright 1994 Kluwer Academic Publishers, reprinted by permission.

Published by the University of Minnesota Press
111 Third Avenue South, Suite 290, Minneapolis, MN 55401–2520
Printed in the United States of America on acid-free paper

Library of Congress Cataloging-in-Publication Data

Monster theory : reading culture / Jeffrey Jerome Cohen, editor.
p. cm.
Includes bibliographical references and index.
ISBN 0-8166-2854-8 (hardcover). — ISBN 0-8166-2855-6 (pbk.)
1. Monsters in literature. 2. Abnormalities, Human, in literature. 3. Grotesque in literature. 4. Difference (Psychology) in literature. I. Cohen, Jeffrey Jerome.
PN56.M55M55 1996
809′.93353—dc20 96–21914

Contents

III. Monstrous Inquiry

IV. Monstrous History

Preface: In a Time of Monsters

We live in a time of monsters.

Channel-surf for a moment. Britain's Channel Four reports a new menace of the technological to be practiced against the organic: Russia has developed a terrorist's dream weapon, a nuclear bomb the size of a baseball that utilizes a mysterious compound called red mercury to "destroy human life but leave buildings and machinery intact." This explosive device contributes to the widespread fear that the synthetic and mechanistic is destined to eradicate its own creators—an anxiety that could be labeled Frankenstein's monster syndrome. Dr. Sam Cohen, the inventor of the neutron bomb, declares, "I find the entire business terrifying."[1]

The highest-grossing film of 1993—indeed, of all time—is Steven Spielberg's *Jurassic Park*. The plot of this movie-cum-marketing juggernaut involves the technology-assisted return from the dead of primordial monsters who menace the integrity of the American family by threatening to devour its children. That *Jurassic Park* would have been a far superior piece of cinema if its computer-animated velociraptors had in fact ingested the kids they merely threaten suggests that these monsters arrive at a time when traditional nuclear families perhaps need to be troubled.

"On November 2, 1993, Cincinnati voters amended the city's charter to bar the city council from enacting or enforcing laws that give equal legal protection to lesbian, gay, or bisexual citizens in seeking employment, housing, and public accommodations."[2] Colorado struggles with its own similar ban, while Hawaii debates the legality of same-sex marriages and the U.S. military wonders if straight soldiers are safe sharing the same dormitories and showers as gays.

When serial killer Jeffrey Dahmer was tried for his crimes, the press repeatedly linked his monstrousness (defined both psychologically and legally) to his sexuality; "normal" serial killers prey upon women and children (e.g., Ted Bundy, John Wayne Gacy). Jeffrey's father Lionel recently published *A Father's Story*, a biography that examines the early life of his cannibalistic son.[3] The book puzzles over how a boy who as a child seemed sweet and docile could turn out so terribly wrong.

The famous "surgeon's photo" of the Loch Ness monster has been revealed, through a deathbed confession, to have been a fake—a construction of twigs bound to a toy submarine. No explanation yet why three thousand other people have testified to seeing Nessie since the 1934 photograph was taken. Meanwhile, the yeti, sasquatch, and Champ (the monster of Lake Champlain) remain at large.

Support groups for men and women who have been abducted and maltreated by aliens are meeting in New York, Boston, and San Francisco. A Harvard psychiatrist who runs such gatherings recently published a book validating their experiences.[4]

Some new and recent films: *Bram Stoker's Dracula, Wolf, Mary Shelley's Frankenstein, Interview with the Vampire, Mary Reilly, Species,* and *Nightmare on Elm Street VI.*

This collection of cultural sound bites, taken almost at random from the media barrage constitutive of postmodern living, embodies (in monstrous form) a commentary upon fin de siècle America, a society that has created and commodified "ambient fear"—a kind of total fear that saturates day-to-day living, prodding and silently antagonizing but never speaking its own name.[5] This anxiety manifests itself symptomatically as a cultural fascination with monsters—a fixation that is born of the twin desire to name that which is difficult to apprehend and to domesticate (and therefore disempower) that which threatens. And so the monster appears simultaneously as the demonic disemboweler of slasher films and as a wide-eyed, sickeningly cute plush toy for children: velociraptor and Barney.[6]

The contributors to this volume acknowledge that we live in a time of monsters. Together, we explore what happens when monstrousness is taken seriously, as a mode of cultural discourse. This examination necessarily involves how the manifold boundaries (temporal, geographic, bodily, technological) that constitute "culture" become imbricated in the construction of the monster—a category that is itself a kind of limit case, an extreme version of marginalization, an abjecting epistemological device basic to the mechanics of deviance construction and identity formation. Although the methods vary and the modes of interrogation span a wide range of critical praxes, what unites all of the contributors (regardless of the specific temporal or spatial boundaries of their discourse) is an insistence that the monster is a *problem* for cultural studies, a code or a pattern or a presence or an absence that unsettles what has been constructed to be received as natural, as human. As a group we have been especially interested in those time periods that are currently underrepresented in cultural studies (especially the Middle Ages and early modern period), but we realize that if we turn to the past—even the recent past—as a place to do our monstrous work, it is only because the monsters of the present have beckoned us to those paths.

The contents of this book are arranged under loose, suggestive rubrics that are meant to instigate a chain of resonances rather than delimit singular meanings. The most obvious organization for a book of this kind would perhaps be a chronological ordering of its contents, but such a valorization of time as the primary determinant of meaning goes against what much of this collection asserts. The monster is a category that is not bound by classificatory structurations, least of all one as messy and inadequate as time. To order the contents of this volume diachronically would implicitly argue for a progress narrative that, as I state in "Monster Culture (Seven Theses)," does not—*cannot*—exist. One of my objectives as editor of this collection is to counter the presentism that characterizes contemporary cultural studies, its mistaken apotheosis of the postmodern Now over a Past it dismisses as irrelevant. Premodern and early modern periods are typically ignored in essay collections like this one, but in a book on monsters such an omission would doom the project to failure. The monster is that uncertain cultural body in which is condensed an intriguing simultaneity or doubleness: like the ghost of Hamlet, it introjects the disturbing, repressed, but formative traumas of "pre-" into the sensory moment of "post-," binding the one irrevocably to the other. The monster commands, "Remember me": restore my fragmented body, piece me back together, allow the past its eternal return. The monster *haunts*; it does not simply bring past and present together, but destroys the boundary that demanded their twinned foreclosure. Joan Copjec makes a similar argument within a psychoanalytic paradigm, in terms of "what Freud would call the latency of historical time with regard to its own comprehension":

> This notion of latency must not be positivized, as though something lay dormant but already formed in the past, and simply waited to emerge at some future time; this would indeed be a continuist notion. Instead, latency designates our inaccessibility to ourselves, and hence our dependence on others—on other times as well as other subjects.[7]

We can go further and predict that the repression of these "other times" and "other subjects" will be fatal to cultural studies if its uncritical use of the temporal as a disciplinary marker is not challenged.

Given that monstrosity challenges a coherent or totalizing concept of history, what else could contain the monstrous contents of this book beside suggestive and *provisional* groupings? The three essays grouped under the rubric "Monster Theory" foreground the critical underpinnings of their inquiry. My own "Monster Culture (Seven Theses)" is a kind of toolbox: a series of reconfigurable postulates about the relationship between monstrous and cultural bodies. Freely blending the medieval with the postmodern (*Beowulf* with *Alien*, Richard III with Lestat), I argue that the monster is best understood as an embodiment of difference, a breaker of category, and a resistant Other known only through process and movement, never through dissection-table analysis. In "*Beowulf* as Palimpsest," Ruth Waterhouse draws out one of the central concerns of the collection, antidiachronicity: following the insights of the deconstructionists and the theorists of intertextuality, she argues that we can and should read backward from the present, in a "progression" that makes a problem of temporality rather than simply reinscribes it. And so Grendel is filtered through such intervening texts as *Dracula* and *Dr. Jekyll and Mr. Hyde.* In "Monstrosity, Illegibility, Denegation," David L. Clark problematizes the relationship between monster and text even further, by arguing for the monstrous nature of language itself; through a close reading of a poem by bp Nichols, he argues that language—the thing that speaks us, as speaking subjects—is inherently inhuman. Language, monstrosity, *demonstration*—these are the links that bind monster theory, and the collection.

Part II, "Monstrous Identity," gathers four essays exploring how the categories "human" and "monster" are coincipient, mutually constitutive, monstrously hybrid. Anne Lake Prescott ("The Odd Couple") scrutinizes the conjoining of giants and dwarves in Renaissance England. This strange admixture creates an "anamorphic monster" that in turn validates the "paradoxical virtues of defect." Allison Pingree's "America's 'United Siamese Brothers'" examines the ambiguous place between the "normal" and the monstrous that conjoined twins create and relates the nineteenth-century fascination with Chang and Eng's domestic life to postwar anxieties over national identity: the inseparability of Chang and Eng condenses anxieties about the unification of the North and South after the Civil War. David A. Hedrich Hirsch's "Liberty, Equality, Monstrosity" delivers a political reading of the body of that most famous of all monsters, Victor Frankenstein's despairing creature. In Hirsch's reading, familial structuration becomes entangled in the ideological apparatus of a state that extends sympathy only toward "certain people defined as one's kin, one's *patrie*." Family values exclude the monster, the Other who does not fit the construction of Selfsame.

Part III, "Monstrous Inquiry," conjoins epistemology, the discourses of science, and the process of cultural self-identification. Stephen Pender's "'No Monsters at the Resurrection'" scrutinizes some early modern doubled bodies that call into question boundary demarcations of all kinds. Through a careful analysis of public reaction to monstrous births, Pender undermines the prevailing critical notion that scientific discourse had "rescued" the monster from its embeddedness in a rhetoric of miracle and marvel by the late sixteenth century. Lawrence D. Kritzman's "Representing the Monster" relocates Montaigne's notions of deformity away from the physical and toward the cognitive. Through a provocative account of Montaigne's version of the Martin Guerre story, Kritzman argues that the monster offers a challenge not only to the "will to totality," but to the very nature of gender and subjectivity. "Hermaphrodites Newly Discovered," Kathleen Perry Long's contribution to the collection, examines how a satiric account of the court of Henri III, written across the doubly sexed body of the hermaphrodite, conducts a complex inquiry into the artificiality of both gender roles and language. Mary Baine Campbell ("*Anthropometamorphosis*") links John Bulwer's seventeenth-century treatise on "cosmetology" to the rise of the science of anthropology; at the birth of the discipline she finds, haunting inquiry, the monster.

The final section, "Monstrous History," brings past and present together in an exploration of how the monster has haunted and continues to haunt, informing (deforming) the very process of historiography. In "Vampire Culture," Frank Grady provides a detailed analysis of Anne Rice's wide-ranging *Vampire Chronicles* that converts an economic narrative into a monstrous one. The essay explores the place of the monster in late capitalism, its relation to a system that tries to make sense of art and value as both commodified history and aesthetic surplus. William Sayers explores the phenomenon of the revenant in Old Norse culture in his essay "The Alien and Alienated as Unquiet Dead." In the family sagas that form his field of interrogation, Sayers finds an attempt at "ethnogenesis," at creating a usable past that makes sense of a difficult present. Michael Uebel ("Unthinking the Monster") unpacks how this process of identity formation was conducted in another field of medieval historiography, in the writing of horrifying anti-Muslim polemic that purported to give an accurate account of the interaction between Christendom and Islam. By monsterizing Saracen alterity, Christians constructed their image of Self; Uebel turns to this field of "unthought" (what is abjected in the process of becoming Christian, what is constructed as monstrous) to build a theoretical framework for the reading of monsters more generally. Finally, John O'Neill's "Dinosaurs-R-Us" brings us all the way back to the moment of creation, to our own modern myth of Genesis in the dream of genetic engineering. O'Neill links this regressive fascination with the infantilization of science and the darker side of consumer culture. Monsters, he reaffirms, still serve as the ultimate incorporation of our anxieties—about history, about identity, about our very humanity. As they always will.

Notes

1. Quoted in *San Jose Mercury News*, April 13, 1994, 1F (from Reuters). It is likely that "red mercury" is a hoax (*Boston Globe*, August 25, 1994, 2), a monstrous imaginary substance that embodies and excites all kinds of anxieties about the changing world order; but even the insubstantial can be deadly, as the chain of murders in South Africa attributed to the quest for "red mercury" demonstrates (*Philadelphia Inquirer*, August 21, 1994, AO2). I am grateful to Mark Cohen for helping me pinpoint these references.

2. *Perspectives* (American Historical Society Newsletter) 32 (February 1994): 1.

3. Lionel Dahmer, *A Father's Story* (New York: William Morrow, 1994). This book is listed in the HOLLIS (Harvard Library) electronic catalog under the following suggestively linked topics that perhaps say everything about familial life in late-

twentieth-century America: "Fathers—United States—Biography," "Serial murders—Wisconsin—Milwaukee—Case studies," and "Murderers—Wisconsin—Milwaukee—Family relationships."

4. John E. Mack, *Abduction: Human Encounters with Aliens* (New York: Scribner's, 1994).

5. See Brian Massumi, "Everywhere You Want to Be: Introduction to Fear," in *The Politics of Everyday Fear,* ed. Brian Massumi (Minneapolis: University of Minnesota Press, 1993), 3–37.

6. Portions of this preface and of chapter 1, "Monster Culture (Seven Theses)," have twice been delivered as part of conference presentations. Invariably the audience giggles at the juxtaposition—so seemingly absurd—of the friendly mascot of PBS (Barney) and the equally but oppositely fictionalized dinosaur who thinks like a human and shreds flesh like the Alien (velociraptor). "That's not funny," I chide them, knowing full well that it is; what anxiety, then, do we hide by the laughter? What does the dismissal by declaration of absurd mismatch allow us *not* to have to think about?

I would like to take this opportunity to thank the members of the audiences at the Twenty-seventh Annual Center for Medieval and Early Renaissance Studies Conference (Binghamton, N.Y., October 1993) and the "Reading Monsters, Reading Culture" Conference at the University of Cincinnati (April 1994, where much of this introduction was the keynote address) for their helpfulness in thinking through this monstrous text.

7. Joan Copjec, "Introduction," in *Supposing the Subject,* ed. Joan Copjec (London: Verso, 1994), ix.

I Monster Theory

1 Monster Culture (Seven Theses)

Jeffrey Jerome Cohen

What I will propose here by way of a first foray, as entrance into this book of monstrous content, is a sketch of a new *modus legendi*: a method of reading cultures from the monsters they engender. In doing so, I will partially violate two of the sacred dicta of recent cultural studies: the compulsion to historical specificity and the insistence that all knowledge (and hence all cartographies of that knowledge) is local. Of the first I will say only that in cultural studies today history (disguised perhaps as "culture") tends to be fetishized as a *telos*, as a final determinant of meaning; post de Man, post Foucault, post Hayden White, one must bear in mind that history is just another text in a procession of texts, and not a guarantor of any singular signification. A movement away from the *longue durée* and toward microeconomies (of capital or of gender) is associated most often with Foucauldian criticism; yet recent critics have found that where Foucault went wrong was mainly in his details, in his minute specifics. Nonetheless, his methodology—his archaeology of ideas, his histories of unthought—remains with good reason the chosen route of inquiry for most cultural critics today, whether they work in postmodern cyberculture or in the Middle Ages.

And so I would like to make some grand gestures. We live in an age that has rightly given up on Unified Theory, an age when we realize that history (like "individuality," "subjectivity," "gender," and "culture") is composed of a multitude of fragments, rather than of smooth epistemological wholes. Some fragments will be collected here and bound temporarily together to form a loosely integrated net—or, better, an unassimilated hybrid, a monstrous body. Rather than argue a "theory of teratology," I offer by way of introduction to the essays that follow a set of breakable postulates in search of specific cultural moments. I offer seven theses toward understanding cultures through the monsters they bear.

Thesis I: The Monster's Body Is a Cultural Body

Vampires, burial, death: inter the corpse where the road forks, so that when it springs from the grave, it will not know which path to follow. Drive a stake through its heart: it will be stuck to the ground at the fork, it will haunt that place that leads to many other places, that point of indecision. Behead the corpse, so that, acephalic, it will not know itself as subject, only as pure body.

The monster is born only at this metaphoric crossroads, as an embodiment of a certain cultural moment—of a time, a feeling, and a place.[1] The monster's body quite literally incorporates fear, desire, anxiety, and fantasy (ataractic or incendiary), giving them life and an uncanny independence. The monstrous body is pure culture. A construct and a projection, the monster exists only to be read: the *monstrum* is etymologically "that which reveals," "that which warns," a glyph that seeks a hierophant. Like a letter on the page, the monster signifies something other than itself: it is always a displacement, always inhabits the gap between the time of upheaval that created it and the moment into which it is received, to be born again. These epistemological spaces between the monster's bones are Derrida's familiar chasm of *différance:* a genetic uncertainty principle, the essence of the monster's vitality, the reason it always rises from the dissection table as its secrets are about to be revealed and vanishes into the night.

Thesis II: The Monster Always Escapes

We see the damage that the monster wreaks, the material remains (the footprints of the yeti across Tibetan snow, the bones of the giant stranded on a rocky cliff), but the monster itself turns immaterial and vanishes, to reappear someplace else (for who is the yeti if not the medieval wild man? Who is the wild man if not the biblical and classical giant?). No matter how many times King Arthur killed the ogre of Mount Saint Michael, the monster reappeared in another heroic chronicle, bequeathing the Middle Ages an abundance of *morte d'Arthurs.* Regardless of how many times Sigourney Weaver's beleaguered Ripley utterly destroys the ambiguous Alien that stalks her, its monstrous progeny return, ready to stalk again in another bigger-than-ever sequel. No monster tastes of death but once. The anxiety that condenses like green vapor into the form of the vampire can be dispersed temporarily, but the revenant by definition returns. And so the monster's body is both corporal and incorporeal; its threat is its propensity to shift.

Each time the grave opens and the unquiet slumberer strides forth ("come from the dead, / Come back to tell you all"), the message proclaimed is transformed by the air that gives its speaker new life. Monsters must be examined within the intricate matrix of relations (social, cultural, and literary-historical) that generate them. In speaking of the new kind of vampire invented by Bram Stoker, we might explore the foreign count's transgressive but compelling sexuality, as subtly alluring to Jonathan Harker as Henry Irving, Stoker's mentor, was to Stoker.[2] Or we might analyze Murnau's self-loathing appropriation of the same demon in *Nosferatu,* where in the face of nascent fascism the undercurrent of desire surfaces in plague and bodily corruption. Anne Rice has given the myth a modern rewriting in which homosexuality and vampirism have been conjoined, apotheosized; that she has created a pop culture phenomenon in the process is not insignificant, especially at a time when gender as a construct has been scrutinized at almost every social register. In Francis Coppola's recent blockbuster, *Bram Stoker's Dracula,* the homosexual subtext present at least since the appearance of Sheridan Le Fanu's lesbian lamia (*Carmilla,* 1872) has, like the red corpuscles that serve as the film's leitmotif, risen to the surface, primarily as an AIDS awareness that transforms the disease of vampirism into a sadistic (and very medieval) form of redemption through the torments of the body in pain. No coincidence, then, that Coppola was putting together a documentary on AIDS at the same time he was working on *Dracula.*

In each of these vampire stories, the undead returns in slightly different clothing, each time to be read against contemporary social movements or a specific, determining event: *la décadence* and its new possibilities, homophobia and its hateful imperatives, the acceptance of new subjectivities unfixed by binary gender, a fin de siècle social activism paternalistic in its embrace. Discourse extracting a transcultural, transtemporal phenomenon labeled "the vampire" is of rather limited utility; even if vampiric figures are found almost worldwide, from ancient Egypt to modern Hollywood, each reappearance and its analysis is still bound in a double act of construction and reconstitution.[3] "Monster theory" must therefore concern itself with strings of cultural moments, connected by a logic that always threatens to shift; invigorated by change and escape, by the impossibility of achieving what Susan Stewart calls the desired "fall or death, the stopping" of its gigantic subject,[4] monstrous interpretation is as much process as epiphany, a work that must content itself with fragments (footprints, bones, talismans, teeth, shadows, obscured glimpses—signifiers of monstrous passing that stand in for the monstrous body itself).

Thesis III: The Monster Is the Harbinger of Category Crisis

The monster always escapes because it refuses easy categorization. Of the nightmarish creature that Ridley Scott brought to life in *Alien,* Harvey Greenberg writes:

> It is a Linnean nightmare, defying every natural law of evolution; by turns bivalve, crustacean, reptilian, and humanoid. It seems capable of lying dormant within its egg indefinitely. It sheds its skin like a snake, its carapace like an arthropod. It deposits its young into other species like a wasp. . . . It responds according to Lamarckian *and* Darwinian principles.[5]

This refusal to participate in the classificatory "order of things" is true of monsters generally: they are disturbing hybrids whose externally incoherent bodies resist attempts to include them in any systematic structuration. And so the monster is dangerous, a form suspended between forms that threatens to smash distinctions.

Because of its ontological liminality, the monster notoriously appears at times of crisis as a kind of third term that problematizes the clash of extremes—as "that which questions binary thinking and introduces a crisis."[6] This power to evade and to undermine has coursed through the monster's blood from classical times, when despite all the attempts of Aristotle (and later Pliny, Augustine, and Isidore) to incorporate the monstrous races[7] into a coherent epistemological system, the monster always escaped to return to its habitations at the margins of the world (a purely conceptual locus rather than a geographic one).[8] Classical "wonder books" radically undermine the Aristotelian taxonomic system, for by refusing an easy compartmentalization of their monstrous contents, they demand a radical rethinking of boundary and normality. The too-precise laws of nature as set forth by science are gleefully violated in the freakish compilation of the monster's body. A mixed category, the monster resists any classification built on hierarchy or a merely binary opposition, demanding instead a "system" allowing polyphony, mixed response (difference in sameness, repulsion in attraction), and resistance to integration—allowing what Hogle has called with a wonderful pun "a deeper play of differences, a nonbinary polymorphism at the 'base' of human nature."[9]

The horizon where the monsters dwell might well be imagined as the visible edge of the hermeneutic circle itself: the monstrous offers an escape from its hermetic path, an invitation to explore new spirals, new and interconnected methods of perceiving the world.[10] In the face of the monster, scientific inquiry and its ordered rationality crumble. The monstrous is a genus too large to be encapsulated in any conceptual system; the monster's very existence is a rebuke to boundary and enclosure; like the giants of *Mandeville's Travels,* it threatens to devour "all raw & quyk" any thinker who insists otherwise. The monster is in this way the living embodiment of the phenomenon Derrida has famously labeled the "supplement" (*ce dangereux supplément*):[11] it breaks apart bifurcating, "either/or" syllogistic logic with a kind of reasoning closer to "and/or," introducing what Barbara Johnson has called "a revolution in the very logic of meaning."[12]

Full of rebuke to traditional methods of organizing knowledge and human experience, the geography of the monster is an imperiling expanse, and therefore always a contested cultural space.

Thesis IV: The Monster Dwells at the Gates of Difference

The monster is difference made flesh, come to dwell among us. In its function as dialectical Other or third-term supplement, the monster is an incorporation of the Outside, the Beyond—of all those loci that are rhetorically placed as distant and distinct but originate Within. Any kind of alterity can be inscribed across (constructed through) the monstrous body, but for the most part monstrous difference tends to be cultural, political, racial, economic, sexual.

The exaggeration of cultural difference into monstrous aberration is familiar enough. The most famous distortion occurs in the Bible, where the aboriginal inhabitants of Canaan are envisioned as menacing giants to justify the Hebrew colonization of the Promised Land (Numbers 13). Representing an anterior culture as monstrous justifies its displacement or extermination by rendering the act heroic. In medieval France the *chansons de geste* celebrated the crusades by transforming Muslims into demonic caricatures whose menacing lack of humanity was readable from their bestial attributes; by culturally glossing "Saracens" as "monstra," propagandists rendered rhetorically admissible the annexation of the East by the West. This representational project was part of a whole dictionary of strategic glosses in which "monstra" slipped into significations of the feminine and the hypermasculine.

A recent newspaper article on Yugoslavia reminds us how persistent these divisive mythologies can be, and how they can endure divorced from any grounding in historical reality:

> A Bosnian Serb militiaman, hitchhiking to Sarajevo, tells a reporter in all earnestness that the Muslims are feeding Serbian children to the animals in the zoo. The story is nonsense. There aren't any animals left alive in the Sarajevo zoo. But the militiaman is convinced and can recall all the wrongs that Muslims may or may not have perpetrated during their 500 years of rule.[13]

In the United States, Native Americans were presented as unredeemable savages so that the powerful political machine of Manifest Destiny could push westward with disregard. Scattered throughout Europe by the Diaspora and steadfastly refusing assimilation into Christian society, Jews have been perennial favorites for xenophobic misrepresentation, for here was an alien culture living, working, and even at times prospering within vast communities dedicated to becoming homogeneous and monolithic. The Middle Ages accused the Jews of crimes ranging from the bringing of the plague to bleeding Christian children to make their Passover meal. Nazi Germany simply brought these ancient traditions of hate to their conclusion, inventing a Final Solution that differed from earlier persecutions only in its technological efficiency.

Political or ideological difference is as much a catalyst to monstrous representation on a micro level as cultural alterity in the macrocosm. A political figure suddenly out of favor is transformed like an unwilling participant in a science experiment by the appointed historians of the replacement regime: "monstrous history" is rife with sudden, Ovidian metamorphoses, from Vlad Tepes to Ronald Reagan. The most illustrious of these propaganda-bred demons is the English king Richard III, whom Thomas More famously described as "little of stature, ill fetured of limmes, croke backed, his left shoulder much higher then his right, hard fauoured of visage. . . . hee came into the worlde with feete forward, . . . also not vntothed."[14] From birth, More declares, Richard was a monster, "his deformed body a readable text"[15] on which was inscribed his deviant morality (indistinguishable from an incorrect political orientation).

The almost obsessive descanting on Richard from Polydor Vergil in the Renaissance to the Friends of Richard III Incorporated in our own era demonstrates the process of "monster theory" at its most active: culture gives birth to a monster before our eyes, painting over the normally proportioned Richard who once lived, raising his shoulder to deform simultaneously person, cultural response, and the possibility of objectivity.[16] History itself becomes a monster: defeaturing, self-deconstructive, always in danger of exposing the sutures that bind its disparate elements into a single, unnatural body. At the same time Richard moves between Monster and Man, the disturbing suggestion arises that this incoherent body, denaturalized and always in peril of disaggregation, may well be our own.

The difficult project of constructing and maintaining gender identities elicits an array of anxious responses throughout culture, producing another impetus to teratogenesis. The woman who oversteps the boundaries of her gender role risks becoming a Scylla, Weird Sister, Lilith ("die erste Eva," "la mère obscuré"),[17] Bertha Mason, or Gorgon.[18] "Deviant" sexual identity is similarly susceptible to monsterization. The great medieval encyclopedist Vincent of Beauvais describes the visit of a hermaphroditic cynocephalus to the French court in his *Speculum naturale* (31.126).[19] Its male reproductive organ is said to be disproportionately large, but the monster could use either sex at its own discretion. Bruno Roy writes of this fantastic hybrid: "What warning did he come to deliver to the king? He came to bear witness to sexual norms. . . . He embodied the punishment earned by those who violate sexual taboos."[20] This strange creature, a composite of the supposedly discrete categories "male" and "female," arrives before King Louis to validate heterosexuality over homosexuality, with its supposed inversions and transformations ("Equa fit equus," one Latin writer declared; "The horse becomes a mare").[21] The strange dog-headed monster is a living excoriation of gender ambiguity and sexual abnormality, as Vincent's cultural moment defines them: heteronormalization incarnate.

From the classical period into the twentieth century, race has been almost as powerful a catalyst to the creation of monsters as culture, gender, and sexuality. Africa early became the West's significant other, the sign of its ontological difference simply being skin color. According to the Greek myth of Phaëton, the denizens of mysterious and uncertain Ethiopia were black because they had been scorched by the too-close passing of the sun. The Roman naturalist Pliny assumed nonwhite skin to be symptomatic of a complete difference in temperament and attributed Africa's darkness to climate; the intense heat, he said, had burned the Africans' skin and malformed their bodies (*Natural History*, 2.80). These differences were quickly moralized through a pervasive rhetoric of deviance. Paulinus of Nola, a wealthy landowner turned early church homilist, explained that the Ethiopians had been scorched by sin and vice rather than by the sun, and the anonymous commentator to Theodulus's influential *Ecloga* (tenth century) succinctly glossed the meaning of the word *Ethyopium*: "Ethiopians, that is, sinners. Indeed, sinners can rightly be compared to Ethiopians, who are black men presenting a terrifying appearance to those beholding them."[22] Dark skin was associated with the fires of hell, and so signified in Christian mythology demonic provenance. The perverse and exaggerated sexual appetite of monsters generally was quickly affixed to the Ethiopian; this linking was only strengthened by a xenophobic backlash as dark-skinned people were forcibly imported into Europe early in the Renaissance. Narratives of miscegenation arose and circulated to sanction official policies of exclusion; Queen Elizabeth is famous for her anxiety over "blackamoores" and their supposed threat to the "increase of people of our own nation."[23]

Through all of these monsters the boundaries between personal and national bodies blur. To complicate this category confusion further, one kind of alterity is often written as another, so that national difference (for example) is transformed into sexual difference. Giraldus Cambrensis demonstrates just this slippage of the foreign in his *Topography of Ireland*; when he writes of the Irish (ostensibly simply to provide information about them to a curious English court, but actually as a first step toward invading and colonizing the island), he observes:

> It is indeed a most filthy race, a race sunk in vice, a race more ignorant than all other nations of the first principles of faith.... These people who have customs so different from others, and so opposite to them, on making signs either with the hands or the head, beckon when they mean that

> you should go away, and nod backwards as often as they wish to be rid of you. Likewise, in this nation, the men pass their water sitting, the women standing. . . . The women, also, as well as the men, ride astride, with their legs stuck out on each side of the horse.[24]

One kind of inversion becomes another as Giraldus deciphers the alphabet of Irish culture—and reads it backwards, against the norm of English masculinity. Giraldus creates a vision of monstrous gender (aberrant, demonstrative): the violation of the cultural codes that valence gendered behaviors creates a rupture that must be cemented with (in this case) the binding, corrective mortar of English normalcy. A bloody war of subjugation followed immediately after the promulgation of this text, remained potent throughout the High Middle Ages, and in a way continues to this day.

Through a similar discursive process the East becomes feminized (Said) and the soul of Africa grows dark (Gates).[25] One kind of difference becomes another as the normative categories of gender, sexuality, national identity, and ethnicity slide together like the imbricated circles of a Venn diagram, abjecting from the center that which becomes the monster. This violent foreclosure erects a self-validating, Hegelian master/slave dialectic that naturalizes the subjugation of one cultural body by another by writing the body excluded from personhood and agency as in every way different, monstrous. A polysemy is granted so that a greater threat can be encoded; multiplicity of meanings, paradoxically, iterates the same restricting, agitprop representations that narrowed signification performs. Yet a danger resides in this multiplication: as difference, like a Hydra, sprouts two heads where one has been lopped away, the possibilities of escape, resistance, disruption arise with more force.

René Girard has written at great length about the real violence these debasing representations enact, connecting monsterizing depiction with the phenomenon of the scapegoat. Monsters are never created *ex nihilo,* but through a process of fragmentation and recombination in which elements are extracted "from various forms" (including—indeed, especially—marginalized social groups) and then assembled as the monster, "which can then claim an independent identity."[26] The political-cultural monster, the embodiment of radical difference, paradoxically threatens to *erase* difference in the world of its creators, to demonstrate

> the potential for the system to differ from its own difference, in other words not to be different at all, to cease to exist as a system.... Difference that exists outside the system is terrifying because it reveals the truth of the system, its relativity, its fragility, and its mortality.... Despite what is said around us persecutors are never obsessed with difference but rather by its unutterable contrary, the lack of difference.[27]

By revealing that difference is arbitrary and potentially free-floating, mutable rather than essential, the monster threatens to destroy not just individual members of a society, but the very cultural apparatus through which individuality is constituted and allowed. Because it is a body across which difference has been repeatedly written, the monster (like Frankenstein's creature, that combination of odd somatic pieces stitched together from a community of cadavers) seeks out its author to demand its raison d'être—and to bear witness to the fact that it could have been constructed Otherwise. Godzilla trampled Tokyo; Girard frees him here to fragment the delicate matrix of relational systems that unite every private body to the public world.

Thesis V: The Monster Polices the Borders of the Possible

The monster resists capture in the epistemological nets of the erudite, but it is something more than a Bakhtinian ally of the popular. From its position at the limits of knowing, the monster stands as a warning against exploration of its uncertain demesnes. The giants of Patagonia, the dragons of the Orient, and the dinosaurs of Jurassic Park together declare that curiosity is more often punished than rewarded, that one is better off safely contained within one's own domestic sphere than abroad, away from the watchful eyes of the state. The monster prevents mobility (intellectual, geographic, or sexual), delimiting the social spaces through which private bodies may move. To step outside this official geography is to risk attack by some monstrous border patrol or (worse) to become monstrous oneself.

Lycaon, the first werewolf in Western literature, undergoes his lupine metamorphosis as the culmination of a fable of hospitality.[28] Ovid relates how the primeval giants attempted to plunge the world into anarchy by wrenching Olympus from the gods, only to be shattered by divine thunderbolts. From their scattered blood arose a race of men who continued their fathers' malignant ways.[29] Among this wicked progeny was Lycaon, king of Arcadia. When Jupiter arrived as a guest at his house,

Lycaon tried to kill the ruler of the gods as he slept, and the next day served him pieces of a servant's body as a meal. The enraged Jupiter punished this violation of the host-guest relationship by transforming Lycaon into a monstrous semblance of that lawless, godless state to which his actions would drag humanity back:

> The king himself flies in terror and, gaining the fields, howls aloud, attempting in vain to speak. His mouth of itself gathers foam, and with his accustomed greed for blood he turns against the sheep, delighting still in slaughter. His garments change to shaggy hair, his arms to legs. He turns into a wolf, and yet retains some traces of his former shape.[30]

The horribly fascinating loss of Lycaon's humanity merely reifies his previous moral state; the king's body is rendered all transparence, instantly and insistently readable. The power of the narrative prohibition peaks in the lingering description of the monstrously composite Lycaon, at that median where he is both man and beast, dual natures in a helpless tumult of assertion. The fable concludes when Lycaon can no longer speak, only signify.

Whereas monsters born of political expedience and self-justifying nationalism function as living invitations to action, usually military (invasions, usurpations, colonizations), the monster of prohibition polices the borders of the possible, interdicting through its grotesque body some behaviors and actions, envaluing others. It is possible, for example, that medieval merchants intentionally disseminated maps depicting sea serpents like Leviathan at the edges of their trade routes in order to discourage further exploration and to establish monopolies.[31] Every monster is in this way a double narrative, two living stories: one that describes how the monster came to be and another, its testimony, detailing what cultural use the monster serves. The monster of prohibition exists to demarcate the bonds that hold together that system of relations we call culture, to call horrid attention to the borders that cannot—*must* not—be crossed.

Primarily these borders are in place to control the traffic in women, or more generally to establish strictly homosocial bonds, the ties between men that keep a patriarchal society functional. A kind of herdsman, this monster delimits the social space through which cultural bodies may move, and in classical times (for example) validated a tight, hierarchical system of naturalized leadership and control where every man had a functional place.[32] The prototype in Western culture for this kind of "geographic" monster is Homer's Polyphemos. The quintessential xenophobic rendition of the foreign (the *barbaric*—that which is unintelligible within a given cultural-linguistic system),[33] the Cyclopes are represented as savages who have not "a law to bless them" and who lack the *techne* to produce (Greek-style) civilization. Their archaism is conveyed through their lack of hierarchy and of a politics of precedent. This dissociation from community leads to a rugged individualism that in Homeric terms can only be horrifying. Because they live without a system of tradition and custom, the Cyclopes are a danger to the arriving Greeks, men whose identities are contingent upon a compartmentalized function within a deindividualizing system of subordination and control. Polyphemos's victims are devoured, engulfed, made to vanish from the public gaze: cannibalism as incorporation into the wrong cultural body.

The monster is a powerful ally of what Foucault calls "the society of the panopticon," in which "polymorphous conducts [are] actually extracted from people's bodies and from their pleasures . . . [to be] drawn out, revealed, isolated, intensified, incorporated, by multifarious power devices."[34] Susan Stewart has observed that "the monster's sexuality takes on a separate life";[35] Foucault helps us to see why. The monster embodies those sexual practices that must not be committed, or that may be committed only through the body of the monster. *She* and *Them!*: the monster enforces the cultural codes that regulate sexual desire.

Anyone familiar with the low-budget science fiction movie craze of the 1950s will recognize in the preceding sentence two superb films of the genre, one about a radioactive virago from outer space who kills every man she touches, the other a social parable in which giant ants (really, Communists) burrow beneath Los Angeles (that is, Hollywood) and threaten world peace (that is, American conservatism). I connect these two seemingly unrelated titles here to call attention to the anxieties that monsterized their subjects in the first place, and to enact syntactically an even deeper fear: that the two will join in some unholy miscegenation. We have seen that the monster arises at the gap where difference is perceived as dividing a recording voice from its captured subject; the criterion of this division is arbitrary, and can range from anatomy or skin color to religious belief, custom, and political ideology. The monster's destructiveness is really a deconstructiveness: it threatens to reveal that difference originates in process, rather than in fact (and that "fact" is subject to constant reconstruction and change). Given that the recorders of the history of the West have been mainly European and male, women (*She*) and nonwhites (*Them!*) have found themselves repeatedly transformed into monsters, whether to validate specific alignments of masculinity and whiteness, or simply to be pushed from its realm of thought.[36] Feminine and cultural others are monstrous enough by themselves in patriarchal society, but when they threaten to mingle, the entire economy of desire comes under attack.

As a vehicle of prohibition, the monster most often arises to enforce the laws of exogamy, both the incest taboo (which establishes a traffic in women by mandating that they marry outside their families) and the decrees against interracial sexual mingling (which limit the parameters of that traffic by policing the boundaries of culture, usually in the service of some notion of group "purity").[37] Incest narratives are common to every tradition and have been extensively documented, mainly owing to Lévi-Strauss's elevation of the taboo to the founding base of patriarchal society. Miscegenation, that intersection of misogyny (gender anxiety) and racism (no matter how naive), has received considerably less critical attention. I will say a few words about it here.

The Bible has long been the primary source for divine decrees against interracial mixing. One of these pronouncements is a straightforward command from God that comes through the mouth of the prophet Joshua (Joshua 23:12ff.); another is a cryptic episode in Genesis much elaborated during the medieval period, alluding to "sons of God" who impregnate the "daughters of men" with a race of wicked giants (Genesis 6:4). The monsters are here, as elsewhere, expedient representations of other cultures, generalized and demonized to enforce a strict notion of group sameness. The fears of contamination, impurity, and loss of identity that produce stories like the Genesis episode are strong, and they reappear incessantly. Shakespeare's Caliban, for example, is the product of such an illicit mingling, the "freckled whelp" of the Algerian witch Sycorax and the devil. Charlotte Brontë reversed the usual paradigm in *Jane Eyre* (white Rochester and lunatic Jamaican Bertha Mason), but horror movies as seemingly innocent as *King Kong* demonstrate miscegenation anxiety in its brutal essence. Even a film as recent as 1979's immensely successful *Alien* may have a cognizance of the fear in its underworkings: the grotesque creature that stalks the heroine (dressed in the final scene only in her underwear) drips a glistening slime of K-Y Jelly from its teeth; the jaw tendons are constructed of shredded condoms; and the man inside the rubber suit is Bolaji Badejo, a Masai tribesman standing seven feet tall who happened to be studying in England at the time the film was cast.[38]

The narratives of the West perform the strangest dance around that fire in which miscegenation and its practitioners have been condemned to burn. Among the flames we see the old women of Salem hanging, accused of sexual relations with the black devil; we suspect they died because they crossed a different border, one that prohibits women from managing property and living solitary, unmanaged lives. The flames devour the Jews of thirteenth-century England, who stole children from proper families and baked seder matzo with their blood; as a menace to the survival of English race and culture, they were expelled from the country and their property confiscated. A competing narrative again implicates monstrous economics—the Jews were the money lenders, the state and its commerce were heavily indebted to them—but this second story is submerged in a horrifying fable of cultural purity and threat to Christian continuance. As the American frontier expanded beneath the banner of Manifest Destiny in the nineteenth century, tales circulated about how "Indians" routinely kidnapped white women to furnish wives for themselves; the West was a place of danger waiting to be tamed into farms, its menacing native inhabitants fit only to be dispossessed. It matters little that the protagonist of Richard Wright's *Native Son* did not rape and butcher his employer's daughter; that narrative is supplied by the police, by an angry white society, indeed by Western history itself. In the novel, as in life, the threat occurs when a nonwhite leaves the reserve abandoned to him; Wright envisions what happens when the horizon of narrative expectation is firmly set, and his conclusion (born out in seventeenth-century Salem, medieval England, and nineteenth-century America) is that the actual circumstances of history tend to vanish when a narrative of miscegenation can be supplied.

The monster is transgressive, too sexual, perversely erotic, a lawbreaker; and so the monster and all that it embodies must be exiled or destroyed. The repressed, however, like Freud himself, always seems to return.

Thesis VI: Fear of the Monster Is Really a Kind of Desire

The monster is continually linked to forbidden practices, in order to normalize and to enforce. The monster also attracts. The same creatures who terrify and interdict can evoke potent escapist fantasies; the linking of monstrosity with the forbidden makes the monster all the more appealing as a temporary egress from constraint. This simultaneous repulsion and attraction at the core of the monster's composition accounts greatly for its continued cultural popularity, for the fact that the monster seldom can be contained in a simple, binary dialectic (thesis, antithesis . . . no synthesis). We distrust and loathe the monster at the same time we envy its freedom, and perhaps its sublime despair.

Through the body of the monster fantasies of aggression, domination, and inversion are allowed safe expression in a clearly delimited and permanently liminal space. Escapist delight gives way to horror only when the monster threatens to overstep these boundaries, to destroy or deconstruct the thin walls of category and culture. When contained by geographic, generic, or epistemic marginalization, the monster can function as an alter ego, as an alluring projection of (an Other) self. The monster awakens one to the pleasures of the body, to the simple and fleeting joys of being frightened, or frightening—to the experience of mortality and corporality. We watch the monstrous spectacle of the horror film because we know that the cinema is a temporary place, that the jolting sensuousness of the celluloid images will be followed by reentry into the world of comfort and light.[39] Likewise, the story on the page before us may horrify (whether it appears in the *New York Times* news section or Stephen King's latest novel matters little), so long as we are safe in the knowledge of its nearing end (the number of pages in our right hand is dwindling) and our liberation from it. Aurally received narratives work no differently; no matter how unsettling the description of the giant, no matter how many unbaptized children and hapless knights he devours, King Arthur will ultimately destroy him. The audience knows how the genre works.

Times of carnival temporally marginalize the monstrous, but at the same time allow it a safe realm of expression and play: on Halloween everyone is a demon for a night. The same impulse to ataractic fantasy is behind much lavishly bizarre manuscript marginalia, from abstract scribblings at the edges of an ordered page to preposterous animals and vaguely humanoid creatures of strange anatomy that crowd a biblical text. Gargoyles and ornately sculpted grotesques, lurking at the crossbeams or upon the roof of the cathedral, likewise record the liberating fantasies of a bored or repressed hand suddenly freed to populate the margins. Maps and travel accounts inherited from antiquity invented whole geographies of the mind and peopled them with exotic and fantastic creatures; Ultima Thule, Ethiopia, and the Antipodes were the medieval equivalents of outer space and virtual reality, imaginary (wholly verbal) geographies accessible from anywhere, never meant to be discovered but always waiting to be explored. Jacques Le Goff has written that the Indian Ocean (a "mental horizon" imagined, in the Middle Ages, to be completely enclosed by land) was a cultural space

> where taboos were eliminated or exchanged for others. The weirdness of this world produced an impression of liberation and freedom. The strict morality imposed by the Church was contrasted with the discomfiting attractiveness of a world of bizarre tastes, which practiced coprophagy and cannibalism; of bodily innocence, where man, freed of the modesty of clothing, rediscovered nudism and sexual freedom; and where, once rid of restrictive monogamy and family barriers, he could give himself over to polygamy, incest, and eroticism.[40]

The habitations of the monsters (Africa, Scandinavia, America, Venus, the Delta Quadrant—whatever land is sufficiently distant to be exoticized) are more than dark regions of uncertain danger: they are also realms of happy fantasy, horizons of liberation. Their monsters serve as secondary bodies through which the possibilities of other genders, other sexual practices, and other social customs can be explored. Hermaphrodites, Amazons, and lascivious cannibals beckon from the edges of the world, the most distant planets of the galaxy.

The co-optation of the monster into a symbol of the desirable is often accomplished through the neutralization of potentially threatening aspects with a liberal dose of comedy: the thundering giant becomes the bumbling giant.[41] Monsters may still function, however, as the vehicles of causative fantasies even without their valences reversed. What Bakhtin calls "official culture" can transfer all that is viewed as undesirable in itself into the body of the monster, performing a wish-fulfillment drama of its own; the scapegoated monster is perhaps ritually destroyed in the course of some official narrative, purging the community by eliminating its sins. The monster's eradication functions as an exorcism and, when retold and promulgated, as a catechism. The monastically manufactured *Queste del Saint Graal* serves as an ecclesiastically sanctioned antidote to the looser morality of the secular romances; when Sir Bors comes across a castle where "ladies of high descent and rank" tempt him to sexual indulgence, these ladies are, of course, demons in lascivious disguise. When Bors refuses to sleep with one of these transcorporal devils (described as "so lovely and so fair that it seemed all earthly beauty was embodied in her"), his steadfast assertion of control banishes them all shrieking back to hell.[42] The episode valorizes the celibacy so central to the authors' belief system (and so difficult to enforce) while inculcating a lesson in morality for the work's intended secular audience, the knights and courtly women fond of romances.

Seldom, however, are monsters as uncomplicated in their use and manufacture as the demons that haunt Sir Bors. Allegory may flatten a monster rather thin, as when the vivacious demon of the Anglo-Saxon hagiographic poem *Juliana* becomes the one-sided complainer of Cynewulf's *Elene*. More often, however, the monster retains a haunting complexity. The dense symbolism that makes a thick description of the monsters in Spenser, Milton, and even *Beowulf* so challenging reminds us how permeable the monstrous body can be, how difficult to dissect.

This corporal fluidity, this simultaneity of anxiety and desire, ensures that the monster will always dangerously entice. A certain intrigue is allowed even Vincent of Beauvais's well-endowed cynocephalus, for he occupies a textual space of allure before his necessary dismissal, during which he is granted an undeniable charm. The monstrous lurks somewhere in that ambiguous, primal space between fear and attraction, close to the heart of what Kristeva calls "abjection":

> There looms, within abjection, one of those violent, dark revolts of being, directed against a threat that seems to emanate from an exorbitant outside or inside, ejected beyond the scope of the possible, the tolerable, the thinkable. It lies there, quite close, but it cannot be assimilated. It beseeches, worries, fascinates desire, which, nonetheless, does not let itself be seduced. Apprehensive, desire turns aside; sickened, it rejects. . . . But simultaneously, just the same, that impetus, that spasm, that leap is drawn toward an elsewhere as tempting as it is condemned. Unflaggingly, like an inescapable boomerang, a vortex of summons and repulsion places the one haunted by it literally beside himself.[43]

And the self that one stands so suddenly and so nervously beside is the monster.

The monster is the abjected fragment that enables the formation of all kinds of identities—personal, national, cultural, economic, sexual, psychological, universal, particular (even if that "particular" identity is an embrace of the power/status/knowledge of abjection itself); as such it reveals their partiality, their contiguity. A product of a multitude of morphogeneses (ranging from somatic to ethnic) that align themselves to imbue meaning to the Us and Them behind every cultural mode of seeing, the monster of abjection resides in that marginal geography of the Exterior, beyond the limits of the Thinkable, a place that is doubly dangerous: simultaneously "exorbitant" and "quite close." Judith Butler calls this conceptual locus "a domain of unlivability and unintelligibility that bounds the domain of intelligible effects," but points out that even when discursively closed off, it offers a base for critique, a margin from which to reread dominant paradigms.[44] Like Grendel thundering from the mere or Dracula creeping from the grave, like Kristeva's "boomerang, a vortex of summons" or the uncanny Freudian-Lacanian return of the repressed, the monster is always coming back, always at the verge of irruption.

Perhaps it is time to ask the question that always arises when the monster is discussed seriously (the inevitability of the question a symptom of the deep anxiety about what is and what should be thinkable, an anxiety that the process of monster theory is destined to raise): Do monsters really exist?

Surely they must, for if they did not, how could we?

Thesis VII: The Monster Stands at the Threshold . . . of Becoming

"This thing of darkness I acknowledge mine."

Monsters are our children. They can be pushed to the farthest margins of geography and discourse, hidden away at the edges of the world and in the forbidden recesses of our mind, but they always return. And when they come back, they bring not just a fuller knowledge of our place in history and the history of knowing our place, but they bear self-knowledge, *human* knowledge—and a discourse all the more sacred as it arises from the Outside. These monsters ask us how we perceive the world, and how we have misrepresented what we have attempted to place. They ask us to reevaluate our cultural assumptions about race, gender, sexuality, our perception of difference, our tolerance toward its expression. They ask us why we have created them.

Notes

1. Literally, here, *Zeitgeist*: Time Ghost, the bodiless spirit that uncannily incorporates a "place" that is a series of places, the crossroads that is a point in a *movement* toward an uncertain elsewhere. Bury the Zeitgeist by the crossroads: it is confused as it awakens, it is not going anywhere, it intersects everyplace; all roads lead back to the monster.

2. I realize that this is an interpretive biographical maneuver Barthes would surely have called "the living death of the author."

3. Thus the superiority of Joan Copjec's "Vampires, Breast-feeding, and Anxiety," *October* 58 (Fall 1991): 25–43, to Paul Barber's *Vampires, Burial, and Death: Folklore and Reality* (New Haven, Conn.: Yale University Press, 1988).

4. "The giant is represented through movement, through being in time. Even in the ascription of the still landscape to the giant, it is the activities of the giant, his or her legendary actions, that have resulted in the observable trace. In contrast to the still and perfect universe of the miniature, the gigantic represents the order and disorder of historical forces." Susan Stewart, *On Longing: Narratives of the Miniature, the Gigantic, the Souvenir, the Collection* (Baltimore: Johns Hopkins University Press, 1984), 86.

5. Harvey R. Greenberg, "Reimaging the Gargoyle: Psychoanalytic Notes on *Alien*," in *Close Encounters: Film, Feminism, and Science Fiction*, ed. Constance Penley, Elisabeth Lyon, Lynn Spigel, and Janet Bergstrom (Minneapolis: University of Minnesota Press, 1991), 90–91.

6. Marjorie Garber, *Vested Interests: Cross-Dressing and Cultural Anxiety* (New York: Routledge, 1992), 11. Garber writes at some length about "category crisis," which she defines as "a failure of definitional distinction, a borderline that becomes permeable, that permits of border crossings from one (apparently distinct) category to another: black/white, Jew/Christian, noble/bourgeois, master/servant, master/slave. . . . [That which crosses the border, like the transvestite] will always function as a mechanism of overdetermination—a mechanism of displacement from one blurred boundary to another. An analogy here might be the so-called 'tagged' gene that shows up in a genetic chain, indicating the presence of some otherwise hidden condition. It is not the gene itself, but its presence, that marks the trouble spot, indicating the likelihood of a crisis somewhere, elsewhere" (pp. 16–17). Note, however, that whereas Garber insists that the transvestite must be read *with* rather than *through*, the monster can be read only *through*—for the monster, pure culture, is nothing of itself.

7. These are the ancient monsters recorded first by the Greek writers Ktesias and Megasthenes, and include such wild imaginings as the Pygmies, the Sciapods (men with one large foot with which they can hop about at tremendous speed or that they can lift over their reclining bodies as a sort of beach umbrella), Blemmyae ("men whose heads / Do grow beneath their shoulders," in Othello's words), and Cynocephali, ferocious dog-headed men who are anthropophagous to boot. John Block Friedman has called these creatures the Plinian races, after the classical encyclopedist who bestowed them to the Middle Ages and early modern period. *The Monstrous Races in Medieval Art and Thought* (Cambridge: Harvard University Press, 1981).

8. The discussion of the implication of the monstrous in the manufacture of heuristics is partially based upon my essay "The Limits of Knowing: Monsters and the Regulation of Medieval Popular Culture," *Medieval Folklore* 3 (Fall 1994): 1–37.

9. Jerrold E. Hogle, "The Struggle for a Dichotomy: Abjection in Jekyll and His Interpreters," in *Dr. Jekyll and Mr. Hyde after One Hundred Years,* ed. William Veeder and Gordon Hirsch (Chicago: University of Chicago Press, 1988), 161.

10. "The hermeneutic circle does not permit access or escape to an uninterrupted reality; but we do not [have to] keep going around in the same path." Barbara Herrnstein Smith, "Belief and Resistance: A Symmetrical Account," *Critical Inquiry* 18 (Autumn 1991): 137–38.

11. Jacques Derrida, *Of Grammatology,* trans. Gayatri Chakravorty Spivak (Baltimore: Johns Hopkins University Press, 1974).

12. Barbara Johnson, "Introduction," in Jacques Derrida, *Dissemination,* trans. Barbara Johnson (Chicago: University of Chicago Press, 1981), xiii.

13. H. D. S. Greenway, "Adversaries Create Devils of Each Other," *Boston Globe,* December 15, 1992, 1.

14. Thomas More, *The Yale Edition of the Complete Works of Thomas More,* vol. 2, *The History of King Richard III,* ed. Richard S. Sylvester (New Haven, Conn.: Yale University Press, 1963), 7.

15. Marjorie Garber, *Shakespeare's Ghost Writers: Literature as Uncanny Causality* (New York: Routledge, Chapman & Hall, 1988), 30. My discussion of Richard is indebted to Marjorie Garber's provocative work.

16. "A portrait now in the Society of Antiquaries of London, painted about 1505, shows a Richard with straight shoulders. But a second portrait, possibly of earlier date, in the Royal Collection, seems to emblematize the whole controversy [over Richard 's supposed monstrosity], for in it, X-ray examination reveals an original straight shoulder line, which was subsequently painted over to present the raised right shoulder silhouette so often copied by later portraitists." Ibid., 35.

17. I am hinting here at the possibility of a feminist recuperation of the gendered monster by citing the titles of two famous books about Lilith (a favorite figure in feminist writing): Jacques Bril's *Lilith, ou, La Mere obscure* (Paris: Payot, 1981), and Siegmund Hurwitz's *Lilith, die erste Eva: Eine Studie uber dunkle Aspekte des Weiblichen* (Zurich: Daimon Verlag, 1980).

18. "The monster-woman, threatening to replace her angelic sister, embodies intransigent female autonomy and thus represents both the author's power to allay 'his' anxieties by calling their source bad names (witch, bitch, fiend, monster) and simultaneously, the mysterious power of the character who refuses to stay in her textually ordained 'place' and thus generates a story that 'gets away' from its author." Sandra M. Gilbert and Susan Gubar, *The Madwoman in the Attic: The Woman Writer and the Nineteenth Century Literary Imagination* (New Haven, Conn.: Yale University Press, 1984), 28. The "dangerous" role of feminine will in the engendering of monsters is also explored by Marie-Hélène Huet in *Monstrous Imagination* (Cambridge: Harvard University Press, 1993).

19. A cynocephalus is a dog-headed man, like the recently decanonized Saint Christopher. Bad enough to be a cynocephalus without being hermaphroditic to

boot: the monster accrues one kind of difference on top of another, like a magnet that draws differences into an aggregate, multivalent identity around an unstable core.

20. Bruno Roy, "En marge du monde connu: Les races de monstres," in *Aspects de la marginalité au Moyen Age,* ed. Guy-H Allard. (Quebec: Les Éditions de l'Aurore, 1975), 77. This translation is mine.

21. See, for example, Monica E. McAlpine, "The Pardoner's Homosexuality and How It Matters," *PMLA* 95 (1980): 8–22.

22. Cited by Friedman, *The Monstrous Races,* 64.

23. Elizabeth deported "blackamoores" in 1596 and again in 1601. See Karen Newman, "'And Wash the Ethiop White': Femininity and the Monstrous in Othello," in *Shakespeare Reproduced: The Text in History and Ideology,* ed. Jean E. Howard and Marion F. O'Connor (New York: Methuen, 1987), 148.

24. See Giraldus Cambrensis, *Topographia Hibernae (The History and Topography of Ireland),* trans. John J. O'Meara (Atlantic Highlands, N.J.: Humanities Press, 1982), 24.

25. See Edward Said, *Orientalism* (New York: Pantheon, 1978); Henry Louis Gates Jr., *The Signifying Monkey: A Theory of Afro-American Literature* (New York: Oxford University Press, 1988).

26. René Girard, *The Scapegoat,* trans. Yvonne Freccero (Baltimore: Johns Hopkins University Press, 1986), 33.

27. Ibid., 21–22.

28. Extended travel was dependent in both the ancient and medieval world on the promulgation of an ideal of hospitality that sanctified the responsibility of host to guest. A violation of that code is responsible for the destruction of the biblical Sodom and Gomorrah, for the devolution from man to giant in *Sir Gawain and the Carl of Carlisle,* and for the first punitive transformation in Ovid's *Metamorphoses.* This popular type of narrative may be conveniently labeled the fable of hospitality; such stories envalue the practice whose breach they illustrate through a drama repudiating the dangerous behavior. The valorization is accomplished in one of two ways: the host is a monster already and learns a lesson at the hands of his guest, or the host becomes a monster in the course of the narrative and audience members realize how they should conduct themselves. In either case, the cloak of monstrousness calls attention to those behaviors and attitudes the text is concerned with interdicting.

29. Ovid, *Metamorphoses* (Loeb Classical Library no. 42), ed. G. P. Goold (Cambridge: Harvard University Press, 1916, rpr. 1984), I.156–62.

30. Ibid., I.231–39.

31. I am indebted to Keeryung Hong of Harvard University for sharing her research on medieval map production for this hypothesis.

32. A useful (albeit politically charged) term for such a collective is *Männerbunde,* "all-male groups with aggression as one major function." See Joseph Harris, "Love and Death in the *Männerbund*: An Essay with Special Reference to the *Bjarkamál* and *The Battle of Maldon,*" in *Heroic Poetry in the Anglo-Saxon Period,* ed. Helen Damico and John Leyerle (Kalamazoo: Medieval Institute/Western Michigan State University, 1993), 78. See also the *Interscripta* discussion of "Medieval Masculinities," moderated and edited by Jeffrey Jerome Cohen, accessible via WWW: http://www.george-

town.edu/labyrinth/e-center/interscripta/mm.html (the piece is also forthcoming in a nonhypertext version in *Arthuriana*, as "The Armour of an Alienating Identity").

33. The Greek word *barbaros*, from which we derive the modern English word *barbaric*, means "making the sound *bar bar*"—that is, not speaking Greek, and therefore speaking nonsense.

34. Michel Foucault, *The History of Sexuality*, vol. 1, *An Introduction*, trans. Robert Hurley (New York: Vintage, 1990), 47–48.

35. Stewart, *On Longing*. See especially "The Imaginary Body," 104–31.

36. The situation was obviously far more complex than these statements can begin to show; "European," for example, usually includes only males of the Western Latin tradition. Sexual orientation further complicates the picture, as we shall see.

Donna Haraway, following Trinh Minh-ha, calls the humans beneath the monstrous skin "inappropriate/d others": "To be 'inappropriate/d' does not mean 'not to be in relation with'—i.e., to be in a special reservation, with the status of the authentic, the untouched, in the allochronic and allotropic condition of innocence. Rather to be an 'inappropriate/d other' means to be in critical deconstructive relationality, in a diffracting rather than reflecting (ratio)nality—as the means of making potent connection that exceeds domination." "The Promises of Monsters," in *Simians, Cyborgs, and Women: The Reinvention of Nature* (New York: Routledge, 1991), 299.

37. This discussion owes an obvious debt to Mary Douglas, *Purity and Danger: An Analysis of the Concepts of Pollution and Taboo* (New York: Routledge & Kegan Paul, 1966).

38. John Eastman, *Retakes: Behind the Scenes of 500 Classic Movies*, 9–10.

39. Paul Coates interestingly observes that "the horror film becomes the essential form of cinema, monstrous content manifesting itself in the monstrous form of the gigantic screen." *The Gorgon's Gaze* (Cambridge: Cambridge University Press, 1991), 77. Carol Clover locates some of the pleasure of the monster film in its cross-gender game of identification; see *Men, Women, and Chain Saws: Gender in the Modern Horror Film* (Princeton, N.J.: Princeton University Press, 1992). Why not go further, and call the pleasure cross-somatic?

40. Jacques Le Goff, "The Medieval West and the Indian Ocean," in *Time, Work and Culture in the Middle Ages*, trans. Arthur Goldhammer (Chicago: University of Chicago Press, 1980), 197. The postmodern equivalent of such spaces is Gibsonian cyberspace, with its MOOs and MUSHes and other arenas of unlimited possibility.

41. For Mikhail Bakhtin, famously, this is the transformative power of laughter: "Laughter liberates not only from external censorship but first of all from the great internal censor; it liberates from the fear that developed in man during thousands of years: fear of the sacred, fear of the prohibitions, of the past, of power." *Rabelais and His World*, trans. Hélène Iswolsky (Indianapolis: Indiana University Press, 1984), 94. Bakhtin traces the moment of escape to the point at which laughter became a part of the "higher levels of literature," when Rabelais wrote *Gargantua et Pantagruel*.

42. *The Quest for the Holy Grail*, trans. Pauline Matarasso (London: Penguin Books, 1969), 194.

43. Julia Kristeva, *The Powers of Horror: An Essay on Abjection*, trans. Leon S. Roudiez (New York: Columbia University Press, 1982), 1.

44. Judith Butler, *Bodies That Matter: On the Discursive Limits of "Sex"* (New York:

Routledge, 1993), 22. Both Butler and I have in mind here Foucault's notion of an emancipation of thought "from what it silently thinks" that will allow "it to think differently." Michel Foucault, *The Use of Pleasure,* trans. Robert Hurley (New York: Vintage, 1985), 9. Michael Uebel amplifies and applies this practice to the monster in his essay in this volume.

2 *Beowulf* as Palimpsest

Ruth Waterhouse

Beowulf includes a palimpsest of Grendel, in that in 107a, Scribe A originally wrote that Grendel was proscribed "in chames cynne [because of Ham's kin]."[1] The manuscript was altered from "chames" to "caines" ("because of Cain's kin"), as Ham (who was the second son of Noah) seemed less relevant than "Cain" to a reader, given the following lines with their reference to the killing of Abel.[2] Even during the period of the text's inscribing, an early reference to Grendel became a palimpsest, as one interpretation succeeded another for reasons we can now only deduce from context.[3]

The interpretation of Grendel has been changing from the beginning, as he has been recontextualized, especially since Tolkien popularized him as a monster.[4] The palimpsest concept has by extension come to allude not only to reinscribings such as the literal and physical reference to Grendel's being of Cain's rather than Ham's kin, but also as an extended metaphor for what has been increasingly recognized in recent years, that studies of Old English texts reveal as much about the period of and cultural influences on the decoder as about the Anglo-Saxon period itself.[5]

There is a continuity between *Beowulf* and later literature, but not an unbroken line, and in present-day preoccupations with literary and cultural studies, that tenuous link needs to be recontextualized continually to take account of the gap of time and cultural change that separates us from a poem a thousand years older.[6] Not least important is how our present situation in the cultural milieu of the Western society of the late twentieth century makes of *Beowulf* a palimpsest on which we cannot help but inscribe our twentieth-century presuppositions.

Intertextuality

An approach from the present backward through time is a reversal of one of the happiest hunting grounds of Anglo-Saxon studies, searching for sources, and presupposes a chronological movement from past to present. But the more recent concept of intertextuality does not necessarily function as a one-way movement through time. Culler has defined literary works as "intertextual constructs . . . A text can be read only in relation to other texts, and it is made possible by the codes which animate the discursive spaces of a culture."[7] Although intertextuality assumes relationships between one text and others, it does not presuppose that those relationships are only linear and chronological. If for an individual a more recent text is a starting point for the exploration of older texts, that intertextuality is as relevant as any other.

Monsters in Society and Culture

A key feature in *Beowulf* and in other discourses is the position of monsters in society and culture. Their ontological challenge to the late twentieth century is a continuing one, especially when the dominant place of film and television in modern Western culture makes it inevitable that monsters such as the Incredible Hulk, King Kong, and even Darth Vader are household names. Knowledge of them will for most people precede knowledge of some of their possible intertexts. For instance, the Incredible Hulk can be seen as the obverse of Dr. Jekyll's Mr. Hyde, and at a greater remove of Frankenstein and his monster and eventually of a subverted Pygmalion myth. Another type of monster is Dracula, who may initially seem only tangentially related to the others, but, like Frankenstein, has become so well known that he regularly features in parodies as well as in serious discourses that overtly use Dracula as their main intertext. Such names may point to archetypes; they are now best known by the names given them in specific literary texts, whether or not a decoder knows that particular text.[8]

The term *monster*, according to the *OED*, suggests a range of meanings. The semantic field combines various possibilities, such as the following:

– natural or human
\+ deformity (physical and/or moral)
\+ large size

Not all of these need be copresent; for instance, cruelty and wickedness are not necessarily applicable to animals—like the original King Kong—who lack moral awareness and whose behavior is appropriate to their nonhuman status. The definitions stress that monsters are Other, as contrasted with the subjectivity of Self that classes them as alien in some way, though they do not include one aspect relevant to most "monsters": the emotive impact that they make as Other, usually terror or dread, while an aura of mystery also surrounds them. The response to a monster may be influenced by any or all of the aspects of the semantic field, and may be modified within the discourse, as when by the end of *Frankenstein* the monster excites pity as well as revulsion, but the terrifying impact that a monster has on both the protagonists within the text and the audience/reader is an important part of the overall signification of the term.

It is easy to see how even the ex-Jedi knight Darth Vader can be labeled "monster," because he is large, wears a masklike helmet that hides his deformed face, and is evil, an instance of the Dr. Jekyll/Mr. Hyde paradigm in which Mr. Hyde has all but overcome Dr. Jekyll. The fear he inspires is also relevant to his twentieth-century "monster" status, and an element of mystery surrounds him for most of his period on screen.

We can also see why Grendel's nonnatural hugeness and depravity and the reactions of awe and dread have placed him for so long in the category to which Frankenstein's monster can be assigned; further, like Dracula and other vampires, the dragon (OE *draca*) mortally wounds his victim, Beowulf, by biting his neck. Modern monsters do not offer such a close parallel for Grendel's mother, a point to be considered later.

Stevenson's *The Strange Case of Dr. Jekyll and Mr. Hyde*

Stevenson's story *The Strange Case of Dr. Jekyll and Mr. Hyde* is presented through a series of embedded narratives in which discourse time disrupts story time markedly.[9] It opens with Mr. Utterson, the lawyer, whose first recorded speech is, "I incline to Cain's heresy. . . . I let my brother go to the devil in his own way" (29). His kinsman Mr. Enfield's account of his first meeting with Mr. Hyde includes the remark that Hyde's trampling on the girl child "was hellish to see" (31) and that Hyde carried it off "really like Satan" (32). When Utterson asks for a description of him, Enfield says, "He must be deformed somewhere; he gives a strong feeling of deformity, although I couldn't specify the point" (34). When Utterson himself meets Hyde, his description of him is that "Mr. Hyde was pale and dwarfish; he gave an impression of deformity without any namable malformation" (40). Dr. Lanyon's posthumous narrative records of Hyde that "there was something abnormal and misbegotten in the very essence of the creature" (78), and Jekyll's own posthumously recorded statement says that Hyde's pleasures "soon began to turn towards the monstrous" (86). Every major protagonist in the text chooses signifiers that point to the deformity and evil that fit Hyde into the monster paradigm, even though his dwarfish size is also a feature remarked on more than once.

Stevenson's monster is an alter ego of Dr. Jekyll,[10] closer to him than Frankenstein's monster is to Frankenstein, in that Jekyll and Hyde are mutually exclusive; they cannot coexist, but engage in a perpetual power struggle in which Hyde progressively gains in strength and Jekyll is only just successful through his suicide. Predating Freud, Stevenson emphasizes the deliberate and willed separation of Self from Other within the same individual. The choice of one individual to split himself between his better and his worse aspects has an impact not merely upon himself but also on others, as the monstrous Other preys upon society as well.

The Self-Other relationship is not simple in the gothic novel, for it can be an alienated relationship within the individual, as in Dr. Jekyll and Mr. Hyde (where Other is perceived as the perversion of reason, even madness); within the individual's society (where Other is perceived as antisocial, breaking society's rules, or nonsocial, going beyond society's norms); or within the individual's normal physical context (where Other is perceived as non- or supernatural).[11] Mr. Hyde does not overtly embody this last Other, as do most of the other monsters to be considered, but the first two encapsulate his monstrous aspects.[12]

Such a paradigm of what is monstrous reflects facets of the increasingly uncertain cultural mores of the late Victorian period and the approach of modernism, with its emphasis upon the metafictional exploration of consciousness itself and how Other is comprehended; Stevenson cannot keep the damage that a self-created monster wreaks confined to its creator, but (as with Oscar Wilde's Dorian Gray) shows how individual and society constantly interact.[13]

Shelley's *Frankenstein*

Mary Shelley's *Frankenstein,* written some two generations earlier, is about a monster, though the name she has assigned to his creator has been transferred to him (where Dr. Jekyll and Mr. Hyde maintain their separate entities, though only one appears at any one time), in recognition that the two are inextricably related.[14] Shelley presents her monster within a series of retrospective embedded narratives, framed by Captain Walton's letters to his sister, and includes not only Frankenstein's first-person narration of his life but also a long section in which the monster himself is allowed to relate his experiences from his own subjective stance. There is no real question about the status of the creature: *monster* is, the term most frequently applied to Frankenstein's creation, and is repeatedly applied to him by Frankenstein himself and also by Captain Walton (492); the creature speaks of "the deformity of my figure" (379) and, most poignantly when he sees himself reflected in a pool, he says, "I became fully convinced that I was in reality the monster that I am" (379). At the end he says of himself that "the fallen angel becomes a malignant devil" (494). He fits the parameters of "monster" in his not truly human status, his murderous crimes, and his size, and particularly in the terror and dread he evokes in those he meets.

The creature and Hyde share many similarities: both are (or give the impression to those who describe them) deformed; both commit crimes, leading in the end to murder; both are associated with evil, the reverse of Christian virtue. But they are also differentiated: Frankenstein's "wretch" (another term used frequently of him) is not coexistent with his creator, and is not his alter ego; he lives his own separate life. He is not totally evil, as his period with his "cottagers" shows. His crimes are presented not as they affect society in general but as a direct attack upon Frankenstein's own family and friend. He is created as Other to Frankenstein's Self in individual terms and, not wishing to live once Frankenstein is dead, he goes off to perish on his own funeral pyre. He is Other who differs from Hyde's Otherness. He is a human creation with his own consciousness and ability to learn, and he reflects the romantic period in which Mary Shelley was writing, with its confidence in the creative ability of the Self, as represented by the poets.

The self-confident assertion of the individual artist's right to usurp the power of society has influenced Mary Shelley's mere mortal who tries to usurp the power to create life, and she simultaneously elevates and deconstructs the Self who asserts the ability and right to create Other as another human—but in fact creates a monster. She also suggests a key difference between romanticism, with its concern with Self, and gothicism, which is fascinated with Other.

Beowulf's Monsters

To approach *Beowulf* through twentieth- and nineteenth-century paradigms of a monster is to make of the earlier poem a palimpsest that is influenced by these later monsters (and by many others I have not dealt with here). Beowulf's monsters can easily be recontextualized in accordance with certain aspects of those already considered. The third, the dragon, has seemed problematic, partly because it is so mysterious, and scarcely described,[15] and many aspects of the dragon have evoked a tremendous amount of discussion: for instance, it can be perceived as an exteriorization of the vices of greed, pride, and presumption,[16] or as merely a monster of the marvellous type found in the *Liber Monstrorum*.[17] It fits most closely with the imaginary animal. As befits its animal status and contrary to Tripp's suggestion that it is a man-dragon, it is not loaded with the negative Christian terms that abound in the earlier sections about Grendel and his mother.[18] From a twentieth-century perspective, the monster it most resembles is Dracula (whose very name suggests a diminutive of *draca*). This resemblance is most marked when the dragon meets Beowulf for the third time:

> þa wæs þeodsceaða þriddan siðe,
> frecne fyrdraga fæhða gemyndig,
> ræsde on ðone rofan, þa him rum ageald,
> hat ond heaðogrim, heals ealne ymbefeng
> biteran banum; he geblodegod wearð
> sawuldriore, swat yðum weoll. (2688–93)

> [Then for the third time the enemy of the people, the fearsome fire-dragon, hot and battle-fierce, mindful of the feud, rushed on the brave one, when the opportunity was given him, enclosed all his neck with his sharp teeth; he was bloodied with his life-gore, his blood welled out in waves.]

Stoker's *Dracula*

The vampirelike action of the dragon leads to the retaliation by Beowulf and Wiglaf that causes its own death, and in other ways the dragon does not fit the paradigm associated with Count Dracula in the text given his name:[19] it is not human, and it does not depend on blood for its continuing life. But there are other intertextual aspects that draw attention to themselves from a twentieth-century standpoint. At the beginning, before his nature is known to the main protagonists, Count Dracula locates treasure troves by the supernatural means of the blue flame hovering over them, and the fire-breathing dragon is introduced in relation to its discovery of the treasure hoard:

Hordwynne fond
eald uhtsceaða opene standan
se ðe byrnende biorgas seceð,
nacod niðdraca, nihtes fleogeð
fyre befangen; hyne foldbuend
(swiðe ondræ)da(ð). (2270b-75a)

[The old twilight predator, the naked hostile dragon, found the pleasurable hoard standing open, he who, flaming, seeks barrows, flies at night, encompassed with fire; him the people in the land fear greatly.]

The climax to the Dracula story (built on a series of different perspectives, such as diaries and letters, all of which present Dracula from subjective viewpoints, none from an objective third-person narrator) has Jonathan Harker and Quincey Morris both using their knives to "shear through the throat" and "plunge into the heart" of Dracula (447) to destroy him; Beowulf's sword having failed, he and Wiglaf attack the dragon with their battle knives, and each plunges his weapon into the dragon to kill it. Morris is mortally wounded in the fight, and Beowulf also receives his death wound. It is necessary to cut off the heads of the undead who have become vampires, and, switching monsters momentarily, we find that Beowulf in the hall of Grendel's mother cuts off the head of the dead Grendel and also the head of his mother.

Earlier in the poem, there is reference to that other dragon slayer, Sigemund (884), but it is explicitly stated there that he is alone on that exploit, for Fitela is not with him (889). It is not part of a contemporary convention that the poet is following in having two warriors together slaying the dragon, just as Harker and Morris together attack Dracula's throat and heart. Is this coincidence, or is it an archetypal motif, or is there a possibility that Bram Stoker is recalling earlier intertexts? Dracula, relating to Harker the history of his race, says: "Here, too, when they came, they found the Huns, whose warlike fury had swept the earth like a living flame, till the dying peoples held that in their veins ran the blood of those old witches, who, expelled from Scythia, had mated with the devils in the desert" (41). And Van Helsing, in giving the history of vampirism, says that the vampire follows "the wake of the berserker, Icelander, the *devil-begotten* Hun, the Slav, *the Saxon*, the Magyar" (286; emphasis mine). The references to miscegenation allude to the tradition associated with exegesis of Genesis 6:4, where the *filii dei* and the *filiae hominum* intermingle, giving birth to giants. This is a part of the monstrous genealogy that the *Beowulf* poet attaches to Grendel, making him "caines cynne."[20]

Self-Other Relationships

The Dracula story reflects a different culture from that of *Beowulf*, one closer to Stevenson's, with the monster figure's depredations affecting not only the individuals but also their society. But unlike the Self-Other relationship that is so close in *Dr. Jekyll and Mr. Hyde*, in *Dracula* the predominant point of view of the Self (Selves) representing what Varnado calls "the orderly, rational bourgeois life of the West" is differentiated from Other with his combination of legendary, historical, and Eastern dimensions.[21] The sign on Mina's forehead that signifies her partial taking over by the monstrous Other does not disappear until that Other has been finally destroyed. The power struggle between Self and Other has been realized with Other given great intertextual power as an archetype, thus suggesting the gothicism of the text. Neither Dracula nor the dragon plays a major role in the text in which he occurs, but both become very powerful signs for the monstrous but fascinating dread that Other generates, though Dracula does not have to compete with figures such as those in the Grendel family in evoking that awe.

The mysterious dimension of Grendel is a crucial part of how he is presented in Beowulf.[22] There is no overt close description of him, though his eyes, his hands, and of course his head are foregrounded in the discourse, and though he seems to be huge, able to seize thirty men at once and carry them in his monstrous "glof," his size is left vague. From a twentieth-century stance, an awareness of this lack of specific description is as much an indication of our current expectations as it is a comment on the contemporary society.[23] More important is Grendel's relationship to Beowulf, and the extent to which the two can be regarded as obverse and reverse of the same paradigm, or as doubles or second selves.[24]

It is clear, however, that because Grendel has been raiding Heorot for twelve years before Beowulf's arrival, he cannot be classed either as deriving from Beowulf in the way that Frankenstein's monster is derived from Frankenstein or as his alter ego, like Mr. Hyde. Yet if Beowulf and Grendel are linked as analogous to Self and Other, the modern monsters can suggest something about Grendel. He is large, he is explicitly and frequently linked (by the third-person narrator as well as by the protagonists) with evil, and his superhuman aspects, such as his strength and the terror he evokes, are all part of the paradigm of the monster. Major differences from the more recent monsters are not only Grendel's attack upon the society of the Danes prior to Beowulf's arrival, but also the variety of attributed motives for his depredations: the torment of hearing the revel in the hall (86–89a), the seeking out of the Danes after the beer banquet (115–17), his malice and hostility (146–61), and the references to his eating of those he kills (though it is not made clear whether the eating of human flesh is essential for his well-being, as the drinking of blood is for Dracula).

Assuming that the pejorative terms attributed to Grendel by the narrator and the ameliorative terms attributed to the Danes and especially to Beowulf can be perceived as an Other/Self distinction, the controlling point of view of the poem and of its narrator is that of the whole society in which Self is fashioned, a society under attack from all three types of Other already suggested, even though the multivalent motives of Other's attack may contain some justification, as when the society and culture are themselves shown to be flawed, with the treachery of Hrothulf and Unferth and the impotence of Hrothgar embedded in them.

The vexed question of the Christianness of *Beowulf* is part of the issue. Given the uncertainty of the dating of the poem, the extent to which the ideology of the society for whom the poet is writing is Christianized is problematic, but if even a writer as late as Ælfric inveighs against pagan practices, then the society is still one in which Christian beliefs *can* come under physical attack from heathen and can hardly be taken for granted as the unchallenged basis for society. The attack is that of an anti-Christian representative, an evil and mysterious Other, against a society that is only semi-Christianized, and one that perverts the central rite of Christianity with the eating of the body and blood of members of the society. It is a fundamental attack that cannot be countered from within the original society (either by Hrothgar or by Unferth) and needs the assistance of one who both has links with it (as Beowulf does by way of his father) and is also the obverse of that Other itself.

The wide-ranging nature of the attack of such an Other upon individual and society and even upon the natural milieu (so that the hart is not prepared to enter the mere in which Grendel lives) has been more and more narrowed in more recent monsters, but in *Beowulf* it is presented as being much more fundamentally against the structure of society and culture, and the sheer length of the discourse devoted to the lead-up to Beowulf's fight with Grendel is important for showing how widespread and terrifying is the perception of that attack in the Self's response to a threat to the whole fabric of society.

The Second Monster in *Beowulf*

The second monster in *Beowulf* is one for whom there is no real parallel in nineteenth- and twentieth-century monsters.[25] This is strange. Mary Shelley, the creator of Frankenstein's monster, was a woman, and Frankenstein's refusal to complete his creation of an Eve figure, a female mate, for the monster leads to the latter's vendetta against Frankenstein's closest family and friend. The vampire Lucy, who is taken over by Other after death (and the other vampires who become surrogates for Dracula), and Mina, who embodies within herself the Self/Other conflict in a Jekyll/Hyde manner, are both crucially important in *Dracula* as instances of the perversion of Self. The disappearance of the mark on Mina's forehead is the signifier of Dracula's destruction. In *Dr. Jekyll and Mr. Hyde,* women are as marginalized as on the whole they are now perceived as being in the society and culture of the Victorian and early twentieth-century periods.

Though Grendel's mother is a monster who, like Hyde, Frankenstein's wretch, and Dracula, kills, she differs strikingly from the women in the recent monster discourses because unlike Lucy, who in *Dracula* is drawn into Otherness only after her death, she is, together with Grendel, associated from the start with Otherness (though, like Lucy, her head, with Grendel's, is cut off by the representative of Selfness);[26] but she also participates in a relationship that is parallel to that of other women associated with Selfness, such as Wealtheow and Hildeburh, in that the son of each is destined for death. But it is only Grendel's mother, the Other, who is able to achieve vengeance upon the impotent Self of Hrothgar's court for the death of her son, and in her fight against the hero representative who comes in from beyond that society she comes closer to success than her son does in the first struggle between Self and Other. The perpetual gender power struggle within society and culture does not allow the female to overcome the male in physical combat, but the female is in no way as weak an Other as the female of the Self.

The narrator overtly spells out that the terror evoked by Grendel's mother is commensurately less than that evoked by her son (1282–87), and this is a reflection of the contemporary attitude toward women; but it could also be an ironic comment on the heroic ideology, if women were not expected to take part in actual combat.[27] That a monster *could* be female for the Anglo-Saxons (instead of a female becoming a monster, as in later texts) suggests that women were not as marginalized as they came to be in the later periods. Mary Shelley's significant spelling out of Frankenstein's refusal to complete a female for his monstrous creation is a recognition that it was not possible in her society to allow a woman monster to be created, as the Other of femaleness was sufficient to cause the Self of maleness to quail, without giving a female any further power such as Stoker allows his perverted female vampires (though under the control of a male). That Stevenson does not include a woman (of any significance) within his text suggests that in his society the patriarchal hegemony has in the late Victorian period achieved its maximum suppression of the Otherness of the female.

The palimpsest that is the poem of *Beowulf* is able to reflect back a decoder's own society and culture as well as hint at aspects of its contemporary cultural-social attitudes. The retellings of the fight with Grendel's mother that, as in more recent monster texts, disrupt chronological progression show that the text inscribes into its own discourse palimpsestic reinterpretations of a contest that is analogous to a Self/Other struggle.[28] The epistemological challenge joins the ontological challenge to come to terms with monsters and with what and how they signify as they have been presented in literary discourse over the past thousand years.

Notes

I would like to thank Dr. Michael Flint for his help in searching out the relevant monsters for this piece. This essay was originally published in *In Geardagum* (June

1992). The editors, Loren Gruber and Dean Loganbill, have granted me permission to reprint it in a shortened form.

1. Quotations from *Beowulf* in what follows are taken from Fr. Klaeber, *Beowulf and the Fight at Finnsburg*, 3rd ed. (Boston: D. C. Heath, 1950), with the line numbers of that edition. Translations are mine.

2. See Ruth Mellinkoff, "Cain's Monstrous Progeny in *Beowulf*: Part II, Post-Diluvian Survival," *Anglo-Saxon England* 9 (1981): 183–97, especially 194, where she discusses the confusion between Cain and Ham in various texts. Phillip Pulsiano, in "'Cames cynne': Confusion or Craft," *Proceedings of the PMR Conference* 7 (1985 for 1982): 33–38, argues precariously for the original reading.

3. See Kevin S. Kiernan, *Beowulf and the Beowulf Manuscript* (New Brunswick, N.J.: Rutgers University Press, 1981), especially his argument that folio 182 (BL numbering) is a palimpsest joining two originally separate poems.

4. J. R. R. Tolkien, "*Beowulf*: The Monsters and the Critics," *Proceedings of the British Academy* 22 (1936): 245–95; reprinted in *An Anthology of Beowulf Criticism*, ed. Lewis D. Nicholson (Notre Dame, Ind.: University of Notre Dame, 1963), 51–103; and in *Interpretations of "Beowulf": A Critical Anthology*, ed. R. D. Fulk (Bloomington: Indiana University Press, 1991), 14–44.

5. See, for instance, the collection of essays edited by Allen J. Frantzen, *Speaking Two Languages: Traditional Disciplines and Contemporary Theory in Medieval Studies* (New York, 1991), and the introduction to R. D. Fulk, ed., *Interpretations of "Beowulf": A Critical Anthology* (Bloomington: Indiana University Press, 1991). Much earlier, Kemp Malone, in "A Reading of *Beowulf* 3169–3182," in *Medieval Literature and Folklore Studies: Essays in Honor of Francis Lee Utley*, ed. Jerome Mandel and Bruce A. Rosenberg (New Brunswick, N.J.: Rutgers University Press, 1970), 35–38, brought out how scholars reconstruct text; Andreas Haarder, in *Beowulf: The Appeal of a Poem* (Copenhagen: Akademisk Forlag, 1975), details the history of *Beowulf* criticism, relating it finally to political, sociological, and literary contexts.

6. Bernice L. Webb, "James Bond as Literary Descendant of Beowulf," *South Atlantic Quarterly* 67 (1968): 1–12; and James R. Hurt, "Grendel's Point of View: *Beowulf* and William Golding," *Modern Fiction Studies* 13 (1967): 264–65, both note parallels between *Beowulf* and modern prose fiction. Lee A. Warren, in "Real Monsters Please: The Importance of Undergraduate Teaching," *Journal of General Education* 31 (1979): 23–33, argues for leading beginning students to earlier works by way of texts such as Camus's *The Plague*, which provides a comparative approach to *Beowulf*.

7. Jonathan Culler, *The Pursuit of Signs: Semiotics, Literature, Deconstruction* (London: Routledge & Kegan Paul, 1981), 38.

8. It is also relevant to canonical Anglo-Saxon studies that Frankenstein, Dr. Jekyll, and Dracula were not in earlier decades of the twentieth century accepted into the literary "canon," presumably because they were perceived as part of "pop" culture. Another such example from the earlier twentieth century is Tarzan, who is tangentially related to monsters, given his supernatural strength and noncivilized setting.

9. Robert Louis Stevenson, *The Strange Case of Dr. Jekyll and Mr. Hyde* (1886; Harmondsworth: Penguin, 1979). Page numbers from this edition are cited in what follows.

10. However, Jerrold E. Hogle, in "The Struggle for a Dichotomy: Abjection in

Jekyll and His Interpreters," in *Dr. Jekyll and Mr. Hyde after One Hundred Years*, ed. William Veeder and Gordon Hirsch (Chicago: University of Chicago Press, 1988), argues strongly for the process of abjection throughout the novella.

11. Marshall Brown, in "A Philosophical View of the Gothic Novel," *Studies in Romanticism* 26 (1987): 275–301, examines Kantian categories within gothic novels, without using the Self/Other concept.

12. Stevenson's period was when science was coming to be highly regarded, and not only is Jekyll a doctor, but there is an emphasis on the scientific feasibility of Jekyll's transformation into Hyde.

13. This is a point that Hogle examines in "The Struggle for a Dichotomy."

14. Mary Shelley, *Frankenstein; or, The Modern Prometheus* (1818; Harmondsworth: Penguin, 1968). Page numbers cited in text are from this edition.

15. My "Spatial Perception and Conceptions in the (Re-)presenting and (Re-)constructing of Old English Texts," *Parergon* 9, no. 1 (1991): 87–102, deals with the lack of specific description in OE texts. Though I do not deal with the dragon in that essay, it too is not specifically described.

16. See, for instance, Margaret Goldsmith's interpretations, as in "The Christian Perspective in *Beowulf*," *Comparative Literature* 14 (1962): 71–90; subsequently in *Studies in Old English Literature in Honor of Arthur G. Brodeur*, ed. Stanley B. Greenfield (Eugene: University of Oregon Press, 1963), 71–90; reprinted in Fulk, *Interpretations of "Beowulf"*, 103–19; and her *The Mode and Meaning of Beowulf* (London: Athlone, 1970), especially when she deals with the allegorization of the poem.

17. L. G. Whitbread, in "The *Liber Monstrorum* and *Beowulf*," *Medieval Studies* 36 (1974): 434–71, discusses the relationship of the two texts, though from the viewpoint of an early date for *Beowulf*. See Ann Knock, "The *Liber Monstrorum*: An Unpublished Manuscript and Some Reconsiderations," *Scriptorium* 32 (1978): 19–28; and the definitive discussion by Michael Lapidge, "*Beowulf*, Aldhelm, the *Liber Monstrorum* and Wessex," *Studi Medievali*, 3rd ser., 23 (1982): 151–92. William E. Brynteson, in "*Beowulf*, Monsters, and Manuscripts: Classical Associations," *Res Publica Litterarum* 5, no. 2 (1982): 41–57, also sets the *Beowulf* codex in the tradition of "monster books."

18. Raymond P. Tripp Jr., *More about the Fight with the Dragon: Beowulf 2208b-3182, Commentary, Edition, and Translation* (Lanham, Md.: University Press of America, 1983).

19. Bram Stoker, *Dracula* (1897; Harmondsworth: Penguin, 1979).

20. I am indebted to Dr. Jeffrey Cohen for pointing out the earlier reference in *Dracula*, and for his very pertinent comments on the two passages.

21. S. L. Varnado, *Haunted Presence: The Numinous in Gothic Fiction* (Tuscaloosa: University of Alabama Press, 1987), 102.

22. Wayne Hanley, in "Grendel's Humanity Again," *In Geardagum* 11 (1990): 5–13, argues that Grendel is a man; the term *monster*, however, as has been shown, is not restricted to nonhumans. Earlier writers who have considered Grendel's attributes as a monster include G. Storms, "Grendel the Terrible," *Neuphilologische Mitteilungen* 73 (1972): 427–36. In a private communication, Professor Jane Roberts has indicated to me that the bulk of OE terms signifying monsters occur in *Beowulf*.

23. See Waterhouse, "Spatial Perception."

24. See Katherine O'Brien O'Keeffe, "*Beowulf*, Lines 702b–836: Transformations

and the Limits of the Human," *Texas Studies in Literature and Language* 23 (1981): 484–94; and S. L. Dragland, "Monster-Man in *Beowulf*," *Neophilologus* 61 (1977): 606–18. Criticism of Beowulf himself can both strengthen and weaken the parallel; see James Smith, "*Beowulf* I," ed. Martin Dodsworth, *English* 25 (1976): 203–29, and "*Beowulf* II," ed. Martin Dodsworth, *English* 26 (1977): 3–22, especially his treatment of the monsters. Norma Kroll, in "*Beowulf*: The Hero as Keeper of Human Polity," *Modern Philology* 84 (1986): 117–29, sees Beowulf and his monsters as doubles or second selves.

25. Recent discussion that reappraises Grendel's mother includes Kevin S. Kiernan's "Grendel's Heroic Mother," *In Geardagum* 6 (1984): 13–33; and Jane Chance's *Woman as Hero in Old English Literature* (Syracuse: Syracuse University Press, 1986), which includes her earlier "The Structural Unity of *Beowulf*: The Problem of Grendel's Mother," first printed in *Texas Studies in Language and Literature.* See especially Chance's chapter 7, to which I am deeply indebted for what follows.

26. From a feminist point of view it is significant that this is not narrated as part of the fight with her, but is part of Beowulf's retrospective narration to Hygelac (2138–40).

27. Contradictions in the presentation of the heroic society are suggested by Harry Berger and H. Marshall Leicester Jr. in "Social Structure as Doom: The Limits of Heroism in *Beowulf*," in *Old English Studies in Honour of John C. Pope*, ed. Robert B. Burlin and Edward B. Irving (Toronto: University of Toronto Press, 1974), 37–79.

28. Rosemary Huisman, "The Three Tellings of Beowulf's Fight with Grendel's Mother," *Leeds Studies in English* 20 (1990): 217–48.

3 Monstrosity, Illegibility, Denegation: De Man, bp Nichol, and the Resistance to Postmodernism

David L. Clark

> absolutely incomprehensible if I were not forced to confess that I suffer from a morbid horror of the pen, and that this work is for me an experience of sheer torture, quite out of proportion to its relative unimportance.
>
> FERDINAND DE SAUSSURE, "On a Torn, Undated Page"[1]

De Man's Denegation

In a theoretical age often enamored of the "playfulness" of the sign and the "pleasure" of the text, Paul de Man's last writings stand out as darkly sobering, driven as they are by an almost ascetic desire to bring thinking into proximity with what he calls, after Walter Benjamin, "*reine Sprache*," pure language (TT, 92),[2] or, in Carol Jacobs's terms, "that which is purely language—nothing but language."[3] From the stringent and self-canceling perspective afforded by de Man's late essays, the Nietzschean rhetoric of play and gaming often associated with postmodernist theory and literary practice registers the work of a deeply rooted aesthetic ideology that determines the play of signs primarily as the play of *meaningful* signs, that is, legible signs that are happily and familiarly available to comprehension. What is familiarly known about signification may not be not properly known, however, for the simple reason that this familiarity represses the *un*happy possibility that "language is not exhausted by the thought of the human."[4]

De Man's essays written after "Shelley Disfigured" (1979) take as their *Aufgabe,* their impossible task, the articulation of linguistic "play" as something truly serious, stripped of all humanistic categories. With an acuity that makes him the closest of close readers, de Man focuses on the nonsignifying elements of discourse, down to the senseless differential markings formed by the unpredictable appearance of individual letters within words, elements that "act" as the condition of the possibility of meaningful language but that ineluctably remain on the far side of that meaningfulness. De Man asks what language must be and what it means that language "is," not because he expects any positive answers to these overlapping questions but because by asking them in a radical way he opens a route or path of thinking that leads to a nullity about which nothing positive (or, for that matter, negative) can be said. This absolute negation, which negates even what can be said negatively about language, this *denegation*, then, de Man calls several things: "the play of the letter as inscription," the "materiality of the letter," and, more complexly, "the positional power of language." De Man advances the counterintuitive argument that language is hardly a site of *jouissance* but much rather a region of negativity more originary than the *not* of logical negation. This unnamed and unnamable Other, moreover, can always, at any turn, performatively disrupt human pretensions to knowledge—especially where these pretensions concern language. Language's denegation possesses the eventlike character of an accident that suddenly and irrevocably interrupts life: unpredictable, unmotivated, prosaically indifferent to human desire, yet often experienced in a mood of pathos and fear. As Fredric Jameson has recently remarked, in imagining what language "might look like in our own absence," de Man confronts "some *monstrous thing* we cannot imagine seeing from the outside—that nameless alien being we domesticate by means of the more banal anthropomorphic concepts of reasons, choices, motives, leaps of faith, irresistible compulsions, and the like."[5] The fact that Jameson resorts to a figure of monstrosity is not incidental, for de Man's rhetoric is marked by tropes conveying the specifically *teratological* threat that language's Other poses for the understanding. The "monstrous" here functions as a philosopheme, a conceptual-figural strand linking quite disparate texts in unexpected ways and revealing a hidden coherence with regard to the relationship between language and the human. In evoking the spectacular possibilities of "the undoing of cognition and its replacement by the uncontrollable power of the letter as inscription" (RT, 37), de Man points to a negative power of language that can be anticipated only in the form of an absolute risk.

Thus he does not evoke the limitless pleasure of the text, but a momentary horror of it. In the wake of de Man's last writings, is a "Nietzschean affirmation . . . of a world of signs without fault, without truth, and without origin" truly possible?[6] Or does this affirmation point to a deeper crisis, one inadvertently brought to the surface by the postmodern critique of the sign, against which its optimistic claims are defensively asserted? bp Nichol's radically open-ended poem *The Martyrology* is a productive place to examine these questions, for two reasons: first, although the poem has been accurately described as an exemplary expression of the Canadian literary avant-garde, a "compendium of ever changing and newly created forms,"[7] at certain points it appears genuinely uneasy with its own linguistic experimentation, as if shrinking from an impending catastrophe; second, *The Martyrology* bears its own complex witness to just such a catastrophe at the illegible point of its conclusion—a conclusion that was contingently imposed by Nichol's premature, accidental death.[8] (But how could that death be anything but "premature," given that it will always have happened too soon, "before" its radical suddenness could be cognized, cured, or matured by thought? This twist in temporality is a question to which we will return.) It is here, where *The Martyrology* concludes, or rather stops, that something like de Man's notion of the risk of writing is concealedly revealed.

The Death of the Author

How to begin to read a poem that ended without being at an end? Now that *The Martyrology* is finished, which is to say neither complete nor incomplete, not so much a fragment of a whole as *other* than whole, now that Nichol's long poem has miscarried, the task of the reader becomes more than ever to begin to read the poem, the final shape of which having only recently been unalterably imposed by the author's unforeseen and unforeseeable death. Indeed, that shape was unlooked-for to the precise extent that the death was unexpected. Unhappily, readers of Nichol are in a better position since his death to see what must have always been the case: that a radically open-ended poem like *The Martyrology* will need to test its commitment to its chosen status by remaining open, finally, to the one thing that it could not and yet was compelled to be open-ended to: the death of the author. In other words, *The Martyrology* is most truly a life's work at the point of its accidental closure by the author's death: Nichol is dead, and that fatality reveals itself as his poem's ownmost possibility. How to think this negativity? Even if we do not or cannot think it, as readers we have no choice but to find ourselves caught in its dreadful shadow; today, when we read *The Martyrology*, we commence by reading (of) Nichol's end, itself utterly senseless and unrepresentable and yet fully inscribed in a poem whose final form is what it is exactly because of it.

A Dream of Dismemberment

"Taking the notion of open-form writing to its logical extreme," as Nichol once said of his poem, meant, finally, exposing *The Martyrology* to the extremity of death.[9] Yet the abrupt ending of Nichol's poem serves to remind us that the text will have been from the beginning a kind of death sentence ever more about to be pronounced. Certainly the sense of an ending, and of the hazard of life's triumph over art, is not confined to the entirely exorbitant "place" where Nichol's death interrupts *The Martyrology*. As Stephen Scobie has argued about the first five books, the narrative of the poem is itself fraught with the weight of destitution, moments of "desolation caused equally by the death of the saints, the failure of language, and the abandonment by the father."[10] I want to begin my remarks with one of these moments, obvious enough to be easily missed.[11] I want to begin with the prefatory material of Book 5, which comprises a detailed map of downtown Toronto, four epigraphs, and two title pages. The first of these epigraphs is a simple word game:

blue
        bluer
                bloor

Arranged on the page as a stepped sequence, the epigraph seems to tumble out of itself, auguring the textual strategy that will come to dominate Book 5, the "ear-y" way in which language invariably sounds itself beyond or before sense. On a separate page, Nichol next reprints an anecdote from Caxton about the risk of miscommunication that follows logically from the shifty relationship between the signifier and the signified. That language is characterized by an endless process of "dyversite & chaunge" is put to us by the passage itself, which reproduces Caxton's archaic word usage and orthography. Immediately below this epigraph, Nichol cites Cocteau's declaration that "the greatest literary masterpiece is no more than an alphabet in disorder," a remark that not only decanonizes canonical works by reducing them to the meaningless linguistic atoms making them up, but also, more interestingly, declines to inform us as to whether this reduction is the occasion of satisfaction or regret. Which has suffered the most, one might well ask, the alphabet's order in being rearranged into meaningful words, or the "greatest literary masterpiece" for being dismantled into so many blank letters? And from that unanswered question the reader turns to the second title page and finds a letter from a friend, quoted in full, which concludes with a startling image of the writer alone before an annihilatory violence hidden within his own writing: "I had a sudden image of your poetry capturing you like the Minotaur in the labyrinth," Nichol's correspondent concludes, "—and started wondering what is the relationship of someone to the mythology they make up? Anyway. Best, Matt."

Is there not a narrative faintly constructed here between and along these epigraphs, or at least a circling about and a deepening of the sense of a certain hazard inherent in the task of writing? From the harmless pun on "bluer/bloor" (Bloor is the name of a major street in Toronto, a homely reference to Nichol's home), we turn to Caxton's politely acknowledged problem of the shiftiness of words, and from there to the dismemberment of the "literary masterpiece" at the hands of its own materiality, and then finally to the unhomely phantasmagoria of Matt(Cohen)'s letter, where the dream of the Minotaur is related and a kind of warning made. But of what? A curious "image" this, whose hallucinatory power seems tied to its very suddenness. Ordinarily, prefaces are places where writers indulge in the fantasy that they are the masters of their own texts. Here, however, it is the text, not the author, who is powerful. Matt's dream of dismemberment is at the very least an inauspiciously ambivalent way to begin Book 5 of *The Martyrology*, a volume that is more obviously given over to the felicitous life of words, not their threatening, much less monstrous, otherness. Nichol would seem to celebrate the erring paths of the signifier, once, as he writes, the "hazardous connections to their signifieds / are severed" (Chain 1); why then *begin* with a warning, as if one hazard only concealed another? A large part of the Minotaur's repulsiveness comes from its grossly indeterminate status, neither human nor nonhuman, but both at once. What is so threateningly *alien* about one's own poem that it can be thought of as similarly monstrous? What cruelty lurks at the heart of the labyrinth of language?

A Terror Glimpsed: *La folie de Saussure*

These are difficult issues to raise, it seems, even for Nichol, who after all displaces them into Matt's voice. I want to argue that the later work of Paul de Man, which might usefully be described as an unfinished theory of language's threatening otherness, is extraordinarily germane to the probing questions and darkening mood that Nichol's prefatory remarks evoke. De Man's last public lecture is a case in point: in the course of discussing Walter Benjamin's unsettling observation that translators—and, by extension, all who wrestle with words—face a "*monstrous* and originary danger" in their work, de Man is led to the disconcerting conclusion that it "is not at all certain that language is in any sense human" (TT, 87). In a slightly earlier essay, de Man argues that Ferdinand de Saussure's most radical linguistic research had brought him perilously close to this very "danger," the risk of "cognitive dismemberment" at the hands of "the uncontrollable power of the letter as inscription" (HI, 37). Part of the task facing readers of de Man will continue to be the unpacking of the significance of remarks like these, whose typically lurid figures of destruction are matched only by their unsparing compression. But this much is clear: de Man's later rhetorical readings all reflect what Barbara Johnson calls his "central insight: that language, since it is . . . *constitutive* of the human, cannot itself be entirely 'human.'" As Johnson argues, language

> is neither inside nor outside the subject, but both at once. As the ground of possibility of expressive intentionality, language cannot itself be entirely reduced to interpretability. This does not mean that language *never* means, but rather that beyond the apparent meaning . . . there can always be a residue of functioning. . . . that is not a *sign* of anything, but merely the outcome of linguistic rules, or even of "the absolute randomness of language." Not that language is always absolutely random, but that we can never be sure that it isn't.[12]

A disturbing and freakishly counterintuitive notion, this: that language is not human, or more problematically, that we are not in a position to determine decisively whether it is human or not. For de Man the "residual" or "material" linguistic functioning that makes the concept of subjectivity *as* a concept available to thought radically exceeds the subject, remaining other than and irreducible to it. Moreover, the perilous surety of human being is achieved only by turning away from the inconceivable blankness of this linguistic materiality, a turning that enables the mind to "shelter itself from self-erasure" (SS, 770). As if to resist this "troping," de Man attends to the materiality of the sign, stressing the hidden threat that its radical senselessness inescapably poses for reading, for cognition, and for what is reassuringly familiar about the fundamentally humane (or "phenomenal") space that is constituted by language. For de Man, even to suggest that language "speaks"—as Heidegger famously wrote[13]—automatically humanizes and recuperates what it says, because such speaking could only be *for* us and *to* us as the sole creatures in a position to listen. What language says, if anything, is not something we can determine with any certainty. Whatever language *is*, is therefore at best an anthropomorphizing postulate about it rather than a quality that could as such be perceived, described, or known.

After "Shelley Disfigured" (1979), de Man's essays in effect circle about a fundamental question: Why is there language rather than ubiquitous blankness? It is a question whose answer is to be found in the asking of it. It is only in thinking (of) language *as* a question, as an indeterminate opening rather than as something given to perception, that de Man can turn his critical gaze to the unique site at which language takes place, the movement or act that unfolds the space in which articulation occurs: "the materiality of the letter" is one of the several odd names he gives this originary linguistic moment. The unstable object of de Man's attention escapes conceptual location, but it might just as easily be described using a phrase Nichol himself employs in *The Martyrology*: "adrift *between* the signifier & the signified" (*Book* 5, Chain 3). Because this minimal space of random movement is the very condition of the distinction between signifier and signified, it is itself radically *in*articulate and illegible; certainly the relation of its nonsignifying betweenness to language's phenomenal appearance in signs could not be understood by a reading that, after all, reads only (about) language. For de Man, language is indistinguishable from the forgetting of the condition of its possibility in this inaugural breaching; it thus functions at two levels that are unaccommodated to each other and yet inextricably interinvolved: on the one hand, the inhuman lacuna that is signification's possibility and, on the other, the blotting out of the intolerable blankness of this lacuna so that language may occur and the subject—among all other conceptualizations—may appear. The prephenomenal character of the opening of language makes its nature into something like a bare act, irreducibly singular, opaque, and, as de Man insists, "uncontrollable." What bears emphasis, then, is that the materiality of the letter is utterly heterogeneous to that which is articulated in language. A rift divides language from the material condition of its possibility, rendering arbitrary and contingent all phenomenal forms that inevitably come to be imposed upon it. What would it be to read the unreadable origin of language, to traverse language's unfathomable self-estrangement? Nichol's word "adrift" seems just right, conveying as it does the originary indifference to meaningfulness out of which the sign suddenly forms and to which, according to de Man, it is ultimately answerable. As de Man concludes in "Shelley Disfigured," amid this betweenness, "nothing, whether deed, word, thought, or text, ever happens in relation, positive or negative, to anything that precedes, follows, or exists elsewhere, but only as a random event whose power, like the power of death, is due to the randomness of its occurrence" (SD, 122).

At the conclusion of my remarks I want to circle back to why de Man so readily compares the materiality of the letter to death—in this case the death of Shelley while writing *The Triumph of Life*—and how that comparison illuminates the final disposition of *The Martyrology*. After "Shelley Disfigured," de Man's unique notion of the sign's materiality never ceases to guide his work. What varies is the way in which the hazard of its gross indeterminacy ripples through individual texts. Arguably the clearest explication of linguistic materialism comes in his discussion of Saussure's research on anagrams, the so-called other or crazy Saussure. Since Jean Starobinski's publication of his commentary on Saussure's notebooks in 1971—under the title *Les mots sous les mots*[14]—it has become well known that in the years leading up to his seminal lectures on general linguistics Saussure was obsessed with the strange possibility that Latin verse concealed key words and proper names through various mechanisms of anagrammatic and hypogrammatic dispersal. Although Saussure wanted to believe that these names were thematically relevant to the texts in which they were deviously buried, and that their appearance was thus governed by a set of definable linguistic rules, he found finally that he could not dismiss the possibility that what he saw, or thought he saw, was of his own invention. The more he looked, the more language seemed to be a potentially limitless significative field, inscribed not only with names, but with any number of other patterns and articulations whose meaningfulness or meaninglessness depended entirely on the will of the reader to make them so. Unable to distinguish conclusively between what were the random effects of a disordered alphabet—as Nichol's epigraph from Cocteau might suggest—and a bona fide system of codification, Saussure felt compelled to suspend judgment over the whole matter and to keep his research unpublished. As he wrote in a letter, "I make no secret of the fact that I myself am perplexed—about the most important point: that is, how should one judge the reality or phantasmagoria of the whole question."[15]

For de Man, Saussure's "perplexity" is the outward cognitive response to an inner necessity of language. For a linguistic pattern to have one meaning or another—indeed, for a linguistic pattern to operate significatively at all—fully presupposes "the movement of the *sign-function*"[16] or "positional power," senseless in itself, that makes that meaning possible. Saussure's suspended question about the "reality" or "phantasmagoria" of what he saw in the repetitions and patterns of Latin verse brings him to the threshold of apprehending this material precondition of language, the armature of meaning whose erasure paradoxically enables signification—and therefore language—to take place. Not that language's positional power could ever itself be read or understood, given that the object of reading is always language and nothing less. "That language *is*, is not comprehensible," writes Hans-Jost Frey, identifying linguisticality—what language is at its effaced origin—with the sheer senselessness of its power to mean.[17] The materiality of the letter amounts to a virtual or nonsignificative "act" in which the question of language's having taken place is held in abeyance and remains unthought. As Marc Redfield argues, linguistic materialism "consists in the necessary though impossible possibility that a sign may not be a sign."[18] The "sign that may not be one" is the very blankness haunting Saussure's reading, as his hypogrammatic gaze widens to include more and more hidden words and meanings—until it becomes impossible to determine at what point signification stops or starts. Adrift between the signifier and the signified, Saussure's gaze glazes, turns into a stare, halted and perplexed by the linguistic proliferation it is itself responsible for triggering. Where does reading begin? Saussure's question is unanswerable until he can determine with any certainty whether or where language *has* taken place, but this proves to be the most difficult question of all.

A Maze of Messages: Nichol after de Man

My remarks about the materiality of the letter may seem to have moved my argument away from Book 5 of *The Martyrology*, but I have in fact arrived at the heart of the poem's textual strategies. What Saussure appears to have glimpsed—and subsequently repressed, coming as this glimpse did on the eve of the more "rational" linguistic science that would come to bear his name[19]—was a profound revision of how signifying systems operate, one that strikingly anticipates the exorbitant treatment of language characterizing Book 5. One could argue that what is a "chimerical obsession"[20] in Saussure becomes a radical poetics—not without its own obsessional qualities—in Nichol. Like the linguist, Nichol treats the text as if it were hypogrammatic or paragrammatic, that is, indeterminately bound with several competing signifying strands. As Leon S. Roudiez writes, language is paragrammatic "in the sense that its organization of words (and their denotations), grammar, and syntax is challenged by the infinite possibilities provided by letters or phonemes combining to form networks not accessible through conventional reading habits."[21] For Nichol the text is always unpredictably underwritten by other texts, *les mots sous les mots*; here words are everywhere making themselves heard beneath or within other words, writing re-sounding itself as if in a vast echo chamber. The extent to which Nichol's poem is open to these reverberating "possibilities" is perhaps no more evident than in the case of what Steve McCaffery calls his "charades," where phrases, words, and letters are compelled to yield new significations simply through the redistribution of the blank spaces in which the signifying material is inscribed.[22] McCaffery provides an extraordinary example:

> Flamingo: pale, scenting a latent shark.
> Flaming, opalescent in gala tents—hark.[23]

As Nichol writes in Book 5:

> this multiplication
> attention to a visual duration
> comic stripping of the bare phrase
> the pain inside the language speaks
> ekes out meaning phase by phase
> make my way thru the maze of streets & messages
> reading as i go
> creating narratives by attention to a flow of signs)
>
> each street branches in the mind
> puns break
>   words fall apart
> a shell

sure as hell's
ash ell
when i let the letters shift sur face
is just a place on which im ages drift (*Book* 5, Chain 3)

"Puns break / words fall apart": ironically echoing Eliot's *Burnt Norton*,[24] Nichol notes that words are subject to a built-in imprecision, their semantic depth constantly threatened by the slipperiness of their lettered "sur face." Here, for example, "a shell" yields the colloquial "sure as hell's," only to break up into the nonsense of "ash ell." Describing his poetic strategy, Nichol writes of "looking out across the surface of words," and of how he "mine[s] the language for the heard world:"

writers struggle as i do
make a mend
join the torn letters of the language (*Book* 5, Chain 1)

Working with signs that are surveilled, mined, torn, and (a)mended, the poet reifies writing, as if he were *doing* things with words as much as writing them. Stripping (or "shell[ing]") language of its prior semantic determinations, and focusing instead on the play of its subsemantic constituents, Nichol compels reading matter to become, at the moment of its manipulation, merely linguistic matter. Occasionally a metapoetic description is followed by a quoted example, in a curious anticipation of the "activity" of critical discourse about *The Martyrology*, including my own:

lionel was tracking the word shift: 'laughter in slaughter' (*Book* 5, Chain 2)

Perhaps most reminiscent of Saussure's hypogrammatic gaze, however, is the poet's "tracking" of concealed proper names, especially the names of saints. Beginning in the opening books of *The Martyrology*, Nichol often divests the conventional meanings of words that happen to start with the consonant cluster *st*, only literally to (re)canonize them as the names of saints: "storm" and "stranglehold," for example, are christened "St. Orm" and "St. Ranglehold."

Both the game of the saint's name and its witty verbal equivalents in *The Martyrology* are generally considered to be a primary expression of Nichol's willingness to "admit into the poem a radical sense of linguistic free play and dissemination which is central to a poststructuralist theory of language."[25] Without question, Nichol luxuriates in the pleasure of the text by liberating it from the notion of a fixed and stable meaning. *The Martyrology* becomes a site where sentences, phrases, and words are recast as an expansive, nontotalizable writing field in which the material elements of the language endlessly combine, dissolve, and coalesce again to form new significations quite apart from those that are available to more familiar reading strategies. Yet to describe *The Martyrology* in this way blunts the full force of its disarticulating tactics, and for reasons whose underlying defensiveness would need to be discussed in the context of postmodernist theory and literary practice. It is of course true that hypogrammatic reading reminds us that at any point the referentiality of a text is jeopardized by another dimension of language functioning next and counter to that referentiality; there could be no end to the words one could "playfully" assemble out of any given chain of signifiers.

Nevertheless, the process of "looking across the surface of words" ineluctably remains a form of *reading*, and reading is always a case of *déjà lu*: How else could we know that we were reading anything, unless the signifiers in front of us were recognizable as language? But as Saussure's curious experience with the anagrams suggests, it is exactly the surety of that recognition—essential to the intelligibility of language—that is unsettled once the text has been dismantled into a disordered alphabet, and thus exposed to the sheer random occurrence and aggregation of individual letters, syllables, and words. What language actually is *before* it becomes readable, which is to say before one word or another is read *into* its accidentality, is not comprehensible. Nevertheless, the pressure of this unintelligibility makes itself felt precisely because once the text is hypogrammatically unsealed it becomes impossible to halt the "multiplication" of words generated along its "sur face." As Wlad Godzich notes, Saussure "considered his anagrammatic research a failure," not only because it had succeeded in demonstrating that "a string of signifiers [was] . . . capable of yielding a great many different signifiers" but also because "it refuse[d] to give them a hierarchy."[26] The second part of Saussure's difficulty is for him the most disconcerting, for without this "hierarchy" there is no way to discern the phenomenal shape of individual significative patterns (whether words or phrases) in the otherwise heterogeneous blur of the linguistic material.

Saussure's research "failure" is of course the linguistic windfall behind Nichol's poetic success. Yet by affirming the poet's "radical sense of linguistic free play" in the name of "poststructuralism" or "postmodernism," critical discussions of Nichol risk missing the underlying recuperative aspect of *The Martyrology*'s exorbitant textual strategies: the poem's very readability, the fact that it is composed of legible signs, attests to Nichol's own careful hierarchization of the nonhierarchical possibilities that his poetic tactics are responsible for opening up. The poet "make[s]" his "way thru the maze of . . . messages," as he says in Chain 3, but this labyrinth of information cannot be traversed everywhere, all at once; there will always be an interminable number of ways not taken. In other words, Nichol cannot read all the messages and be one reader because reading is expressly a question of choosing a path. For the sake of intelligibility *a* way must be made and will always be made through the maze, some "messages" ignored while others are deciphered. What would it mean, then, to be lost in the labyrinth, without a way through its endless signifying turns? By not forging a route of any kind—which is to say, by suspending the process of discrimination between signifying and non-signifying patterns upon which reading as such depends—Nichol would approximate Saussure's "perplexity" about Latin texts, the aimless moment in which meaningful language has been overwhelmed by the blank infinity of the sum of its possible significations. Captured by the unrestrained excess of the linguistic material before sense can be made of it, Nichol would in effect surrender to the monstrous thoughtlessness hidden within the maze's heart.

Saussure will not have it. But as I have suggested, in his own way neither will Nichol, for all his emphasis on the disseminative potential of language. Faced with what Godzich accurately describes as "a heterogeneous, non-reductive field which [did] . . . not lend itself to the conceptualization of a model,"[27] Saussure appears to have fled to the comforting rationality of linguistics. As de Man suggests, the swerve in his research career "supports the assumption of a terror glimpsed" (HI, 37). To the extent that Saussure's own "maze of messages" escapes conceptualization, it is unrecognizable as writing, which is one of the connotations of de Man's strange remark that it "is not at all certain that language is in any sense human." What begins as play for Nichol, the "comic stripping of the bare phrase," likewise leads to a cryptically grim disclosure: "the pain inside the language speaks." What the nature of this pain could be is difficult to articulate because it is, in its bareness, where the poem as readable language "begins," the maze before a "way" through it has been chosen. But Nichol's hypogrammatism gives it a muted voice, insofar as the poet's frolic among possible readings at every point bears the trace of a deeper undecidability: the labyrinthine prospect of a truly infinitized free play that is irreducible to and unregulated by any system of signification. In this intolerable realm the semiotic condition of the sign is eclipsed and language rendered into a kind of textual blur or smudge that extinguishes understanding. To experience language in its radical bareness is itself incomprehensible, for, as de Man writes, "We would then have witnessed . . . the undoing of cognition and its replacement by the uncontrollable power of the letter as inscription" (RT, 37).

De Man's point is that cognition, readability, and conceptualization are always already the refusal of this monstrously unsettling possibility. Insofar as "linguistic free play" can be said to describe *The Martyrology*'s hypogrammatism, it too is unavoidably an expression of the disavowal of the "letter as inscription" because it restricts itself to destabilizing the *manner* but not the *fact* of language's signifying function. From the perspective of the "work" of conventional reading habits, Nichol's word games are unarguably playful; yet the difference between "work" and play dissolves once we remember that both forms of apprehension are identically *readings*. Whether playful or laborious, reading presumes the legibility of the text and thus shelters *The Martyrology* from the "pain" of the "bared phrase" precisely because its agony could never be apprehended by a reading that reads only language. In other words, whatever label we give *The Martyrology*, legibility remains the humane bound of intelligibility within which the promised "freedom" of its "play" is unavoidably circumscribed. That Nichol's practice of a "poststructuralist theory of language" is so readily described as *play* (or "charades") pinpoints the limits to its "radical" nature, because the metaphor of gaming names language as the medium and object of the one who *plays*. In the manner of Friedrich Schiller, we might ask, What could be more essentially human (and humanizing) than *Spiel*?[28] *Homo significans* and *Homo ludens*: under these companionable and intimately interlinked signs we preserve the humane space of language by finding in it the reflection of our deepest selves not only as makers of signs, but also as the sole, privileged creatures in the position to luxuriate in their polysemy.

And yet the threat of the text's undoing by "the power of the letter as inscription" often seems close to the surface, and never more so than in those moments in Book 5 when Nichol seems taken aback by the momentum of his own linguistic free play:

t he
hee hee
    ha ha
        ho ho
            tho i know its no laughing matter some days
a sum of ways
weights the measured writing of the poem (*Book 5*, Chain 3)

Here "laughter" is literally found in "slaughter," onomatopoeic mirth in the literal dismemberment of the article "the." As McCaffery economically describes it, "spacing . . . inaugurates a radical split in the phonic direction, introducing in the second line an investment in a different sound whose end profit is a different meaning that generates its own chain of playful implications."[29] Yet Nichol is quick to note that there is a certain unhappy price for this playfulness, as he feels the sudden gravity or "weight[iness]" of the incalculable and labyrinthine "sum of ways" language might go once its hypogrammatism is unleashed. Held up against the measurelessly random possibilities that the letter insists upon language, even Nichol's manifest playfulness must come off more soberly as a "measured writing." Writing *as* writing is exactly the measure of intelligibility that is imposed upon the chaotic linguistic matter out of which it is made. Nichol:

looking out across the surface of the words today
the letters are not my n m e (*Book 5*, Chain 1)

Language is neither his ("my n"/mine) nor him ("m e"/me); but even as Nichol's letters acknowledge that they are not his foe or "n m e" either, he introduces the possibility that in their openly admitted otherness they might well become so; in the next several lines, the poet tentatively compares himself (and us) to "narcissus," making "the surface of words" into a fatally attractive simulacrum of the self:

narcissus as it was so long a go
                        e go
        and maybe even i go
                        o go s poe goed
                        edgarrishly
                        all'a narcissistically
so u go

Much could be said about how Nichol proceeds in these few lines, which are in many ways an exemplary instance of how Book 5 "unfolds"—if that is the right verb to describe the poet's halting movement through language's maze of messages. Nichol is in fact obliged to invent a verb to characterize how it is that he and his letters "go": "o go s poe goed," after the mythical Okanagan creature Ogopogo.[30] One might say then, by way of paraphrase, that the poem proceeds *monstrously*. Or, as Nichol also suggests, it unfolds "edgarrishly," deviantly, like the excessive characters in stories by "[P]oe," or like the language of Gloucester's half-crazed son in *King Lear,* whose nonsensical echolalia on the heath appears playful while also sounding the destruction of a more general coherence.[31] Surely that way lies *la folie de Saussure*; but as de Man notes in what is undoubtedly his own most garish essay, "no degree of knowledge can ever stop this madness, for it is the madness of words" (SD, 122).

Scrapped Script and a New Saint Axe

By dismembering words into letters, Nichol brings out the relationship between meaningfulness and the literal, material properties of language; new words and meanings are generated by the "playful" manipulation of letters and syllables that are themselves quite without the sense they receive once they are manipulated. What is the nature of the textual material, then, and what are words such that they can be made out of it? Considered strictly as a *game*, Nichol's text only affirms the fairly obvious fact that signifiers are capable of yielding multiple meanings; what always goes without saying, however, is that the difference between what a text says and what it is construed to mean leaves open in principle the strange notion of the signifier freed from all significance—freed even and especially from being merely insignificant, a mark whose meaninglessness is relative rather than absolute, wholly a function of its difference from those that have been construed as meaningful. To read this (absolutely) blank signifier would be precisely *not* to read; it would be to leave open the question of language, and, impossibly, to "see" the text in its sheer materiality. Neither comprehending nor not-comprehending, this *denegated* vision would approach what de Man calls, after Kant, *Augenschein,* the "stony gaze" under which meaningful language "fragments" into the radically meaningless material condition of its possibility (PMK, 144). For de Man, language is always and everywhere the phenomenal monument to this materiality, marking its ineluctable operation precisely by annulling it.

Nichol's hypogrammatism, which amounts, finally, to a sustained attention to the purely random distribution of letters and syllables in the linguistic field, reproduces Kant's *Augenschein*, insofar as that is possible. Certainly no attempt is made, as is the case in Saussure's notebooks, to rescue language from itself by anchoring its hypogrammatism in a particular poem's extralinguistic thematic concerns; the words that Nichol deciphers from other words are randomly generated by the text's senseless capacity to produce meaningless clusterings of letters, linguistic scraps whose significance as readable words can come only after the accidental fact of that clustering. As I have suggested, Saussure is repulsed by the measurelessness of this linguistic phenomenon; but Nichol presses on, exploring the outermost limits of language by "taking the notion of open form writing," as he says prosaically, "to its logical extreme."[32] Once the incommensurability of the signifier and the signified is demonstrated, as it undoubtedly is when words are read into chance accumulations of linguistic matter, the nonsignifying object of Kant's "stony gaze" would seem theoretically possible; yet it is not until Book 5's penultimate chain that that "extreme" comes closest to being realized. In these pages (see Figure 3.1), I would argue, the fragmentation of language into a disordered alphabet is chastening and precipitous as much as it is "playful," for in their scattering of single, isolated letters (chipped off from the ends of unconnected words) the reader is brought to the very threshold across which language in its materiality passes into cognition and readability. Where "laughter" was once playfully "tracked" in "slaughter," now all that remains are dismembered signs, the detritus of scrapped script (or "scrapture," as Nichol calls it).

The emptiness of this lettered space discloses more clearly than ever the fundamental discrepancy between meaning and the constituents of meaning; reading is here reduced to near zero-degree apprehension, a mere spelling out of single, meaningless letters.[33] Nevertheless, *as* an identifiable part of the alphabet, the letter *as* letter is already well on its way to language; that is why linguistic materiality "appears" not in the actual mark on the page, which is, after all, readable as a letter, but in the utter incommensurability of even this minimal significance and what that mark must be—senseless in itself—in order to bear meaning at all. "Such marks cannot be known to *signify* and cannot be said to be *per-*

Figure 3.1. Reprinted from *The Martyrology: Book 5* (Toronto: Coach House Press, 1977), by permission of Eleanor Nichol

ceived," Cynthia Chase notes, "since their form, their shape, their phenomenal status, is a function of an intentionality or semiotic status that can only be postulated for them rather than perceived, described, or known."[34] In other words, language's "semiotic status"—what I have been calling its readability—amounts to a "postulation" about these marks, a human or "intentional" imposition of meaningfulness on that which lies beyond or before perception, description, and knowledge. The altogether absent continuity between these marks and conceptualization, beginning with the notion of "language" but extending to all manner of thinking, including the notion of the human subject, undoes phenomenal apprehension, disfiguring it by exposing the contingent nature of its impositional character. Utterly indifferent to what is postulated about it, the materiality of the letter thus operates as the indeterminate background against which language and knowledge appear not positively, as the object of apprehension, but negatively, as a kind of sustained hallucination about and defensive gesture against the disarticulating force of the power of inscription.

If language is, as Nichol admits, "not a spell" but "an act of desperation,"[35] then "What *is* the relationship of someone to the mythology they make up?" The answer to this question, which introduces Book 5, naturally finds a focus in the poet's myth of the saints, and particularly in the game of the saints' names. The fact that playing with names forms such an important part of Nichol's hypogrammatism is significant, because of all the parts of language it is the name that most lends itself to the comforting notion that language is essentially a nomenclature, a system of signs pointing to things that are already given to comprehension in advance of signification. Nothing could be further from the truth in Nichol's name game, where the real question could be described as what is given to language in advance of comprehension. Here Nichol thematizes as play the fact that words can always be recovered from the purely accidental combination of letters and syllables. Of course, the names of the saints are not already *there* to be recognized and read—although it is interesting to note how difficult it is to speak of hypogrammatism as anything but a process of "decipherment," as if one were disclosing something fully formed but "concealed" in the textual material. As in the case of Saussure's anagrams, the game of the name demonstrates instead that language as such is not given to perception at all, but must be made to appear through the arbitrary decision to impose meaningfulness upon some articulations—meaningless in themselves—and not on others. Nichol's wordplay thus raises the question of what must be there for the name, for any meaningful word or pattern, to be brought into legibility *in the first place.* Where does reading—"conventional," "postmodernist"—*as* reading begin? That multiple, or rather, infinite significances can be conferred upon linguistic patterns, even in the absence of any communicable meaning, necessarily implies a moment of inertial opposition or resistance about language in which the question of what is determined to be significant, and thus what is *in*significant, is left open. To pass from "stranglehold" to "St. Ranglehold," for example, the reader must move through a sort of linguistic apogee, which, like the turning point at the height of a parabolic arc, is essentially dimensionless, imperceptible as such. Neither one word nor the other, neither noun nor proper name, this pivotal linguistic moment "between the signifier & the signified" is itself unreadable, yet logically necessary for the new signification to have been conferred upon the same aggregate of letters. Evident only in its effacement, this moment is not a sign and thus certainly not language, but what might be called "pure phonic datum," the condition of the possibility of signification.

"Pure phonic datum" is Sylvère Lotringer's term for the materiality of the letter, and deliberately recalls Benjamin's "*reine Sprache*." In his discussion of Saussure's unresolved perplexity about the significative status of the proper names that he had tracked in this datum, Lotringer asks two questions with a punning flourish worthy of any wordplay in *The Martyrology*:

> What is to be done with the disturbing repetitions of the pure phonic datum, with the "regular distribution of vowels and consonants" glimpsed in the Saturnian and certain formula lines of Homeric poetry? To which saint should they be dedicated—if not to a new *Saint-Axe* [i.e., "syntax"]?[36]

The French would say: *Ne savoir à quel saint se vouer*, meaning, roughly, "to be at one's wits' end." Lotringer's question deliberately echoes Saussure's undecidability about the "phantasmagoria" or "reality" of what suddenly looms before him in his hypogrammatic research: unable to decide whether what he gazes at remains significant—that is, language—or not, and thus unwilling to determine what to "do" with it, the linguist finds himself exposed to the unintelligible possibility of "pure phonic datum." The moment is itself intolerable because it marks the end of wit, and unsustainable because even the minimal imposition of names like "datum," "materiality," or "the sign that may not be one" settle out the radical indeterminacy that these terms name. What is to be done? There is nothing to do except *read*, which is to say *inflict* sense of some kind upon the utter senselessness of the materiality of the letter by choosing a path through its unbounded possibilities. Language is precisely the consecration of the materiality by which it is subtended, or, to use Lotringer's metaphor, the endless spiriting away of "pure phonic datum" through its dedication to one saint or another.

Perhaps this includes even a dedication to a "new *Saint-Axe*," whose grim name recalls the threat of dismemberment that is language's originary task to sublate. To which saint, indeed, if not this one, should we commit Nichol's fragmentation of language into the random sequences of its letters, and the reassembly of these fragments into words and names—especially the names of saints? We read these names; what remains unread is that which language must be in order for it to be read, for such names to be read "in" it. In other words, if reading is always reading language, then what the lettered space of the hypogrammatized text is in principle "before" functioning as legible writing remains inaccessible—blotted out so that language can take place and reading begin. The paradox is that the game nevertheless points well beyond itself while effacing the conditions that allow it to be played. Rather than simply functioning as a ludic element in the text, Nichol's hypogrammatism discloses the more general phenomenon by which the work of reading, whether conventional or playfully unconventional, is made possible, for the transparently arbitrary "discovery" of the saints' names reminds us that reading prethinks the resolution of the undecidability about whether what lies before us is significant or not, and thus whether language has occurred.

The game of the saint's name represents an uncanny literalization of language's founding consecration of its materiality. As a naming, the game repeats the inaugural scene of nomination in which the passage from the materiality of the letter to phenomenal, readable language is everywhere effected: to read is always already to give a name—"Readability"—and a face—"language"—to that which is absolutely nameless and faceless, the blank materiality of language that Rodolphe Gasché characterizes as "the *texte brut* [literally, "the bare phrase"], . . . the text before it starts to signify and prior to the established meanings that the community of interpreters has inflicted upon it."[37] Reading renders familiarly human that which is in-human within language, or more exactly that which lies on the far side of determining what is human about it or not: namely, "the uncontrollable power of inscription." What needs to be emphasized, therefore, is that although the face of language makes this power phenomenally legible, the shape in which it appears is thoroughly alien to it; indeed, next to the sheer random occurring of the letters s-t-u-t-t-e-r, for example, the readable word in the shape of a saint's name—St. Utter—looks like a completely arbitrary and contingent fiction. Nor is the accidentality from which the legible word is drawn in any sense the cause or origin of what is formed, no more than the saints' legends in *The Martyrology* are caused by the phonic datum out of which their names are abruptly and arbitrarily articulated. Their genealogies are grounded in nothing substantial, but in the accidental aggregation of letters that amounts to a start, a starting, but not an origin, that is, in a textual event that conditions meaning but does not itself possess meaning. In conferring the name of Readability and the face of language on the *texte brut* we assign the capacity for reference to something that is in essence pure, material occurrence, like a random sequence of letters, and that therefore acquires meaning or reference only after the fact. The game of the saint's name paradoxically serves the "decanonizing" function of remembering the imposed or conferred character of that face, exposing it to be a massive and sustained figure for that for which there could be no literal expression.

"Some unheard of, monstrous species of things are involved," Saussure writes,[38] figuring the dread of his own hypogrammatism in a language that seems uncannily similar to Nichol's in the epigraph to Book 5. What is brutish and inaudible here augurs an incomprehensible muteness at the core of language, its monstrosity a figure for the pure otherness of that which cannot be assimilated to any system of intentions or motives or signifying codification. Similarly, when Nichol writes that in focusing on the moment "when the word forms" he is "bringing into light what has been in darkness,"[39] the "darkness" to which he refers is a metaphor for the senseless materiality of language that escapes even the minimal recuperation as the absence of the light of sense; lying beyond the phenomenal opposition of visibility and invisibility, and, for that matter, audibility and inaudibility, it is a blankness within the labyrinth of language that, strictly speaking, escapes understanding as such. At what point *does* a disordered alphabet become a masterpiece? One cannot say, because it (always) goes without saying: as Kevin Newmark observes in the course of a discussion about the random surfacing of concealed words in Blanchot, "we have no language in which to speak of the conditions of language, to speak meaningfully of the moment in which meaningless letters become meaningful words."[40]

We have no language, perhaps, except language itself, which for de Man is everywhere an "allegory" (in his highly idiosyncratic sense of the term) of its own taking-place, a sustained canceling out of the nonsignifying materiality of the letter so that the phenomenal word may appear. The game of the saint's name and the attendant legends that game makes possible amount to an extension of this allegory of reading; the stories of the saints are tied to names whose status in the poem is openly acknowledged to be the result of an arbitrary decision to "form" the word out of text's "darkness." And from this inaugural delusion Nichol constructs a widening and increasingly meaningful narrative in the saints' legends, which are themselves easily assimilable to multiple levels of interpretation, whether, for example, as a figure for the poet's struggle with his vocation or as an expression of Nichol's "postmodernism," in short, to all the conceptions—at once necessary and hallucinatory—that facilitate and enhance the fundamentally reassuring notion that what we are reading is not an in-human accident but language and a poem at that. There is no overcoming this resistance to postmodernism because postmodernism is *itself* this resistance. The fact that the text is titled *The Martyrology* is one sign that the saints' stories and name game form a *mise en abyme* in which the entire poem's constitution *as* readable language is rehearsed, repeated from within. But because language's taking-place conditions meaning but is itself without meaning, it is available only retrospectively, in the poem we actually read. *The opening of language occurs and language means, but we will never be in a position to read language occurring, because by becoming legible language performs the erasure of its having taken place.*[41] The term *postmodern,* or, for that matter, *poem,* though necessary, remains inadequate to describe the *texte brut,* because the readability it fully implies can hardly account for the opening of language as that which is other than and irreducible to what is readable. Because the materiality of the letter is radically indifferent to thought, marking only the text's capacity for "reference prior to designating the referent" (RT, 7–8), it levels without compromise all distinctions on the basis of genre (*The Martyrology* as long poem), literary history or national affiliation (the "Canadian postmodern"), or subject matter ("the failure of language").[42] De Man's radical position would therefore seem monstrously unpalatable to literary critic and author alike: certainly no figure in contemporary theory has been more demonized than de Man—or less well read, the two phenomena being complexly related in overdetermined ways that I cannot explore here. As Carol Jacobs has said, de Man's writings "are an aegis to which the head of the Medusa is affixed and which we contemplate at our own risk."[43] But readers miss exactly half of de Man's central insight if they conclude that in his hands deconstruction becomes merely nihilistic destruction. It cannot be emphasized enough that for de Man reading is unavoidable to the precise degree that it is impossible. What saves his position from simply doing "literature a disservice by placing it in a realm remote from its physical, emotional, and moral contexts," as D. M. R. Bentley has said of post-modernist theory in Canada,[44] is that for de Man we have *no choice but* to locate literature in these and other similarly humanistic contexts, because literary criticism, like all forms of reading, crucially relies upon them in order to ensure the legibility of the text.

The categorical imperative to read, and thus to "discover" in language's legibility a fundamental confirmation of the humanity that we believe ourselves to be, fully implicates de Man's writings and the critical reception of those writings—my own included. There being nothing outside humanism, his work is hardly immune to the processes of monumentalization and aestheticization that he describes as sheltering the human in his target texts. It may even be the case, as Heidi Kreuger has recently argued, that "despite the current tendency to polarize deconstruction and humanism, the rejection of pathos" in de Man is "made on essentially human, and humanist grounds."[45] De Man's fascination with *reine Sprache* represents an attempt to unsettle the fundamental at-homeness of the human with language, *not* to think "beyond" the human—as if that could be accomplished—but more clearly to bring out the uniquely duplicitous position of the human within the domicile of legibility, at once precarious and well founded. Reading with de Man means that the home momentarily becomes a labyrinth, but this displacement is unavoidably imbued with a pathos whose very familiarity returns us home again—or reminds us that we have never left it and that we never could leave it. The persistence of a certain humanism is never more evident than at those points where de Man's extreme analytic rigor, which calls for a hyperascetic resistance to the seductions of the aesthetic ideology, coincides with a conspicuously pathetic rhetoric of monsters and monstrous threats. De Man warns that the dismemberment, disfigurement, and defacement about which he writes are linguistic, not literal, but this proviso does little to contain the hazardous mood that his insistently corporeal rhetoric evokes. The concluding paragraphs of de Man's essay on Kleist are a case in point. Here a scene of meliorative play—Schiller's image of "a well-executed English dance"—is forced to give way to one of lifelessness and "mutilation" (AF, 263, 288): Kleist's puppets in unthinking, mechanical motion, and the strange figure of a legless man given prostheses so that he might simulate Schiller's dancers. Typically, for de Man, this scene of "hidden violence" is powerfully teratogenic, reminding him as it does of the "sheer monstrosity" of "the eyeless philosopher Saunderson in Diderot's *Lettre sur les aveugles*," who is in turn described as "one more victim in a long series of mutilated bodies that attend on the progress of enlightened self-knowledge, a series that includes Wordsworth's mute country-dwellers and blind city-beggars" (AF, 288–90). As Neil Hertz points out, however, de Man appears to conjure up this disfigured parade only so that he may deny its obviously affective dimension. "One should avoid the pathos of an imagery of bodily mutilation," de Man writes, "and not forget that we are dealing with textual models, not with historical and political systems that are their correlate. The disarticulation produced by tropes is primarily a disarticulation of meaning; it *attacks* semantic units such as words and sentences" (AF, 289; emphasis added).

It may be that one *should* avoid this pathos (yet whence comes this ascetic duty?), but the fact is that de Man's argument continues to draw significant rhetorical power from it, right up to his use of the visceral metaphor of assault in the verb *attacks*. Perhaps de Man is simply being ironic, given that he here relies on a distinction between literal and figural violence that his work massively renders problematic. In any case, figural or not, why would "the dismemberment of language by the power of the letter"—and thus the annihilation of thinking—be any *less* monstrously horrifying or destructive than "bodily mutilation"? De Man readily concedes that his resistance to the aesthetic ideology in the name of "the senseless power of positional language" is "made all the more pious for . . . [its] denial of piety" (SD, 122). This denegating gesture, in which denial reinscribes its own object, is crucial to the critical operation of de Man's last essays. As he says in the context of Benjamin's work on translation, the strictly a-pathetic and machinelike work of sheer language is "*best* analyzed in terms of the inhuman, dehumanized language of linguistics, rather than in the language of imagery, or tropes, of pathos, or drama" (TT, 96). Yet this "dehumanized language" unavoidably reintroduces what it is trying to avoid, for no language—*as* language—could enable the reader to step out of his or her humanity into the realm—imaginary, as such—of *reine Sprache*. De Man urges his readers not to think of the "'inhuman' . . . [as] some kind of mystery, or some kind of secret; the inhuman is: linguistic structures, the play of linguistic tensions, linguistic events that occur, possibilities which are inherent in language—independently of any intent or any drive or any wish or any desire we might have" (TT, 96). But he is clearly drawn to an affectively charged teratological rhetoric whenever he evokes the unthinkable possibility of *reine Sprache*, in part because monstrosity not only effectively figures forth the radical alterity of the inhuman, but also renders threateningly unfamiliar what M. H. Abrams rightly believes "is the most human of all the things we find in the world" (TT, 99)—namely, language. How better to represent that which is indifferent to human desire except as monstrous?

But the monstrous is somewhat more than a defamiliarizing device in de Man, who also asks, What is more monstrous, the indifferent alterity of sheer language or the more or less lurid catachreses that are blindly "made" of that alterity, and then instantly mistaken for knowledge and the thought of the human? In de Man's later essays there is certainly no *reine Sprache* as such, and thus no representation of it; but there is no *not* re-presenting it either, caught as he is in a language machine generating an expanding field of figures that "impose[s] . . . on the senseless power of positional language the authority of sense and of meaning" (SD, 117). These figures do not share the slightest similarity to that "nameless, alien being"[46] of which they are figures: sense displaces (and de-faces) senselessness, in a chain of violent substitutions out of which finally emerges a "system of truth, virtue, and understanding" (*AR*, 289). As he says, "The strategy of denegation which calls a threat a shelter in the hope of thus laying it to rest is all too familiar" (WV, 86)—all too familiar because constitutive and protective of the human. The monstrous, I would argue, is an exemplary instance of this denegating strategy, at once a threat and the palliation of that threat: the monstrous evokes the inhuman, but it also humanizes it, in a negative mode, by bringing it dialectically within the orbit of the human as a threatening Other. The a-pathetic glimpse of an Other "within" language becomes the primary means by which to reflect upon the situation of the human, contingently exposed to a linguistic system it cannot entirely control, understand, or do without—a situation, in other words, of maximum pathos. Monstrosity is thus not only a figure of alterity, but also a figure for the uncontrollable figuration of alterity; it brings out how every attempt to represent sheer language—and, in a sense, there is nothing but this attempt—will be more or less lurid, and more or less sheltering in nature. The monstrous is thus a figure that dis-figures or de-faces, in de Man's denegated sense of these key terms: it covers up to the exact extent that it discloses.

Pure language anonymously obliges us to perform the task of making sense, a task whose most general name is "the human." Approaching the inhuman origin of that compulsory labor is difficult, but it is, as Benjamin sees, "*Die Aufgabe des Übersetzers*" par excellence. We see why Benjamin functions as de Man's best image of himself reading. At the risk of an abyssal loss of sense, Benjamin concentrates on the materiality of language. What he says of this radically reconceived notion of "translation" amounts to an uncanny description of the work of de Man's later essays:

> Literality thoroughly overthrows all reproduction of meaning with regard to the syntax and threatens directly to lead to incomprehensibility. In the eyes of the nineteenth century, Hölderlin's translations of Sophocles were monstrous examples of such literality. . . . the demand for literality is no offspring of an interest in maintaining meaning.[47]

Hölderlin's bizarre, word-for-word translations, which Benjamin characterizes as exemplarily attentive to pure language, render the target text illegible, and thus are *monstrously* at odds with mimetic models of the communication of meaning: "A teratogenesis instead of conventional, natural, reproduction results in which the limbs of the progeny are dismembered, all syntax dismantled."[48] So too in de Man's "translations" of Shelley, Kleist, Saussure, and others. This monstrous work "should avoid pathos," but cannot; like Benjamin, de Man unavoidably evokes *reine Sprache* in "the language of imagery, or tropes, of pathos, or drama." Describing Benjamin, de Man describes himself: "To the extent that this text is human, all too human in the appeal it makes to you, and its messianic overtones to name something which is essentially nonhuman, it displaces our sense of what is human, both in ourselves and in our relationship to other humans" (TT, 96). Paradoxically, the monstrous inhuman goes to the heart of the *ethical* undercurrent of de Man's work, his resolute attempt to describe in ever more exacting and self-complicating terms the *ethos* or dwelling place of the human and its others. Caught between exposing a threat and building a shelter, the (de)constructive task of the translator is not a means of sacrificing the human, as some of de Man's most inattentive readers have recently suggested. Kreuger is exactly right when she points out how de Man's underlying concern is much rather "that we not abuse the trope of the 'human,' that we not purchase our pathos too cheaply."[49]

An Act of Desperation

In his *Aesthetische Theorie,* Theodor Adorno writes that "a fragment is a work that has been tampered with by death."[50] Because it was conceived and composed as a *life's* work, and thus exposed at every point to the possibility of interruption by Nichol's death, *The Martyrology* in its open-endedness will always have been fragmentary in Adorno's sense. Death has tampered with *The Martyrology* to be sure, but death was always tampering with *The Martyrology,* its sheer unknowable otherness and brutal contingency lurking around the next turn of the labyrinth—or the next—like that Minotaur that "sudden[ly]" captures the poet in Matt's strange premonitory dream. Writing without a view to finishing, Nichol availed himself of only one ending, whose mortal hazard for *The Martyrology,* as for its author, was its randomness and its inexplicability: the death of the author is precisely that which cannot be *viewed,* that which is utterly unavailable to phenomenality and cognition. Without Kant's *Augenschein,* without that impossibly "stony gaze" of noncomprehension, Nichol's death as such remains inaccessible. But the phenomenal shape of the poem, which is to say whatever it is that we make of the text now that it has been "completed," is paradoxically and irrevocably answerable to that death, the disarticulating force of which decisively articulates *The Martyrology,* determining where the poem as such ends, and thus begins. The poem does not—cannot—negotiate Nichol's death, because that would be to suggest that the one is intelligible to the other. And yet it cannot help but negotiate it, insofar as the poem is *intersected* by the death of the author, crossed suddenly, incomprehensibly, by its annihilatory force: this exorbitant point of intersection remains unthought and unknown, except as a kind of interference effect in the phenomenal form of *The Martyrology* itself. We read *The Martyrology,* now, and because we *read* we impose an unavoidable intelligibility upon the death's senseless intervention by annulling it. "To read is to understand, to question, to know, to forget, to erase, to deface, to repeat," de Man writes in "Shelley Disfigured" (122). We cannot stop making a certain strange sense of death while we read, although as de Man also notes with regard to Shelley's unfinished poem *The Triumph of Life,* this process of "monumentalization" (SD, 120) is inevitably carried out after the fact, and as an arbitrary and contingent fiction. As critical readers or as friends of Nichol, we can neither gaze stonily at his death nor share in its noncomprehension; instead, we are compelled to read "into" it.

Let me try to say this differently. Nichol's death shares no relationship with the poem whose shape it nevertheless articulates; it did not "mean" that shape. How, then, to read the altogether absent continuity between the "act" of the author's death and the poem as it stands today? Death tampers with *The Martyrology*, but the tampering as such proves almost impossible to think. De Man's point, however, is that we are always reading of this tampering in the exorbitant convergence of the materiality of the letter and its phenomenal effacement in language: death, like the uncontrollable power of inscription, is the absolute alterity that conditions the poem and threatens it with fragmentation—and yet forms no part of its phenomenal shape. As de Man luridly overstates it in "Autobiography as De-Facement," "Death is a displaced figure for a linguistic predicament" (81). Not that death is "only" a matter of words, but that the "predicament" of language—the erasure of the opening in which signification occurs—is indistinguishable from the phenomenality of the word *death*; both terms are figures for the senselessness for which there is no literal term. De Man might just as easily have written that the "predicament of language" is a "displaced figure for death," because each metaphor functions as a phenomenal displacement of what cannot be experienced meaningfully. Death *happens* inexplicably and precipitously, like the inaugurating predicament of language and like the purely random clusterings of letters and syllables that in their randomness serve as a figure for that predicament. What intelligibility we make of these nonsignifying events amounts to a human, all too human, "act of desperation," an imposition of meaning upon the radical darkness and *in*humanity of their thoughtlessness. To the precise extent that *The Martyrology* is readable, and therefore a monument to the unintelligibility it erases, it is an example of this imposition, a displaced figure for Nichol's death. "The poem is written in spite of / ," Nichol writes, the line trailing off into the blankness of what the poem is literally unable to name but is nevertheless composed against. Nichol's death, like the materiality of the letter, constitutes the most fundamental point of resistance to the poem's reading. Its blank unthinkability *disfigures The Martyrology*, in de Man's queer sense of the term, defacing or marking the text precisely by unmasking its readability as a humane figure imposed upon a monstrously indifferent otherness.

How to begin to read a poem that ended without being at an end?

Notes

Peter Babiak, Daniel Fischlin, Kevin Newmark, and Marc Redfield all read versions of this essay, and I am very grateful for their invaluable criticisms and suggestions. Eleanor Nichol kindly gave me permission to reproduce two pages from Book 5 of bp Nichol's *The Martyrology*. This essay was prepared for publication with the able assistance of Carolyn Brendon and with the support of the Social Sciences and Humanities Research Council of Canada.

1. Quoted by Jean Starobinski in *Words upon Words: The Anagrams of Ferdinand de Saussure*, trans. Olivia Emmet (New Haven, Conn.: Yale University Press, 1979), 3.

2. Page numbers for quotations from the works of Paul de Man are given in the body of the text and in notes with the following abbreviations. TT is "'Conclusions': Walter Benjamin's 'The Task of the Translator'"; HI is "Hypogram and Inscription"; and RT is "The Resistance to Theory," all in *The Resistance to Theory* (Minneapolis: University of Minnesota Press, 1986). SS is "Sign and Symbol in Hegel's Aesthetics"; AD is "Autobiography as De-Facement"; SD is "Shelley Disfigured"; AF is "Aesthetic Formalization: Kleist's Über das Marionettentheater"; and WV is "Wordsworth and the Victorians," all in *The Rhetoric of Romanticism* (New York: Columbia University Press, 1984). PMK is "Phenomenality and Materiality in Kant," in *Hermeneutics: Questions and Prospects*, ed. Gary Shapiro and Alan Sica (Amherst: University of Massachusetts Press, 1986). *AR* is *Allegories of Reading: Figural Language in Rousseau, Nietzsche, Rilke, and Proust* (New Haven, Conn.: Yale University Press, 1979).

3. Carol Jacobs, "The Monstrosity of Translation," *MLN* 90 (1975): 761.

4. Marc W. Redfield, "Humanizing de Man," *diacritics* 19, no. 2 (1989): 51.

5. Fredric Jameson, *Postmodernism: or, The Cultural Logic of Late Capitalism* (Durham, N.C.: Duke University Press, 1991), 248–49.

6. Jacques Derrida, "Structure, Sign and Play in the Discourse of the Human Sciences," in *Writing and Difference*, trans. Alan Bass (Chicago: University of Chicago Press, 1978), 292.

7. Douglas Barbour, "bp Nichol: In Memoriam," *Canadian Poetry: Studies, Documents, Reviews* 23 (1988): iii–iv.

8. In 1988, bp Nichol died suddenly of complications arising from surgery. He was forty-three years old.

9. bp Nichol, "After Reading the Chronology," in *Tracing the Paths: Reading ≠ Writing the Martyrology*, ed. Roy Miki (Vancouver: Talonbooks, 1988), 339–40.

10. Stephen Scobie, *bp Nichol: What History Teaches* (Vancouver: Talonbooks, 1984), 117.

11. References to bp Nichol's poem *The Martyrology: Book 5* (Toronto: Coach House, 1977) appear in the text with the abbreviation *Book 5*. Because Nichol's poem is without pagination, quotations are identified in the text by chain number.

12. Barbara Johnson, *A World of Difference* (Baltimore: Johns Hopkins University Press, 1987), 6.

13. Martin Heidegger, *Poetry, Language, Thought,* trans. Margaret Waller (New York: Columbia University Press), 196–97.

14. Published in English as *Words upon Words: The Anagrams of Ferdinand de Saussure.*

15. Quoted in Starobinski, *Words upon Words,* 105–6.

16. Jacques Derrida, *Of Grammatology,* trans. Gayatri Chakravorty Spivak (Baltimore: Johns Hopkins University Press, 1974), 60.

17. Hans-Jost Frey, "Undecidability," *Yale French Studies* 69 (1985): 132.

18. Redfield, "Humanizing de Man," 44.

19. Sylvère Lotringer, in "The Game of the Name," *diacritics* 3 (Summer 1973): 8, argues that "the *Anagrams* weren't published: linguistics was born of that exclusion." De Man responds by suggesting that "rather than a 'mere' repression, Saussure's retheorization of the question in the *Cours* can more charitably be seen as the insistence of theoretical discourse in the face of the dangers it reveals" (HI, 37). Extending de Man's point, I argue that the postmodernist affirmation of linguistic play similarly amounts to a negative knowledge of "the dangers it reveals."

20. Jonathan Culler, *Framing the Sign: Criticism and Its Institutions* (Norman: University of Oklahoma Press, 1988), 224.

21. Leon S. Roudiez, "Twelve Points from Tel Quel," *L'Esprit Créatur* 14 (Winter 1974): 300; quoted by Julia Kristeva, *Revolution in Poetic Language,* trans. Margaret Waller (New York: Columbia University Press, 1984), 265n.

22. Steve McCaffery, "The Martyrology as Paragram," *Open Letter,* sixth series, nos. 5–6 (Summer–Fall 1986): 196–97.

23. Ibid., 196.

24. T. S. Eliot, *The Complete Poems and Plays 1909–1950* (San Diego: Harcourt Brace Jovanovich, 1971), 121.

25. Scobie, "bp Nichol," 127.

26. Wlad Godzich, "Semiotics/Semiotext: The Texture of a Weaving Song," *Semiotext(e)* 1 (1975): 82.

27. Ibid.

28. Friedrich Schiller, *On the Aesthetic Education of Man,* trans. Reginald Snell (New York: Ungar, 1965), especially Letters 26 and 27, 124–40.

29. McCaffrey, "The Martyrology as Paragram," 193.

30. Scobie, "bp Nichol," 132.

31. LEAR: Judicious punishment! 'twas this flesh begot
Those pelican daughters.
EDGAR: Pillicock sat on Pillicock-hill.
Halloo, halloo, loo, loo!

Edgar's words simply echo the sounds of Lear's. As the Fool rightly observes about this nonconversation, "This cold night will turn us all to fools and madmen" (3.4.74–7, 78–9).

32. Nichol, "After Reading the Chronology," 339.

33. De Man writes: "When you spell a word you say a certain number of meaningless letters, which then come together in the word, but in each of the letters the word

is not present. The two are absolutely independent of each other. What is being named here as the disjunction between grammar and meaning, *Wort* and *Satz*, is the materiality of the letter: the independence, or the way in which the letter can disrupt the ostensible stable meaning of a sentence and introduce in it a slippage by means of which that meaning disappears, evanesces, and by means of which all control over that meaning is lost" (TT, 89).

34. Cynthia Chase, *Decomposing Figures: Rhetorical Readings in the Romantic Tradition* (Baltimore: Johns Hopkins University Press, 1986), 105.

35. bp Nichol, *The Martyrology: Books 1 & 2* (Toronto: Coach House, 1977), Book 2.

36. Lotringer, "The Game of the Name," 104.

37. Rodolphe Gasché, "In-difference to Philosophy: de Man on Kant, Hegel and Nietzsche," in *Reading de Man Reading*, ed. Lindsay Waters and Wlad Godzich (Minneapolis: University of Minnesota Press, 1989), 265. As Gasché argues, a reading for the *texte brut*, "one that focuses on the nonphenomenal and autonomous potential of language, rather than producing noumena, exhibits a fragmentary chaos of meaningless linguistic matter, repetitive mechanical rules, and absolutely opaque linguistic events" (282).

38. Quoted in Jean Starobinski, *Les mots sous les mots: Les anagrammes de Ferdinand de Saussure* (Paris: Èditions Gallimard, 1971), 31; quoted in de Man, HI, 37, de Man's translation.

39. bp Nichol, "The Pata of Letter Feet, or The English Written Character as a Medium for Poetry," *Open Letter*, sixth series, no. 1 (Spring 1985): 82–83.

40. Kevin Newmark, "Resisting, Responding," in *Responses: On Paul de Man's Wartime Journalism*, ed. Werner Hamacher, Neil Hertz, and Thomas Keenan (Lincoln: University of Nebraska Press, 1989), 347.

41. I paraphrase de Man's crucial formulation: "Language posits and language means (since it articulates) but language cannot posit meaning; it can only reiterate (or reflect) it in its reconfirmed falsehood" (SD, 117–18).

42. Scobie, *bp Nichol*, 117.

43. Carol Jacobs, "On Looking at Shelley's Medusa," *Yale French Studies* 69 (1985): 166.

44. D. M. R. Bentley, "Preface: 'Along the Line of Smoky Hills': Further Steps Towards an Ecological Poetics," *Canadian Poetry: Studies, Documents, Reviews* 26 (1990): vi.

45. S. Heidi Kreuger, "Opting to Know: On the Wartime Journalism of Paul de Man," in *Responses: On Paul de Man's Wartime Journalism*, ed. Werner Hamacher, Neil Hertz, and Thomas Keenan (Lincoln: University of Nebraska Press, 1989), 310–11.

46. Jameson, *Postmodernism*, 249.

47. Walter Benjamin, *Gesammelte Schriften* (Frankfurt: Suhrkamp Verlag, 1972), 4.1, 17–18; quoted in Jacobs, "The Monstrosity of Translation," 761, Jacobs's translation.

48. Jacobs, "The Monstrosity of Translation," 761.

49. Kreuger, "Opting to Know," 311.

50. Theodor Adorno, *Aesthetic Theory*, trans. C. Lenhardt (London: Routledge & Kegan Paul, 1984), 493.

II Monstrous Identity

4 The Odd Couple: Gargantua and Tom Thumb

Anne Lake Prescott

Background

Giants and pygmies are ambiguously monstrous: strange "here" but normal "there," where their species is at home, whether Scythia, Africa, Brazil, Lilliput, or Brobdingnag. The fact of merely situational monstrosity was not lost on earlier writers, who could joke about spatial relativity (the thirty-foot Ascapart in *Bevis of Hampton* leaves home because he is too short) or more soberly deduce from it the value of ethnic humility (in the thirteenth century Jacques de Vitry wrote that "just as we consider Pygmies to be dwarfs, so they consider us giants. . . . And in the land of the Giants, who are larger than we are, we would be considered dwarfs by them").[1] But if setting the gigantic against the minuscule encourages thoughts about perspective and outlook, rhetorically coupling a giant and a pygmy can create a monster even more apt to amuse, horrify, instruct. I will describe how one "monster," Gargantua, was juxtaposed to Tom Thumb (or a nameless pygmy) with enough frequency in early Stuart England to project—linguistically, for one cannot well imagine him—a single anamorphic and unimaginable figure we might call "Gargatom." Tom is an English minimidget, not a member of an exotic race. Yet English writers comfortably named him in contexts where others might say "pygmy," even though "pygmy" can evoke the known world's edges, while "Tom Thumb" evokes chapbooks and doggerel.

Europeans had in fact long associated giants and pygmies, for both inhabit distant or doubtful terrain and both raise questions about size's relation to status (especially as traditional pygmies could be tiny—half a cubit, said one authority).[2] But play with big and little particularly suits an age of developing optical discovery and perspective, a time of *curiosa* collections and exploration, a time when the title page of Hobbes's *Leviathan* could picture society as a giant comprising citizen homunculi. Understandably, then, many references to Gargantua and Tom (or some pygmy) show an interest, serious or whimsical, in the relation of the immense to the nugatory, of plethora to dearth, *ultra* to *citra*, and in what this might say about tumescent pride, misused language, and social confusion. The viewpoint is often conservative in that most of the writers, discontented with modern times, look back to something better; it is often radical in the sense that regularizing the disproportion would mean upsetting even the rich and powerful by requiring them to behave. On the whole, however, and despite some perhaps inadvertent ambiguities, Gargatom—whether noted (often sourly) by the educated or (more cheerfully) by the semi-"popular"—serves the King Arthurs of the world, not its Pyms, Cromwells, or Winstanleys.

The "Gargantua" in the passages I will cite is almost certainly the hero of a series of semiparodic chapbooks with a relationship to Rabelais's own works too shifty for modern notions of authorship. The most elaborate was *Les croniques admirables du puissant Roy Gargantua*, compiled in the early 1530s, perhaps by François Girault. The English knew it well, probably as a now lost translation made in the late 1560s and called something like *The History of Gar[a]gantua.*[3] As this Gargantua is now unfamiliar, a précis might be handy:

> Atop the tallest mountain in the East, his hammer going like lightning, Merlin forges the giants Grangosier and Galemelle out of whales' bones, some of Lancelot's blood, twelve pounds or so of Guenevere's nail clippings, and moss wet with sperm from the god Genius. When Grangosier spies a wound between his wife's legs, he lovingly probes it with the suddenly usable probe attached to his own body, thus conceiving Gargantua. Instructed by Merlin, they set off to seek Arthur, Galemelle giving birth with the help of mountain fauns and celebrities like Morgan, Cybele, and Proserpine. At the Christening, performed by a nearby hermit, attendant fairies name the newborn Gargantua, Greek for "You have a handsome son." Passing through Beauce, where the giants' mare levels a forest with her tail, they reach the Norman coast. Gargantua kills a whale for supper, but his parents soon die for lack of suppositories; now they lie under the rocks they had carried with them—Mont Saint Michel and Tombelaine.
>
> After visiting Paris and playing with the bells of Notre Dame like a baby with a rattle, Gargantua asks Merlin's aid. First quelling a ship-eating giant, he is transported by the magician to Arthur's court, where he battles

the king's enemies, the Gots and Magots; his club is 107 feet long, with an end as big as the mouth of Notre Dame's bells. When he glimpses a picture of the ancient giant rebels piling up hills to reach Heaven, "bon" (i.e., loyal) Gargantua piles up seventeen hills so Arthur can see all the way to Paris. After feeding him, the king dresses him as befits a giant who had reached 367 cubits at three years old; his purse belt, for instance, is made of 1,780 bull penises. Gargantua exchanges verses with a local girl, who, being only 300 cubits, rejects him; so he weds the king of Utopia's daughter. Helped by Merlin, he fights the Irish and Dutch, killing one with a fart (his farts can knock over three loads of hay or run four windmills) and using his penis as a bridge on which the British army can cross home. When he accidentally swallows a gunboat, Merlin sends doctors inside to investigate and then, after the giant is positioned with his rear toward the enemy city, a torch is applied to a heap of matches in his mouth and the resulting explosion burns the town. Now a challenger arrives, sent by the father of giants who lives on the Black Mountain in the land of Prester John. Traveling east, Gargantua reaches the mount where giants drink clouds to save earth from flood. Returning home, he defeats another giant and then leaves for Avalon to live with Arthur, Morgan le Fay, Ogier the Dane, and Huon of Bordeaux.

Admirables is a happy book, "popular" in the sense that enjoying it demands little learning and less reverence but inscribing enough sophisticated distance from itself to have appealed to the educated in the 1530s.[4] Its hero was rhetorically or imaginatively usable in England precisely because he has a double nature. Neither a saint like Christopher nor God's enemy like Goliath, he gets along with Christians although his parents were in large part whale and his mentor a magician. He knows both Paris and the eastern mountains where other giants are found. He is both adult enough to seek a wife and baby enough to rattle Notre Dame's towers. He means well, but he can crush walls and kill people. He is a second-generation and slightly brighter Frankenstein's monster, a warmer and funnier Terminator II. No wonder the English read him in very different ways: a complex world can use a complex giant, especially one so much bigger than ordinary Renaissance giants and hence more entertaining to deflate.

Thus an early English reference to Gargantua mischievously shrinks the giant. In an epistle to Lord Lumley prefaced to a handsome 1569 treatise on prodigies, Edward Fenton grumbles that although God has inscribed his creation with legible marvels, "We see in daily experience, with how great earnestnesse and delight the unlearned sorte runne over the fruitlesse Historie of king Arthur and his round table Knights, and what pleasure they take in the trifeling tales of Gawin and Gargantua: the which besides that they passe all likelihode of truth, are utterly without either grave precept or good example."[5] The book that follows has an amazing array of portents and wonders; the Gargantuan Chronicles are only slightly less credible, although, as Dering says, not so edifying. And, given that Gawain was sometimes thought to have been a giant, this reference to "trifling" tales concerning him and Gargantua seems like an unfriendly oxymoron.[6]

Fenton's dismissal of romance marvels on behalf of his own signifying and exemplary monsters or portents raises a question: Did he think Gargantua a monster? The giant was sometimes called one, for in a human community he is anomalous, if not a "sign" or *monstrum* pointing to some readable truth or warning. The line between giants and humanity could waver, however, to the point where in *Amadis de Gaule* there are mixed marriages. But whatever their quasi-hominid status, giants are what most people mean by "monsters," with gaping orifices and indistinct boundaries. As a giant, then, Gargantua can be read in terms of Renaissance teratology—as much a monster as the whales and giraffes included in Ambrose Paré's book on monsters.[7] Yet one could also argue that, like those same whales and giraffes in the view of many authorities, he is sooner a *lusus naturae*, a sport of nature, belonging despite his odd ancestry to a distinct species of humanoid with understood and ancient origins.[8] Moreover, as sports of nature, giants and pygmies have a link to illusion, fantasy, and ingenuity that further justifies Gargantua's and Tom's frequent association with problematic aspects of the imagination and with jesting wit or device. This connection parallels, and was strengthened by, the old uneasy awareness that perspective, like poetry, works through illusion to deceive or accommodate the fancy. Stephen Gosson merely echoes Plato's *Republic* X when he objects that plays make "thinges as never were" or condense and expand events "according as the Poet blowes them up with his quill, for aspiring heades; or minceth them smaller, for weaker stomakes."[9]

Encounters and Juxtapositions

It may have been Richard Johnson, singer of London's merchant worthies, who first introduced Tom Thumb to Gargantua. Indeed, he claims that Tom is older, a "Tom of more antiquity" than "that monster of men"

"Garragantua."[10] His *History of Tom Thumb* (1621) centralizes the small by displacing the large. Tom is now the servant and champion of King Arthur in that golden age when a plowman could "come uncontroled to a Royal Princes presence" and a farmer could be "of the Kings Counsell" and give judgments "in his russet Coate." Johnson was no revolutionary, but his joking nostalgia, as well as his replacement of the big by the little, might have had political resonance for his implied audience of city tradesmen and apprentices. And as it was Merlin who forged Gargantua's parents, so it is now he who helps Tom's parents find a son. Outfitted as smartly for his size as the chronicle Gargantua had been for his, Tom sets out on adventures that, like the giant's, involve considerable scatology: here, too, the pygmy has tried to overtake Gargantua, although in another reversal he is the victim of farts and swallowings, not their perpetrator. Perhaps because the story's narrative and social perspective rises from so near ground level, Johnson's giants are the murderous boasters and eaters of legend. One, a cannibal, sits alone in his deeply moated castle, not so much liminal as absolute and self-enclosed in his power to disjoint and consume, "boyling, broyling and roasting the joynts and quarters of men, devouring them all one after another, legs, armes and heads bit by bit till they were all eaten up at last" (p. 15). Despite his taste for cooked meat and his classy residence, he bears an oak branch, lacks candles, and roars out in the darkness, "Now fi, fee, fau, fan."

Vomited up by this giant, swallowed and disgorged by a fish (his own version of the whale that figures in both Rabelais and the Gargantuan Chronicles), and now "a Courtier" with magic equipment and a coach, Tom encounters Gargantua one day as the giant is out riding "to solace himselfe, his horse being of that great bignesse, as is described in the booke of his honourable deedes, and himselfe being in height not inferiour to any steeple" (p. 24). But Gargantua has changed. No longer a royal champion, he is now the traditional folklore enemy, a threat to civilization that towers above yet gapes like an abyss. Even though he identifies himself as "the onely wonder of the world, the terror of the people," he does not seem to think of Tom as food (Johnson's giants divide their race's traditional characteristics between them: one a cannibal, the other a braggart). Rather, perhaps dimly recognizing a folklore sibling who has ousted him as Arthur's pet, he carries on like any giant windbag.

What ensues is a contest between big and little, violent domination and abstemious cunning. Gargantua asks "who [is] the better man, and

[can] doe the most wonders." "I can," he brags, "blow downe a Steeple with my breath, I can drowne a whole towne with my pisse, I can eate more then a hundred, I carry more then a hundred, I can kill more then a hundred: all this can I do, now tell what thou canst doe?" (p. 25). Gargantua's boasts recall his old prowess with piss and throat, as well as giants' connection with wind and steeples, but the bullying is not typical of his chronicle (or Rabelaisian) self. As for Tom, he simply refuses to take excess seriously, subverting it with ironic diminuendo, abstention, and cunning (in fact good giant-killing technique). Even sexual knowledge is displaced from Gargantua and his giant codpiece to the tiny voyeur who operates through lack and absence and whose capacities as a spy—a disconcerting touch—must be particularly useful at court:

> I can doe more then this, saide Tom Thumbe, for I can creepe into a keyhole, and see what any man or woman doe in their private chambers, there I see things that thou art not worthy to know. I can saile in an egge-shel, which thou canst not: I can eate lesse then a Wren, and so save victuals: I can drinke lesse then a Sparrow, and therefore I am no drunkard: I cannot kill a Rat with my strength, and therefore am no murtherer: these qualities of mine are better then thine in all mens judgements, and therefore great monster I am thy better.

Baffled by a logic that defines the good by negation, lack, and "lesse"—confusing to one defined by excess and "more"—Gargantua is furious, and "would with his foote have kicked downe the whole wood, and so have buried Tom Thumbe." But Tom immobilizes him with a spell and then, leaving him standing foolishly on one foot (half detached from the natural origin of giants), returns to court to recount his adventure to an "amazed" Arthur. And so the book ends, although Johnson promises a sequel, never written or now lost. From the rather pallid verse version of 1630 we know that Tom will die and be taken off to Fairyland. Here, too, he follows in giant footsteps, for of course the chronicle Gargantua will spend eternity in Avalon. Even in death, Tom has conquered, a victory in large part accomplished by the author's decision to make Gargantua a conventional creature of unintelligent bravado whom even a tiny lowborn Englishman can outboast and outwit, perhaps on behalf of all those other tiny and lowborn Toms who make up, or are too impressed by, such a leviathan as Gargantua.

Others also associated Gargantua with Tom or with other minuscule figures, and although some of the texts are generically a cut above

Johnson's breezy chapbook, none is more provocative in affirming the paradoxical virtues of defect. For the most part it is the grotesque indecorum of conjoining them that troubles or amuses these writers. One simply rejects the monstrous of either sort: Robert Farley's 1628 Neolatin poem on educating the young urges the schoolmaster to avoid sterile and witless *nugae*, whether very little "figmenta" like "Polliculus" ("Thumbkin") or big ones like "Gargantua."[11] Despite the pale academic wit of calling Gargantua nugatory or of finding the Latin for "Tom Thumb," Farley's elegant neoclassical verses are sober stuff and his rejection of grotesque or monstrous follies a predictable echo of wider cultural and pedagogical prejudices that are with us yet. Yet his warning is perhaps also indirect evidence that some teachers were resorting to popular *nugae*: an imaginative or desperate schoolmaster or schoolmistress might find *Tom Thumb* and even *Gargantua* reliably attention grabbing for younger readers.

Farley would have dismissed the chapbooks of Martin Parker as the silliest of "figmenta," but to a more relaxed eye some have a raffish if shallow charm. *Harry White His Humor* (1637), not Parker at his best, is a brief gathering of comments ascribed to White.[12] The opinions are meant to be down-to-earth yet verbally playful, as though Piers Plowman had hired a gag writer (sample zingers: "Item: He cares not much for a dancing-schoole, because if need be [rather than fast] he can eat Mutton without capers"; "Item. He is loath to marry a Widow because he will not taste of that which another man dyed after"; sigs. A6-A7). White has read the chapbooks, although I am not sure if we are to think his response satirical or naive: "Item. He is of this opinion, that if the histories of Garragantua and Tom Thumbe be true, by consequence Bevis of Hampton, and Scoggins Jests must needes bee Authenticall" (sig. A8). Whatever the exact aim of Parker's laughter (he himself wrote pamphlets about Arthur, Guy of Warwick, and Robin Hood), the absurdly implausible giant and pygmy are company for both knights and tricksters and, like them, both the object and means of thinking about the logic of imagination. Yoked to each other by a preposition, Gargantua and Tom together figure a comic superfiction that raises the stakes of arguments over feigning and authenticity; whether alluding to their tales glances at the gullibility of the lower orders or at their sturdy skepticism is hard to say.

Less insipid is Parker's experiment in nonsense writing, *Legend of Sir*

Leonard Lack-wit, published in the year 12000, says the title page (the *Short-Title Catalogue* says 1633) and usefully "Translated out of all Christian Languages into the Kentish tongue." Like Edward Lear and Lewis Carroll, although writing in the tradition of French *coq-à-l'âne* satires and *mundus inversus* broadsides, Parker knows that the secret of literary nonsense is to keep the form and syntax familiar while making the manifest statement impossible or incomprehensible. A burlesque not just of a variety of genres but of books' material appearance, the *Legend* has liminal poetry and dedications, a list of authorities (such as Cock Robin, Elinor Rumming, Ignatius Loyola, Robin Goodfellow, Xantippe, and Zoroaster), and errata (e.g., "for merchant read a meere cheater," and "for Poetry read poverty"). He also enjoys mixing categories ("The Turkish Sultan led an army into Plutarches Morals"; sig. A8^{v}), mild irreverence toward the famous ("An invincible navy of Gnats . . . landed at Rotterdam; which so amazed Erasmus, that he turned over twelve leaves of his Booke"; sig. B2),[13] reversals such as making Gogmagog a pygmy (sig. C1^{v}), and Hudibrastic rhymes ("I that lived like a Lord among thy Laquies, / Now know not at what rate a pint of Sacke is," or "Ide have thee know that I am man of note am, / My father once was Alderman of Gotam" (sig. B5^{v}).

But, Parker wonders, will readers doubt what he has been recounting? If so, let them

> survey the wonderfull and incredible true Histories of Garagantua, Tom Thumbe, Bevis of Southampton, with a thousand more, and they shall finde that unlesse there bee lyes in them, this must needs bee true. Yet the Authors who published those, thought they had wit enough: but I in my Title confesse lacke of wit; and therefore I hope I am the more excusable; but howsoever tis not my purpose to ravish your beleefe, and to bee plaine, I hardly give credit to't my selfe. (sig. C2)

Once again, Gargantua and Tom ambiguously sustain (together with the Saxon hero Bevis) the problematic world of unreality. Perhaps in 1633 Parker was not yet upset by England's growing political divisions, but his later royalist writings suggest that he thought his burlesques, nonsense reversals, and romances pleasantly unpuritanical, "popular" in the way bells, bonfires, football, and May games were "popular," and subversive not of kings and bishops but of their sober enemies.[14] Gargatom, precisely because he is a grotesque, a carnivalesque figment, may retain here his old job as a king's loyal servant.

Figuring Unease: The Politics of the Anamorphic

At times the pairing of opposites even more functionally indicates some disquietude or desire. Here too giants are ambiguous, representing to different people at different times the desirable new life or the dreaded new disorder: reform or entropy. Giants, archaic though they are, stand at the brink of the new, their very malformation hinting that a new shape may be being born, whether as rough beast or divine child. That is why, although it would seem from their size and antiquity that they should represent parents (we have all been Toms or Thumbellinas to someone else's Gargantua and Badebec), giants are unexpectedly allied to the infantile.[15] Guarding, blocking, or simply marking the threshold, they appear terrifyingly inflated because the future is as yet imaginary, unknown, perhaps even desirable; and like a giant, it is going to swallow us up. This may be a further reason for Gargantua's appearances in attacks on romances (like monsters and the future, structures of illusion and the imaginary) and why the early modern period, punctuated by an especially large number of transitions, seems to have had such an interest in giants and their inverted doubles, the pygmies.

Several appearances of Gargantua and Tom (or a nameless pygmy) show the possibilities and the ambiguity. Thomas Nashe the younger's *Quaternio* (1633) is a dialogue on four different walks of life that stops for engaging quotations and anecdotes from writers such as Chaucer, Erasmus, More, and Du Bartas. At one point conversation turns to hierarchal arrangements in families and the commonwealth. The "word Father," says the lawyer, means "as well a politicke as a naturall father," so that the laws "binde Subjects in loyall obedience to their Soveraignes, servants to their Maisters, Pupils to their Tutors, are hence propagated and derived, as well as those Lawes which doe binde Children to their Parents" (1639 ed., sigs. S1–S1^{v}). Laws enjoin the inferior to honor the superior but also the superior to have "vigilant care" for subordinates, "not to place age where youth should fit, nor yet youth where age should fit; Mars where Mercurie should fit, nor yet Mercurie where Mars should fit, for that were to put the Gyants habit upon the little Pigmee, and the Pigmees habit upon the great Gargantua." It is not clear precisely what Nashe's lawyer means by Mars and Mercury. War and letters? The military and the mercantile? His insistence on responsible hierarchy is, however, unmistakable. Nashe himself was to support Charles when the civil war came, and he doubtless agreed that giants should remain giants and pygmies (that is, most of us), pygmies.

Yet Nashe's analogy relies on monsters whose categories were already uncertain; the lawyer's argument may suffer from his examples—if Gargantua is a joke and if no one has seen a real pygmy, if all who inhabit England are men and women, then possibly the relation of rulers and ruled needs rethinking. Nor is the comparison of authority to Gargantua comfortable: this leviathan sounds like the chronicle giant, but even Rabelais's Gargantua swallows people. To oppose him to a pygmy, furthermore, sets up so radical a difference between governor and governed that there is little room for hierarchy itself, for intermediary and mediating bodies (such as parliaments, mothers, teaching assistants). The political implications are unnerving if unintentional. The very monstrosity of Nashe's Gargatom, swamped by clothes or unable to cover his nakedness, shows some joviality but also an ambivalence that betrays the logic: Gargantua is a father figure to give any pygmy pause, and can we be sure that it is not mere clothes that make the giant, that Gargantuan ermines and scarlet never conceal an inward tininess of political understanding?

Another unsteady perspective on big and little, this time glancing at economics, invigorates a moment in Thomas Randolph's comedy *Hey for Honesty*, an expansion and modernization of Aristophanes' *Plutus* composed in the late 1620s. The play's political relevance only increased as Britain's constitutional crisis worsened, so in the late 1640s one F.J. updated it further, and the new version saw print in 1651.[16] In one scene, three bumpkins, a rich parson, and Poverty debate curing the blindness of Plutus, the god of wealth who now distributes his favor with so little insight. Because a sharp-eyed Plutus might revise the economic system, the conversation turns to equality (F.J. adds a reference to the Levelers). Poverty argues:

> Plutus makes men with puffed faces, dropsy bodies, bellies as big as the great tub at Heidelberg; . . . besides, they have eyes like turkeycocks, double-chins, flapdragon cheeks, lips that may spare half an ell, and yet leave kissing-room enough. Nay, 'tis the humour of this age; they think they shall never be great men unless they have gross bodies. Marry, I keep men spare and lean, slender and nimble; mine are all diminutives, Tom Thumbs; not one Colossus, not one Garagantua amongst them; fitter to encounter the enemy by reason of their agility, in less danger of shot for their tenuity, and most expert in running away, such is their celerity.[17]

Sharp words, in the 1640s, although the exact political resonance is hard to hear. *Honesty* is anti-Cromwellian in some regards, but Poverty's boast is unstable. Is it best to be poor? Then we would do our Gargantuas a favor by making them Toms. F.J. seems to prefer the old order, but even a new order would wrestle with similar issues: How can one fatten the little without turning it into the old bigness? Must old priest be writ large as new presbyter? Will parliamentary Toms swell into new Gargantuas? Just as the prologue makes Aristophanes' Cleon a sort of deflated giant, a once fat jumped-up populist plutocrat whose very breath could impoverish others, Poverty thinks of Gargantua not as the people, the civic stuff of which cities are made, the ancient chthonic power in all its ambiguity, but as a social problem. (Not that wealth alone makes a Gargantua; one "Erastophil" says in his *Apologie for Lovers* [1651] that men are microcosms with a longing to be macrocosms. Take Alexander: "What a Monster had this been, if his body had been but of the same tumid and swelling bulk with his mind? Certainly Garagantua had been a meer Pigmie to him" [sig. D12v].)

William Habington's comedy *The Queene of Arragon* (1640) incorporates a similarly diverting conversation about size, one with more muted but still audible political undertones. Here we meet a servant, Brumsilldora, a dwarf with the nickname "Gargantua," whose family pride suits English stereotyping of Spain but whose size suits his nation's now diminished fearsomeness. Asked about his family, he replies, "My Ancestors were Giants, Madam. Giants / Pure Spanish, who disdain'd to mingle with / The blood of Goth or Moore. Their mighty actions / In a small letter Nature Printed on / Your little Servant" (I.i). Given that Spain, home of the famous giant Geryon, had likewise been "tumid and swelling" in the days of that great Armada often compared to a giant, and that its inhabitants shared the Flemish taste for huge processional figures, it is not surprising to find a Spanish giant, although it is startling to find one this short. Why is he so small? "By the decay of Time," he says, and the effect of the "barren hills / Of Biskay." He keeps his name to preserve the memory of his forebears: "They shall live / In me contracted." Tiny "Gargantua" contains his own *concordia discors*, reconciling dwarf and giant through *descent* in every sense and, furthermore, expressing this condition in terms recollecting the age's images and techniques of contraction (he is a living box where ancestors compacted lie, a miniature book of the sort popular with curiosity collectors, a text written in Nature's equivalent of the shorthand invented not so many decades earlier).[18]

The younger Nashe had imagined inverted hierarchy as a pygmy and giant, impossibly, swapping clothes; others fancied a giant outfit dwarfing or deforming its human wearer and thus revealing his inadequacy, making him, so to speak, play Tom Thumb to his costume's Gargantua. As so often, giants figure some moral or social disproportion on which a writer can offer an amused or dismayed perspective. In *Purchas His Pilgrim: Microcosmus, or the Historie of Man* (1619), for instance, Samuel Purchas plays off not only big and little but other and same. The native inhabitants of what was now Virginia, he says, have taught some to wear the "sinister Love-Locke," a "gallantrie" that Tomocomo, an Indian, told Purchas his tribe had learned from its devil. But because Purchas knows that to foreigners the English themselves are "other," and because he has a semisatirical agenda, he shifts perspective for an instant. If Indians are vain, he asks, what of the European? What might a "Traveller thinke of his Gargantuan bellyed-Doublet with huge huge sleeves, now with a contrarie smalnesse imprisoning his body? and the then Ghost-like, skin-close Breeches, since volumniously swolne into Rolles, Slops, Barratashes, Bumbasted Plaits, and Sailers knee-sacks."[19] Purchas is less unsettling than Montaigne on cannibals, but his momentarily reversed line of sight is refreshing.

Gender

Richard Brathwait was likewise disturbed by modern dress. One concern of his *English Gentlewoman* (1631) is to maintain gender difference and hierarchy in the face of a riot of ruffs, hoods, and fancy materials. He does not warn his lady against literal cross-dressing, but his insistence that she be plain and moderate—ungigantic, as it were—is meant to keep her feminine. The book itself is allowed to dress up, however. Adopting a sort of cross-dressing of his own, Brathwait imagines his tract as a lady "adorned" with "divers ornaments" and "many choice endowments," if without "painted pretences" or "Phantasticke habits or forraine fashions" that might "disfigure" her. This idealized lady (Brathwait's book, that is, and also the lady it will fashion) has "made a covenant with her eyes never to wander," is unambitious, and shows her good lineage through gracious self-government. The lady/text, adds Brathwait, will walk with the lady/reader and tell her "time-beguiling Tales." One such tale comes in a section urging the avoidance of "Phantastike" and "outlandish" dress. A good woman, we read, will "wear" Christ, not the soft silks that create soft minds, for "delicacy in the habit begets an effeminacy in the heart" (sigs. C1^{v}–C3^{v}). As Brathwait intends to discipline a lady, not a gentleman, in good and virtuous fashion, this warning might seem pointless. By "effeminate," however, he probably means sexually ambiguous. A lady should be feminine in chaste modesty and—although Brathwait does not quite put it like this—masculine in self-control; but she must not relax into a sensuality that dulls the edges of gender.

On the next page Brathwait turns to "Superfluity of Apparell." Further beggaring the famished while inflating themselves, he says, many "will have long garments, purposely to seeme greater" (sig. C4). This reminds him of the "diminutive Gentleman, who demanding of his Tayler, what yards of Sattin would make him a Suite, being answered farre short in number of what he expected: with great indignation replied, 'Such an one of the Guard to my knowledge had thrice as much for a Suite, and I will second him.'" With an eye on the leftover cloth, the tailor agrees to make "a Gargantua's Suite for this Ounce of mans flesh, reserving to himselfe a large portion of shreads, purposely to forme a fitter proportion for his [i.e., the short gentleman's] Ganimede shape" (sig. C3^{v}). "Gargantua" connotes "bigger than a self-important little person," but what of "Ganimede"? Zeus's abduction of him was sometimes read as intellectual rapture or the union of body and soul, but in ordinary language the name more often indicated, pejoratively, the youthful male object of male desire.[20] What is the allusion doing here? "Ganimede" means "too little for such big cloth," but the reference to Zeus's cupbearer and not, say, to Tom Thumb or a pygmy hints that gender itself is unstable when we dress outlandishly: monstrosity in costume refashions a woman as "other," as a Ganymede who thinks (s)he is Gargantua.

In Henry Glapthorne's *The Hollander* (1635, printed 1640), Gargantua and Tom appear, less directly, in the context of a more outrageously comic confusion over gender. The "Hollander" of the title is Sconce, a deep drinker and "Gallant naturalized Dutchman" of great girth who boasts an ancestry going back almost sixty years (why he swears in French—"mon Dieu," "Foutra"!—is unexplained; bad company?). Irascible Captain Pirke, on the other hand, is short, a "Tom Thumbe"; together, he and Sconce are Gargatom, pygmy and giant (or a waspish Asterix and even dumber Obelix). As part of a complex scheme to rob the Dutchman,

Pirke volunteers to pretend to knight Sconce. His coconspirators find the disparity in size risible, but they agree, asking what the little captain will dub the big Hollander. Pirke replies, "I dub him Gargantua."[21] Fair enough: Sconce is large and noisy. The end of the comedy, however, maneuvers this Gargantua-figure into an arresting scene of shifting sexual identities. Sconce has, for convoluted reasons, been married in female disguise to a woman dressed as a man. Bewildered, the Hollander says to his new spouse, "But let me see and feele you better, it is no periwigge this but are you my husband, a woman, wife?" Dismayed to find her indeed female, he asks for an unguent "that will eat off the wen of manhood, make all whole before . . . I would faine be a Hermaphrodite, or a woman to escape this match." Rabelais's Gargantua had worn the figure of an androgyne as an earring; Sconce wants to be one. This poor "Gargantua," however, cannot achieve a female w/holeness and must keep his male "wen."[22]

Gargatom has retired from rhetorical duty, but the fascination with the humor and terror of size remains: dads shrink kids, Woody Allen slips on a bioengineered giant banana peel, atomic radiation causes six-foot ants, tiny astronauts invading a planet in the Twilight Zone return to a ship marked "NASA." Such images express our own culture's pleasures, interests, and worries as well as a traditional humbling or satirical relativism, although the effect sought is less often illegitimate juxtaposition than humor or terror (Spielberg's T-rex eating a moral pygmy of a lawyer may offer both). In Stuart England, when a French giant and an English midget teamed up as an odd couple the result was a double-bodied grotesque, figuring not so much a set of cultural situations as the mingled or contradictory feelings about them that only monstrously contradictory fictions can express.

Notes

1. Quoted by John Block Friedman, *The Monstrous Races in Medieval Art and Thought* (Cambridge: Harvard University Press, 1980), 163–64. The thirteenth-century *Image du monde* says that "the geaunts that ben in some place have right grete mervaylle of this that we be so lytil ayenst them; lyke as we mervaylle of them that ben half lasse than we be. . . . And they ben the Pygmans whiche ben but iii foot longe. And in lyke wise mervaylle they of us of that we ben so grete, & repute us also for geaunts." (I quote Caxton's translation of a later prose version, *Mirrour of the World*, ed. Oliver H. Prior [London, 1913], 97.) For more on relativism, see

Mary Campbell, *The Witness and the Other World: Exotic European Travel Writing, 400–1600* (Ithaca, N.Y.: Cornell University Press, 1988), 155–58. In this essay I omit extended analysis of giants as such. Susan Stewart's *On Longing: Narratives of the Miniature, the Gigantic, the Souvenir, the Collection* (Baltimore: Johns Hopkins University Press, 1993) offers postmodern and Marxist ruminations, such as the brilliant comment that the A-bomb is a giant weapon powered by the tiny atom. Some of Stewart's statements are inaccurate (e.g., on the giant Gogmagog) or oversimplifying (e.g., that in the Renaissance the "gigantic is appropriated by the state and its institutions and put on parade with great seriousness, not as a representative of the material life of the body, but as a symbol of the abstract social formations making up life in the city"; 81) See also Jean Céard, "La querelle des géants et la jeunesse du monde," *Journal of Medieval and Renaissance Studies* 8 (1978): 37–76; Walter Stephens, *Giants in Those Days: Folklore, Ancient History, and Nationalism* (Lincoln: University of Nebraska Press, 1989); and Daniel Woolf, "Of Danes and Giants: Popular Beliefs about the Past in Early Modern England," *Dalhousie Review* 71 (1991): 167–209.

2. Friedman, *The Monstrous Races*, 195. Friedman stresses the spatial and definitional marginality of monsters; he quotes Ranulf Higden's *Polychronicon*: evidently Nature "plays with greater freedom secretly at the edges of the world" (43).

3. See Huntington Brown, *François Girault's Tale of Gargantua and King Arthur* (Cambridge: Harvard University Press, 1932); Marcel de Grève, "La légende de Gargantua en Angleterre au XVIe siècle," *Revue belge de philologie et d'histoire* 38 (1960): 765–94; and my "Reshaping Gargantua," in *Mélanges offerts a Marie-Thérèse Jones-Davies: L'Europe de la renaissance: cultures et civilizations* (Paris: Touzot, 1988), 477–91, some paragraphs of which I borrow here.

4. What "popular" means for the sixteenth century is hard to say; Mikhail Bakhtin's formulations in *Rabelais and His World*, trans. Helene Iswolsky (Cambridge: MIT Press, 1965) are too binary. Even later, as Peter Burke argues in *Popular Culture in Early Modern Europe* (New York: Harper, 1978), Europe was divided less between the elite or official and the popular than between the few to whom a range of discourses were available and the many living in a narrower world. Compare Natalie Z. Davis, "Printing and the People," in *Society and Culture in Early Modern France* (Stanford, Calif.: Stanford University Press, 1975); Jean-Paul Berlioz, "Aspects populaires des Croniques Gargantuines," *RHR* 11 (1980): 63–74; and Woolf, "Of Danes and Giants."

5. *Certaine Secrete Wonders of Nature*, trans. largely from Pierre Boaistuau, sig. A3–A3[v].

6. On Gawain's size, see Thomas Nashe, *Strange Newes* (1592), in *The Works of Thomas Nashe*, ed. R. B. McKerrow (Oxford: Basil Blackwell, 1966), 1:258 and note.

7. On distinguishing the types of monsters and the instability of the science dealing with them (teratology), see Jean Céard, "Tératologie et tératomancie au XVIe siècle," in *Monstres et prodiges*, ed. Marie-Thérèse Jones-Davies (Paris: Touzot, 1980), 5–15.

8. On the *lusus naturae*, its ties to science, play, illusion, and the cultural need for a place to put what is not monstrous but still anomalous (e.g., outsize like giants or hermaphroditic like snails), see Paula Findlen, "Jokes of Nature and Jokes of Knowledge: The Playfulness of Scientific Discourse in Early Modern Europe," *SRen* 43 (1990):

292–331. Not everyone enjoys play or illusion, however, and early modern references to the gigantic can show an anxiety or scorn that Findlen may underestimate.

9. *Playes Confuted in Five Actions* (1582), sig. D5ᵛ.

10. See Stanley J. Kahrl, ed., *Merie Tales of the Mad Men of Gotam* / Curt Bühler, ed., *The History of Tom Thumb* (Evanston, IL: Northwestern University Press, for the Renaissance English Text Society, 1965), 1–2; the date reads 1621, but Bühler thinks wear on the title page suggests long use. For more on Tom, see Stewart, *On Longing*, 46 (although Bühler cites a 1579 notice of Tom that precedes the 1584 one by Reginald Scott she calls the earliest published); Stewart notes a 1697 almanac record of a 1593 duel between Tom and Gargantua (178).

11. *Neanica* (Edinburgh, 1628), sig. B2ᵛ.

12. I cannot identify White. Parker, a prolific ballad writer, wrote the popular royalist "When the King Enjoys His Own Again."

13. This is a reference to the seated statue of the great scholar; local children, I hear, say that at midnight he turns one page of the book he holds.

14. See Leah S. Marcus, "Introduction," in *The Politics of Mirth: Jonson, Herrick, Milton, Marvell, and the Defense of Old Holiday Pastimes* (Chicago: University of Chicago Press, 1989).

15. Mary Campbell links the medieval romance's taste for the monstrous, for "sub- and superhuman figures," to the genre's role as "a vehicle for infantile fantasies of singularity." Campbell, *The Witness*, 183–84.

16. On dating and authorship of this work, see G. E. Bentley, *The Jacobean and Caroline Stage*, 7 vols. (Oxford: Clarendon, 1941–68), under "Randolph."

17. *Poetical and Dramatic Works of Thomas Randolph*, ed. W. Carew Hazlitt, (London, 1875), 2: 422–23. Because it is fairly close to lines 557–61 in the *Plutus*, although Aristophanes has no giant or pygmy, it is likely that Randolph wrote this bit.

18. On how such books relate microcosm to macrocosm, see Stewart, *On Longing*, 37–44. Compare the bully in *Lady Alimony* (anon., printed 1659) who melts into punctilious civility when defied: "How this Gargantua's spirit begins to thaw! Sirrah, you punto [i.e., point, dot] of valour!" (I.ii–iii in Dodsley's *Old English Plays*, ed. W. Carew Hazlitt [reprint, New York: B. Blom, 1964], 14: 282–84).

19. Sigs. S5–S6. Purchas likes contractions: "And doth it not delight us more, more ravish us, to see Homers Iliads in a Nut-shell, then in spacious Volumes?" (sig. C6ᵛ).

20. On how the myth infolds same/same and same/other, see Leonard Barkan, *Transuming Passion: Ganymede and the Erotics of Humanism* (Stanford, Calif.: Stanford University Press, 1991). Calling Ganymede an *ounce* of *man*'s flesh adds tonal peculiarities, as though a boy were a piece of his older lover, perhaps the small part that penetrates him.

21. Henry Glapthorne, *Plays and Poems*, 2 vols. (London, 1874), 1:84, 111, 135. The play may inscribe recent tensions between England and the Netherlands.

22. Glapthorne, *The Hollander*, 1: 154. Stephen Greenblatt associates an interest in gender shifts to a concern for prodigies; see "Fiction and Friction," in *Shakespearean Negotiations: The Circulation of Social Energy in Renaissance England* (Berkeley: University of California Press, 1988), 76. His discussion helps explain the interest in giants: "Where the modern structuralist understanding of the world tends to sharpen its sense of individuation by meditating upon the normative, the Renaissance tended

to sharpen its sense of the normative by meditating upon the prodigious" (77). Sconce himself regrets that sex is *not* as fluid as we are told Renaissance authorities thought it was. Laura Levine, in "Men in Women's Clothing: Anti-theatricality and Effeminization from 1579 to 1642," *Criticism* 28 (1986): 121–43, finds opponents of the stage afraid both that gender is labile and that sexual monstrosity might be permanent and essential. See also Stephen Orgel, "Nobody's Perfect: Or Why Did the English Stage Take Boys for Women?" *South Atlantic Quarterly* 88 (1989): 7–29.

5 America's "United Siamese Brothers": Chang and Eng and Nineteenth-Century Ideologies of Democracy and Domesticity

Allison Pingree

In the early 1830s, as spectators lined up in towns across the United States for the celebrated event, they found for sale a publicity pamphlet purporting to give "an historical account," based on "actual observations," of the human exhibit they were about to see. The cover and title page greeted them with a familiar sight: an eagle, sporting a banner reading "E Pluribus Unum" in its beak, with the motto "'United We Stand'" inscribed below (see Figure 5.1). Such an image, of course, was unmistakably American: though the nation was only a few decades old, already these symbols circulated widely, having first appeared on the federal government's Great Seal in 1782, and impressed on coins as early as 1795; likewise, "E Pluribus Unum" was considered the national motto for decades (Kane 567, 394).

The placement of the image in this particular context, however, was curious; this was not a government document, after all, but a brochure for a human "spectacle." The persons it advertised were not Americans but citizens of an exotic "otherland," Siam. Moreover, these young men were "monstrous," joined below the chest by an armlike band of flesh approximately eight inches in diameter and five inches in length (Wallace & Wallace 14). These brothers, the "original Siamese Twins," were nearly eighteen years old when first taken from their homeland by an enterprising British merchant and an American trader who foresaw the boys' lucrative possibilities. Arriving in Boston in August 1829, Chang and Eng began a life in the United States that was split between making profits through public exhibition (traveling extensively throughout the country and Europe) and through more private, domestic forms—marrying a

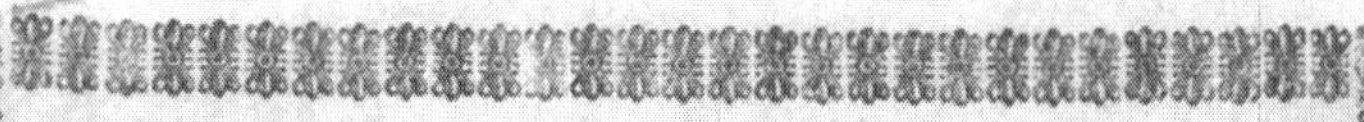

AN

HISTORICAL ACCOUNT

OF THE

Siamese Twin Brothers,

FROM

ACTUAL OBSERVATIONS.

"UNITED WE STAND."

Copy-right secured.

PRICE 12½ CENTS.

FOR SALE ONLY AT THE EXHIBITION

NEW-YORK:

Elliott & Palmer, Printers, 20 *William-street.*

1831.

Figure 5.1. Publicity pamphlet cover, 1831

pair of sisters, buying slaves and successfully working farmland in North Carolina, and fathering a total of twenty-one children. By the time they died in 1874, the twins had gained a staggering level of popularity, some of which derived from working for impresario P. T. Barnum; according to Irving Wallace, Chang and Eng were "more renowned than any of Barnum's exhibits except Tom Thumb" (117). By midcentury, then, most Americans were aware of the twins—either from reading about them or seeing them in person. The spectacle of their fused, "monstrous" bodies thus contained substantial symbolic potential.

Not surprisingly, the twins inspired far more than this initial *Historical Account* pamphlet (written by their first business manager, James Hale). As Robert Bogdan describes, Chang and Eng were some of the nineteenth century's "most studied human beings. Almost from the moment they stepped off the boat in Boston they were probed, pinched, pictured, and pondered by physicians and other scientists presenting the spectrum of learned associations" (296 n. 1). During their life—and after their death—Americans viewed, read and collected lithographs, newspaper articles, cartes de visit, satires, poetry, drama, photographs, novels, and cartoons regarding the twins, and even dressed as them for masquerade parties.[1]

Given this background, then, it seems less surprising that the eagle and motto—an emblem of unity among separate states—would be applied to the conjoined brothers who offered a convenient and potent embodiment of an American ideal. That is, what at first seems like a bad joke (these brothers had no choice *but* to "stand united") reveals more upon closer inspection: here, not only is patriotism employed to sell the twins, the twins themselves are used to sell democratic nationalism.

This cultural exchange points to a broader pattern that emerges in the representations of the twins during the early nineteenth century. The bonded brothers from Siam evoked in the American public issues hotly contested and values passionately held. More specifically, at that time, the country focused intently on tensions that Chang and Eng bore out in their very bodies. Even as the spectacle of the twins constantly raised the question "Are they two or one?" so America struggled with its own configurations of government (divided states within a united nation) and domesticity (marriage in particular). Each representation of the brothers operated at a variety of cultural levels; moreover, each contained, sometimes unwittingly, its own internal tensions. That is, even as the twins' bond was appropriated by a unionist enterprise that urged fusion of the states, it also posed an alternative interpretation—that connecting the states too closely was "monstrous" and excessive. Similarly, even as the twins posed an endearing version of the romantic ideal of finding one's "other half," their own marriages raised the specters of incest, homoeroticism, adultery, and exotic orgies of flesh that profoundly confronted the heterosexual marital norms of Victorian America. In short, even as the *symbol* of the twins was used to support certain dominant values, their literal *bodies* presented other puzzles and contradictions for the country to solve—ones that, ironically, undermined many of those same norms. Ultimately, a reading of the antebellum representations of Chang and Eng reveals an intriguing, broader model of the complicated transactions between American culture and its "monsters."

"One and Inseparable": The Bonds of Democratic Brotherhood

The intense focus, in early-nineteenth-century America, on the strange phenomenon of Chang and Eng's bodies had a long precedent. For many centuries, scientists, physicians, and philosophers have been both plagued and fascinated by conjoined twins' confounding mathematics of personhood—the fact that they are "more than one" yet "not quite two." Teratological studies ranging from Ambroise Paré's *On Monsters and Marvels* (1573) to Gould and Pyle's *Anomalies and Curiosities of Medicine* (1897) include extensive taxonomies of various types of "in-betweenness"—of bodily absence and overabundance (of arms, legs, heads, genitals, and so on). Curiously, sometimes a case is described as a singular person laden with "extra" or "supernumerary" parts (a "three-headed boy"), whereas others are termed dual beings with "missing" parts ("double monsters").[2] Various criteria for "personhood" are given—the number of heads, or of hearts, for example—yet such standards continually prove inadequate or inconsistent. For instance, Paré, referencing the number of hearts, pronounces someone "having two heads, two arms, and four legs" but "only one heart" to be "only one child" (13–14). Paré's verdict seems particularly odd given that such a "child" presents significant evidence for two selves, given the two sets of legs and the two heads.

In like manner, from its national beginnings, the United States has been subject to political debates generated by the paradoxes of division and unity, of democratic individualism and sameness. The "American experiment" was founded on an ideology of clearly defined and recognizable individuals, each of whom is responsible for his or her own actions, yet is also equal to and representative of all others. That is, the very bodies of conjoined twins foreground the tensions inherent in an entity calling itself the "United States"—an entity informed by both a desire for cohesion and an impulse toward separation.

During the first few decades of the nineteenth century, political rhetoric took on a particularly feverish pitch regarding division and connection. Sectionalist fervor emerged in some regions, particularly the South, that both addressed specific economic issues and staked broader claims about the relative importance of state sovereignty over national unity (Garraty 147). Those highly invested in emphasizing national unity, on the other hand, frequently drew on the rhetoric of fratricide to persuade their listeners. Indeed, the symbolism of "brother fighting against brother" in a ruthless embrace of violence—most often associated with the Civil War itself—actually played a part in national debates much earlier. For example, George Forgie argues in *Patricide in the House Divided* that such imagery "was older than the conflict between the sections over slavery," and claims that even as early as the Revolutionary period, "disunion was Washington's greatest dread" (205).

Massachusetts senator Daniel Webster voiced a similar concern a few decades after Washington felt this "dread." In Senate debates of January 1830, Senator Robert Hayne of South Carolina lobbied for low tariffs specifically, and for states' rights in general. In response, Webster defended the tariff not in economic terms but by praising the sacredness of the union—and by implying that too much loyalty to states' rights was akin to treason (Garraty 168): "It is to that Union that we are chiefly indebted for whatever makes us most proud of our country. . . . It has been to us all a copious fountain of national, social, personal happiness" (*Speeches* 83–84). Webster then claimed that he did not dare look at the possibilities that Hayne and other sectionalists proposed, afraid of "what might lie hidden in the dark recesses behind. . . . I have not accustomed myself to hang over the precipice of disunion, to see whether, with my short sight, I can fathom the depth of the abyss below." Further, Webster conjured up the image of his own deathbed, illustrating how damaging a separation would be to the national body: "May I not see . . . the broken and dishonored fragments of a once-glorious Union . . . states dissevered, discordant, belligerent . . . a land rent with civil feuds, or drenched, it may be, in fraternal blood!" Instead, Webster urged loyalty to the "sentiment, dear to every true American heart—Liberty *and* Union, now and forever, one and inseparable!" (*Speeches* 83–84).

Webster's final sentence in this oration, a hyperbolic triad of claims for the union, became immensely popular after the speech—even being printed in *McGuffey's Reader* and memorized by young schoolchildren.[3] More peculiar, however, was its appearance six years later on the cover of another pamphlet publicizing Chang and Eng: *A Few Particulars Concerning Chang-Eng, the United Siamese Brothers* (see Figure 5.2). The link between the twins and this phrase was even richer than that created with the motto on *An Historical Account* ("United we stand"); Chang and Eng indeed would live together "now and forever," their bodies were indeed "one and inseparable." Strikingly, Webster's line is inverted in this context: "Liberty and Union" from the speech becomes "Union and Liberty" on the pamphlet cover. By thus using (and altering) Webster's language, Chang and Eng's promoters could nudge the public into recalling the awful prospects of disunion imagined by Webster in his speech, as well as present the twins as a calming reassurance of brothers unquestionably united.

This conflation of the "inseparability" of Chang and Eng with an agenda of national unity continued in the majority of material on the twins created in the 1830s and 1840s. Indeed, such material insinuates that despite slight exceptions, they really were one person. This impression is created, first of all, through a detailed account of the characteristics of the fleshy band itself:

> On the lower edge of the band, exactly in its centre, is situated the umbilicus or navel; (there being but ONE in common between them;) a pressure upon the lower part of the band . . . would be equally felt by each. . . . There is . . . a considerable degree of nervous sympathy between the two bodies. (Hale 6–7)

By highlighting the twins' "nervous sympathy" and shared navel, this description asserts that at the most basic levels of existence, the brothers are utterly fused.

The twins' reflection of the broader, national story also emerges in how these publicity pamphlets represent the possibility of the twins' being surgically separated. Almost all the material emphasizes the harm and even fatality of such an undertaking, just as Webster saw disunion as

A FEW PARTICULARS

CONCERNING

CHANG-ENG,

THE UNITED SIAMESE BROTHERS,

PUBLISHED UNDER THEIR OWN DIRECTION.

" Union and Liberty, one and inseparable, now and for ever."

NEW YORK:

PRINTED BY J. M. ELLIOTT, 6 LITTLE GREEN STREET.

1836.

Figure 5.2. Publicity pamphlet cover, 1836

a dark "abyss." One passage in Hale's pamphlet explains that a "question has arisen, which has been discussed with some warmth, whether they could be separated with safety. We think they could not. . . . it would be attended with the most dangerous consequences" (16).

The story of Chang and Eng's fiancées' prohibiting the brothers' surgical division similarly portrays division as perilous. When Chang and Eng were about to be married in 1843, they traveled to the College of Surgeons in Philadelphia and adamantly demanded separation. According to biographer Kay Hunter, just as the operation was about to begin, their wives-to-be arrived on the scene. These women, "almost out of their minds with worry," had come to "beg and plead with them to abandon the whole idea of separation." The twins argued back, but "eventually the ladies won the day. The twins decided, in the face of the girls' anxiety and loyalty, to give up their idea of being cut asunder. They would stay together in safety, and the four of them would work out a way of life between them—somehow." The sisters were "delighted at their victory, and Chang and Eng, relieved of the terror of a dubious operation, [were] still United Brothers!" (Hunter 86–87).

Even much later in their lives, the prospect of dividing Chang and Eng was volatile enough that Barnum capitalized on it, using it as a successful marketing ploy; indeed, he claims in his autobiography that the great popularity that followed the twins during the European tour they took in the late 1860s was "'much enhanced, if not actually caused, by extensive announcement in advance that the main purpose of Chang-Eng's visit to Europe was to consult the most eminent medical and surgical talent with regard to the safety of separating the twins'" (quoted in Wallace & Wallace 257). Such publicity strategies played on the audience's fear that such a division would surely result in fatality, thus reiterating once again the value of national cohesion and loyalty.

The nationalist agenda for unity was further implied in the explorations, appearing in articles and pamphlets, of the many characteristics the twins shared. For example, Hale claims that many observers of Chang and Eng have

> the impression that they were actuated by only one mind, so simultaneous were they in all their movements. They play at chess and draughts remarkably well, but never in opposition to each other: having been asked to do it, they replied that no more pleasure would be derived from it, than by playing with the right hand against the left. (8–9)

Here, the twins become so joined as to be one person composed of right and left sides. Hale further exploits this collapse:

> They never enter into conversation or discussion with each other, because, possessing as before observed the same quantum of intellect, and having been placed constantly in the same circumstances, precisely the same effects have been produced upon the mind of each. (10)

Hale concludes his sketch of an utterly merged identity with the claim that the twins' "likings or distastes for particular food are the same precisely," that they "invariably feel hunger and thirst at the same times," and that both "feel the desire to sleep simultaneously and they always awake at the same moment" (11). From the beginning, then, the twins were packaged as one unit, blurred into one set of tastes, thoughts, and impulses—therein offering to the American audience the invitation to affirm its own national cohesion.

Stories within the pamphlets further elaborated on and encouraged ideals of closeness and harmony. For example, Hale claims that neither brother "possesses the slightest degree of superiority over the other. The wisdom of Providence is herein strongly manifested; for did any mental superiority exist, it would necessarily lead to contentions and struggles for pre-eminence." Another pamphlet similarly professes that Chang and Eng "never thwart or oppose each other in any way, . . . they present one of the few, if not indeed the only case, in which two persons have lived together twenty-five years, without even one little quarrel" (*A Few Particulars* 12).

A final instance of the twins' supposed harmoniousness emerges in the results of an exam conducted by a Professor Tucker in 1836, published in the *Proceedings of the American Philosophical Society* (1841). The twins were questioned simultaneously on various topics by different examiners, and their answers recorded separately. Professor Tucker concludes that

> they differed in opinion but seldom, and only on such occasions as those in which an individual may in a short time differ from himself. . . . With these rare exceptions, there was an entire concurrence in their wishes, not merely from the similarity of their tastes and desires, but also from the unwillingness felt by each to contravene the desires or purposes of the other. . . . These brothers thus furnish the *most perfect example of disinterested friendship that has ever existed*, and they exhibit a *phenomenon of moral beauty* that is singularly pleasing. (Ludlow & Mitchell 26–27; emphasis added)

Drawing on a sentimentalized language of perfect friendship and moral beauty, such a representation extols, by implication, a doctrine of national unity and the silencing of conflict.

But representations of the twins did not always work so monolithically, as some internal contradictions within Tucker's language demonstrate. Ironically, the twins' "moral beauty" that is "singularly pleasing" is created through their utter *lack* of singularity; similarly, although Tucker claims the twins' friendship is "disinterested," it can be nothing of the sort, because devotion to one's conjoined twin is, in many ways, devotion to oneself.

A similar complication of layers of meaning within representations of the twins arises in depictions of their homeland, Siam. Lengthy explorations of the country, including descriptions of its climate, economy, dress, and customs, were frequently included in material on the twins. But although such information was common to many "freak" publicity pamphlets (Bogdan 19), in the twins' case, particularly acute attention was given to Siam's governance, specifically the despotic excesses of its rulers. For example, Hale provides this description:

> [The house] of the King is enclosed within walls about two miles in circumference; . . . The person of the King is considered so sacred, that when he leaves the precincts of the palace, (about twice a year), the streets are cleared of people, the doors and windows of all buildings closed, and any person found guilty of looking at his most excellent Majesty, is punished with immediate death.
>
> The government of Siam is probably one of the most despotic and cruel in the world. (5)

The pamphlet then gives "an instance of the tyranny of the King": when the prince of Laos revolted, he was taken prisoner with thirteen members of his family, and all "were confined in an iron cage, loaded with heavy chains," and threatened with cruel death by hanging, spikes, and boiling oil (5–6). Such horrific descriptions offered the American viewing public an implicit affirmation of its own democratic legal system, articulated by the Founding Fathers, protecting against such cruel and unusual punishment.

In a similar pamphlet, Judge J. N. Moreheid discourses at length on the judicial system of Siam, ultimately implying the superiority of American practices:

> The Siamese mode of evidence is, in some respects, similar to the practice of the ancients. . . . The most remarkable custom is . . . practiced, generally, by boiling water or red hot iron. . . . the person accused is required to take up a stone immersed in the former a certain depth, or carry the latter a certain distance. His hand is then wrapped up, and the covering sealed for three days. If there appear, on examination, no marks of burning, he is pronounced innocent; if otherwise, guilty. The trial by cold water is different. Into this the culprit is thrown, his feet and his hands being tied. If he swims, he is guilty; if he sinks, he is considered innocent. (8–9)

Moreheid concludes his condemnation of these outlandish practices as he indirectly affirms the American alternative: "To us, it appears extraordinary that any innocent person could ever be acquitted by the one trial, or any criminal be convicted by the other" (8–9).

With such accounts, the American public could feed its curiosity on macabre details while at the same time gaining confidence in its own democratic principles. In contrast to Siam, the implied message was, the American legal system is just: regulated by a Constitution created out of a purportedly fortuitous union, it offers people due process of law, a fair trial, and the benefit of being innocent until proven guilty. The image of Chang and Eng, depicted as savage immigrants coming to a more civilized world, thus lent support to democratic ideologies.

Yet, ironically, it is precisely this jurisprudential security that, in turn, the twins themselves called into question. That is, the fusion of their bodies was such that the actions of one could not be separated from the actions of the other; each suffered the consequences of the other's behavior. Many stories of such blurred agency circulated during the twins' lives and afterward. For example, during one of their tours in Philadelphia in the early 1830s, a spectator squeezed Chang's hand so intensely that Chang punched him, knocking him down. Incensed, the man hauled the twins to a magistrate on a charge of assault and battery. But the twins' conjunction—instead of working as an emblem of a harmonious and united democracy—obfuscated usual democratic legal practices:

> The magistrate, after studying the twins' connecting band, addressed the complainant. The judge agreed that Chang could be jailed for assault, but added that if Eng were also jailed it would amount to false arrest and the complainant himself would have to be prosecuted. Needless to say, the injured party dropped his charges. (Wallace & Wallace 105)[4]

By appealing to the tenet of not punishing the innocent, the twins here embody ominous possibilities—of the guilty going free. Ironically, such a representation unravels the democratic principles the twins also are used to promote. The threat of lawlessness and chaos, conjured by their conjoined bodies, critiques the notion that a person is to be held accountable for only his or her own acts—and thus ultimately critiques individual agency and responsibility as a whole.

Another widely circulated story, recalled in a *Life* magazine article several decades after the twins' death, works similarly:

> Chang-Eng boarded a railroad train carrying only one ticket. Around their shoulders they wore generous cloaks . . . concealing their connecting band. The conductor first asked Eng for his ticket. He said he didn't have one and the conductor told him to get off. "Very well," said Eng tranquilly. He rose to go, naturally accompanied by his brother. "But *I* have a ticket," Chang protested, "and if you put me off, I'll sue the railroad." (Robertson 70–71)

Once again, even as the twins were used to tout the beauties of democratic brotherhood—escaping a despotic land for the safe and civilized world—their physical conjunction also complicated and undermined the ideals of individual agency implicit in that very same system. Indeed, the twins' very inseparability, appropriated so artfully for a unionist national agenda, proved dangerous in the courtroom, and more broadly to the whole legal system on which such a unified democratic nation was based.

"A Copulative Conjunction": Domestic Habits of the Siamese Twins

Just as the emblem of Chang and Eng reflected the national struggle over political connection and separation, so too did it offer a fruitful symbol of intimacy and closeness for the domestic realms of America. Indeed, the brothers' bond, praised as a "most perfect example" of friendship and "moral beauty," represented for many observers an attractive illustration of the fantasy of finding one's "other half" in romance and marriage. Ironically, however, the twins' own romantic pursuits and marriages posed a severe challenge to those same norms, because they were all too literally each other's "other half."

The trope of romantic love as a search for one's "other half" has a long history; it derives from a section of Plato's *Symposium*, where Aristophanes proposes that "the primeval man was round, his back and sides forming a circle; and he had four hands and four feet" (354). These circular, primitive people were mighty and strong, so much that the gods felt threatened, prompting Zeus to "'cut them in two'" so they would be "'diminished in strength and increased in number'" (354). Thus, the smaller, weaker beings that resulted were, in actuality, halves—and thus began the search: "So ancient is the desire of one another which is implanted in us, reuniting or original nature, making one of two, and healing the state of man. Each of us when separated . . . is but the indenture of a man and he is always looking for his other half" (355). As this ancient myth about "making one of two" has been received in later periods, it most often is appropriated as a metaphor of the quest for romantic (and usually heterosexual) love.[5]

In the early decades of nineteenth-century America, a popular farce drew on the twins to promote similar fantasies of romance and domesticity. In Gilbert Abbott À Beckett's *The Siamese Twins,* the image of Chang and Eng serves as a vehicle for bringing a young couple together in marriage. The play's protagonist, Captain Vivid, dresses his friends up and ties them together, disguised as "the Siamese Twins"—all in order to win the admiration of a Mr. Forceps, who is the guardian of Marian, the woman Vivid loves. Not surprisingly, À Beckett describes this romantic venture in language highly evocative of Chang and Eng's condition; for example, Vivid imagines a future when he and Marian will be "bound by irrevocable bonds" (13)—scheming that even as he "cut[s] one couple in two, I'll go and secure the formation of another" (15). Vivid's plan is to offer to perform for Forceps a miraculous "surgery," splitting the twins apart, but only on one condition: "that, in dissolving one union, you will sanction another—that of myself and your ward" (16). Forceps eagerly responds that he would love to see the twins "come in two" and would be "proud of an alliance with so distinguished a personage" (as Vivid)—and thus grants Vivid Marian's hand (16). In the wake of this pairing, Simon—one of Vivid's friends who has posed in the Siamese charade—is also inspired by romance: "Now I've got rid of the worst part of me [referring to his feigned 'twin'], I can't do without a better half," he claims, and turns to Sally, Marian's maid, to propose marriage. Throughout the play, then, À Beckett uses Chang and Eng's conjunction as a punning and playful gimmick, an extremized exhibition of the closeness that creates and guarantees more culturally inscribed symbolic bonds of matrimony.

Through it, Vivid and Marian, and Simon and Sally, become each other's "other half."

Chang and Eng themselves were often depicted in similar terms of romantic playfulness. From the beginning, the twins' striking physical appearance was stressed (using terms of normalcy, not aberration): "These Youths . . . are in possession of full health and extraordinary bodily strength; display all the faculties of the mind in their fullest extent; and seem in fact in every respect to enjoy a state of perfect happiness and contentment" (Hale 3). Such appeal quickly took on a romantic and sexual edge, as the public material presented them as sensitive, handsome, and eligible bachelors (see Figure 5.3). For example, Hale describes that the twins' "feelings are warm and affectionate, and their conduct amiable and well-regulated. They are very susceptible, and an act of kindness or affectionate treatment of any description is never forgotten" (10). Ultimately, Hale claims that "ladies of the first rank, both in Europe and America, have visited them daily in great numbers; and of all who have honoured them with the company, *none have appeared more gratified than the gentler sex*" (13; emphasis added).

Thus, the heterosexual, physical appeal of the twins played a prominent role in their representations. A widely circulated story supplied the American public's imagination with further romantic evidence: "A chamber-maid at the hotel where they were staying, tapped their heads and jokingly told them they should be her sweethearts, which caused them much amusement, and at one and the same time they both kissed her" (Thompson 83). Similarly, in a letter they wrote in 1842, the twins noted, "'We enjoy ourselves pretty well but have not as yet got married. But we are making love pretty fast, and if we get a couple of nice wives we will be sure to let you know about it" (quoted in Hunter 80).

But just as the twins' symbolizations of democratic brotherhood and national unity were confounded by their actual lives, so too their romantic appeal and flirtatiousness were complicated by other, contradictory messages. That is, whereas in À Beckett's farce the twins' conjunction is a temporary and public exhibition creating permanent, private bonds of intimacy, the twins themselves experienced no such distinction. Rather, the processes usually saved for the most intimate spaces and times—such as romance, sexuality, and reproduction—were for them always a shared experience, on public display. As such, the sexuality of either man, because witnessed—and thus to some extent participated in—by

Figure 5.3. Lithograph of Chang and Eng by A. Hoffy. (By permission of the College of Physicians, Philadelphia.)

the other, presented prospects transgressive to the Victorian American culture in which they lived: homosexuality (because both were male), incest (because they were brothers), and adultery (because each would, in a sense, be sleeping with a woman not his wife).

Therefore, even as the twins were used as emblems of sexual and romantic appeal, their own potential romantic pursuits and marriages were seen as monstrous and perverse. For example, one illustration that portrays them wearing attractive blue berets, green jackets, and yellow vests is labeled only "A Copulative Conjunction." The implied message here is that the twins' bond supplants or warps "normal" heterosexual copulation. Indeed, just as the use of the twins to affirm democratic values unravels into a specter of legal confusion, so too do their constructions as romantic and domestic ideals belie the contradictions to that system inherent in the twins' condition.

More specifically, the language and images of matrimony that emerge in various quips and anecdotes about the twins imply the limits of such domestic forms and practices. For example, biblical phrases such as "They TWAIN shall be ONE flesh" and "What's join'd together, let no man put asunder" (Sammons, epigraph) are applied to the twins in various contexts, but such an alignment questions the process of matrimonial joining altogether, because such depictions are made uncomfortably literal by Chang and Eng. Two other rhymes work similarly: "Lament of the Siamese Twins" portrays the twins mourning, "No modest maid, or widowed wife / Could wed us both, or either; / Fate doomed us to a *single* life / By *coupling two* together" ("Lament"); another advises the twins to "get wives at once, / Why, why defer it when / Unmarried though you should remain, / You can't be *single men*" (Sammons, lines 33–36).

In like vein, when Chang and Eng began to court the young women who would become their wives, the surrounding community was outraged. When the twins appeared in public with Adelaide and Sarah Yates, daughters of a minister who lived near their home in North Carolina, "word of the brazen spectacle" spread quickly (Wallace & Wallace 173). Neighbors of the Yates family, "angry and righteous" and "appalled at the thought of two of their fairest maidens pairing up with freaks, gathered together, hotly discussed the matter, and determined to protest" (Wallace & Wallace 173). Indeed, a few men "took matters further, and, refusing to believe that [Mr.] Yates was not actually encouraging his daughters, smashed some windows at his farm house," eventually threatening to "burn his crops if he did not promise to control his daughters," and end their "friendship" with Chang and Eng (Hunter 83).

Even to Charles Harris, a former manager and close friend of the twins, "the idea of the twins, bound together by a five-inch ligament, unable to act except in tandem, actually marrying two normal young women seemed too bizarre, and an invitation to disaster" (Wallace & Wallace 171). The fact that the twins were courting sisters must have augmented the transgressive nature of the arrangement. The public imagination could fantasize about the sex acts of the foursome, where three—if not four—persons always would be present, and where sisters might watch and participate with sisters, brothers with brothers, and in-laws with in-laws.

The cover image of the previously mentioned Moreheid pamphlet strongly implies such transgressiveness. First of all, after emphasizing "Domestic Habits of the Siamese Twins" in its title, it presents an image of a large plantation house, which it describes as the singular "Residence of the Siamese Twins, Surry County, N.C." (see Figure 5.4). Published in 1850, this image and its claim are technically inaccurate in their implication that the twins and their families shared only one home; in reality, by 1846—after three years of marriage—they had built two houses in Surry County, just over a mile apart, and migrated back and forth between them, staying three days at a time in each (Hunter 89–90). But the cover's titillating image of a single house for four married people plays out, nonetheless, the erosion of the boundaries of domestic propriety that the twins' marriages represented.

Moreover, within the first few paragraphs of this pamphlet, as he describes the twins' homeland, Moreheid emphasizes the fact that the household of the Siamese king "consists of about three thousand individuals, of whom *seven hundred are his wives*" (7). By highlighting this description of monstrously excessive polygamy, Moreheid conflates the twins with the Siamese king—implying that in their supposed single "mansion," the conjugal relations are also wanton and transgressive. Indeed, just as a description of Siam's legal system, in other parts of the pamphlet, offered the American public confidence of America's superiority even as the twins themselves posed a threat to that more "civilized" world, so the pamphlet presents Siamese polygamy as an alien practice against which the American ideal of monogamous matrimony could be affirmed—even as the reality of the twins' lives contradicted that system.

Even when explanations were offered of how the twins may have avoided sexual indecorum, such defenses only betrayed the underlying anxiety that necessitated such justifications in the first place. For example, Dr. William Pancoast asserted that through the use of a system of

LIVES, ADVENTURES, ANECDOTES, AMUSEMENTS, AND

DOMESTIC HABITS

OF THE

SIAMESE TWINS:

ONE OF THE GREATEST WONDERS OF THE PRESENT TIME, BEING TWO PERFECTLY FORMED PERSONS, WHOSE BODIES, BY A SINGULAR CAPRICE OF NATURE, ARE UNITED TOGETHER AS ONE.

Residence of the Siamese Twins, Surry county, N. C.

THESE GENTLEMEN, AFTER TRAVELING EXTENSIVELY IN THIS AND OTHER COUNTRIES, FINALLY MARRIED AND LOCATED THEMSELVES ON A FARM IN SURRY COUNTY, NORTH CAROLINA, WHERE THEY AND THEIR WIVES ARE AT PRESENT RESIDING.

"Distinct as the Billows, yet one as the Sea."

BY HON. J. N. MOREHEID.

RALEIGH, N. C.:
PRINTED AND PUBLISHED BY E. E. BARCLAY.
1850.

Figure 5.4. Cover of Moreheid pamphlet, 1850

"alternative mastery" (where one twin would blank out and surrender control to the other twin), instead of what seemed "most immoral and shocking that the two should occupy the same marital couch with the wife of one," there were no "improper relations between the wives and the brothers" (Wallace & Wallace 183). But such justifications only reminded their audience of the high level of "immoral" and "shocking" acts that indeed might have been taking place in Chang and Eng's household.

The twins presented a threat not only to domestic ideologies regarding heterosexual romance, but also to those regarding reproduction. One narrative details that on a European tour, Chang and Eng were not allowed into France

> on the grounds that such an exhibition would not only deprave the minds of any children who saw it, but it would also have a disastrous effect upon pregnant women. Presumably this fear was based upon the old superstition that if an expectant mother saw something physically unpleasant, her baby would be accordingly disfigured, and France was taking no chances. (Hunter 60)

In a similar vein, one pamphlet relates that in Newport, Kentucky, "a case occured [*sic*] in which the mother alleged that her interest in seeing the famous Siamese twins made such an impression on her that the birth of her Siamese twins was the result" (Teel 15). Thus, even as the twins were normalized to a certain extent, other representations of their conjoined bodies implied, too, that they could undermine and distort "healthy" reproduction—turning births into grotesque replications of their own monstrousness.

Representations of the twins' relationships with their own children displayed a similar vacillation between domestic normalcy and transgression. On the one hand, as their families "increased in size," so their "reputations as good . . . fathers grew," according to one biographer (Smith 30). Another biography emphasizes that their extreme fatherly devotion led them to return to exhibiting themselves in later life—despite their abhorrence of the prospect—in order to earn enough money for their children's education (Graves, cited in Smith 35). On the other hand, however, many noticed that the twins recorded the names of their children, as they were born, "in their Family Book, simply listing them by their Christian names, and not stating to which brother they belonged. It was as though no child belonged to Chang or to Eng, but to

Figure 5.5. Photograph by Mathew Brady, c. 1865. Chang (*right*) is seated next to his wife, Adelaide; Eng is next to his wife, Sarah. In front of Chang and Adelaide is their son Albert; in front of Eng and Sarah is their son Patrick Henry. (By permission of Circus World Museum, Baraboo, Wisconsin.)

them both" (Hunter 91). Even as the twins are used as emblems of intimate kinship structures of matrimony and reproduction, then, this "family book" ironically presents an ambiguity about who really fathered whom—even posing the possibility that the twins themselves might not know the answer. Thus, while in one sense the family book implies an inclusive image of one big happy family—where uncles are as devoted as fathers—in another, it awakens the threat of mistaken paternity and incest.

Not surprisingly, once Chang and Eng had children old enough to travel, the twins' business manager suggested they display their children with them—to "pique audience curiosity anew" (Wallace & Wallace 253) and thus win more business. Of equal interest was the photograph, made for publicity purposes, in the famed studio of Mathew Brady, of the twins, their wives, and two of their children (Wallace & Wallace 254; see Figure 5.5). Such representations reveal the ways in which the American public, in the first decades of the nineteenth century, found both endearing and horrifying the domestic transgressions that Chang and Eng, each other's literal "other half," always posed.

In probing the cultural functions of various forms of monstrosity, Leslie Fiedler makes a claim about the particular hold that conjoined twins have on their audiences:

> Standing before Siamese Twins, the beholder sees them looking not only at each other, but—both at once—at him. And for an instant it may seem to him that he is a third brother, bound to the pair before him by an invisible bond; so that the distinction between audience and exhibit, we and them, normal and Freak, is revealed as an illusion, desperately, perhaps even necessarily, defended, but untenable in the end. (36)

It is certainly true that even as early-nineteenth-century America observed Chang and Eng, so too the twins—and the representations of them—reflected back onto American culture. This mutual gaze attests to the fact that when America stared at the twins, they saw a spectacle that told the national story in its very flesh and bone. Indeed, the possibility of merged selves—in either the political or the domestic sphere—is simultaneously an American fantasy and an American nightmare. Conjoined twins exemplify both the ideal of closeness and sympathy and the specter of an attachment that is stifling or incestuous.

Throughout their long life, Chang and Eng offered an open canvas on which America could encode its dominant ideologies of democracy and domesticity. Ironically, however, even as the "United Siamese Brothers" were presented as idealized literalizations of brotherhood and sameness, and of romantic and matrimonial stability, their contorted, fused bodies also offered, to such ideals, deep challenges indeed.

Notes

In writing this essay, I benefited from many sources of support, insight, and encouragement. I would like to thank, in particular, the Francis Clark Wood Institute for the History of Medicine of the College of Physicians of Philadelphia for a fellowship that funded my research; the staffs at the Library of the College of Physicians of Philadelphia, the National Library of Medicine, and the Harvard University Theatre Collection; and Margaret Reid, Sacvan Bercovitch, Lynn Wardley, Jack Eckert, Gretchen Worden, and my colleagues in the Harvard History and Literature Writing Group.

1. Repositories for the best sources on Chang and Eng, ranging from clippings to pamphlets and unpublished manuscripts to scrapbooks and photographs, are located at the Circus World Museum (Baraboo, Wisconsin), the College of Physicians of Philadelphia, the Harvard University Theatre Collection, the National Library of Medicine (Bethesda, Maryland), and the Southern Historical Collection at the Library of the University of North Carolina at Chapel Hill. A sample of published,

longer works either on or inspired by the twins includes Gilbert Abbott À Beckett's play *The Siamese Twins: A Farce in One Act*; poems "The Siamese Twins: A Chapter of Biography," by William Linn Keese, and "The Siamese Twins: A Satirical Tale of the Times," by Edward Bulwer-Lytton; Mark Twain's satire "The Siamese Twins" and novella *Those Extraordinary Twins*; and Shepherd M. Dugger's narrative *Romance of the Siamese Twins*. Regarding masquerades of the twins, see the *San Francisco Daily Morning Call*, February 19, 1874, listing Richard and Otto Alexander, dressed as "the Siamese Twins" at the "tenth annual Bal Masque of the Eureka Social Club" ("Eureka Masquerade").

2. Puzzlingly, at times within the very same classification of deformity, one example is labeled plural ("twins" born in Paris in 1570 are baptized "Louis and Louise" and referred to as "they") and another is called singular (a "double female monster" born in Salisbury, England, in 1664 is labeled "it" and "the wonderful child") (Gould & Pyle 181–82).

3. For example, see *McGuffey's Sixth Eclectic Reader* (1879), 364. I wish to thank Edward Widmer for alerting me to Webster's speech and to the extreme popularity of its final lines.

4. Such legal dilemmas and ironies are, of course, the subject of Mark Twain's "The Siamese Twins" and *Those Extraordinary Twins*. Although an analysis of both pieces is crucial to a full understanding of the uses of Chang and Eng (and other conjoined twins) in American culture, I focus here on antebellum representations of Chang and Eng, for reasons of both space limitation and historical coherence.

5. John Donne's "The Dissolution" (1635) and Percy Bysshe Shelley's *Epipsychidion* (1821) are two well-known examples of the use of the "other half" metaphor in later literary discourse.

Works Cited

À Beckett, Gilbert Abbott. *The Siamese Twins: A Farce in One Act*. New York: Samuel French, n.d. (performed in the 1840s).

Bogdan, Robert. *Freak Show: Presenting Human Oddities for Amusement and Profit*. Chicago: University of Chicago Press, 1988.

Bulwer-Lytton, Edward. *The Siamese Twins: A Satirical Tale of the Times, with Other Poems*. New York: J. & J. Harper, 1831.

Donne, John. "The Dissolution." 1635. In *The Complete English Poems*. Ed. A. J. Smith. Harmondsworth, Middlesex, England: Penguin, 1971.

Dugger, Shepherd M. *Romance of the Siamese Twins*. Burnsville, N.C.: Edwards, 1936.

"Eureka Masquerade." *San Francisco Daily Morning Call*, February 19, 1874.

A Few Particulars Concerning Chang-Eng, the United Siamese Brothers, Published under Their Own Direction. New York: J. M. Elliott, 1836.

Fiedler, Leslie. *Freaks: Myths and Images of the Secret Self*. New York: Simon & Schuster, 1978.

Forgie, George B. *Patricide in the House Divided: A Psychological Interpretation of Lincoln and His Age*. New York: Norton, 1979.

Garraty, John. *A Short History of the American Nation*, 3rd ed. New York: Harper & Row, 1981.

Gould, George M., and Walter L. Pyle. *Anomalies and Curiosities of Medicine.* Philadelphia: W. B. Saunders, 1897.
Graves, J. F. *Life of Eng and Chang Bunker, the Original Siamese Twins.* Mount Airy, N.C.: Surry County Historical Society, n.d.
Hale, James W. *An Historical Account of the Siamese Twin Brothers, from Actual Observations.* New York: Elliott & Palmer, 1831.
Hunter, Kay. *Duet for a Lifetime: The Story of the Original Siamese Twins.* New York: Coward-McCann, 1964.
Kane, Joseph Nathan. *Famous First Facts: A Record of First Happenings, Discoveries, and Inventions in American History*, 4th ed. New York: H. W. Wilson, 1981.
Keese, William Linn. "The Siamese Twins: A Chapter of Biography." In *The Siamese Twins and Other Poems.* New York: Edwin W. Dayton, 1902.
"Lament of the Siamese Twins." Unidentified newspaper clipping in scrapbook compiled by George Buckley Bolton, 1830. National Library of Medicine, Bethesda, Md.
Ludlow, Dr., and Dr. Mitchell. [Report on "Psychological Observations on the Siamese Twins, Cheng [*sic*] and Eng, made in 1836."] *Proceedings of the American Philosophical Society* 2.15 (1841): 22–28.
McGuffey's Sixth Eclectic Reader, rev. ed. Cincinnati: Van Antwerp, Bragg, 1879.
Moreheid, J. N. *Lives, Adventures, Anecdotes, Amusements, and Domestic Habits of the Siamese Twins.* Raleigh, N.C.: E. E. Barclay, 1850.
Paré, Ambroise. *On Monsters and Marvels.* 1573. Trans. Janis L. Pallister. Chicago: University of Chicago Press, 1982.
Plato. *Symposium.* In *The Works of Plato.* Ed. Irwin Edman. Trans. Benjamin Jowett. New York: Modern Library, 1928.
Robertson, Archie. "Chang-Eng's American Heritage." *Life*, August 11, 1952, 70–72, 77–82.
Sammons, W. L. "An Address to the Siamese Brothers." In *Fairburn's Authentic and Copious Account of the Extraordinary Siamese Twins, Eng and Ching* [*sic*] . . . Broadway: Ludgate Hill, 1829.
Shelley, Percy Bysshe. "Epipsychidion." 1821. In *English Romantic Writers.* Ed. David Perkins. New York: Harcourt Brace Jovanovich, 1967. 1038–46.
Smith, J. David. *Psychological Profiles of Conjoined Twins: Heredity, Environment and Identity.* New York: Praeger, 1988.
Speeches of Hayne and Webster in the United States Senate, on the Resolution of Mr. Foot. January, 1830. Also, Mr.. Webster's Celebrated Speech on the Slavery Compromise Bill, March 7, 1850. Boston: A. T. Hotchkiss & W. P. Fetridge, 1853.
Teel, Jay. *Sideshow Freaks and Features.* Ansted, W.V.: Petland, 1930.
Thompson, C. J. S. *The Mystery and Lore of Monsters.* London: Williams & Norgate, 1930.
Twain, Mark. *Pudd'nhead Wilson and Those Extraordinary Twins.* 1894. Ed. Sidney E. Berger. New York: Norton, 1980.
———. "The Siamese Twins." 1868. In *Sketches New and Old: The Writings of Mark Twain*, vol. 23. New York: P. F. Collier & Son, 1917. 248–53.
Wallace, Irving. *The Fabulous Showman: The Life and Times of P. T. Barnum.* New York: Knopf, 1959.
Wallace, Irving, and Amy Wallace. *The Two.* New York: Simon & Schuster, 1978.

6 Liberty, Equality, Monstrosity: Revolutionizing the Family in Mary Shelley's *Frankenstein*

David A. Hedrich Hirsch

> History has all too often recounted nothing but the actions of ferocious beasts, among whom on rare occasions it recognizes heroes. We have reason to hope that with us begins the history of men, of brothers.
>
> COMTE DE MIRABEAU, 1789

The institution of new social orders has always gone hand in hand with the reinvention of foundation narratives, and according to Socrates, foremost among such literary "cures/poisons [*pharmakois*]" useful in the generation of a republic are myths of humanity's essential kinship, whereby citizens may be taught to "regard the other citizens as their brothers and children of the self-same earth."[1] Let there be Enlightenment, said the creators of French republicanism, believing that the establishment of a more humane, revolutionary order depended upon the resurrection and secular conversion of an idea of social brotherhood associated with early Christianity. The *Catéchisme républicain* redefined baptism as "the regeneration of the French begun on July 14, 1789," penitence as "the banishment of all those monsters who, unworthy to inhabit the land of Liberty . . . , will soon be driven out of every corner of the globe," and communion as "the association proposed to all peoples by the French Republic henceforth to form on earth only one family of brothers."[2] Born-again revolutionaries sought to redefine *le genre humain* through *fraternité*, but how to make the words flesh, and what might be lost in the translation?

Consider the effort of Anacharsis Cloots, who collected thirty-six representatives of *le genre humain*—Prussian, English, Sicilian, Dutch, and

Polish émigrés, among others, and most scandalously an Arab and a Chaldean, each dressed in his national costume—who would embody the Revolutionary spirit of fraternity at the Feast of the Federation, on the anniversary of the Bastille's fall. To late-twentieth-century eyes benumbed by ads touting the "United Colors of Benetton," this sort of spectacle might seem a naively multicultural representation of liberal brotherhood, yet to Cloots and his contemporaries, it was revolutionary, even apocalyptic. He declared that "this civic solemnity will be not solely the festival of the French, but moreover the festival of *le Genre Humain.* The trumpet which sounded the resurrection of a great people resounded to the four corners of the world, and the joyous songs of a choir of twenty-five million free men have woken the peoples long buried in slavery."[3] The *novus ordo sæclorum* begins where the word of the New Testament leaves off. Cloots transforms the Book of Revelation into the text of Revolution; his description of the Revolution as a new genesis depends on the resurrection of dead ideas of human(e) kinship, which had been buried and largely forgotten in the everyday practice of the politically elitist French church.

Keeping in mind Cloots's prophetic vision, now consider the effort of Mary Shelley's "modern Prometheus," Victor Frankenstein, who likewise seeks to form a new genre of humanity by modeling himself after mythological and biblical creators. His aspiration is not, significantly, to resurrect a single Lazarus, the already integral body of a dead individual. God's promise to the pile of bones in Ezekiel 37:6, "I will lay sinews upon you, and will bring up flesh upon you, and cover you with skin, and put breath in you"—a symbolic vow to regenerate an entire people or nation—is a more appropriate comparison here, for by scavenging from dissecting rooms and mortuaries the body parts of myriad individuals, and then confederating these individual parts into a new, conglomerate mass, Frankenstein, like Cloots, seeks to bring to life, in spectacular form, an ideal of *le genre humain* that transcends the bounds of the individual. In the modern myth of creation, the division process recounted in Genesis will be reversed: William Blake suggests in *The Four Zoas* that the fall of the Universal Man into division, into Selfhood, will be redeemed by the human imagination's capacity to lead Man, as a universal concept, toward "his Resurrection to Unity." To view the reformed social body in this way, as Fredric Jameson has argued, is to take a perspective "in which the imagery of libidinal revolution and of bodily transfiguration once again becomes a figure for the perfected community. The unity of the body must once again pre-figure the renewed organic identity of associative or collective life."[4] Frankenstein's creation might be viewed as the literalization of this revolutionary metaphor, for he, like Cloots, would redeem humankind by reuniting the dead into a new social corporation with the words, "I am making the whole of creation new" (Revelation 21:5).[5]

"What then is to hinder man, at each epoch of civilization, from making a stand, and new modelling the materials, that have been hastily thrown into a rude mass?" Mary Wollstonecraft asked in 1794.[6] The ultimate failure of Cloots's and Frankenstein's attempts to remake the social body, I would like to suggest, has everything to do with the instability of the Revolutionary key word *fraternité,* which simultaneously connotes competing designations of the locus of social cohesiveness and responsibility. Taken in one sense, *fraternité* indexes traditional structures of social order grounded upon family status and birthright, and is thus a term implicated in what Michel Foucault has termed the "*deployment of alliance*: a system of marriage, of fixation and development of kinship ties, of transmission of names and possessions," the hereditary strongholds of monarchical, aristocratic, and more generally patriarchal systems of rule.[7] Fraternity, from this perspective, presumes a common subjection to a parental superior: God, king, father, mother, or some amalgamation of these. In its revolutionary sense, *fraternité* suggests an equality based not upon citizens' common subjection or filiation, but upon their constitutional or natural rights as members of *le genre humain,* a form of political solidarity or affiliation often at odds with literal kinship ties and the ideology of the private family. As revolutionists would point out, even Christianity, in its early, radical form, posits a conflict of interest between private family interests and the demands of Christian brotherhood.[8]

This double sense of *fraternité* marks a shift in eighteenth-century conceptions of sympathy that would have profound implications for traditional conceptions of family and state structure:

> The place assumed by fraternity in the Revolution was occupied, in the Enlightenment, by beneficence and sensibility. . . . But classical beneficence, the binding force of hierarchical societies, can only move down the social ladder, from benefactor ("father" or "mother") to beneficiary ("child"); so the Revolutionary practice of fraternity is to be seen as a logically necessary egalitarian corrective within those moral codes regulating good relation-

ships in the community, which were previously structured on the non-egalitarian model of parents and children.[9]

Cloots's spectacle of *le genre humain* explicitly called into question traditional notions of blood kinship and national identity, leading some members of the French Assembly, who found the dark faces of the Arabian and Chaldean representatives a humiliating figuration of the new French citizen, to question the political stakes in allowing "strangers" in Paris to represent the oppressive conditions of foreign countries. Cloots's response, "The only strangers I know of are other species of animals," was greeted by a burst of laughter.[10] This laughter might be read as a defensive denial of the terror elicited by Cloots's positing of an essential likeness between the Assembly members and their strange "brothers," a likeness that would necessarily call into question hereditary designations of racial and national subjectivity. The Abbé Barruel, more terrified than humored by the Revolution's secular version of Christian brotherhood, would later suggest that the universal fraternity advanced by the purported founder of Jacobinism, Adam Weishaupt, indicates such a man's inability to love his own country and family, "and he will substitute that universal love because he is no more attached to [his blood relatives] than he is to the Chinese, the Tartar, or the Hottentot."[11] Metaphorical brotherhood threatens to dissolve the naturalness of literal, descent-based concepts of kith, kin, and kind.

This conflict of interests between blood relatives and monstrous others is central to Shelley's novel as well. Frankenstein's creature, described in terms ("dull yellow eye . . . yellow skin . . . his hair was of a lustrous black, . . . his teeth of a pearly whiteness; . . . straight black lips") commonly encountered in colonial depictions of Asian, Indian, and African "savages," is terrifying not merely in his physical otherness but more profoundly in his call for recognition as a humane, if not also human, being.[12] In his solicitation of *fraternité*, the creature becomes monstrous by undermining determinations of membership within *le genre humain* that depend on familial status (and, by extension, racial or national membership): his call for inclusion within the Frankenstein and DeLacey families threatens the very definition of the closed family unit upon which traditional social structures are grounded. *Frankenstein* suggests that Victor's and the Revolution's ultimately self-destructive reconstructions of *le genre humain* result from mistranslations of *fraternité* that fail to realize the egalitarian spirit of the radical Christian or republican ethos. Without the holy spirit of *fraternité* (the third term in the republican trinity), the genesis of a commonwealth that Hobbes figured as "an artificial man, though of greater stature and strength than the natural," will so closely "resemble that *Fiat* or the 'let us make man,' pronounced by God in the creation" that the fratricide of Cain and Abel, as Chamfort remarked during the Revolution, cannot be far behind.[13]

Politics and the Revolutionary Family

Recent analyses of *Frankenstein* have argued persuasively that the novel's depiction of a terrifying, man-made monster is a response to the overweening confidence of Enlightenment utopianism and to the Terror that destroyed many republicans' belief in the French Revolutionary project. In the most influential of such readings, Lee Sterrenburg examines Shelley's appropriation of rhetoric used by political conservatives including Edmund Burke, who metaphorized the Revolution and British republicans like Shelley's parents, William Godwin and Mary Wollstonecraft, as "a species of political monster, which has always ended by devouring those who have produced it."[14] Other analysts have read Shelley's "modern Prometheus" as a critical figuration of a different philosophical forefather of the Revolution, Rousseau, whom Wollstonecraft praised as "the true Prometheus of sentiment" in her unfinished novel *Maria*, but also denounced as an unnatural father who rejected his own children.[15] While agreeing that *Frankenstein* is critical of the Revolution's failure to realize its utopian promise, I would, however, like to stress that Shelley's understanding of Victor as the "modern Prometheus" also draws upon *pro*-Revolutionary rhetoric, and thereby to suggest that his Promethean-Revolutionary aspiration to re-create *le genre humain* may not, in and of itself, be the central object of the novel's critique.

During the Revolutionary period, the figure of a modern Prometheus was linked to freedom in texts such as Erasmus Darwin's *The Botanic Garden* (1789–91), which describes American and French revolutionaries, newly confederated by the electrical charge of patriotism, taking on the "giant-form" of the "warrior, Liberty," a figure that Mary Wollstonecraft resurrected in *An Historical and Moral View of the Origin and Progress of the French Revolution*.[16] Both of these texts, like *Frankenstein*, describe the collection of individuals into a new "colossal form" of man charged by a Promethean flame, who challenges the integrity of older structures of human social order. "FREEDOM" is the "new Prometheus" through which "social man a second birth shall find," wrote Wollstonecraft's American friend Joel Barlow in his epic *Columbiad*, and this secular version of rebirth entails the denaturalization of traditional familial, religious, and political power structures: "No proud privilege from birth can spring, / No right divine, nor compact form a king."[17]

The Columbiad's opposition of freedom and birth privilege underlines an issue central to Revolutionary-era debate over the idea of *le genre humain*: the propriety of using metaphorical rhetoric in the naturalization of traditional structures of monarchical and familial order, both founded upon hereditary transmission of power. Pursuing the type of paternalistic metaphor advanced earlier by Robert Filmer's *Patriarcha*, Edmund Burke argued the conservative position in his *Reflections on the Revolution in France* (1790), which appropriates traditional family order to prove the naturalness of hereditary monarchy:

> Our political system is placed in a just correspondence and symmetry with the order of the world, and with the mode of existence decreed to a permanent body composed of transitory parts. . . . By adhering in this manner and on those principles to our forefathers, we are guided not by the superstition of antiquarians, but by the spirit of philosophic analogy. In this choice of inheritance we have given to our frame of polity the image of a relation in blood; binding up the constitution of our country with our dearest domestic ties; adopting our fundamental laws into the bosom of our family affections; keeping inseparable, and cherishing with the warmth of all their combined and mutually reflected charities, our state, our hearths, our sepulchres, and our altars.[18]

Moving quickly by way of "philosophic analogy" from the constitutional state to bodily constitution, and then to an image of blood relationships and domestic ties, Burke grounds his promonarchical argument on those two most natural organizations, the composite body and the domestic family. Although Burke's trope of a massive social body composed of otherwise separate pieces has a well-established rhetorical lineage, we shall see in a moment how *Frankenstein* makes monstrous this metaphorical representation of familial and social order, effectively unmasking this classical figuration of the social body and revealing its grotesque double. For the time being, it will suffice simply to emphasize Burke's grounding of monarchical rule upon the apparent naturalness of the domestic unit: the order of the hierarchical family is a crucial link in the great signifying chain of being.

Whereas Burke considered Jacobin challenges to paternalist hierarchy monstrous, British republicans effectively reversed this polemic, arguing that the real political monster was the system of so-called natural inheritance. Burke's system of primogeniture, like a "species of imaginary consequence," Thomas Paine argued, "is the law against every other law of nature": children other than the firstborn son, who should be considered "flesh and blood of their parents" by *nature's* laws, are "nothing akin to them" under "the monster" of primogenitureship. "To restore, therefore, parents to their children, and children to their parents—relations to each other, and man to society—and to exterminate the monster Aristocracy, root and branch—the French constitution has destroyed the law of PRIMOGENITURESHIP. Here then lies the monster; and Mr. Burke, if he pleases, may write its epitaph."[19] Wollstonecraft's description of the effects of hereditary property also speaks of monsters: "Man has been changed into an artificial monster by the station in which he was born, and the consequent homage that benumbed his faculties"; hereditary definitions of status produce monsters who cannot sense that true happiness arises "from the friendship and intimacy which can only be enjoyed by equals."[20] Countering Burke's defense of inheritance, Wollstonecraft argues that the "perpetuation of property in our families," far from being natural, is the source of civic monstrosity. Class distinctions informing aristocratic notions of "family" are a form of cultural narcissism: "The mind must have a very limited range that thus confines its benevolence to such a narrow circle, which, with great propriety, may be included in the sordid calculations of blind self-love."[21]

William Godwin pursues these ideas much further in his *Enquiry Concerning Political Justice*, by stating that hereditary systems and the false titles of feudalism were "a ferocious monster, devouring, wherever it came, all that the friend of humanity regards with attachment and love," and then even more radically by denaturalizing the very nature of family upon which Burke (as well as Paine and Wollstonecraft, albeit to a much lesser extent) attempted to base analogical arguments of natural social structures.[22] Godwin's vision of a properly anarchic society (adapted from Socrates' recommendations in the *Republic*) posits the chimerical institution of the family as but one example of classification systems that separate citizens. Nepotism, hereditary obligation, and other institutionalized forms of preference are overvaluations of particular people that prevent citizens from seeing that the worth of an individual is measured only in the context of the state. "What magic is there in the pronoun 'my'?" Godwin asks, translating Socrates; "My brother or my father may be a fool or a profligate, malicious, lying or dishonest. If they be, of what consequence is it that they are mine?" Although common sense might argue "in favour of providing, in ordinary cases, for my wife and children, my brothers and relations, before I provide for strangers," it is only by rationally purging from the language and structure of a republican ethos the false magic of the genitive "my"—and thus by dissolving the Burkean monsters of feudal (en)titlement—that truly liberated and impartial justice can be effected.[23] Should *brother* refer only to one's legal or biological kin, Godwin, like Cain, would disavow the responsibility of being his brother's keeper, and in doing so uphold the impartial responsibilities of social fraternity.

Thus, although in the late 1790s, as Sterrenburg has shown, conservatives would commonly use the figure of a monster to describe the uncontrolled, parricidal Revolution, it is important to recognize also that Republican sympathizers used the term *monster* to figure the unnatural offspring of heredity-based definitions of identity and status. English republicans' depictions of hereditary monstrosity—which challenge political conservatism's home base in family-centered transmissions of power and status—suggest a radical interrogation of the family as the institutional origin of inequality and political tyranny. In *Frankenstein,* Mary Shelley suggests along the same lines that closed systems of intrafamilial distribution of wealth and beneficence—processes of socioeconomic inbreeding—are akin to institutionalized incest in their production of monstrosities of birth. Without going as far as her father and calling for the abolition of the family (even Godwin would eventually step back from that position), Shelley probes the conflicting relations between the family and ethical/political definitions of citizenship, social orders grounded upon either literal (blood-based) or metaphorical (revolutionary) definitions of kinship and *fraternité.* Shelley's project in *Frankenstein* is not, as some readers have argued, the depoliticization of the monster tradition by shifting from politics to psyche—"Political revolution has been replaced by a parricidal rebellion within the family," Sterrenburg asserts[24]—but rather an uncovering of the ideological linkages elucidated by British republicans between family and state structures, and an inquiry into the family's responsibility in the creation of monstrosity. An argument such as Sterrenburg's accedes to the bourgeois hypothesis that the family can exist in insular security as part of the private realm, noncontingent with the place of the political—a view held by liberal followers of Locke but explicitly rejected by theorists from Plato to Godwin who argued that there is but one place, one topic, within which family and state organizations exist, so that "replacement" can be understood only as a false escape from one realm to another. "To represent the 'Jacobin monster' in domestic and psychological terms," Sarah Goodwin argues, "is not to exclude the political, but to enlarge it."[25]

The prevailing tradition of *Frankenstein* criticism, however, upholds this division between the private and public realms, championing the closed family circle as a domestic paradise lost when the two foremost exemplars of Promethean spirit in the novel, Victor Frankenstein and Robert Walton, attempt to escape from boundaries (the limits of prevailing scientific knowledge, career destinations chosen by fathers, and the constriction of traditional family bonds) that have been imposed to curtail their pursuits by those who uphold convention. Typical of most readings of the novel is a blind acceptance of the moral offered by Percy Shelley's preface to the first edition, which asserts the author's intentions as "avoiding the enervating effects of the novels of the present day, and . . . the exhibition of the amiableness of domestic affection" (7). Shelley's preface suggests that the novel of terror, not unlike the political manifestation of Terror during the Revolution, aims to enforce an ideological uniformity upon those subject to its representational regime: the horrific function of this novel about a monster is apparently to rouse the enervated novel reader to a reactive, if not perhaps reactionary, appreciation for "the amiableness of domestic virtue" typified by the private family. It would appear that much of *Frankenstein*'s popularity has been a function of its success in embodying the then nascent, now firmly entrenched, ideology of bourgeois "family values," and even many feminist readers of the novel, otherwise attentive to the family's restriction of women's freedom, have championed domestic interiority as the only locus for human tranquillity.

Victor's Ulyssean "voyage of discovery to the land of knowledge" (55), his asexual construction of a creature without women's agency, has been frequently interpreted as a gynephobic attack on woman-centered family domesticity. Margaret Homans, for one, stresses the psychologically regressive character of Frankenstein's scientific foray outside the boundaries of "*normal* heterosexual procreation": "To bring a composite corpse to life is to circumvent the *normal* channels of procreation; the demon's 'birth' violates the *normal* relations of family, especially the *normal* sexual relation of husband and wife."[26] The normalizing force of such a reading is emphasized in Anne K. Mellor's assertion that men like Walton and Frankenstein "have diverted their libidinal desires away from normal erotic objects": "In place of a heterosexual attachment to Elizabeth, Victor Frankenstein has substituted a homosexual obsession with his creature."[27] Although on the whole Mellor's analysis provides a much-needed interrogation of the ideological contradictions within *Frankenstein*'s representations of the "normal" family—she stresses that "the bourgeois family is founded on the legitimate possession and exploitation of property and on an ideology of domination . . . that render it innately hierarchical,"[28] an argument advanced, as we have seen, by Shelley's own parents, Wollstonecraft and Godwin—her psychoanalysis of Frankenstein is itself dependent upon notions of normativity and hierarchical domination (the compulsory heterosexuality definitive of the family as opposed to a "monstrous" homosexuality defined by abnormal libidinal objects) that characterize the bourgeois regime's deployment of sexuality, as Foucault has argued.

The dominant tradition of feminist analysis of *Frankenstein* misrepresents the origin of monstrosity as a function of "abnormal" creation rather than a failure of postpartum bonding, an argument that, expanded from the "private" realm of the household to the "public" realm of national politics, is in line with critics' assertion that Shelley rejected the idea of revolution itself, rather than the Revolution's failure to establish true *fraternité*. (Contrary to Homans and Mellor, one could even develop an argument, following Shulamith Firestone, that Frankenstein's technological discoveries could liberate women from the childbearing function and allow humanity to "outgrow nature" and the biology-based gender inequalities underwriting traditional family structure.)[29] Readings of the novel as championing the "normal relations of family," I would argue, actually subscribe to an (aristocratic) ethos of descent-based identity opposed by Shelley in *Frankenstein* and her later republican novels *Valperga* and *The Last Man*. Victor Frankenstein's construction of an abstract figure of humanity—through generic association rather than lineal kinship—is less a symptom of gynephobia than a realization of Paine's conviction that "*the unity of man*; by which I mean that men are all of *one degree*, and consequently that all men are born equal, and with equal natural right," will be obscured by an aristocracy-based ideology of blood, race, and heredity unless we can imagine that "posterity had been continued by *creation* instead of *generation*."[30]

The frequency of readers' pathologization of Frankenstein's scientific exploration as a "perverse," "abnormal," inverted, "debased," against-nature, "narcissistic" breach of "the boundaries of the benevolent family" might raise the question of exactly *whose* narcissism is at stake here; after all, Ovid's Narcissus does not suffer from an illness intrinsic to himself, but is instead cursed to death by others whose *own* self-love is threatened by Narcissus's lack of interest.[31] Recalling Wollstonecraft's critique of the "perpetuation of property in our families," of the confining of such families' "benevolence to such a narrow circle, which, with great propriety, may be included in the sordid calculations of blind self-love," *Frankenstein* consistently suggests that the private family might *itself* be considered the central locus of narcissism. Among recent feminist analyses of the novel, Kate Ellis's "Monsters in the Garden: Mary Shelley and the Bourgeois Family" is unique in its suggestion of a countermoral to the novel: "Shelley seems to suggest that, if the family is to be a viable institution for the transmission of domestic affection from one generation to the next, it must redefine that precious commodity in such a way that it can extend to 'outsiders' and become hardy enough to survive in the world outside."[32] Challenging readers' acceptance of Percy Shelley's prefatory assertion that the novel is chiefly concerned with "the exhibition of the amiableness of domestic affection," Ellis argues that "if Shelley meant to be descriptive, he was certainly reading *Frankenstein* selectively. . . . Mary Shelley was at least as much concerned with the limitations of that affection as she was with demonstrating its amiableness."[33] Regardless of the fact that a self-centered character like Victor is the product of tranquil domesticity or that a family life devoid of parental love can somehow issue forth the saintly Justine Moritz, readers of *Frankenstein* consistently uphold the private domestic family as the only natural foundation for social tranquillity. Yet, building upon Ellis's analysis, I would like to suggest that the domestic insularity that defines familial happiness might also be the very cause of that family's self-destruction.

Familiality and Contempt

Ironically, most readers' conviction that Frankenstein's production of the creature is narcissistically "antifamily" repeats the power dynamics of familial proscription presented in the novel itself, dynamics of boundary marking and normative bondage that in the first place prompt Walton and Frankenstein to look elsewhere for creative possibility and freedom. Had he obeyed his father's deathbed injunction forbidding him from becoming a naval explorer, Walton's life "might have been passed in ease and luxury" (12), but such a life of ease is subsequently qualified in Shelley's 1831 revision as an overrefined insularity. Walton tells Margaret that a "youth passed in solitude, my best years spent under your gentle and feminine fosterage, has so refined the groundwork of my character, that I cannot overcome an intense distaste to the usual brutality exercised on board ship," let alone his distaste for "wholly uneducated" and "ignorant" men of the working classes (230, 232). The criticism Walton then directs at his sister—"You have been tutored and refined by books and retirement from the world, and you are, therefore, somewhat fastidious" (232)—and his derision of the lieutenant's "national and professional prejudices" (14) are apt criticisms of Walton's own fastidious aversion to manners foreign to his own experience. Victor Frankenstein similarly recounts an early life structured by the family as "remarkably secluded and domestic; and this had given me invincible repugnance to new countenances." This prejudicial education restricts Victor's ability to love anyone outside the narrow domestic circle. "I loved my brothers, Elizabeth, Clerval; these were 'old familiar faces;' but I believed myself totally unfitted for the company of strangers." Like Walton, Frankenstein early on finds his intellectual desires countered by his father's "indefinite censure" (33) and his adopted sister Elizabeth's disinterest: the domestic Eden is maintained by enforced ignorance of anything outside its inward-looking boundaries.

If Joel Barlow had argued that freedom is the new Prometheus, Mary Shelley suggests that the modern Prometheus's freedom is bound by his family's blind self-love: intellectual freedom in *Frankenstein* is antithetical to bourgeois notions of normality and is therefore repeatedly proscribed by the family over the course of the novel, with earthly fathers playing God in the domestic Eden. Opposing the values espoused by his father, who believes that "learning [is] superfluous in the commerce of ordinary life," Henry Clerval finds that his "own mind was all the possession that he prized, beautiful and majestic thoughts the only wealth he coveted—daring as the eagle and as free, common laws could not be applied to him; and while you gazed on him you felt his soul's spark was more divine—more truly stolen from Apollo's sacred fire, than the glimmering ember that animates other men" (39). This modern Prometheus, like Barlow's, desires freedom from the ordinary definitions of status and wealth characteristic of inherited social orders and valued by his mercantile father: Clerval evinces "a restrained but firm resolve, not to be chained to the miserable details of commerce" (240). Safie, another of the novel's Promethean characters bound and chained by familial tyranny, runs away from a home headed by a Turkish father who would have her "immured within the walls of a haram, allowed only to occupy herself with puerile amusements," hoping instead "to aspire to higher powers of intellect, and an independence of spirit" in the state of relative freedom offered by republican Geneva, "where women were allowed to take a rank in society" (119). Each of these narratives suggests that the purported paradise of bourgeois domesticity is, from a certain perspective, a realm of imprisonment that forbids family members from pursuing goals other than those that fall within the private family's desire for conformity.

The narcissism of this drive to reproduce the status quo is evident even in the rare instances of the family's extension of itself to incorporate an outsider: despite her foreign birth, Safie as a Christian can be absorbed within the DeLacey family without calling that family's self-definition into question, just as Elizabeth Lavenza (in the first edition, Victor's first cousin) is sufficiently "of a distinct species" from her "dark-eyed, hardy little vagrant" Italian foster siblings—"fairer than a garden rose among dark-leaved brambles" (235)—to warrant not only her adoption as Victor's sister, but also her being chosen, on the basis of Caroline Frankenstein's "desire to bind as closely as possible the ties of domestic love" (29), as Victor's future wife. Far from being antithetical to familial order, incest (as Freud would later note) is the drive par excellence through which "the members of a family hold together permanently and become incapable of contact with strangers."[34] The family's policing of the bounds of property and propriety so rigorously follows what Wollstonecraft called "the sordid calculations of blind self-love" that it renders any nonfamily members unrecognizable. Happy families are all alike; familiality breeds contempt for any *un*familiar faces, Shelley suggests, laying the groundwork for a republican critique of classism and racism (although potentially raising the specter of contemporary anti-Semitic rhetoric as well).[35]

These examples of the family's attempt to maintain its insularity might be read as the bourgeois translation of aristocratic modes of hereditary privilege: the blue-bloodedness definitive of pre-Revolutionary ideas of "family" and power has been translated into bourgeois identity politics surrounding race, nation, and class. Consider this: Percy Shelley added to Mary's manuscript lines stating that the "republican institutions of our country have produced simpler and happier manners than those which prevail in the great monarchies that surround it," and that this republican simplicity so decreases the "distinction between the several classes" that a "servant in Geneva does not mean the same thing as a servant in France and England" (60). The rest of the novel contradicts this, however. The ease with which the Frankenstein family accepts the outrageous circumstantial evidence that their servant Justine, formerly "loved and esteemed as [a] sister" (81), has murdered little William in order to steal a cameo depicting his mother suggests an underlying fear that even the most trusted members of the working class, when allowed into the domestic sanctuary, are likely to disrupt the middle class's conservative transmission of property from generation to generation. Even in a republican state, protection of the insular status of the private bourgeois family overrules any public ideal of classless egalitarianism. The class interest shared by the magistrates overseeing Justine's trial and by the Frankenstein family—"one of the most distinguished" of the Genevan republic (27), so distinguished that William's response to the "monster" takes the form of an elitist threat: "My papa is a Syndic . . . he would punish you" (139)—is ultimately a stronger public force than any of Elizabeth's depictions of the servant as "my more than sister." All that is needed to convince even Justine of her guilt is the court's provision of a father-confessor, who "threatened and menaced, until I began to think that I was the monster that he said I was" (82). The monster has traditionally been defined as a figure disruptive of traditional social categories of rank and distinction, as Mary Douglas has shown: little did Justine realize that her ambiguity as a servant within the domestic circle, the mere *metaphoricity* of her kinship to Elizabeth, William, and Victor, always underwrote the possibility of her being read as a monstrous simulacrum of a family member. Her threat as a servant to the "literal" definition of family, one might argue, lies in the etymological kinship between *family* and the Latin term for female slave, *famula.* In other words, Justine's inclusion in and exclusion from the Frankenstein family perform a genealogy of the metaphoricity of the "literal" family itself, as well as a history of the narrowing of the concept of family to the exclusion of household members not linked by blood or marriage. The unjust execution of Justine is a violent and ineffectual attempt to resecure the boundaries of the family proper and its private possession of property, an attempt to exclude metaphorical monstrosity from the familial and political domains of *nomos* and *logos.* Her supposed theft of William's cameo *likeness* of Caroline Frankenstein reveals that property and the proper sense of a word—in this case, family or (blood) fraternity—are "next of kin within the same semantic network," as Paul Ricoeur has argued.[36]

This conflict between metaphorical and literal designations of kinship is most forcibly brought home in the narrative offered by Frankenstein's creature, the figural embodiment of the republican Revolution's aspiration toward a new form of social federation. The creature's narrative hinges upon his failed attempt to be adopted within the hearth and hearts of the DeLacey family, descendants of "a good family in France" who were forced into exile and poverty after the eldest son, Felix, rescues Safie's father, a Turkish merchant sentenced to death less because of "the crime alleged against him" than because of the foreigner's "religion and wealth" (117–18). Mellor's dating of the events recounted in *Frankenstein* would suggest that the French government responsible for the Turk's execution order and the DeLacey family's status as émigrés is that of the Montagnards, who under Robespierre would later institute the infamous Reign of Terror.[37] In what initially seems to be a contrast to this increasingly exclusive Revolutionary government (which ultimately reacted violently to any threat of civil nonuniformity, and to the *sans-culottes*' growing demand for a share in the bourgeois power structure), Shelley depicts the DeLaceys as a progressive family who champion Cloots's ideal of *le genre humain* in risking their own well-being to secure justice for Safie's father, a religious and national foreigner. Despite their former affluence under the Bourbon regime, the DeLaceys are so infused with the republican spirit of the Revolution's early stage that they teach Safie to speak French by referring to Volney's *Ruins*, Plutarch's *Lives*, and a translation of Milton's *Paradise Lost.* Eavesdropping upon Safie's instruction, Frankenstein's creature "learned that the possessions most esteemed by your fellow-creatures were, high and unsullied descent united with riches": "I heard of the division of property, of immense wealth and squalid poverty; of rank, descent, and noble blood" (115). The DeLacey family's acceptance of Safie into their private hut would suggest that they are exempt from Wollstonecraft's accusation of aristocratic families' "blind self-love," and, as many readers have noted, Shelley's description of the DeLacey hut comes closer than any other familial arrangement depicted in the novel to the ideal of a nonhierarchical domestic space.

Yet Frankenstein's creature is barred from entering even this illusory Paradise, despite DeLacey *père*'s promise that "the hearts of men, when unprejudiced by any obvious self-interest, are full of brotherly love and charity." "You raise me from the dust by this kindness," the creature responds (130), suggesting that brotherly love would be the true source of the creature's birth into humanity. But the humane lessons in republican brotherhood that the creature learns from the DeLaceys are ultimately overwritten by a more brutal human proclivity toward class and familial protectionism: neither republican justice (as the execution of Justine suggests) nor the republican family is as blind as old DeLacey. The DeLaceys show a firm sense of the idea "of brother, sister, and all the various relationships which bind one human being to another in mutual bonds" (116–17), but like the primitive family described by Rousseau in his *Essay on the Origin of Languages*, the sighted members of the family seem incapable of abstracting from the creature's compassionate nature the idea of a man. "Their hut contained all their fellow beings," Rousseau explains; "a stranger, a beast, a monster, were for them the same thing: outside of themselves and their family, the whole universe was nothing to them."[38] Young Felix might be eager to shelter his beautiful Arabian fiancée Safie beside the family hearth—"as a fair exotic is sheltered by the gardener, from every rougher wind," perhaps (233–34)—but on seeing the creature clinging to his father's knee he is transformed into a violent defender of the family's insularity.

Exiled from the domestic Paradise, the creature, "like the arch fiend, bore a hell within me," yet unlike Milton's Satan, the creature has yet to act upon any violent thoughts stemming from jealousy for the father's favored son. It is Felix, in fact, who appears the more Cain-like here, whose self-interest in violently delimiting the boundaries of family privilege overrules any inclination toward brotherly love and charity. As if to symbolize the fruits of the family's tendency to cultivate only its own garden (its *hortus conclusus*), and the way in which the happy family's exclusivity can produce a hell within anyone barred from the domestic hearth, the creature destroys "every vestige of cultivation in the garden" and sets the hut aflame once he realizes that his "protectors" have abandoned him (134–35).[39] It is "thanks to the lessons of Felix," the creature explains to Frankenstein, "and the sanguinary laws of man, [that] I have learned to work mischief" (138). Thus begins the conversion of a benevolent creature—who if allowed to partake of "the interchange of kindness, . . . would bestow every benefit upon [humanity] with tears of gratitude" (141)—into a revolutionary *enragé* whose communitarian claims will soon be transformed into a veritable reign of terror.

Of Monsters and Men

The "sanguinary laws of man" suggest to the creature that his only hope for sympathetic kindness lies in discovering his blood kin. But given his failure to be bound by blood ties or legal contract to the Frankensteins, and his subsequent reliance on metaphorical, rather than literal, definitions of familial responsibility, this final hope is ultimately without grounds. Particularly interesting about the creature's solicitation of sympathy from Frankenstein is that, rather than base his arguments on the grounds of natural *fraternité*, he has learned enough from the DeLacey family's lessons in household management to appropriate the rhetoric of blood kinship, speaking as a child to its parent, as well as the rhetoric of legal contract, speaking as wife might appeal to her spouse: "You, my creator, detest and spurn me, thy creature, to whom thou art bound by ties only dissoluble by the annihilation of one of us" (94). Underlying the creature's metaphorical program is his sense that Frankenstein might be moved by a Burkean "philosophic analogy" linking the image of a "body composed of transitory parts" to the naturalness of "our dearest domestic ties" and, by extension, paternalistic political regimes. "I am thy creature, and I will be even mild and docile to my natural lord and king, if thou wilt also perform thy part, the which thou owest me," he argues (95). Speaking *as* a family member, the creature is initially able to forge metaphorical bonds with and around his creator, much as the Frankenstein family had done earlier in Victor's life: the modern Prometheus would once again be bound by familial obligation.

The supreme irony is that Victor's attempt to form a revolutionary "new species" or *genre humain*, a new social order free from the conservatism of familial reproduction, has resulted in a monstrous translation of the very same ties that previously constricted him. "No *father* could claim the gratitude of *his child* so completely as I should deserve their's," he says of this "new" species (49; emphasis added); his conception of revolution is that of a beginner who, according to Marx, in learning a new language always retranslates it into his mother (or in this case his father) tongue. Far from creating a new fraternal order, Frankenstein's behavior toward "his child" unwittingly reproduces the same structures of paternal proscription that had earlier opposed Victor's claim to be a person in his own right. "The tradition of all the dead generations weighs like a nightmare on the brain of the living," Marx would write of a later failed revolution, in a statement that is as applicable to Frankenstein as to his creature. "And just when they seem engaged in revolutionizing themselves and things, in creating something that has never yet existed, precisely in such periods of revolutionary crisis they anxiously conjure up the spirits of the past . . . to present the new scene of world history in . . . borrowed language."[40] As Frankenstein's nightmare condensation of the faces of Elizabeth, his dead mother, and his "monster" had prophesied earlier, the confederated creature has become a monstrous metaphor for, and defamiliarization of, the literal family. Unless "the past is severely curtailed in its powers to dominate present and future," writes Edward Said, the seemingly "direct genealogical line" of "parenthood and filiation . . . , whether in language or in the family, will produce a disguised quasi-monstrous offspring, that is farce or debased language, rather than a handsome copy of the precursor or parent."[41]

Pulled between the ties of metaphorical kinship to the creature and literal kinship to his family, Victor finds himself in a double bind: by using the Burkean tool of philosophic analogy, the creature has temporarily rendered the metaphorical/literal split indistinguishable. If Burke's chain of being is to remain intact, the same cohesive power binding up the transitory parts of the microcosmic body should be translatable without loss to "the image of a relation in blood; binding up the constitution of our country with our dearest domestic ties; adopting our fundamental laws into the bosom of our family affections." Victor explains his dilemma as follows: "I created a rational creature, and was bound towards him, to assure, as far as was in my power, his happiness and well-being. This was my duty; but there was another still paramount to that. My duties towards my fellow-creatures had greater claims to my attention" (214–15). Yet the creature's rhetoric, the fact that his autobiographical relation "proved him to be a creature of fine sensations" (142), has already rendered this a false opposition of duties; this narrative proof of the creature's humane sensitivity implies that he must be a man and a brother, a "fellow-creature."

Victor's subsequent attempt to protect his literal family is as much an expression of Schillerian naïveté as Elizabeth's fantasy that, "quiet in our native country, and not mingling in the world, what can disturb our tranquillity?" (89). This lapse into the comforting fiction of the family's radical detachment from the political realm is a denial of the terrible truth Elizabeth had come to see following Justine's execution:

> I no longer see the world and its works as they before appeared to me. Before, I looked upon the accounts of vice and injustice, that I read in books or heard from others, as tales of ancient days, or imaginary evils; at least they were remote, and more familiar to reason than to the imagination; *but now misery has come home, and men appear to me as monsters thirsting for each other's blood*. . . . Alas! Victor, when falsehood can look so like the truth, who can assure themselves of certain happiness? (88; emphasis added)[42]

When the metaphorical and the literal become indistinguishable, when political misery comes home, there is no Paradise to be regained because Paradise is revealed as always already lost. Yet the family, desperate to believe in the security of its tranquil hut, refuses to acknowledge the flip side to Elizabeth's terrifying transvaluation: if men can appear as monsters, then certainly monsters can appear as men. Rather than pursue the defamiliarizing implications of her metaphorical critique, however, Elizabeth recants: "Yet *I* am certainly unjust" for questioning the court's judgment of Justine, she says, in an attempt to resecure the distinction between human justice and inhuman monstrosity. But all this recantation can enact is a self-contradictory assertion of her own (in)humanity, for if "men" are to justice as "monsters" are to injustice, then Elizabeth's retraction "I am unjust" both *ad*jures and *ab*jures her own capacity for monstrous behavior.

If indeed the human is monstrous and the "monster" is human, then the paranoid dis*owning* of this fact by Frankenstein and his family represents an expansively defined *homo*phobia, fear of the same, through which Brothers and Others are discriminated by a disavowal of similarity and an externalizing projection of internal difference. The monstrosity of metaphoric resemblance is its capacity to denaturalize what had passed for literal identity. Even further, metaphor's proliferation of aberrant meanings, through a sympathetic (miscegenational?) cathexis between things that "should not" be kin, has the potential to displace so-called natural kinship altogether: "One of the first results of those sympathies for which the dæmon thirsted would be children, and a race of devils would be propagated upon the earth, who might make the very existence of the species of man a condition precarious and full of terror" (163). The very existence of the species of "man" is in question, not only materially but in an ontological and epistemological sense as well. It is horribly appropriate, then, that Victor's defensive refusal to recognize his own monstrosity—his inability to read *fraternité* metaphorically, terrified that such a reciprocal exchange with the Other would shatter the imaginary, oppositional integrity of his own human(e)ness—leads directly to the death of virtually every other character in the novel who would call Victor "brother." In a fleeting moment of temporary insanity, Victor recognizes this: Elizabeth, William, Justine, Clerval—"they all died by my hands" (182). *Fraternité* denied, *fraternité* bound and reduced to the literalness of the "old familiar faces" of Victor's childhood, has been translated into fratricide. Victor never comes to a full understanding of what Justine's unloving mother had recognized earlier, "that the deaths of her favourites was a judgment from heaven to chastise her partiality" (61).

In this light, Walton's renunciation of his quest to locate someone "to love . . . as a brother," "as the brother of my heart" (22), after the dying Frankenstein denies that any "new ties" or "fresh affections" could ever be as familial as his dead sister and brothers (209), seems to signify the defeat of republican *fraternité* by private family interests, and it is at this point, significantly, that the novel returns to its epistolary format, with Walton's discourse projected once again toward his "beloved sister" Margaret. His very impulse to write these letters has been his inability to locate a state of fraternity outside the bounds of familial, "national and professional prejudices": "I desire the company of a man who could sympathize with me; whose eyes would reply to mine. *You* deem me romantic, my dear sister, but . . . I greatly need a friend who would have sense enough *not* to despise me as romantic" (13–15; emphasis added). If there exists an explicit location in the novel for the beginnings of a feminist critique, it would be here, as Ellis has suggested, in *Frankenstein*'s delimitation of the properly isolated realm of domesticated, feminine subjectivity. Fastidious refinement and "retirement from the world" (232) is at once a fiction-based Paradise and a source of monstrous alienation. "You have a husband, and lovely children; you may be happy," Walton writes to Margaret (210), but what does Walton have, something of an outsider to his married sister's *hortus conclusus*, except for a tale of fraternity lost? What, finally, is the composite text of *Frankenstein*, as a collection of discrete autobiographical parts charting explorers' quest for sympathy—or, for that matter, what is Frankenstein's monstrously failed re-creation of *le genre humain* itself—but the horrifying traces of the very *absence* of fraternity, the narrative relations compensatory to fraternal relations that do not exist?

Walton's explorations and letters call for a fraternally sympathetic reader but are addressed to an unresponsive sibling. Here is a formal manifestation of the novel's inability to resolve the contradiction between literal and metaphorical brotherhood, and it is possible to read this irresolution as the novel's refusal to deploy the rhetorical politics of Terror, which attempt to impose an unequivocal and inescapable subject-position upon those subject to Terror's paranoid discursive regime. Although the novel's structure addresses the reader as Margaret, the reader is also positioned as an outsider to this literal brother-sister dyad, as an extrafamilial monster outside the DeLacey cottage, being taught the lessons of bourgeois domestic order by identifying with a woman reading "in ease and luxury" inside the home, yet exiled from this interior space. Simultaneously inside and outside the closed *oikonomia* of the text, simultaneously human and monster, literal sister and metaphorical brother, the reader's positionality is as uncertain as *Frankenstein*'s position on the defamiliarizing implications of Revolutionary *fraternité*. We have no way of knowing whether Walton—Margaret's *literal* brother in two senses—ever realizes his decision to return to his "dear sister." Can the Wordsworthian ideal of childhood fraternity indeed be resurrected, and if so, can this paradise be regained by any vehicle other than what Walton calls the "poor medium" of *letters*, letters that might very well miss, like Walton, their intended destination? At the novel's conclusion, the reader is cast adrift as if on an Arctic ice raft, forced to imagine whether such a return to unproblematic notions of "literal" immediate kinship is possible once the monstrosity of the metaphor has hit home.

Terror and Republican Family Values

If the "unchangeable constancy" of Burke's chain of being rests upon the integrity of its component links, Shelley's novel suggests not only that his traditional political order was as doomed as the Frankenstein family (beneficent paternalism demanding an unshakably natural parental instinct), but that any "familial" system, including the paranoically exclusive order of *fraternité* under the Montagnard Terror, is liable to collapse upon itself due to the very insularity that defines it. A social chain quite different from Burke's is evident in *The Modern Prometheus*, from the closed domain of the Genevan republic ("The shutting of the gates regularly at ten o'clock . . . had rendered our residence within the walls of Geneva very irksome"; 86) down to the level of Victor's possessive individualism—a chain described in an early Jacobin fraternal initiation as follows:

> With the division of the globe and of its states, benevolence was restrained within certain limits, beyond which it could no longer trespass. . . . In such a state, why not restrain that love within a narrower compass, to citizens living in the same town, or to members of one family; or why even should not each person have concentrated his affections in himself? *We really beheld Patriotism generating localism, the confined spirit of families, and at length Egotism. . . . Diminish, reject that love of the country, and mankind will once more learn to know and love each other as men.* Partiality being cast aside, that union of hearts will once more appear and expand itself—on the contrary, extend the bonds of *Patriotism*, and you will teach man that it is impossible to blame the closer contraction of love, to a single family, to a single person, in a word, to the strictest *Egotism*.[43]

Such a chain need not bind up only national patriotism, but could (and indeed did) also generate later nineteenth- and twentieth-century conceptualizations of race and class. The Abbé Barruel dismisses this perspective as the cant of an "artful and insidious logician" or "sophister, . . . acting the part of Satan to pervert mankind,"[44] much as Victor Frankenstein dismisses "the sophisms of the being [he] created" (163). Yet it is difficult not to wonder how different the finale of the Revolution, or of *Frankenstein*, might have looked had such a perspective been granted a charitable reading. Instead of a story of monsters, might there have begun Mirabeau's "history of men, of brothers"?

However successful the Revolution may have been in overturning age-old systems of aristocratic and monarchical rule, its extension of family love into an ethos of national patriotism brought about not a fraternally (let alone sororally) egalitarian state free of conflict, but rather a reign of nationalistic vainglory separated from, yet intrinsically coexistent with, the "private" realm of narcissistic family love henceforth regarded as the only potential locus of utopian security. Reflecting on the genesis of Terror, Wollstonecraft asks, "What has hitherto been the political perfection of the world? In the two most celebrated nations [France and England] it has only been a polish of manners, an extension of that family love, which is rather the effect of sympathy and selfish passions, than reasonable humanity." Sympathy, in this context, is the restrictive acknowledgment in an other of only those familiar, familial, and likable aspects of one's likeness—not a universal recognition of humankind, but an unreasonable overvaluation of certain people defined as one's kin, one's *patrie*. "And in what has ended their so much extolled patriotism?" Wollstonecraft asks. "In vain glory and barbarity—every page of history proclaims,"[45] whether this page recount the republican Terror of 1793–94 or the "family values" terrorism of more recent Republican national conventions.

Notes

1. Plato, *The Republic*, dual-language ed., trans. Paul Shorey (Cambridge: Harvard University Press, 1982), 3.459e, 3.424e. On the notorious ambiguity of the term *pharmakon*, as the cure/poison of representation, see Jacques Derrida, "Plato's Pharmacy," in *Dissemination*, trans. Barbara Johnson (Chicago: University of Chicago Press, 1981), particularly 143-49, where the *pharmakon* is described as "something not completely dead: a living-dead, a reprieved corpse, . . . the phantasm, the simulacrum," and as the "wayward, rebellious son" of metaphor, who threatens to destroy the father or elder brother.

2. Quoted in James A. Leith, *Media and Revolution: Moulding a New Citizenry in France during the Terror* (Toronto: Canadian Broadcasting Corporation, 1968), 15.

3. Quoted in Georges Avenel, *Anacharsis Cloots: L'Orateur du Genre Humain*, 2 vols. (Paris: Librairie Internationale, 1865), 1:182–83; my translation here and subsequently. Rather than use the English *humankind*, I have left the term *genre humain* untranslated in order to retain the multiple significances of *genre*, of *humain* (similar to the English *humanity*, denoting human and/or humane), and subsequently of the compound *genre humain*.

4. Fredric Jameson, *The Political Unconscious: Narrative as a Socially Symbolic Act* (Ithaca, N.Y.: Cornell University Press, 1981), 74. See also Jameson's "Religion and

Ideology: A Political Reading of *Paradise Lost*," in *Literature, Politics and Theory*, ed. Francis Barker, Peter Hulme, Margaret Iversen, and Diana Loxley (London: Methuen, 1986), 35–56, which reads *Frankenstein* (somewhat reductively) as an "allegory of Jacobin hybris and the dangers of summoning up that very Adamic and Miltonic monster, the mob or the people" (37), a reading no doubt influenced by Franco Moretti's 1983 interpretation in *Signs Taken for Wonders: Essays in the Sociology of Literary Forms*, trans. Susan Fischer, David Forgacs, and David Miller (London: Verso, 1988).

5. On Frankenstein's creature as representative of the revolutionary body politic, see Anne K. Mellor, *Mary Shelley: Her Life, Her Fiction, Her Monsters* (New York: Routledge, 1988), 81–83.

6. Mary Wollstonecraft, *An Historical and Moral View of the Origin and Progress of the French Revolution and the Effect It Has Produced in Europe* (Delmar, N.Y.: Scholars' Facsimiles & Reprints, 1975), 15.

7. Michel Foucault, *The History of Sexuality*, Vol. 1, *An Introduction*, trans. Robert Hurley (New York: Vintage, 1990), 106. Even the fraternity of established Christianity, in contrast to Jacobin fraternity, depends upon vertically intergenerational notions of inheritance: as Ozouf argues (following Michelet), "Christianity rooted fraternity in original sin, in the 'heredity of crime,' and the significance of the Revolution was precisely to have broken with the hereditary principle." Mona Ozouf, ("Fraternity," in *A Critical Dictionary of the French Revolution*, ed. François Furet and Mona Ozouf, trans. Arthur Goldhammer (Cambridge: Belknap/Harvard University Press, 1989), 700.

8. The Abbé Barruel, in his infamous *Memoirs Illustrating the History of Jacobinism*, 4 vols., trans. Robert Clifford (Hartford: Hudson & Goodwin, 1799), was appalled by Jacobins' "blasphemous" citation of Matthew 12:46–50, Mark 3:32–35, and Luke 14:26 to suggest Christ's opposition to tribal notions of family (3:195).

9. Felicity Baker, "Rousseau's Oath and Revolutionary Fraternity: 1789 and Today," *Romance Quarterly* 38 (August 1991): 278.

10. Avanel, *Anacharsis Cloots*, 1:192.

11. Barruel, *Memoirs*, 3:109.

12. Mary Shelley, *Frankenstein, or The Modern Prometheus (The 1818 Text)*, ed. James Rieger (Chicago: University of Chicago Press, 1974), 52. Page numbers for further citations of this work appear in the text.

13. Thomas Hobbes, *Leviathan*, ed. Michael Oakeshott (Oxford: Basil Blackwell, 1957), 5. For Chamfort's famous judgment of the Revolutionists, "la fraternité de ces gens là est celle de Cain et Abel," see Claude Arnaud, *Chamfort* (Paris: Robert Laffont, 1988), 278.

14. See Lee Sterrenburg, "Mary Shelley's Monster: Politics and Psyche in *Frankenstein*" in *The Endurance of* Frankenstein*: Essays on Mary Shelley's Novel*, ed. George Levine and U. C. Knoepflmacher (Berkeley: University of California Press, 1979), 143-71. This collection of essays is henceforth cited as *Endurance* in these notes. Also see Ronald Paulson, *Representions of Revolution (1789-1820)* (New Haven, Conn.: Yale University Press, 1983), 239–47.

15. See David Marshall, *The Surprising Effects of Sympathy: Marivaux, Diderot, Rousseau, and Mary Shelley* (Chicago: University of Chicago Press, 1988), 178–227. For other studies of Rousseau's importance to *Frankenstein*, see Peter Brooks, "'God-

like Science/Unhallowed Arts': Language, Nature, and Monstrosity," in *Endurance,* 205–19; Peter Dale Scott, "Vital Artifice: Mary, Percy, and the Psychopolitical Integrity of *Frankenstein,*" in *Endurance,* 172–202; Paul A. Cantor, *Creature and Creator: Myth-Making and English Romanticism* (Cambridge: Cambridge University Press, 1984); Daniel Cottom, "*Frankenstein* and the Monster of Representation," *Sub-Stance* 28 (1989): 60–71; and James O'Rourke, "'Nothing More Unnatural': Mary Shelley's Revision of Rousseau," *ELH* 56 (Fall 1989): 543–70.

16. Wollstonecraft, *An Historical and Moral View,* 81.

17. Joel Barlow, *The Columbiad* (Philadelphia: C. and A. Conrad, 1807), 4:435–73; 6:39–40.

18. Edmund Burke, *Reflections on the Revolution in France,* ed. Charles W. Eliot (New York: P. F. Collier, 1937), 172–73.

19. Thomas Paine, *The Rights of Man* (Harmondsworth: Penguin, 1984), 81-82. See Wordsworth's contemporaneous reference to primogeniture as an "unnatural monster" in "A Letter to the Bishop of Llandaff," in *The Prose Works of William Wordsworth,* ed. W. J. B. Owen and Jane Worthington Smyser, 3 vols. (Oxford: Clarendon, 1974), 1:43.

20. Mary Wollstonecraft, *A Vindication of the Rights of Men,* in *The Works of Mary Wollstonecraft,* vol. 5, ed. Janet Todd and Marilyn Butler (London: William Pickering, 1989), 10–11. See Fred Botting, *Making Monstrous:* Frankenstein, *Criticism, Theory* (Manchester: Manchester University Press, 1991), 144–45.

21. Wollstonecraft, *A Vindication,* 22.

22. William Godwin, *Enquiry Concerning Political Justice, and Its Influence on Modern Morals and Happiness,* ed. Isaac Kramnick (New York: Penguin Classics, 1985), 476.

23. Ibid., 170.

24. Sterrenburg, "Mary Shelley's Monster," 157.

25. Sarah Webster Goodwin, "Domesticity and Uncanny Kitsch in 'The Rime of the Ancient Mariner' and *Frankenstein,*" *Tulsa Studies in Women's Literature* 10 (Spring 1991): 103.

26. Margaret Homans, *Bearing the Word: Language and Female Experience in Nineteenth-Century Women's Writing* (Chicago: University of Chicago Press, 1986), 101, 103; emphasis added.

27. Mellor, *Mary Shelley,* 109, 122.

28. Ibid., xii.

29. See Shulamith Firestone, *The Dialectic of Sex: The Case for Feminist Revolution* (New York: Morrow, 1970).

30. Paine, *The Rights of Man,* 66.

31. Jean Hall, "*Frankenstein*: The Horrifying Otherness of Family," *Essays in Literature* 17 (Fall 1990): 180–82; Rosemary Jackson, "Narcissism and Beyond: A Psychoanalytic Reading of *Frankenstein* and Fantasies of the Double," in *Aspects of Fantasy: Selected Essays from the Second International Conference on the Fantastic in Literature and Film,* ed. William Coyle (Westport, Conn.: Greenwood, 1986), 48.

32. Kate Ellis, "Monsters in the Garden: Mary Shelley and the Bourgeois Family," in *Endurance,* 140.

33. Ibid., 123.

34. Sigmund Freud, "Extracts from the Fliess Papers," in *The Standard Edition of the Complete Psychological Works of Sigmund Freud,* vol. 1, ed. and trans. James Strachey (London: Hogarth, 1966), 257.

35. In *The Rights of Man,* Paine's denunciation of the incestuous nature of aristocratic systems is explained by comparison to the Jews: "Aristocracy has a tendency to degenerate the human species.—By the universal economy of nature it is known, and by the instance of the Jews it is proved, that the human species has a tendency to degenerate, in any small number of persons, when separated from the general stock of society, and intermarrying constantly with each other" (83). Jane Blumberg, in "A Question of Radicalism: Mary Shelley's Manuscript 'History of the Jews,'" in *Revolution and English Romanticism: Politics and Rhetoric,* ed. Keith Hanley and Raman Selden (New York: St. Martin's, 1990), 131–46, shows how Shelley's inclination toward anti-Semitism is somewhat at odds with her republican sentiments, although the crux of Mary as well as Percy Shelley's critique of established religion is its tendency to become, like the Revolution itself, divorced from its benevolent roots and enlisted in the service of vengeant political aggression. Despite her republicanism, Shelley evinces a class-bound aversion to monstrous foreigners in an 1814 entry in her *Journals,* where she describes "the horrid and slimy faces" of her *petit bourgeois* German traveling companions and indicates that "our only wish was to absolutely annihilate such uncleanly animals, to which we might have addressed the Boatman's speech to Pope—'Twere easier for God to make entirely new men than attempt to purify such monsters as these.'" (*Journals of Mary Shelley, 1814–1844,* 2 vols., ed. Paula Feldman and Diana Scott-Kilvert (Oxford: Clarendon, 1987), 1:20–21.

36. Paul Ricoeur, *The Rule of Metaphor,* trans. Robert Czerny (Toronto: University of Toronto Press, 1977), 285.

37. See Mellor, *Mary Shelley,* 237–38.

38. Quoted in Marshall, *The Surprising Effects,* 203.

39. For the colonialist repercussions of this image of the narcissistic *hortus conclusus,* see Gayatri Chakravorty Spivak, "Three Women's Texts and a Critique of Imperialism," in *"Race," Writing, and Difference,* ed. Henry Louis Gates Jr. (Chicago: University of Chicago Press, 1986), 269.

40. Karl Marx, *The Eighteenth Brumaire of Louis Bonaparte* (New York: International, 1963), 15.

41. Edward Said, *The World, the Text, and the Critic* (Cambridge: Harvard University Press, 1983), 123.

42. Compare Elizabeth's shift in perception here to Wollstonecraft's description of the change in attitude toward the king and courts undergone by the "disenfranchised multitude" in France, who were newly made aware "that those, whom they had been taught to respect as supernatural beings, were not indeed men—but monsters; deprived by their station of humanity, and even sympathy." Wollstonecraft, *An Historical and Moral View,* 36.

43. Quoted in Barruel, *Memoirs,* 3:108.

44. Ibid., 4:342.

45. Wollstonecraft, *An Historical and Moral View,* 15–16.

III Monstrous Inquiry

7 "No Monsters at the Resurrection": Inside Some Conjoined Twins

Stephen Pender

In 1664, a "wonderful creature" was born at Fisherton-Anger in Salisbury. Female twins "perfectly made," with "only one payre of legs coming forth on one side from the middle where they were joined," were born to John and Mary Waterman. This "strange Monster . . . formed Triangular," in the words of a contemporary ballad by a physician, Josiah Smith, had "Two Bodies shaped perfectly," "joyned wondrously," a seemingly miraculous occurrence that demanded both investigation and exhibition.

The Waterman twins were "convey'd / for Chyurgeons to Dissect." On 9 November 1664, Robert Boyle read a letter to the Royal Society that noted that, when the bodies were opened, "they were found to have their parts double." The physicians found "two Hearts, two Livers, and all the inward parts complete," except that the twins shared just two kidneys. The dissection itself was a spectacular affair. After convincing John Waterman that his children should be dissected, the physicians were barely able to perform the operation due to a crowd of onlookers. In fact, Samuel Pepys noted that the children lived for just twenty-four hours, dying, he thought, because they were "being showed too much to people." Thus the twins were not only a curiosity to the medical community of Fisherton-Anger and, later, to the virtuosi of the Royal Society; they also caused a stir among the Watermans' neighbors.

The twins' exhibition did not stop at their death or dissection, however. Ten days after the birth, "*This monster*" was "Imbalmed, and to be brought ['*speedily*'] to London to be seen." Henry Denny, the Fisherton apothecary, had disemboweled and cleaned the bodies, and placed them in "liquor and gums" to retard putrefaction and discoloration. By 18 November, the

Fisherton monster was in London "for his majesty's view, and after, for the whole country that will." In London, there were "Lords, Ladys, and much Gentry to see it"; John Waterman grossed twenty pounds (a large sum in this period), given "by persons of Quality" on the first day of exhibition.

Three years later, Nicholas Fairfax told Henry Oldenburg of the birth of another set of conjoined twins, mentioned in "one of ye books of prodigies." "Methinks," he wrote, "tis easyer to rais a great many questions about his Case yn to answer a few."[1] Conjoined twins, in the words of Jonathan Swift, were bound to raise an "abundance of questions in divinity, law and physic."[2] The kinds of questions such births occasioned became clear in a Fisherton coffeehouse in the late autumn of 1664. On a visit there the morning the Waterman monster was born, William Hann, a correspondent of Robert Boyle, learned the minister at Fisherton had declared the question as to the number of souls the twins possessed the province of divines; before its dissection, the monster was baptized with "two names." Hann could not withhold his indignation: "The divines must be beholden to the physicians for the determination of it." The minister had baptized as *two* what was potentially *one*. Yet for those in the Royal Society who knew about the birth, corporal confusion was rife. Boyle called the "Monstrous Issue," which had already been seen by "a thousand" a few days after birth, "but one Body." Comparing them with a set of twins in "*Rueffus*" (Jakob Rueff), Oldenburg called Martha and Mary "double bodies." This confusion required the correction of authority: not only did the Society wish the "Dissector of this Double-Child" had been more detailed about the description of its "vessels" and other viscera, it wished he had put his name to the account "for ye more authenticknes of ye relation." A similar crisis of verisimilitude is recorded in much of the popular and "scientific" literature about monsters.[3] In the face of obliquity, Oldenburg called for the authority he deemed necessary to "a Royall Society of severe Philosophers." Like William Hann, he recognized that "divines" must defer to physicians, even if access to the inside of the body did not guarantee sure arbitration.[4] Speculation about Martha and Mary's individuality, about the distinctness of their bodies and their souls, at least in part accounted for their popularlity as "freaks."

From the records of the birth, dissection, and display of the Waterman twins, it seems Pepys and the "persons of Quality" who saw the embalmed body were as much absorbed by the birth as those who saw

Martha and Mary Waterman alive. Although natural philosophers displayed an array of new concerns about the precise observation of monstrous phenomena, and in spite of the common characterization of the mid-seventeenth century as the apex of a "scientific revolution," the fascination occasioned by this monstrous birth was similar to that conjured up by human deformity in the sixteenth and early seventeenth centuries. Both educated and uneducated reactions to monstrous births separated by more than a century had more in common than one might assume; both were driven by insatiable curiosity. For reasons of analogy or explanation, for example, virtuosi routinely drew parallels between historically remote monstrous births.

Against what has been characterized as the progressive naturalization of the monstrous, it appears that residual curiosity (as well as fear) persisted in the reception of deformed, strange, and wondrous bodies. Katharine Park and Lorraine Daston's claim that the study of monsters was absorbed by the disciplines of comparative anatomy and embryology seems to me correct in general (if the phenomenon is seen from a distance, from the top down, as it were); nevertheless, it fails to take account of the complex, often conflictual status of the monstrous in the early modern period. The notion that the monster was in some ways a "common ground" between popular and elite cultures points to the continual problem that the preternatural poses for contemporary thinkers. It is not my purpose here, however, to engage in debate about either the causes of monsters or their place in early taxonomy. For most people who saw (or, for that matter, who *bore*) monsters, it would have been difficult to separate various threads of causation, let alone distinguish between the preter- and the supernatural. My point is that as a tradition or traditions, the reception of the monstrous as portentous did not simply expire: the intensification of the case for natural causation in the seventeenth century, for example, was an increasingly complex elaboration of some of the themes present in writing about monsters and miracles since antiquity or the Middle Ages (in Aristotle or Nicole Oresme, for example). Thus the "principal line of development, from monsters as prodigies to monsters as examples of medical pathology," in Park and Daston's terms, seems less certain to me.[5] There appears to be a more fluid interchange between the portentous and the merely anomalous than Park and Daston allow. Despite the fact that there was more continuity than change, there was no clear sequence of historical development in the reception of deformed bodies; the meaning of monsters was renegotiated throughout the early modern period.[6] Catastrophic births were subject to a dialectical understanding: the dynamic attempt to naturalize the monster through the discourses of science ran parallel to, and in some instances ratified, the continued proliferation of accounts of terata as miraculous, strange, and portentous.

What then did it mean to see (or, a more difficult question, to *have*) a deformed body, which in the early modern period would have been called "monstrous"? Of course, there are no easy answers to such a question: not only is there a paucity of evidence about what men and women in the seventeenth century thought about monsters, the clues that do exist are widely dispersed (without regard to *our* divisions of knowledge). Still, it may be useful to begin to chart some of the conceptual changes that occurred in the reception of monstrous births in the seventeenth century and, further, to see in these changes indices of larger, perhaps more ephemeral, historical processes. In what follows I shall argue that the notion of monstrosity in the late sixteenth and seventeenth centuries troubled a particular configuration of embodiment. While the medical and scientific cultures attempted to remake the human body into an object of scientific scrutiny, in popular understanding the body remained a vast and insistent index of natural and political worlds. The disparity between deformed bodies as objects of scrutiny and as portents, however, cannot be solved by invoking a straightforward distinction between popular and elite culture; monsters, and natural history in general, enthralled all classes. Though the dissection of monsters marked the death of a certain kind of "idle" curiosity (and was also part of the response to popular disorder articulated by the practitioners of the "new science"), such practices were in no way decisive in uncovering the cause of human deformity, nor, in the eyes of most, did they diminish the aura that surrounded prodigies.

The remainder of this essay is divided into three parts. In the first, I recover the rudimentary history of monsters that Bacon proposed in the early seventeenth century and argue that monsters both contributed to and troubled the enclosure of facts. I suggest that attempts to normalize monstrous bodies or to invest them with equivalence with respect to other *mirabilia* failed because of their prophetic and political resonance and because *monstrous* bodies were also *human* bodies. I argue in the second section that specific attention to the human body increased in the seventeenth century, in the context of which there emerged a partite view of the human form. Monsters, in particular, dramatized the anxious relationships between insides and outsides, parts and wholes. Finally, I discuss the most celebrated conjoined twins in the seventeenth century, noting the debates about embodiment and individuality they occasioned. My purpose is to demonstrate that, contrary to the notion that they were emptied of political or theological resonance at a certain point in history, monsters continued to exert a specific gravity on the imaginations of men and women in the past.

A History of Monsters

While engaged in a "diligent dissection and anatomy of the world," Francis Bacon suggested that the history of nature is tripartite, composed of the history of nature in course, the history of nature erring or varying, and the history of nature altered or wrought. Nature exists in three states: "The first state refers to the *species* of things; the second to *monsters*; the third to *things artificial*." To many seventeenth-century collectors, natural philosophers, and fairgoers, monsters (or natural marvels) were most numinous. In *The Advancement of Learning* (1605), Bacon laments that nowhere is there "a substantial and severe collection of the Heteroclites or Irregularities of nature, well examined and described," whereas in *Novum Organum* (1620), he begins to chart a history of "errors, vagaries and prodigies," "Deviating Instances" on the way toward "the Interpretation of Nature" by induction. Dismissing the fantastic concoctions of religious writers "and men of that sort," he argues that, from "grave and credible history and trustworthy reports," "a collection or particular natural history of all prodigies and monstrous births of nature; of everything in short that is in nature new, rare, and unusual" must be made. Monsters, as "deviating instances," were the means by which the latent processes of Nature were accessed and recorded. Though many agreed with John Gadbury, who in 1660 thought that the "*order of Nature now*, . . . is obstructed by monsters and prodigies," it is not simply that monsters throw doubt on an ordered perception of a world full of similitudes and correspondences;[7] rather, monsters sustain the world by means of their legible deformity. If nature is "detected in her deviation and the reason thereof made evident," Bacon wrote, "there will be little difficulty in leading her back by art to the point whither she strayed by accident."[8] As a broadside of 1565 declares, "They ar lessons & scholynges for us all (as the word monster sheweth)."[9]

Lorraine Daston has argued that Bacon's rather "incoherent" scheme, one that reduced the anomalous to a mere index of underlying common forms, opened a space for the preternatural in natural history. Bacon's scheme was of course enormously influential. Joshua Childrey, for example, called his volume of nascent "local history" *Britannia Baconica* (1660). Robert Plot, a keeper of the Ashmolean museum and a secretary to the Royal Society, began his natural history of Oxfordshire by invoking a strictly Baconian paradigm. As part of his tripartite program, and as a foundation for a natural history of England, Plot promised to consider nature's "*extravagencies* and *defects*, occasioned either by the Exuberancy of Matter, or Obstinacy of Impediments, as in *Monsters*." Nehemiah Grew, fellow responsible for the Royal Society's repository, was less fashionable (but more Baconian) in his desire that the Society's collections encompass not only "*things strange and rare, but the most known and common amongst us*."[10] Despite Grew's enthusiasm for an attention to the normal, it was the anomalous that held early natural historians in thrall.

Part of what Bacon's program and its heirs may have accomplished with a sustained focus on the anomalous, according to Daston, was the "unvarnishing" of facts, and a Baconian understanding of "facts," even miraculous facts, contributed to the waning of the category of the supernatural throughout the seventeenth century. It seems monsters had been sufficiently naturalized by the 1670s for Nathaniel Wanley to claim that variations in Nature's "mintage," even in "human medals," were indeed wondrous, but nevertheless wholly natural. Yet looking closely at the examples Wanley cites, from conjoined twins to a woman who bore eggs, taking account of the book as a whole, one feels that whatever naturalization has taken place, the ontological status of the monstrous was yet to be determined. The "happy unhappiness" of monsters, in addition to their sheen of wonder, was little diminished by their naturalization.[11] Indeed, in 1697, William Turner asserted that "plausible" deformities might be borne with patience; "when the Abberations are Opprobrious, and carry some notable Deformity and Reproach in their Face," however, "we stand and wonder at the Product." Perhaps that is why he was careful to report a monstrous birth supposedly the result of bestiality. "This young Monster was nailed up in the Church-Porch of the . . . Parish, and exposed to publick view a long time, as a Monument of Divine Judgement."[12] This punitive display was a talisman, an emblem of sin, not simply a curiosity; it was dependent upon a series of "varnished facts," if you will. Part of its power came from its categorical effrontery and the mingling of species, but the intentions of display clearly marked this body as something more than a *fact*. Even if monsters were reduced to indices of the common forms in nature, it was this emotive resonance that accounted for the widespread attention to the anomalous.

One site that was integral to the gradual and episodic immurement of the anomalous was the cabinet of curiosities. Early collectors were alive to "deviating instances" or *jeux de nature* and hence monsters had a prominent place in *wunderkammern*.[13] In fact, the "infectious enthusiasm for the collection of curios" in the seventeenth century extended to the human body. Private cabinets and public repositories usually contained a cross section of monstrous animal and human remains. Sprat's *History of the Royal Society* describes the Society's cabinet as "a General Collection of all the Effects of *Arts*, and the Common, or Monstrous *Works* of *Nature*." The catalog to the cabinet of the physician Pierre Borel had a section titled "raretez de l'homme" that incorporated the bones of a giant, a bicephalous monster, and fragments of a mummy. Bones, livers, the "Entrailes of a Man," and the "Sceleton of a Woman of 17 Yeares old who murdered her son" were exhibited in the celebrated anatomy theater at Leiden.[14] Sir Hans Sloane's collection of "humana" (anatomical specimens and models) increased by some 50 percent in the early years of the eighteenth century. There was even considerable traffic between early collections and the spaces of exhibition.[15] Among the practices associated with natural history, collecting was not unique in its attention to "humana." What does stand out, however, is the combination of a sustained investment in singularity (the strange and the rare) with an attention to the human body.

Early cabinets contained the rudiments of Bacon's "severe collection of the Heteroclites or Irregularities of nature"; as some of the earliest attempts to constitute the world as a "view" or "representation," early collections may afford "a glimpse of nature prior to the scientific revolution."[16] Paradoxically, though tethered to a view of nature increasingly under attack from natural philosophers, collection itself was coupled with the new philosophy. Indeed, according to Lorraine Daston, something as "striking and intractable as the cabinet anomalies was required to make the idea" of factuality conceivable within the parameters of the "new science."[17] The collection and display of monsters occurred during a readjustment of scientific investment in singularity from an attention to objects and bodies themselves to an emergent focus on the ways in which such "ethnographic objects" conformed to taxonomies. In other words, the display of human beings gradually came to depend on both ontological categories (on the difference between the normal and the anomalous) and the frisson of the freakish.[18] Beneath this attention to category, however, the unvarnishing of facts failed to succeed: the monstrous was the privileged site of human transformation (as Ovid knew), and the categorical stress embodied in monstrous forms outgrew schemata employed to regularize them. In one sense, monstrous human bodies may be thought of as the sites across which singularity was, by an almost alchemical process, made to signify the normative rather than the deviant. Monstrosity was periodically, though never completely, transformed from anomaly to disease (or, in Park and Daston's terms, from prodigy to pathology); though both reinforced the singularity of the monster, museum display and public exhibition were integral to this episodic normalization.

The marvelous and the scientific coexisted in the reception and study of monsters and continued to do so long after the monster's absorption by "legitimate" scientific discourses in the eighteenth century. Indeed, as the reasons for the birth of monsters laid out by Paré, Rueff, and Lemnius (for example) indicate, natural, supernatural, and "scientific" causes were thought to play equal parts in the fruition of a monster from at least the sixteenth century on.[19] That monsters ever had "automony" as objects of scientific study is doubtful; monsters were always, in one way or another, imbricated with popular beliefs about miracles, medicine, and the human body. In my view, any naturalization of monstrosity occurred against the most crucial of contemporary developments: an array of new ideas and practices that constituted a shift in the way men and women in the past understood being and having bodies.

Inside and Outside: The Poesis of the Early Modern Body

Francois Jacob has characterized the seventeenth and eighteenth centuries as a period in which human bodies were "scraped clean." "They shook off their crust of analogies, resemblances and signs," he writes, "to appear in all the nakedness of their true outer shape."[20] What if their "true outer shape" was *monstrous*? Did the cluster of resemblances simply wither away? The question is well worth asking in relation to conjoined twins, as so often it was the exterior of their bodies that functioned as evidence for an internal, human, even spiritual life. Real living bodies *were* scraped clean—in preparation for both literal and philosophical dissection. What was found in the viscera, as it were, was that the body did not stop emoting, it did not cease to be evocative, once subjected to analysis, classification, or, to put it *in extremis*, repeated desecration. In this section, I contend that the scrutiny of monsters was an integral part of tectonic conceptual shifts in the seventeenth century, shifts that may have laid bare the conditions for the scraping clean of bodies. Because monsters instantiate a particular relationship between inside and outside, between the deformed interior of the body and the opaque interior, they were the occasion not only for analogical thinking, but for sustained meditation on the dialectics of inside and outside.

David Le Breton has argued that "opening up the body played a very important role in the dynamics of mental civilization." Anatomists, strong as Atlas though more cunning, shifted the Western *episteme*: they distinguished "man from his body." The modern definition of the body "implies that man is cut off from the cosmos, cut off from others, cut off from himself": "The publication of the *Fabrica* by Vesalius in 1543 marks the turning point." Dissection, it has been argued, turned the body into a new kind of "discrete object," a process involving "a degradation of the notion of a self extended into a unique and inviolable corporeal volume, to one in which the self only loosely possessed a body." Before the body could be reconstituted as an object of description, "it first had to be devalued as a vehicle of symbolic meaning." In other words, it had to be scraped clean. The early modern world might thus be called the "self-separated realm."[21]

If the body was made into an anatomical specimen, it was not a disinterested process. Though dissection quickly became the mark of a scientific treatment of a monstrous birth (for example), resistance to dissection was a constant phenomenon throughout the period. Physicians were busy distancing themselves from the source of their material—the gibbet—and often with good reason, because, as Peter Linebaugh has demonstrated for a later period, riots against physicians and surgeons for the bodies of condemned felons were not uncommon.[22] Those who performed dissections were seen by the "lower orders" as punitive actors.

"Men of the lowest classes," in fact, were not only the subject of dissections as executed criminals, they were employed "to wash, dry, skin or scrape the bodies which are to be opened up, or to tie up or hold down living animals and to remove the intestines and entrails."[23] Such resistance was due not only to the notion that the body must remain intact in order to rise on the last day, but also to the punitive, class-based character of dissection. Edward May, physician to Charles I, for example, reserved his utmost anger for lower-class resistance to dissection. Disease might be easily cured using dissection to enhance therapeutic treatment, "if it were not for a babish, or a kinde of cockney disposition in our common people, who think their children or friendes murdered after they are dead, if a Surgion should but pierce any part of their skinnes with a knife." Even in the case of a monstrous birth, the resistance to dissection was formidable. William Durston, a "Doctor in Physick" who reported to the Royal Society on a monstrous birth at Plymouth in 1670, found the children's father reluctant to have their bodies dissected. "Having with some difficulty obtained the Fathers leave to dissect it," Durston, pressed "by the tumultuous concourse of people" who came to see the twins, might have "proceeded to further Observations" if it were not for the "Fathers importunity to hasten the Birth to the Grave."[24]

Despite the resistance to real dissection, metaphorical anatomy was increasingly popular throughout the seventeenth century; indeed, there was a vogue for things anatomical.[25] Rembrandt's anatomies, memento mori scenes (such as the frontispiece to Vesalius's *Fabrica*), the explosion of medical publishing, especially in the vernacular, and *écorchés* (artful depictions of cadavers with skin flayed and dangling from muscle and bone, illustrations of which often accompanied anatomical treatises), for example, all testify to the presence of a heightened awareness of distended, decaying, or pathological bodies. In an early exercise in anthropology, for example, the physician John Bulwer set out to examine the English *habitus* and considered deformity a place to begin. Seeking to uncover the ways in which man had made "a corporal Apostacy from himselfe," Bulwer examined the "Specifical deformities" of peoples that lived in the liminal spaces of the world. He concluded that imperfections contribute to the knowledge of (European) perfection: "If Nature . . . sets us in the way to seek defects, . . . the best improvement of this folly is to make these creatures serve for instruments, to bring us to seek out the Creator." Deformity brings us knowledge of "him who hath none"; the imperfect contributes to the ontology of perfection. Bulwer's main point is to argue that the disfigurement of the outside of the body also disfigures the inside, disrupting, in the process, the resonances between the human and the divine.[26]

In his anatomical-anthropological investigations, Bulwer understood the human body as an agglomeration of parts. In fact, the thrust toward the performance of the body as compartmentalized, even in metaphoric dissection, was ubiquitous in this period. Body parts haunt the Renaissance. At a public anatomy at Bologna in 1540, for example, at which Vesalius was the demonstrator, Matthaeus Curtius declared that "the body as being a whole moulded together, must be divided into its parts so that we might better know each one of them." Helkiah Crooke, noting that there is both historical (real) and scientific (discursive) anatomy, suggests that the object of both is a "Part," "for the Anatomist doth not handle a whole body, but a body divided into members and parts."[27]

The sutured body, however, had its own poetics. Every work that pleases the mind or senses "doth it for some amiable point or quality," but "that cannot be if they discover any illfavourednesse or disproportion to the parts apprehensive," as, for example, when "the shape of a membred body [is] without his due measures and simmetry, and the like of every other sence in his proper function."[28] Excesses and defects, a "membered body" without symmetry, mar the correspondence of the part to the whole; the senses themselves might be harmed by looking upon such deformity. George Puttenham confirmed the notion that disproportion was thoroughly unnatural in a real or rhetorical body: deformity dramatized the fragile relationship between parts and wholes that underlies the partite nature of the body. A monster is that which "has any thing defective or redundant, either in Parts or Magnitude."[29] But dissymmetry also has its aesthetic appeal: as E.K. tells us in *The Shepheardes Calender*, a "dischorde in Musick maketh a comely concordaunce: so great delight tooke the worthy Poete Alceus to behold a blemish in the joint of a wel shaped body."[30] Though he found it difficult to draw any "general Conclusion" from the observation of deformed bodies, in 1754 William Hay, himself deformed, insisted that it was "natural to imagine, that . . . the inward Parts of the Body must in some measure comply with the outward Mould."[31] Parts must be proportionate to wholes, outsides commensurate with insides. The "poetics of the body" is shorthand for a particular way of talking about the dialectics of inside and outside.

Perhaps the popularity of anatomy was symptomatic of the emergence of a set of questions and practices that was, in Barbara Stafford's words, the "heart of a master problem for the Enlightenment": How does one attain "the interior of things?"[32] What did Donne mean when he suggested we better discern ourselves cut up and in pieces than altogether?[33] Were we to (at least metaphorically) "stand and unfold ourselves"? Because to open it up was perhaps to "invalidate" the body itself,[34] the question of interiority was implicit in one of the shibboleths of seventeen-century thinkers, *nosce te ipsum.* To a limited degree, "knowing thyself" meant knowing something of the poetics of the body, of the relationship between surface and depth, outside and in. Othello mistook surface for depth; Hamlet threw open the equation. Throughout the early modern period, human deformity posed the question What is inside? in a particularly difficult manner. How is a "comely" or deformed exterior an index of the inside (which of course includes the intellect and the soul)? In any case, in the context of a new attention to the human body—to the moment of incarnation, for example, to other cultures' bodily dispositions, to the function of the heart, to layers of skin, muscle, and sinew regularly peeled away in anatomical texts—monsters aptly illustrate the dialectic between inside and outside.

In his 1569 translation of Pierre Boaistuau's *Histoires prodigieuses,* Edward Fenton mentions the mixture of terror and pleasure involved in gazing at monsters:

> Amongst all the thinges whiche maye be viewed under the coape of heaven, there is nothyng to be seene, which more stirreth the spirite of man, whiche ravisheth more his senses, whiche doth more amaze him . . . than the mo[n]sters, wonders and abbominations, wherein we see the workes of Nature, not only turned [adverslie?], misshapen and deformed, but (which is more) they do for the most part discover unto us the secret judgem[en]t and scourge of the ire of God.

This experience constrains us "to enter into our selves," "to examin our offices, and have in horrour our misdeedes."[35] More than a remonstrance of the ways in which Nature is misshapen, monsters, like signs in the sun and moon or apparitions in the air, discover "*unto us*" the secret judgment of God. George Purslowe, another monster-gazer, thought that through monsters "God the Almighty doth . . . declare unto us his wrath." God makes some bodies ugly so that "they are to man and woman mockeries of their pride"; "God never gives a sound paiment but it is for a sure fault." To William Pickering, a person's "sure fault" is evident in the shape and on the surface of the body. A "deformed and ill fauored bodie in proportion," he wrote,

> is a lively representation of a vitious and ill disposed nature, so that it is a necessarie consequent, that as his bodie is croked, Crabtree lyke, and growne out of all order, so his mind is monstrus, and stained with manie foul qualities.

For Pickering, as for most of the odd assortment of doctors, poets, natural historians, and clergymen who wrote about monsters, there was no need to examine the offices; the outside of the body *represents* its interior.[36]

In 1635, the reverend Thomas Bedford agreed. During his careful examination of conjoined twins, Bedford declared God's writing evident in the twin boys. God had laid "the black-finger of Deformity upon the body," "written in great Letters the guilt of Sin, and in a deformed body drawn a resemblance to the Soules deformity." According to John Spencer in 1663, "God writes his displeasure against [us] in black and visible Characters."[37] Of course, "the understanding spirit" may not see God's writing without the help of the chirurgeon (or the allegorist). God has inscribed the interior of the body; his writing emerges most succinctly, as Bedford's treatment of this particular birth testifies, in the inventory of the body's internal space.

The fame of the twins Bedford examined "spread all abroad"; "Towne and Countrey commeth in to see" babies born *conjoined*, "in a word, from head to heele (so farre as the eye could discerne) two compleat and perfect bodies, but concorporate and joyned together from breast to belly, two in one" (4). Upon seeing the children, Bedford thought "Art might have caused a just separation of them, for I conceived them to bee no other than two bodies joyned together in one common skin" (4). Contorting the bodies so they faced one another, he began to perceive his error: "I found that they had but one brest-bone common to them both, and by it, as by a partition wall, were their two bodies (as two chambers) both joyned & separated" (4–5). At first, Bedford elaborates an easy exchange between the inside and outside of their bodies, one in which internal organs correspond to the outer disposition of parts and appendages. "Know wee not that the members of the Bodie are the Organs and Instruments of the Soul?" he asks, remembering that God had "drawn a resemblance . . . to the Soules deformity" in a deformed body (17). But when Bedford touched the clavicle of the Persons twins, determining their shared interior, "as by a partition wall" joined and separated, he implied that, contrary to this simple correspondence, the "externall bulke" of the twins" bodies was not in the end an index of their interior. Although most vital organs seemed to arrange themselves to reflect the number of heads and necks exhibited by the conjoined bodies—to reflect, that is, their individuality—the recalcitrant liver was shared by both. That shared, crucial organ led Bedford to the suppression of his earlier intuition that these might be two bodies in order that he might arrive at a just moral. Although the twins possessed "all the parts and members of Consultation, and operation for two persons," "here is one body, one brest, o[n]e belly," the seats of the heart and the bowels. "One," he emphasized, "not in the Identity of substance; but in the conglutination of externall parts from brest to belly" (20–21). Just as "Christians are one spirit," so "these two were one body" (21). He left to speculation whether or not they had two souls, but was certain they shared one body (although he claims to "leave it to the Colledge of Physitians to discover"). The twins are transformed into a lesson for the faithful: in what could be taken as a rather arcane example of the intrarelations of various sects (all in one body, the church), Bedford's contortive speculations were an attempt to leach out a moral from the dead bodies of the twins. One is reminded of Paul's statement to the newly converted Ephesians: Christ "is our peace, who made both one, and hath broken down the middle wall of partition *between us*" (Ephesians 2:14).

The ways in which personhood is subject to embodiment fascinated curiosity seekers and nascent teratologists for the rest of the seventeenth century and throughout the eighteenth century. One monster in particular was the focus of much speculation and debate during this period: into the nineteenth century, Lazarus-Johannes Baptista Colloredo was "the best-known example" of a *thoracopagus parasiticus*. In 1697, John Evelyn even suggested that a medal be cast of "*Lazarus* the *Italian*, whose Brother grew out of his side."[38] In the following section, I trace the reception of Lazarus in London through two popular publications related to his exhibition and then sketch out some of the speculations related to personhood and embodiment that these famous conjoined twins occasioned.

"The Italian Monster Pregnant with His Brother"

In the late autumn of 1637, Londoners were treated to an extraordinary spectacle. On 4 November, Sir Henry Herbert, master of revels, awarded "a license for six months . . . to Lazarus, an Italian, to shew his brother Baptista, that grows out of his navell, and carryes him at his syde."[39] Johannes Baptista was the name of the "imperfect" brother, who emerged laterally from Lazarus's breast so that only one leg (his left) was visible, along with two arms, two imperfect hands, a small thorax and an enormous head.[40] Lazarus was on show in London until late in 1639,[41] after which time he took his royal license to Norwich and, in April 1642, to Aberdeen,[42] exhibiting himself for money. Lazarus is recorded in Strasbourg in 1645, in Basel and Verona in 1645 or 1646;[43] he was shown, as one ballad put it, in "many parts of Christendome."

On 23 November 1637, Robert Milbourne registered "a Picture of *the Italian yong man with his brother growing out of his side* with some *verses* thereunto," a fair description of the extant Latin single-sheet folio "Historia Aenigmatica, de gemellis Genoae connatis." The text describes Lazarus and Johannes as two "unified" brothers, though there is an implication that they are *one* body. Although he is sentient, feeling as the brother feels, healthy when the brother is healthy ("Fratre dolente dolet, Fratre valente valet"), Johannes, the "Monstrum horrendum," is listless, unable to eat, drink, talk, even see. The perfect brother is burdened with Johannes, whom he is compelled to nourish, shapeless and speechless, in perpetual boyhood. The author's emphasis on Johannes's parasitic nature discounts the brothers' somatic unity.

But what did this portent portend? Lazarus was the residuum of the extinguished light of faith, a sign that the monstrous, speechless populous, as well as the clergy, embrace a corrupt, diminished church. Just as the existence of intellect in the imperfect brother was dubious, so too the body of the people carried its own parasite, a degenerate clergy. The inseparable brothers were an emblem of the fate of a Catholic England: the imperfect brother lived on the substance of another, while the perfect brother (England) nurtured a perpetually boyish sibling, believing that if it died, he too would die of stench and putrefaction. In this Latin broadside, Lazarus was treated as an embodiment of religious error, and in this the author no doubt pandered to his learned audience. While the author scrutinized the monster's somatic disposition, he was at pains to

Figure 7.1. Lazarus-Johannes Baptista Colloredo, from Thomas Bartholin, *Historarium Anatomicarum Rariorum Centuria I et II* (The Hague, 1654). (Reprinted with the kind permission of Thomas Fisher Rare Book Library, University of Toronto.)

anatomize its political valence, a concern absent from a contemporary English ballad about the "Italian brothers."

Although Martin Parker, author of "The Two Inseparable Brothers," gestures toward the inseparable brothers as a religio-political phenomenon, his main concern is to present Lazarus as a biological marvel, registering his fascination with his alimentary habits or his reaction to "Quotidian maladies." Parker is most interested in the actions and responses that traverse the boundaries of their bodies, blunting the edge of the brothers' individuality. Lazarus can read, write, sing, and talk, for example, but when he speaks, Johannes's lips, "both Ruby red," move "not in speaking but in action." Just one of Johannes's legs is visible, "and some suppose, / the other is contain'd / Within his brother's body." Nature has "us'd him so to it" that "he never thus is pain'd." Johannes's missing appendage was seen as potentially submerged beneath the skin of his brother; Lazarus has incorporated another complete body. Similar questions were asked about conjoined twins sixty years later by James Paris, an inveterate seeker and collector of curiosities. Seeing a *thoracopagus* exhibited in London in 1698, Paris asked the parasitic twin "if he could feel whether he had thighs and leggs in his brother's body, but he said he felt none." For Paris, as well as for Parker, the spectacle of conjoined bodies raised the question of incorporation.[44]

To one contemporary, Lazarus suggested a set of problems: "a disputable question may arise" in relation to the brothers, that is, "whether they have distinct lives, so they are possessed of two soules; or have but one imparted betwixt them both."[45] If the only way to the inside, to the soul, is through the outside, answering the question of the brothers' individualities was dependent upon their somatic disposition. Following this line of reasoning, Martin Parker accepted the brothers as concorporate, *individual* bodies and proceeded to deploy several devices in order to determine his correctness. "This a strange story to tell," Parker wrote, for "Sometime one's sicke, the other wel": "Th'imperfect" once had small pox, which saddened but did not afflict the perfect brother. Quotidian maladies cannot arbitrate between bodies, so Parker pursues an inquiry initiated in the first part of the ballad. Pinch any part of Johannes's body, Parker notes, he will cry. Pain, though not sensation itself, differentiates the brothers: "And if you nip it by the arme, . . . / (this hath beene tride by many), / It like an infant (with voyce weake) / Will cry out though it cannot speake, / as sensible of paine / Which yet the other feeleth not, / But if the one be cold or hot, / that's common to both twaine." Each body feels localized pain exclusively, like a pinch or a nip (as "hath been tride by many"), but generalized dispositions toward cold or heat are common to both. It is as if the shared interior of the bodies accommodates the interchange of sensations relating to humoral, particularly phlegmatic, undulations, but pain felt on the surface differentiates the brothers. Pain was also used to map the contours of incorporation in the case of conjoined twins in Scotland in the sixteenth century. This monster lived to twenty-eight years; beneath the navel was one body, above it two (at times, the twins were given to arguing). When "hurt beneath the Navel both bodies felt the pain; if above, that body only felt, that was hurt."[46]

Though the classic description of Lazarus suggests the brothers shared viscera,[47] Parker seems less sure, embodying his uncertainty in the word *cleave*: Lazarus is "A perfect proper youth . . . / to which the lesse doth cleaue." Although Parker uses *cleave* to mean "adhere," in an equally popular usage it meant "to split" (for example, in the phrase "a cleaving in peeces").[48] The inseparable brothers were at once conjoined and divided. Perhaps this is why John Cleveland, writing against a group of Puritan divines in 1641 whose concorporation outdoes even Lazarus, referred to "the Italian monster pregnant with his brother" as "Nature's diaeresis half one another." Nature's haphazard partition, in which one organism is half another, brought parturition to Cleveland's mind.[49]

In *A General Collection of the Virtuosi of France* (1664), an English translation of the reports of the "conferences" of Theophraste Renaudot's Parisian Bureau d'Adresse that occurred between 1634 and 1641, Lazarus is called a "two-fold" body, wherein "it appears that each of them hath a brain, heart, and lungs distinct; but they have both but one liver, one stomack, and one set of Intestines."[50] It appears to some of the "virtuosi" that Johannes sucks nourishment from Lazarus by means of "Anastomosis (or Insertion) of his *Vessels* with those of his Brother, as the Child sucks the Maternal Blood by the *Umbilical* Vein" (62). Sorting out these anastomotic bodies proved less difficult than might be imagined. The French investigators conclude that Lazarus-Johannes Baptista Colloredo's twofold body, because it had two brains, "may be rightly call'd two Men, who consequently have two Souls" (63).

The question remained as to whether or not the inseparable brothers were monstrous. To this query, there were two answers: "The same thing may be a Monster *Physically*, inasmuch as it deflecteth from the Laws of Nature, as this doth, though it be not one *Politically*, in that it is capable to make a Will, Inherit, Contract, and to all other Actions civil" (63). Structurally, the Italian brothers were monstrous; functionally, at least according to the Bureau d'Adresse (ignoring, it seems, Johannes's extreme physical limitations), they were not. Questions that arose about his embodiment and subjectivity were resolved by radically redefining what it meant to be monstrous; thus Lazarus was given *two* bodies, one physical and one political.

The final word on Lazarus in the seventeenth century belongs to the Athenian Society, John Dunton's group established to resolve all "nice and curious questions." Number 29 of the *Athenian Mercury* (1691), the Society's periodical, raised the question of bodies and souls succinctly: How will the "*Two brothers*" arise at the day of judgment? After repeating Bartholin's much-cited description of the brothers, the anonymous writer insisted that because no lineaments of a rational soul were found in Baptista, Lazarus "shall rise without him at the Day of Judgment, for there will be no Monsters at the *Resurrection*." If by chance Johannes had an *inactive*, rational soul,[51] "hindered . . . by the unfitness of Improper Organs," he will rise on the final day, ranked among children and idiots. But he will rise "with a perfect Body, not with another Body, but the same specifick Body, adapted and fitly organized for a future State." For the "Athenians," the body was something residual and erroneous, enveloping potential rationality in organic impropriety. If the outside indexes the inside, the argument implies, there will be no monsters at the resurrection.

The Historical Body

Along with a sober warning about the indirect, presumptive, and conjectural knowledge characteristic of historical work, Carlo Ginzburg has identified the anomalous as a privileged zone, a sign or a clue, that allows the penetration of historical totalities at the same time it resists serialization or typicality.[52] Though microhistory has been charged with a penchant for the bizarre (and Ginzburg's audacious claims have yet to win widespread acceptance), I believe it is only in the traffic or noise, if you will, between the concise, the particular, and the general that one realizes that the "bizarre" is nothing of the sort. As there has been some suggestion that the human body itself has been hidden from history,[53] an interrogation of the past that takes the body as its focus might initially appear "bizarre" until the ubiquity and importance of somatic metaphors to social cohesion (for example) is realized. The intrication of anatomy and history has yet to be thoroughly examined (*histos*, after all, means both web and tissue; history and histology may be closer than we imagine). In any case, scrutinizing diverse reactions to the Waterman twins or to Lazarus-Johannes Baptista Colloredo affords a glimpse of the ways in which monstrous births were problems for the seventeenth century, just as the ways in which men and women in the past understood monsters are historical problems now. Human deformity raised a constellation of questions about embodiment, incorporation, personhood, and the afterlife, to mention only some of the issues "on display" alongside monstrous bodies at fairs and taverns and in early collections. As we have seen, none of these questions were definitively answered by the inquiries of natural philosophers, nor did their investigations fully dissolve the residuum of fear and awe that accompanied human deformity.

Despite claims that the absorption of monsters contributed to the suffocation of analogical thinking, to the darkening of the aura that surrounded a preternatural birth, I have argued that monsters continued to occasion "emblematic" thought. Writing about a monstrous child who was "carried about with intent to get some money with the sight of him," Montaigne insisted that "any figure which doth amaze us, hath relation unto some other figure of the same kind, although unknowne unto man."[54] According to the evidence, Montaigne's early faith in similitudes was generalized throughout the seventeenth century, even though it was at odds with some of the emergent scientific constructions of the anomalous in the period. Paradoxically, attention to an analogical way of thinking (particularly the interchange between parts and wholes) may even suggest parallels between popular and elite receptions of monstrous births. Attempts to naturalize monsters may have succeeded in certain historical moments for certain classes of men and women; again and again, however, in cabinets, at birth scenes, and at exhibitions, monsters refused to conform to any categorical imperatives (if indeed there were any). In addition, the political valence of monstrosity, something that I have had little space to discuss, conjured up a cluster of associations with moral depravity that, in part, *sustained* the monster as portentous in excess of efforts toward normalization. The monstrous body was seen as a "condensed approximation" of the body politic.[55]

When Thomas Bedford asserted that God had "in a deformed body drawn a resemblance to the Soules deformity," the body was seen as a sign of some hidden, interior nature, not simply as a fact, a mark of individuality, or a means of expression. Seeing the outside of the body as an index of interiority was at variance with the experimental thrust toward the body as an object of inquiry.[56] Experimental philosophy remade the body into a machine (most often a clock) and recast the wonder occasioned by its working from servile awe into sanctioned curiosity. Still, from the evidence uncovered here (resistance to dissection, for example), the body did not simply and once and for all become a residual source of error after its interior was exposed to the world. Although questions related to monstrosity were partly resolved through increased scrutiny of the viscera, the existence of monsters troubled the understanding of the body as a mass of flesh, an agglomeration of parts or the property of medical science.

"Bodily Deformity is visible to every Eye; but the Effects of it are known to very few; intimately known to none but those, who feel them; and the generally are not inclined to reveal them."[57] In 1754, William Hay reflected on an acute historical problem: there is little direct evidence detailing the ways in which *monsters themselves* felt about their deformity. There remains a need for historians to chart not only the ways in which contemporary culture forms constellations with the past; we need, as Roy Porter suggests, "basic mappings of experience, belief systems, images and symbols," which include an understanding of suffering and illness, living and dying, and the human body and its organs.[58] When such maps are finally produced, we may realize that monsters are clues that aid in recalling the history of man's "corporal Apostacy from himselfe." Just as history knows no regular verbs, in E. P. Thompson's adroit phrase, it might also know no regular bodies.

Notes

1. *The Complete Correspondence of Henry Oldenburg*, 13 vols., ed. A. R. Hall and M. B. Hall (Madison: University of Wisconsin Press, 1965–86), 3:492, 496.

2. Swift to Deane Stearne, 10 June 1708, in *The Correspondence of Jonathan Swift*, ed. Harold Williams, 3 vols. (Oxford: Clarendon, 1963), 1:82. On Helen and Judith, see *PTRS* 50 (1757): 311–22.

3. Martin Lister is finally convinced of the existence of various questionable monsters by his own observations: "Though I now believe there was much truth in

most of them, yet I fear little care was taken to describe exactly the Animals, . . . which has gone a great way in rendring all such stories useless and ridiculous." *Philosophical Collections* 6 (1682): 165.

4. For the preceding account of the Waterman twins, see the following documents: *The Diary of Samuel Pepys,* ed. Robert Latham and William Matthews (Berkeley: University of California Press, 1974), 5:319; "Nature's Wonder" and "The True Picture of a Female Monster," in *The Pack of Autolycus,* ed. Hyder Edward Rollins (Cambridge: Harvard University Press, 1927), 141–45, 140–41; *The Correspondence of Henry Oldenburg,* 2:294, 277, 280, 296, 309; *The Works of Robert Boyle,* 6 vols. (London, 1772), 6:166. The *Journal des scavans* (Amsterdam, 1679; the entry is dated 5 January 1665) reports that the twins were embalmed and carefully preserved ("On a embaume ce monstre, & on le conserve soigneusement").

5. Katharine Park and Lorraine J. Daston, "Unnatural Conceptions: The Study of Monsters in Sixteenth- and Seventeenth-Century France and England," *Past and Present* 92 (1981): 23.

6. Arguing the opposite case (that there was a definitive trajectory in the reception of the prodigious), Lorraine J. Daston posits that "preternatural phenomena were [first] demonized and thereby incidentally naturalized; then the demons were deleted, leaving only the natural causes." "Marvellous Facts and Miraculous Evidence in Early Modern Europe," *Critical Inquiry* 18 (1991): 107.

7. John Gadbury, *Natura prodigiorum* (London, 1660), sig. A5[v]. For the notion that monsters throw doubt on the ability to perceive an ordered world, see Georges Canguilhem, "Monstrosity and the Monstrous," *Diogenes* 40 (1962): 27.

8. Francis Bacon, *Novum Organum,* book 1, aphorism 126, in *The Works of Francis Bacon,* ed. James Spedding, Robert Leslie Ellis, and Douglas Denon Heath (London: Longmans, 1860), 4:110; *The Philosophical Works of Francis Bacon,* ed. John M. Robertson (London: Routledge, 1905), 80; "Aphorisms on the Composition of the Primary History," *The Parasceve,* in *Works,* 4:253; *Novum Organum,* book 2, aphorism 29, in *Works,* 4:169.

9. *The true discription of two monsterous Chyldren Borne at Herne in Kent, in Ballads & Broadsides chiefly Of the Elizabethan Period,* ed. H. L. Collmann (New York: Burt Franklin, 1912), 186.

10. Daston, "Marvellous Facts," 111; Robert Plot, *The Natural History of Oxfordshire, being an Essay Towards the Natural History of England,* 2d ed. (London, 1705), 1; Nehemiah Grew, *Musaeum Regalis Societatis* (London, 1681), preface.

11. Nathaniel Wanley, *The Wonders of the Little World: Or, a General History of Man in Six Books* (London, 1678), 5, passim.

12. William Turner, *A Compleat History of the Most Remarkable Providences* (London, 1697), pt. 2, chap. 27, p. 25.

13. See Bacon's now famous insistence (1594) that a prince must keep a "goodly huge Cabinet" wherein "whatsoever Singularity, Chance and the Shuffle of things hath produced." *Gesta Grayorum 1688* (London: Malone Society Reprints, 1914), 35.

14. Margaret T. Hodgen, *Early Anthropology in the Sixteenth and Seventeenth Centuries* (Philadelphia: University of Pennsylvania Press, 1964), 114; Sprat, *History of the Royal Society* (London, 1667), 251; for Borel, see Krzysztof Pomian, *Collectors and Curiosities: Paris and Venice, 1500–1800,* trans. Elizabeth Wiles-Portier (Oxford:

Polity, 1990), 45–47; *A Catalogue Of all the Cheifest Rarities In the Publick Theater and Anatomie-Hall Of the University of Leyden* (London, 1691).

15. For the Sloane collection, see E. St. John Brooks, *Sir Hans Sloane: The Great Collector and His Circle* (London: Batchworth, 1954), 195.

16. Pomian, *Collectors and Curiosities;* Eilean Hooper-Greenhill, *Museums and the Shaping of Knowledge* (London: Routledge, 1992), 82.

17. Lorraine Daston, "The Factual Sensibility," *Isis* 79 (1988): 462ff. For comprehensive treatment of cabinets of curiosities, see Oliver Impey and Arthur MacGregor, eds., *The Origins of Museums: The Cabinet of Curiosities in Sixteenth- and Seventeenth-Century Europe* (Oxford: Clarendon, 1985).

18. "Exhibition classifications, whether Linnean or evolutionary, shift the grounds of singularity from the object to a category within a particular taxonomy." Barbara Kirshenblatt-Gimblett, "Objects of Ethnography," in *Exhibiting Cultures: The Poetics and Politics of Museum Display*, ed. Ivan Karp and Steven D. Lavine (Washington, D.C.: Smithsonian Institution Press, 1991), 392.

19. See "The Causes of Monsters," in *On Monsters and Marvels*, ed. and trans. Janis L. Pallister (Chicago: University of Chicago Press, 1982 [1573]), 3ff.; Rueff, *The Expert Midwife, or An Excellent and Most Necessary Treatise of the Generation and Birth of Man* (London, 1637 [Latin, 1554]); Lemnius, *The Secret Miracles of Nature: in Four Books* (London, 1658 [Latin, 1581]), book 1, 22.

20. Francois Jacob, *The Logic of Life: A History of Heredity*, trans. Betty E. Spillman (London: Penguin, 1989), 28.

21. David Le Breton, "Dualism and Renaissance: Sources for a Modern Representation of the Body," *Diogenes* 142 (1988): 47–69; Karl Figlio, "The Historiography of Scientific Medicine: An Invitation to the Human Sciences," *Comparative Studies in Society and History* 19 (1977): 277; Barbara Duden, *The Woman beneath the Skin: A Doctor's Patients in Eighteenth-Century Germany* (Cambridge: Harvard University Press, 1991), 10; Philip Fisher, "The Recovery of the Body," *Humanities in Society* 2, no. 2 (1978): 134.

22. Giovanna Ferrari, in "Public Anatomy Lessons and the Carnival: The Anatomy Theatre at Bologna," *Past and Present* 117 (1987):100, argues that public anatomies and executions "spread rapidly during the sixteenth and seventeenth centuries, and are interrelated, not only by a number of similarities, but also by an element that is common to both: the body of the convict." See also Linebaugh, "The Tyburn Riot against the Surgeons," in *Albion's Fatal Tree: Crime and Society in Eighteenth-Century England*, ed. D. Hay et al. (London: Allen Lane, 1975), 65–117.

23. Vidus Vidius the Younger, *De anatome corporis humani* (Venice, 1611), cited in William Brockbank, "Old Anatomical Theatres and What Took Place Therein," *Medical History* 12 (1968): 372.

24. Edward May, *A Most Certaine and True Relation of a Strange Monster* (London, 1639), 36–37; William Durston, "A Narrative of a Monstrous Birth," *Philosophical Transactions of the Royal Society* 5 (1670): 2096–98.

25. See, for example, Devon Hodges, *Renaissance Fictions of Anatomy* (Amherst: University of Massachusetts Press, 1985).

26. John Bulwer, *Anthropometamorphosis: man transform'd; or the artificial changeling* (London, 1650), sigs. $a4^{r}$, $a6^{r}$; 64–65, 75, 147–48; 65; 14–15; 157–58.

27. *Andreas Vesalius' First Public Anatomy at Bologna, 1540*, ed. and trans. Ruben Eriksson (Uppsala, Sweden: Almquist & Wiksells, 1959), 55; Helkiah Crooke, *Microcosmographia: A Description of the Body of Man* (London, 1615), 27.

28. George Puttenham, *The Arte of English Poesie*, ed. Gladys D. Woodcock and Alice Walker (Cambridge: Cambridge University Press, 1936), 261.

29. Samuel Wesley, comp., *The Athenian Oracle: Being an Entire Collection of all the Valuable Questions and Answers in the Old Anthenian Mercuries*, 3 vols., 3rd ed. (London, 1706–16), 3:94.

30. *The Yale Edition of the Shorter Poems of Edmund Spenser*, ed. William A. Oram et al. (New Haven, Conn.: Yale University Press, 1989), 15.

31. William Hay, *Deformity: An Essay*, 2d ed. (London, 1754), 20.

32. Barbara Stafford, *Body Criticism: Imaging the Unseen in the Enlightenment* (Cambridge: MIT Press, 1991), 47.

33. *The Sermons of John Donne*, 10 vols., ed. Evelyn Simpson and George R. Potter (Berkeley: University of California Press, 1962), vol. 1, sermon 1, lines 188–203.

34. See Luke Wilson, "William Harvey's *Prelectiones*: The Performance of the Body in the Renaissance Theater of Anatomy," *Representations* 17 (1987): 62–95. Wilson suggests that the body is invalidated by "any glimpse of the inside," an infraction that is repaired in the performance of the anatomy itself.

35. Edward Fenton, *Certaine Secret Wonders of Nature* (London, 1569), 100ff.

36. George Purslowe, *Gods Handy-worke in Wonders. Miraculously Shewen upon Two Women, Lately Delivered of Two Monsters* (London, 1615), sig. A2[r]-A4[r]; William Pickering, *A Briefe and Necessarie Treatise, Touching the Cure of the Disease called Morbus Gallicus, or Lues Venera* (London, 1585), 60[v]. Thomas Pope Blount, for example, comments that it was "a received Opinion among the ancients that Outward Beauty, was an infallible Argument of inward Beauty; and so on the contrary, That a deformed Body was a true Index of a deformed Mind, or an ill Nature." *Essays on Severall Subjects* (London, 1697), 217.

37. Thomas Bedford, *A True and Certaine Relation of a Strange Birth* (London, 1635), 9, 17; page numbers for further references to this work are included in the text. John Spencer, *A Discourse Concerning Prodigies*, 2d ed. (London, 1665), sig. a3[r].

38. Barton Cooke Hirst and George A. Piersol, *Human Monstrosities*, 4 vols. (Philadelphia: Lea Brothers, 1893), 4:194ff.; John Evelyn, *Numismata* (London, 1697), 277.

39. See Hyder E. Rollins, "Martin Parker, Ballad-Monger," *Modern Philology* 16, no. 9 (1919): 456.

40. The standard for the physical description of Lazarus, one subjoined to medical and cultural discussions of parasitical teratology from the late seventeenth century until today, is Thomas Bartholin's *Historiarum Anatomicarum Rariorum Centuria I et II* (The Hague, 1654), 105ff.

41. The anonymous author of a contemporary pamphlet writes, "I will onely remember unto you a very handsome young man, late (if not now) in Towne, whose picture hath bin publickely set out to the common view, and himselfe to bee seene for money." *A certaine Relation of the Hog-faced Gentlewoman called Mistris Tannakin Skinker* (London, 1640), sig. A4[r].

42. See John Spalding, *The History of the Troubles and Memorable Transactions in Scotland from the Year 1624 to 1645*, 2 vols. (Aberdeen, 1792), 2:4.

43. Eugen Hollander, *Wunder, Wundergeburt und Wundergestalt: In Einblattdrucken des Funfzehnten bis Achtzehnten Jahrhunderts* (Stuttgart: Von Ferdinand Enke, 1921), 103ff.; Bartholin, *Historiarum Anatomicarum*; and Chritophus Graefius, *Disputatio physico-philologica de monstris* (Lipsiae, 1660), para. 68.

44. James du Plessis Paris, *Prodigies & Monstrous Births of Dwarfs, Sleepers, Giants, Strong Men, Hermaphrodites &c* (ca. 1680–1700), fol. 21.

45. *A certaine Relation of the Hog-faced Gentlewoman*, sigs. A3v–A4r.

46. George Buchanan, *The History of Scotland*, trans. James Aikman (Glasgow: Blackie, Fullarton, 1827), 4 vols., 2:227. Wanley, *The Wonders of the Little World*, 5.

47. J. Greene, "Account of a Man with a Child growing out of his Breast," *Gentleman's Magazine* 47 (October, 1777): 482; William Winstanley, *The New Help to Discourse*, 9th ed. (London, 1733), 85–86; both working from Bartholin.

48. Thomas Blount, *Glossographia* (London, 1656), entry for "dissection."

49. John Cleveland, "Smectymnuus, or the Club-Divines," in *The Poems of John Cleveland*, ed. John M. Berdan (New Haven, Conn.: Yale University Press, 1911), 124.

50. *A General Collection of the Discourses of the Virtuosi of France*, trans. G. Havers (London, 1664–65), 61. Page numbers for further references to this work are included in the text.

51. According to the Athenian Society, if human anomalies could "Number, Discourse in Questions and Answers, &c.," they were not monsters; that is, they had rational souls. Wesley, *The Athenian Oracle*, 1:20.

52. Carlo Ginzburg, "Microhistory: Two or Three Things That I Know about It," *Critical Inquiry* 20 (1983): 33; and "Clues: Roots of an Evidential Paradigm," in *Myths, Emblems, Clues*, trans. John Tedeshi and Anne C. Tedeshi (London: Hutchinson Radius, 1990), 106, 123.

53. Francis Barker, *The Tremulous Private Body* (New York: Methuen, 1984), 11.

54. Michel de Montaigne, "Of a monstrous Childe," in *The Essayes or Morall, Politike and Militarie Discourses of Lo: Michaell de Montaigne*, trans. John Florio (London, 1603), 409.

55. Elaine Scarry, *The Body in Pain: The Making and Unmaking of the World* (New York: Oxford University Press, 1985), 245.

56. Roy Porter has claimed that "deformity of the body clearly betokened the derangement of the mind within." "Monsters and Madmen in Eighteenth-Century France," *The Monstrous* (Durham French Colloquies 1) (Durham: Durham University, 1987), 85.

57. Hay, *Deformity*, 2.

58. Roy Porter, "The Patient's View: Doing Medical History from Below," *Theory and Society* 14 (1985): 186.

8 Representing the Monster: Cognition, Cripples, and Other Limp Parts in Montaigne's "Des Boyteux"

Lawrence D. Kritzman

> Cripples are ill-suited to bodily exercises, and crippled souls to mental exercises.
>
> I, 25

> It is from experience that I affirm human ignorance, which is, in my opinion, the most certain fact in the school of the world.
>
> III, 13

> On the loftiest throne in the world we are still sitting only on our rump.
>
> III, 13

Cognition, Miracles, and Monsters

The relationship between the exemplum of cripples and the theme of causality is central to Montaigne's representation of the monster in the essay "On Cripples" (III, 11).[1] If the question of causality is discussed early in the chapter, it is in order to set in motion an epistemological critique whose target is the weakness of human reason. Montaigne focuses specifically on the defects of human understanding and our need to shift attention away from things ("*choses*") in order to reflect more closely on their causes ("*causes*"). Nevertheless, by engaging in this wordplay the essayist ironically links things to causes and thereby transforms reason into a form of amusement incorporating fiction and desire.

> I was just now musing, as I often do, on how free and vague an instrument human reason is. I see ordinarily that men, when facts are put before them, are more ready to amuse themselves by inquiring into their reasons

> than by inquiring into their truth. They leave aside the cases and muse themselves treating the causes. Comical Prattlers. (p. 785)

In differentiating between facts and causes, Montaigne represents the image of a human subject who wishes to establish a concept of being that is conditioned by the artificial contrivances of causality. The essay demonstrates how the quest for causes engages us in a retrospective attempt to inscribe the teleological as the basis for a purposeful and predetermined development. Engaged in a logic based on the affinity of a given sign or act with its specific object, those "comical prattlers" to whom Montaigne refers (as those "*plaisants causeurs*") invoke originary fictions aimed at establishing the sovereignty of reference.

For Montaigne the constitution of meaning for these vanity-stricken subjects is based on the productive power of the imagination, which makes selected judgments circulate and consequently blurs the boundary between representation and reality. Generated by the force of the imagination, what we call "reason" trades upon naive referential assumptions whose fabrications are nothing less than the presumptive passage from cause to effect. "Do not these examples confirm what I was saying at the beginning that our reasons often anticipate the fact, and extend their jurisdiction so infinitely that they exercise their judgment even in inanity and non-being?" (p. 791). The faculty of expression is capable of inventing verbal constructs whose foundation is built on a simulacrum of richness and plenitude derived from the interaction of signs with other signs. With this in mind, Montaigne situates reason in the hyperreality of simulations where images and spectacles nurture a form of thought that is frozen in a sterile process of invented logic that introduces an unnatural force into the economy of living nature.

> Our reason is capable of filling out a hundred other worlds and finding their principles and contexture. It needs neither matter nor basis; let it run on; it builds as well on emptiness as on fullness, and with inanity as with matter. (p. 785)

By associating reason with discourse, Montaigne represents defective thinking, the deformities of the mind, through a trope whose conceptual or explanatory force is derived from the idea of running or the random motion produced by the peripatetic energy derived from error (from the Latin *errare*). "There is nothing so supple and erratic as our understanding" (p. 792). At the very least, a strong affinity is established here between cognition and the kinetic force of language where meaning opens itself up to the vertiginous possibilities of referential aberration through the presumptuous activity of human understanding. If discourse stands in the service of logic, it is in order to project pseudotruths that are the product of the unbridled wandering of the imagination. In the essay "On Idleness," Montaigne states, "so many chimeras and fantastic monsters, one after another, without order or purpose" (I, 8, p. 21).

In the essay "On Cripples," Montaigne uses the figure of deformity to describe the monstrous representations that the imagination is capable of engendering though the power of unbridled speculation. The desire to create something out of nothing produces an effect that is the result of reason's error. "Our reasons often anticipate the fact, and extend their jurisdiction so infinitely that they exercise their judgment even in inanity and non-being?" (p. 791). In describing the exaggerated shape that his own discourse takes, Montaigne relates the epistemological thrust of the rhetorical dimension of language. The inflationary economy of discourse depicted by Montaigne unsettles the solidity of truth and enables it to reverberate in the inflections of a voice that dissociates cognition from performance. Montaigne dramatically proclaims:

> I myself, who am singularly scrupulous about lying and who scarcely concern myself with giving credence and authority to what I say, perceive nevertheless that when I am excited over a matter I have in hand, either by another man's resistance or by the intrinsic heat of the narration, I magnify and inflate my subject by voice, movements, vigor and power of words, and further by extension and amplification, not without prejudice to the simple truth. . . . A lively and noisy way of speaking, such as mine ordinarily is, is apt to be carried away into hyperbole. (p. 786)

The hyperbolic power of language generates a logic of deformation and a deformation of logic; humankind nurtures this monstrous presence through the construction of differences that are merely the effects of rhetorical transformations. "Authors," claims Montaigne, "even the most compact and the wisest—around one good argument see how many others they strew, trivial ones, and if you look at them closely, bodiless" (III, 12, p. 795).

To be sure, the troplogical complexities of Montaigne's text engages in a series of figural exchanges in which architectural metaphors are used to represent the instability of knowledge that is accepted as firmly established. Montaigne draws on an example of so-called fact as it passes from one person to another, and in the act undergoes a decentering process whose sheer excessiveness might be qualified as a form of monstrousness. "Thus the whole structure goes on building itself up and shaping itself from hand to hand; so that the remotest witness is better instructed about it than the nearest, and the least informed more convinced of it than the first" (p. 786). The speed by which knowledge is relayed engages it in a process of infinite substitution whereby the repetition of information creates a newly reinvented truth whose differentiality from its site of conception projects a return that is never that of the same. As stories grow and spread, truth is dissipated, and the "real" derives from the illusion that the further one strays from the truth the closer one gets to it. As Montaigne suggests, when we are challenged regarding the veracity of what was heard, we get "carried away" by the excitement of speaking to the extent that we defend claims that are unsubstantiated by facts.

Within the context of the essay "On Cripples," ignorance thus acquires a strikingly positive value at the expense of absolute knowledge, which is represented as a form of mastery that restrains the production of meaning to the finality prefigured in its beginnings. As Montaigne astutely puts it:

> Nor is wine pleasanter to the man who knows its primary properties. On the contrary, both the body and the soul disturb and alter the right they have to the enjoyment of the world by mixing into it the pretension to learning. Determining and knowing, like giving, appertains to rule and mastery; to inferiority, subjection, and apprenticeship appertains enjoyment and acceptance. (p. 785)

The presumption of knowing inevitably extinguishes pleasure and extricates it from the place where it may achieve a kind of plenitude in the bliss of ignorance. The rejection of mastery situates the subject in a position of apprenticeship (implicitly associated with the act of "essaying") that enables it to transform its inadequacy into a form of enjoyment derived from the absence of "objective" content. Yet humankind's attempt to be causative and to determine meaning provides the basic matrix for the compulsive attitude that imprisons the vain subject in, metaphorically speaking, a "phallic mode" that can never be associated with unmitigated enjoyment. In short, the essay transmits an ethical stance that refuses to cover over the void that is at the core of human subjectivity, a void that ultimately gives rise to the vicissitudes of desire.

Montaigne begins his essay with a discussion of the reform of the calendar by Gregory XIII in 1582 and the uncertainty of being able to establish true chronology and the difficulty of recording a history of the past. What was conceived as an apocalyptic transformation in the way time is measured ended up failing to effect any real change at all. "It is two or three years since they shortened the year by ten days in France. How many changes were supposed to follow this reform! . . . my neighbors find the hour for sowing and reaping, the opportune moment for their business, the harmful and propitious days, exactly at the same point to which they had always assigned them" (p. 784). In essence, the attempt to be causative in reforming the calendar, as Louis Richeome suggests in *Trois discours pour la religion catholique* (1597), is simply an example of a false miracle.[2] Instead of producing a wondrous transformation, what we witness in the reform of the calendar is the epistemological importance attributed to the workings of reason and its attempt to regulate the processing of time. "Neither was the error felt in our habits, nor is the improvement felt" (p. 784). The artificiality of this so-called scientific invention contrasts strikingly with the natural movement intuited through cyclical time. "So much uncertainty there is in all things: so gross, obscure, and obtuse is our perception!" (p. 784). Here Montaigne mocks those who assign cosmic meaning to that which is only a false miracle.

At the center of this essay is a discussion of the nature of miracles. By playing on the etymology of the word *miracle* (derived from the Latin *miraculum*, or object of wonder), Montaigne enables it to intersect with the concept of the monster (derived from the Latin *monstrum*, to show) in order to demonstrate how external representations overdetermine the way in which we witness the world. "If we call prodigies [monsters] or miracles whatever our reason cannot reach, how many of these appear continually to our eyes!" (I, 27, p. 132). To be sure, miracles are admirable, the product of the human imagination and the cause of wonderment.[3] As Richard Regosin suggests, "We can say . . . that Montaigne's monster is that which is shown and which shows itself, and which shows what it is, *that* it is."[4] The force of the imagination thus has a mesmerizing effect, leading to the collapse of boundaries between the visual and the cognitive. "So much uncertainty there is in all things: so gross, obscure, and obtuse is our perception!" (p. 784).

In the writing of the text, the essayist attempts to represent the marvelous as the recognition of an unusual experience, a spectacle that is both different and beyond the scope of our perception. The wonders that give the "strange" sign what value it has are themselves effects of difference that produce a feeling of alienation through a cognitive myopia that draws on our propensity for fear. "Our sight often represents strange images at a distance which vanish as they approach" (p. 787). As I have demonstrated in another context, the monstrous stems from the perception of deviation from the normative; difference, portrayed as a visual "effect," attests to the rarity attributed to the object of the gaze.[5] Faced with the monstrosity of difference, one reduces the perceived aberration of otherness through a process of recuperation that has a neutralizing effect. "We become habituated to anything strange by use and time" (p. 787). What is most startling here is more the change to which strangeness is submitted than that which humankind undergoes. If time and spatial proximity make strangeness familiar, it is because strangeness is but a "symptom" of our own inexperience before the threatening diversity of the world. In "Of a Monstrous Child," Montaigne asserts, "We call contrary to nature what happens contrary to custom; nothing is anything but according to nature, whatever it may be" (II, 30, p. 539).

Throughout the essay, Montaigne's text foregrounds the disintegration of the reliability of the witness and the ability to represent "experience" in language. Initially, deformity is more a function of thinking than it is an anatomical consideration. "It is a marvel from what empty beginnings and frivolous causes such famous impressions ordinarily spring" (p. 787). What is characterized as a miracle in Renaissance thought is integrally linked to the notion of *admiratio* (derived from the Latin for "to wonder or marvel at"), a concept that combines epistemological and causal concerns and that is based more often than not on the visual processing of knowledge.

Drawing upon models found in Aristotle's *Nicomachean Ethics* and Horace's *Epistles*, Montaigne's essay narrates how testimonial stances, produced by the act of seeing, combine perception with incomprehension and transform them into facts that are the result of ignorance.[6] "Iris is the daughter of Thaumas. Wonder is the foundation of all philosophy, inquiry its progress, ignorance its end" (p. 788). By failing to read visual signs with deep understanding, humankind is prone to find greatness in that which is most distant and incomprehensible. To witness a miracle is thus to fall prey to the self-deceiving nature of one's vanity, which ultimately produces a situation in which the viewer looks but does not really quite see and understand. Montaigne's scriptural testimony bears witness to the monstrosity of our judgment and the strangeness of our reason, its "*erreur et estonnement.*" Accordingly, he goes so far at times as to suggest an epistemological equation between "looking" and "lacking." Yet what is perceived as being truly extraordinary, as in the case of divine miracles, should be distinguished from what is merely admirable. "What we call monsters are not so to God, who sees in the immensity of his work the infinity of forms that he has comprised in it; and it is for us to believe that this figure that astonishes us is related and linked to some other figure of the same kind unknown to man" (II, 30, p. 539). Accordingly, Montaigne warns us against trying to understand what is beyond our comprehension without being authorized to do so. "What is beyond his conception and of supernatural effect, he should be believed only when some supernatural approbation has sanctioned him. This privilege that it has pleased God to give to some of our testimonies must not be cheapened and communicated lightly" (p. 789).

In the context of miracles, Montaigne's essay also explores the phenomenon of witchcraft in early modern France by drawing on arguments found in the preface to Jean Bodin's *De la demonomanie des sorciers* (1580), where the author opts for the belief in supernatural effects without grounding them in an accurately defined causality.[7] As Richard Sayce has suggested, Montaigne composed his essay at a time when the belief in witchcraft and the persecution of its followers had reached its peak.[8] In this essay, however, Montaigne indirectly inveighs against Bodin, who attacks those skeptics—the "*maistres doubteurs*"—concerning the "reality" of witchcraft. Quite clearly, Montaigne engages in a critique of those such as Bodin who pursue witches through unusual reasoning and thus ironically provoke their persecution. The immoderation of the believers in witchcraft enables Montaigne not to condemn them for "holding a false opinion" (p. 789); on the contrary, he proclaims with great force: "I accuse them only of holding a difficult and rash one [opinion], and condemn the opposite affirmation, just as they do, if not so imperiously. . . . Let them appear as probable, not be affirmed positively [Cicero]" (p. 789).

To be sure, if Montaigne condemns witch-hunting, his goal is not so much to defend the supernatural acts of the unfortunate witches as it is to question the presumption derived from the belief in certitude. "The witches of my neighborhood are in mortal danger every time some new author comes along and attests to the reality of their visions" (p. 788). In the course of the argument, the supernatural activities of the witches become far less threatening than the monstrous reasoning articulated by their accusers.[9] The abuse of knowledge alluded to here inflicts upon our acts of seeing and functions as an assault on an utterly proofless reality. "Many abuses are engendered in the world, or to put it more boldly, all the abuses in the world are engendered by our being taught to be afraid of professing our ignorance and our being bound to accept everything that we cannot refuse" (p. 788). Abuse derives from our inability to see ourselves for what we are; the power of distortion is demonstrated by the need to know and the desire to tell. General testimony becomes impossible because it becomes difficult to distinguish the true from the false. Accordingly, the essayist's desire for moderation and skepticism before the hyperbolic power of the imagination reveals the extent to which he believes that we are caught up in representations and simulations of the monstrous. "It makes me hate probable things when they are planted on me as infallible. I like these words, which soften and moderate the rashness of our propositions: 'perhaps,' 'to some extent,' 'some,' 'they say,' 'I think,' and the like" (p. 788).

If the identity of the unusual is known only from the projection of external features, it is because we traditionally witness the monstrous as that which resists understanding and categorization within the taxonomies of what culture defines as natural. Within this framework, Montaigne's essay discretely converges epistemological and ontological concerns. "I have no more evident monstrosity and miracle in the world than myself. We become habituated to anything strange by use and time; but the more I frequent myself and know myself, the more my deformity astonishes me, and the less I understand myself" (p. 787). Ironically, the variety of miracles that one perceives outside of oneself emanates from the strangeness within the self, the grotesque way in which we process reality and interpret it according to the whims of our imagination. The chimera and monsters that the mind produces make the essayist a narcissistic observer of his mind's monstrous progeny. "We love to embroil ourselves in vanity, as something in conformity with our being" (p. 786).

The book that Montaigne writes functions as a receptacle paradoxically filled with the "crotesques" (I, 28) that are the result of epistemological and ontological emptiness. "And what are these things of mine, in truth, but grotesques and monstrous bodies, pieced together of divers members, without definite shape, having no order, sequence, or proportion other than accidental?" (p. 135). Within this context, error is the result of humankind's failure to accept the inadequacies of the self, the errors that make humankind what it is. Be that as it may, the only way to cope with the crippled judgment that is endemic to the human condition is to transform oneself into a spectacle, an object to be seen in all its deformity, which ultimately becomes what the word *monster* literally signifies. "Anyone who wants to be cured of ignorance must confess it" (p. 788). The showing that defines the monster and that tries ("*essaie*") to cure us of the malady of ignorance facilitates an attempt to overcome the problematic relationship of language to truth by conferring form on the text of the essay.[10] Montaigne's acceptance of self-deficiency, represented by the rambling and inconstant motion of his mind, enables him to acquire strength through the power of a scriptural gait that proceeds at an uneven pace, "*à saut et à gambades,*" as it stumbles along the circuitous path to self-knowledge. The assumption of Socratic *docta ignorantia* enables the essayist to be seen as he is, and in this exhibitionist pose of self-portraiture (from the Latin *protrahere,* to draw out, disclose, or reveal), he is able to come into much closer contact with the monstrous deformities that might otherwise escape him. The desire to write is concomitant with the monstrous externalization of his inner phantasms. Thus what Montaigne's essay confirms is that the opposition between the natural and the unnatural is artificially constructed and the monstrous is but a manifestation of the diversity within nature itself: "Nothing is anything but according to nature, wherever it may be" (II, 30, p. 539).

Montaigne and Martin Guerre

In the course of the essay, the acknowledgment of the limitations of human inquiry acquires symbolic value; the recognition of impairment carries with it a newly found ability to see. It is therefore not surprising that we find embedded within the essay "On Cripples" a selective retelling of the famous sixteenth-century story of Martin Guerre, a tale derived, in part, from the presiding judge Jean de Coras's legal account, and that allegorizes the epistemological and ontological issues at hand in this chapter. Ostensibly, the insertion of the Toulouse case in the essay appears to be associated with a defense against the persecution of witches. But, as Natalie Zemon Davis points out in her analysis of the Martin Guerre story, as a young man Martin Guerre lived in a household where "he had to cope not just with one but with two powerful male personalities who both had fiery tempers."[11] Having married at an early age, Martin Guerre was a young man who was publicly embarrassed by his precarious sexuality, his inability to achieve an erection and consummate his marriage.[12] Bertrande's marriage bed had been the locus of impotence for eight years when the couple believed that they had become the victims of a magic spell. However, even after he had finally consummated his marriage, Martin Guerre abandoned his wife and newborn son, Sanxi, because of his fear of impending paternal punishment for minor theft. He decided to go off and fight a war in Spain, where he was wounded. During his absence, another man appeared, Arnaud Du Tilh, who declared himself to be the "real" Martin Guerre and was accepted by the villagers and by Guerre's wife. When a disagreement over family property ensued and Martin Guerre's impersonator commited a number of blunders, a trial took place, the outcome of which reaffirmed the false identity of the impostor. It was only when the court was on the verge of accepting this travesty of justice that the real Martin Guerre reappeared, entering the courtroom on crutches, thus belatedly revealing his identity through the visual evidence of lameness. The arrival of the lame man paradoxically dramatizes this exemplary fiction, for it ironically foregrounds Arnaud's "im-posture" by no longer providing him with a "leg" to stand on.

Although Montaigne does not call our attention to the question of Martin Guerre's lameness in his retelling of the narrative, the recognition of lameness and monstrosity for those familiar with the story of the trial become sources of re-vision that ultimately lead to knowledge. Not only does Martin Guerre function as the bearer of truth, but his appearance puts into question the absolutism constituting the posture or inflexibility of our judgment. In a way, Martin Guerre 's deformity carries with it a kind of strength, for the man who stumbles and limps and advances slowly, the tardy cripple who appears at the end of the trial, comes to embody truth.

From the Martin Guerre story emerges a figure who is both erotically and anatomically different. In this text the delusionary nature of conventional masculinity is put into question on a symbolic level, for the monstrosity constituting Martin Guerre's difference derives from the representation of a de-phallicized and de-idealized male body. The man who was incapable of achieving an erection ironically becomes responsible for the "arrest" (the sentence) that stops, stabilizes, and reifies the so-called truth. Ironically, the man who limps and is phallicly limp (and perhaps impotent) symbolically challenges the hypothesis of what we call today the psychoanalytically anchored phallus/penis equation. Like Montaigne, who draws attention to his own sluggishness, and the cripple whose arrival is quite long in coming, the essayist proclaims that the education of the ideal student must become an exercise in learning, one whose path to knowledge must be slow, halting, and undeliberate. "If I had to train children, I would have filled their mouths so much with this way of answering, inquiring, not decisive—'What does that mean? I do not understand it. That might be. Is it true?'" (p. 788). Quite clearly, the de-phallicized approach to knowledge practiced by the essayist is revealed in his relation to the symbolic as it is experienced at the level of the imaginary. "He who imposes his argument by bravado and command shows that it is weak in reason" (p. 789).

Interestingly enough, if Montaigne appears to valorize lameness indirectly, he is also quick to condemn the excesses of justice as exemplified by the judge of Toulouse, who condemns a man to be hanged without the benefit of fully substantiated evidence against him. On the contrary, Montaigne would have opted for suspending his judgment before the lameness of his reason.

> He seemed to me, in describing the imposture of the man he judged guilty, to make it so marvelous and so far surpassing our knowledge and his own, who was judge, that I found much rashness in the sentence that has condemned the man to be hanged. Let us accept some form of sentence which says "The court understands nothing of the matter," more freely and ingenuously than did the Areopagites, who, finding themselves hard pressed by a case that they could not unravel, ordered the parties to come back in a hundred years. (p. 788)

If the cripple is figured as the carrier of truth in this essay, the judge is represented as the arrogant enforcer of the law. "How many condemnations I have seen more criminal than the crime!" (III, 13, pp. 819–20). In this context, the overriding judicial metaphor contributes significantly to a sense of changelessness and the stability associated with phallic identification. The posture (from the Latin *positura*, or position) that Montaigne wishes to put forward derives from the need to extinguish the difference between dominance and opposition. "It is my opinion that we should suspend our judgment just as much in the direction of rejecting as of accepting . . . my belief is not controlled by anyone's fists" (pp. 788, 789). By adapting a more mediocre posture, the essayist allows himself the flexibility that ironically empowers him.

Cripples and Female Desire

If difference is an issue in this essay, the exemplary rarity constituting the monstrous is used as a tool to valorize the representation of female desire. Near the end of the essay, a direct reference is finally made to cripples and the novelty of corporeal imperfections. Here the essayist transforms the female body into the locus of libidinal investment as well as into the object of specular surveillance. He suggests in a somewhat matter-of-fact way the deep pleasure derived from making love with a lame person, whose sexual energy becomes more potent due to the lack of movement of the limbs.

> Apropos or malapropos, no matter, they say in Italy as a common proverb that he does not know Venus in her perfect sweetness who has not laid with a cripple. In that feminine commonwealth, to escape the domination of the males, they crippled them from childhood—arms, legs, and other parts that gave men an advantage over them—and made use of them only for the purpose for which we made use of women over here. I would have said that the irregular movement of the lame woman brought some new pleasure to the business and a spice of sweetness to those who try it. But I have just learned that ancient philosophy . . . has decided the question. It says that since the legs and thighs of lame women, because of their imperfection, do not receive the food that is their due, the result is that the genital parts, which are above, are fuller, better nourished, and more vigorous. Or else that, since this defect prevents exercise, those who are tainted by it dissipate their strength less and come more entire to the sports of Venus. (p. 791)

In a way, the defect associated with "the irregular movement of the lame woman [le mouvement detraqué de la boiteuse]" remarkably acquires an exemplarity by challenging the commensurability of the penis and the phallus in depicting passion. To be sure, the crippling of men by women, as the essay suggests, is an attempt to resist the domination associated with the patriarchal order as it is played out by Martin Guerre's lack. This disfiguration of the male anatomy demystifies the relationship between the phallus and the penis, for the resistance to the phallocentric order can be achieved only through a newfound potency associated with the impaired body. If, in the case of women, the genital parts are fuller and better nourished in this state of imperfection, as Montaigne claims, it is because lameness, no longer considered a deficiency, must be regarded as something to be desired. Montaigne's text rhetorically enacts a displacement through which sexual difference is constituted and maintained by the projection of lack onto a male subject. Finding himself indirectly aligned with the feminine (what Montaigne terms "the pleasure brought to those who try it [l'essayent]") allows the essayist to pose a libidinal and identificatory challenge to what is traditionally conceived of as potency through references to epistemological issues. In this context, the category of "man" becomes a movable one, for maleness is subject to mutation and exception.[13]

This narrative interlude in "On Cripples" is punctuated by an interesting anecdote that converges the *topoi* of cripples, lovemaking, and writing. "The Greeks decried women weavers as being hotter than other woman: because of the sedentary trade they perform, without much bodily exercise . . . the joggling that their work gives them as they are thus seated arouses and solicits them, as the shaking and trembling of their coaches does the ladies" (p. 791). The women weavers' (the *tisserandes*, derived from the curious conversion of the Latin *texere*, to weave, and the Latin *textus*, tissue of a literary work) activity, like that of Montaigne composing his *Essais*, thematizes the symbolic positioning of desire and the denial of castration. The act of braiding, as it is described here, is tantamount to motivating the drive and the energy that are the source of desire. Far from being negatively conceived, this representation of the sedentary female dramatically portrays the passion and strength that is the result of the art of weaving.

Montaigne's essay thus demonstrates through the figuration of the monster a tacit challenge not only to the will to totality, but to conventional male subjectivity and the very "nature" of gender identity. We have learned from post-Freudian psychoanalysis that identity is based on the internalization of a series of images that are first perceived as external to the desiring subject. In the essay "On Cripples," the psychic mapping of the male subject is based upon the identification with unconventionally deformed bodily images, and later with the introjection of a female presence attuned to unrestrained libidinal pleasure. The narrative constructed in this essay finds its power of persuasion in its capacity to illuminate the buried history of the essayist. The politics of desire and identification as they are foregrounded in "On Cripples" therefore presents a re-visionist theory of male gender identity in which the exemplary figures of rarity represented in the text aim at deforming the dominant fictions put forth in the name of the father while constituting a counter-discourse that indirectly expresses defiance of existing conventions. The resistance to the artificially created authority of man is but an attempt for desire to portray itself in the naturalness of its scriptural deformations, and in so doing to converge the desiring subject with the idealized yet imperfect image of the cripple in a kind of specular bliss. The representation of the monster is therefore not based on its isolation from the symbolic order of language but on its inability to be inscribed easily within the paradigms of conventional gender identity. By describing the so-called myth of monstrosity, Montaigne's text proposes a hermeneutic riddle, first disguised as an epistemological question, and finally taking on ontological proportions that suggest that the cultural system in which individual subjects are inscribed is monstrously artificial. In the end, Montaigne's exemplarity derives from the projection of a marvelously imperfect self.

Notes

1. *The Complete Essays of Montaigne*, trans. Donald M. Frame (Stanford, Calif.: Stanford University Press, 1976). Page numbers for further references to this work appear in the body of the text.

2. "Elle [la correction du Calendrier] ne fut non plus miracle . . . combien que beaucoup de simples gens l'estiment fort merveilleuse." Louis Richeome, *Trois discours pour la religion catholique, des miracles, des saincts & des images* (Bordeaux: S. Millanges, 1597), 41. See R. M. Calder, "Montaigne, 'Des Boyteux' and the Question of Causality," *Bibliothèque d'humanisme et Renaissance* 45 (1983): 446 n. 4.

3. On the intersection of the miracle-monster *topoi* I have greatly benefited from the analyses of Richard L. Regosin's "Montaigne's Monstrous Confession," *Montaigne Studies* 1 (1989): 73–87. "This is an essay about seeing, about witnessing and bearing witness to phenomena which are often characterized as miracles and which the essayist against the pressure of common opinion, would reinscribe in the domain of nature or on which he would reserve judgment altogether" (78).

4. Ibid., 77.

5. See my "Montaigne's Fantastic Monsters and the Construction of Gender," in *Writing the Renaissance: Essays on the Sixteenth-Century French Literature in Honor of Floyd Gray*, ed. Raymond C. La Charité (Lexington: French Forum, 1992), 183–96. In *Des monstres, des prodiges, des voyages* (Paris: Livre Club du Libraire, 1964), the sixteenth-century French physician Ambroise Paré proclaims: "Monstres sont choses qui apparaissent outre le cours de Nature (& sont le plus souvent signes de quelque malheur à venir" (181). On the use of the monster metaphor in Montaigne's *Essays*, see Mary B. McKinley, *Words in a Corner: Studies in Montaigne's Latin Quotations*

(Lexington: French Forum, 1981); Gisèle Mathieu-Castellani, *Montaigne: De l'écriture de l'essai* (Paris: Presses Universitaires de France, 1988); Fausta Garavini, "La présence des monstres dans l'élaboration des *Essais*: à propos de I, iii, 'Nos affections s'emportent au-dela de nous,'" in *Le parcours des Essais: Montaigne 1588–1988*, ed. Marcel Tetel and G. Mallary Masters (Paris: Aux Amateurs de Livres, 1989), 33–46. John D. Lyons has treated the question of the exemplary value of monstrosity in Montaigne in *Exemplum: The Rhetoric of Example in Early Modern France and Italy* (Princeton, N.J.: Princeton University Press, 1989). For a general discussion of the monster in literary production, see Marie-Hélène Huet, *Monstrous Imagination* (Cambridge: Harvard University Press, 1993). The most important book on the monster in the Renaissance is Jean Céad's *La nature et les prodiges* (Geneva: Droz, 1977). Also see Katharine Park and Lorraine J. Daston, "Unnatural Conceptions: The Study of Monsters in Sixteenth- and Seventeenth-Century France and England," *Past and Present* 92 (1981): 20–54.

6.See Calder, "Montaigne," 452–54.

7. Jean Bodin, *De la demonomanie des sourciers* (Paris: Jacques du Puys, 1580).

8. Richard A. Sayce, *The Essays of Montaigne: A Critical Exploration* (Evanston, Ill.: Northwestern University Press, 1972), 248.

9. "It is not so much the poor witches who go beyond the natural, as the learned among us. . . . Through science, man goes beyond the natural and becomes unwise." Marianne S. Meijer, "Guesswork or Facts: Connection between Montaigne's Last Three Chapters (III:11, 12 and 13)," *Yale French Studies* 64 (1983): 177.

10. "Le vrai monstre, c'est l'oeuvre qu'il sort de lui-même qui contemple cette oeuvre, née comme hors de lui, en dépit de son désir de modération et d'ordre." Floyd F. Gray, *La balance de Montaigne* (Paris: Nizet), 50.

11. Natalie Zemon Davis, *The Return of Martin Guerre* (Cambridge: Harvard University Press, 1983), 19. On Montaigne's testimony of the Martin Guerre trial in Toulouse, see Emile V. Telle, "Montaigne et le procès Martin Guerre," *Bibliothèque d'humanisme et Renaissance* 37 (1975): 387–419.

12. "For a while Martin and his family might have hoped the impotence would pass. . . . Still nothing happened. Bertrande's family was pressing her to separate from Martin; since the marriage was unconsummated, it could be dissolved after three years and she would be free by canon law to marry again. It was humiliating, and the village surely let them know about it." Davis, *The Return of Martin Guerre*, 20.

13. "In 'Des boyteux' [Of cripples] Montaigne chooses III, xi to classify the chapter on sorcery. It happens that eleven is the digit of the devil because the integer 1 is doubled into 11; but when the author remarks that 10 days have been added to the Gregorian calendar in October 1582, the numerical count can be as much as 10 or 11 days, the number matching the 'bissextile' tension of the chapter." Tom Conley, *The Graphic Unconscious in Early Modern Writing* (Cambridge: Cambridge University Press, 1992), 118–19.

9 Hermaphrodites Newly Discovered: The Cultural Monsters of Sixteenth-Century France

Kathleen Perry Long

The Political and Intellectual Context for "The Island of Hermaphrodites"

Recent works on the figure of the hermaphrodite, especially as manifested in early modern France, have concentrated on the medical and legal bases for depiction of this dual being.[1] When philosophical sources are explored, platonic and neoplatonic sources are emphasized.[2] Thus the hermaphrodite becomes a figure either of menace or of divine completion and wisdom. These views evade many of the epistemological, theological, and political problems raised by ambiguity of gender, problems currently discussed in modern gender theory but already known to Renaissance audiences well versed in skepticism. The gender ambiguities played out in the court of Henri III of France were as much the result of the revolution brought about by the revival of the works of Sextus Empiricus as of any platonic or medical theories. More than an expression of the desire for spiritual wholeness, these ambiguous roles were a direct subversion of society. The evidence for this subversion rests in a satirical novel published decades after Henri's death, as well as in the works of the baroque poets he patronized.

Throughout his satirical novel about the court of Henri de Valois, *Description de l'isle des hermaphrodites, nouvellement découverte* (Description of the island of hermaphrodites, newly discovered), written shortly after 1598, Thomas Artus seems obsessed with the cultural signs of gender—clothing, gesture, language, public behavior—rather than bodily marks of gender or reproductive questions.[3] The barely described hermaphroditic body is pushed, prodded, and primped into its dualistic form. This outward appearance in turn *creates* the hermaphroditic identity, rather than echoing some inherent quality. Thus, although his book is meant to be a conservative critique of the fashionable court and moderate politics of Henri III, in the end, Artus seems to question normative views of gender (and, by extension, of other social issues) without restoring any solid epistemological grounding for these views that he seems at first to support: his narrative takes place in a realm of pure signification. By these means, Artus brings into question virtually all of the structures of the society in which he lives, structures that he links continually to the question of gender.

These doubts are closely connected to philosophical issues that dominated the cultural context of late-sixteenth-century France. In 1562, Henri Estienne had published a Latin edition of Sextus Empiricus's *Outlines of Pyrrhonism.* As Richard Popkin points out, "Sextus Empiricus . . . came to have a dramatic role in the formation of modern thought."[4] Sextus argues that apprehension of meaning is mediated by the senses or by language, and that direct knowledge may therefore not be possible: "Nothing can be apprehended [known] through itself" (that is, the signified cannot signify itself); but, by logical extension of the first rule, "nothing can be apprehended through another thing."[5] That other thing would itself have to be established, in relation either to the first thing or to yet another thing, and thus, "if that through which an object is apprehended must always itself be apprehended through some other thing, one is involved in a process of circular reasoning or in regress *ad infinitum*" (*Outlines*, I, 16, 179). Circular reasoning, for Sextus, is the constant referral from one to the other element of a definition, and back again to the first. Regress ad infinitum, similar but not identical to the Derridean notion of the supplement,[6] is the constant replacement of one element used to define another by yet a third (and the third by a fourth, and so on) in infinite and linear fashion. These two skeptical concepts create a potential basis for questioning cultural constructs of gender in early modern Europe, for the definition of "female" purely in relation to the concept "male" (what Laqueur calls the "one sex model" of gender)[7] calls either for circular reasoning or infinite regress in the search for some form of foundational identity.

Once intellectual dogmatism is put into doubt, all ground is taken out from under any proposition. This groundlessness leads to the skeptical ideal, suspension of judgment, often expressed as "to every argument an equal argument is opposed" (*Outlines*, I, 27, 202). This suspension of judgment, achieved by accepting the impossibility of apprehension of a thing in itself or through another thing, can be linked to the problematic nature of gender roles. This suspension also echoes, even while it surpasses, the refusal of distinctions in academic philosophy (delineated in Cicero's *Academica*), distinctions between subject and object, true and false, real and unreal, alike and different, self and other. These distinctions are impossible to affirm because of the inherent subjectivity and variability in the presumed subjects and/or objects. The list of forms of variability constitutes Sextus's Ten Modes. These modes not only question the possibility of accurate representation or perception, they put into doubt the possibility of existence of stable objects of perception or representation. In short, all of our "knowledge" is based on appearances (our perceptions), which vary constantly in relation to a number of factors and therefore may or may not be linked to any higher truth. What we declare to be the "true" nature of something is simply whatever is apparent to us, a sign rather than the thing itself. For this reason, nothing can be established as foundational, and the skeptical philosopher, in contemplating this regress, achieves suspension of judgment by balancing the multiple possibilities.

The majority of Sextus's examples in his list of Ten Modes are drawn from sexuality or gender; these examples are most important in his discussion of cultural relativism (the Tenth Mode). In particular, he mentions the custom among Persian men of wearing long robes (*Outlines*, I, 148, 87), as well as the Persian acceptance of homosexuality and incest (*Outlines*, I, 152–55, 89–91). He then presents a catalog of diverse customs concerning transvestism, incest, cannibalism, adultery, patricide, and homicide, which is repeated in book III. The lesson of this catalog can be read in a paradoxical fashion: either all of these practices are indifferent, and attitudes toward them merely dictated by culture rather than nature, or these certain practices are abhorrent, and cultures based upon them are inherently self-destructive. Just when the reader seems poised to choose the more conservative reading, Sextus adds an example of moral relativism within the Greco-Roman culture: homicide is punished by law, yet gladiators who kill are rewarded (III, 212, 469). Not only are moral and sexual codes variable, but they seem so arbitrarily imposed by societies that no "true" code could be said to exist at all. Identities based on such codes are fragile indeed.

Sextus discusses cultural relativism in relation to dress, sexual behavior, religious practice, and legal or moral codes. But all of these practices, and indeed most of our experiences, are mediated by language or sign systems, and so he devotes his most careful criticism to the use of such signs. Sextus separates out suggestive signs from indicative ones. Suggestive signs are habitually associated with phenomena; for example, smoke suggests the presence of fire, and a scar suggests the former existence of a wound. Indicative signs are chosen to designate the thing signified, but do not invariably accompany the signified; language is composed entirely of indicative signs (*Outlines*, II, 10, 212–17, for example). Sextus's argument in the first book that nothing can be apprehended by means of another thing argues against the efficacy of language. Invariably, language becomes an empty signifier, a shell divorced from the thing it is used to represent.

Sextus's thought offers a significant source of ideas and examples for Artus, who cleverly makes his hermaphrodites "embody" these skeptical theorems. In turn, this philosophical context casts a skeptical light on the purported conservative program of the *Isle des hermaphrodites.* First, the hermaphrodites are only the appearance of human beings, recognizable only by speech, costume, gesture, and the laws they create—all socially dictated, that is performative, aspects of identity. They also embody the suspension of judgment, in that they are neither male nor female (also not entirely French or alien, or entirely fact or fiction). When the instability of their sexual or gendered identity is recognized, then all other forms of identity, such as familial origins, social rank, and religious faith, are swept away as well. In the end, the emptiness of their identity is grounded in their strange use of language, floating free from any potential signification.

At first, Artus seems to portray cultural, religious, and sexual diversity as the sources of all of France's woes. In particular, he castigates the political moderates of the time, known as the *Politiques*, for their insistence on toleration of religious difference, accusing them of abolishing all religion in France because it seems too harsh to them. This religious tolerance is associated with the general degeneration of morals at the royal court. The reign of the *Politiques*/hermaphrodites has trivialized everything, from the law, through language, even to questions of faith. The accommodating spirit of the *Politiques* is equated here with a sort of early libertine movement, and thus with hypocritical atheism. And Artus encourages the perception of the dishonesty of the *Politiques* by insisting on the dual nature of the hermaphrodite—who seems like a woman, but is also a man; seems religious, but is not; says one thing, but means another. This hypocrisy leads to laws that bend to the mutable wills of the most criminal elements in society, as incest and all conceivable forms of murder are not only permitted, but even encouraged in the realm of the hermaphrodites (*H* 57–61). At least upon first reading, the monstrous hermaphrodite seems to be the figure of a disordered society in which traditional laws and values have been set aside in favor of a feigned moderation, which reveals itself to be excess.

What seems to menace any dogmatically ordered society is the acceptance that there may be more than one perspective on any issue. Acceptance of Protestantism puts the "truth" of Catholicism into doubt—two religious truths cannot exist at one and the same time. If one tolerates the existence of both, one achieves only suspension of judgment, which dissolves hierarchical orderings based on a supposedly foundational truth. Both religions cannot contradict each other and still be true, yet this is purportedly what the *Politiques* want to believe. Similarly, given the coexistence of two genders in one person, the notion of one gender as the "true" sex is canceled out. If the genders are defined only in relation to each other, as they are in the one-sex system, then we are left with a *mise-en-abime* in any attempt to categorize genders.

Without any foundational truth, the subject is left only with appearances by which to judge genders. These appearances are culturally imposed acts or signs; thus Artus seems to demonstrate a notion of gender echoed by postmodern critics such as Judith Butler: "Gender is the repeated stylization of the body, a set of repeated acts within a highly rigid regulatory frame that congeal over time to produce the appearance of substance, of a natural sort of being." Further, this stylization, also in circular fashion, is dictated by power relations and in turn confirms those power relations. This view is also echoed by Butler: "The body gains meaning within discourse only in the context of power relations. Sexuality is an historically specific organization of power, discourse, bodies, and affectivity."[8] Thus bisexuality, transvestism, and hermaphroditism, all situations in which two different signs of gender ("male" and "female" desire; male and female clothing and gesture; male and female genitalia) coexist in problematic relation, both render the artificial or culturally imposed nature of gender evident and undercut the power relations that inform and are informed by gender. Artus is fascinated with the signs of gender and with the disorder that confusion or suspension of these signs can create in society. And, in spite of his proclaimed conservatism, Artus offers no foundational truth to counter these signs. Rather, he creates a proliferation of parodic signs that seems to indicate an effusive joy in the destruction of dogmatic society.

Artus begins his account with a reference to the New World, a discovery that itself shattered the illusion of unity or uniqueness that cradled the Old for millennia (*H* 4–5). Artus deplores the rush to novelty and change that disturbs the presumed stability of the Old World. Yet he contradicts himself a few lines later, mentioning "the continual upheavals which have occurred in Europe for so many years" (*H* 5). One is left with the question of whether these explorers are searching for social novelty or escaping social upheaval. The narrator himself voyages in order to avoid participation in murderous strife (*H* 5). He wanders throughout the world until he hears of the treaty of Vervins (1598). In his attempt to return home, he lands on a sort of anti-utopian island governed by hermaphrodites, one that resembles the court of Henri de Valois (Henri III).[9] This island is not anchored, but floats about in the ocean (*H* 8). The narrator underscores the unreality of the island: "We saw this island everywhere so fertile and flowering that we thought the fable of the Elysian Fields to be absolute truth in comparison" (*H* 9). First placed in evidence is the most immediately visible sign of power, that is, elaborate architecture. The palace is characterized by its "diversity": "The eye that can see everything in an instant was not sufficient to take in all that was contained in this beautiful Palace" (*H* 9). The multiplicity of signs apparent in this palace defies comprehension. Notably, it is at this point that the voyagers discover this is the land of hermaphrodites.

Clothing and the Performative Nature of Gender

Significantly, the narrator's first encounter with a hermaphrodite results not in a view of that mysterious being, but rather of its elaborately described clothing: "un petit manteau de satin blanc chamarré de clinquant, doublé d'une étoffe ressemblant à la pane de soye [a small coat of white satin edged with metallic fringe, lined in a material that resembled silk plush]" (*H* 13). Note that even the lining (*doublure*) only resembles plush, rather than being it. Reality is at two removes from this material, as silk plush was used as a sort of fake fur. Thus this *pane de soye* is an imitation of a fake. Similarly, the creatures themselves exist removed from direct observation. There is a cloth covering a mask that lies on the hermaphrodite's face, so that any (bodily) "reality" is unavailable to public view. The hermaphroditic body is constructed by means of makeup, prosthetic devices, and clothing; it is alternately built up and carved out, and becomes a sort of early modern cyborg.[10] The voyager watches these hermaphrodites being primped, powdered, and tweezed into form. They are rouged and bleached; their beards are thinned and their cheeks filled out (by means of bones attached inside the mouth). They are dressed in silk *chausses* (trousers) and their feet are jammed into tiny shoes. This forcing of the foot into a too-small space could be seen as a parody of the narrow sexual and social roles imposed upon men and women and expressed by means of clothing:[11]

> Un autre vint incontinent après, apporter une petite paire de souliers fort étroits & mignonnement découpés. Je me mocquois en moi-même de voir si petite chaussure, & ne pouvois comprendre à la verité comme un grand & gros pied pouvoit entrer dans un si petit soulier, puisque la regle naturelle veut que le contenant soit plus grand que le contenu, & toutesfois c'étoit ici le contraire. (*H* 20)

> [Another arrived immediately after, to carry in a small pair of shoes, very narrow and cut out in cute fashion. I laughed to myself when I saw such small shoes, and could not understand, in truth, how a large, fat foot could enter into such a small shoe, since the natural rule wills that that which contains be larger than that which is contained, and nonetheless it was the contrary in this case.]

In this image, the hermaphrodites seem to take on a parodic force of their own, and one begins to wonder whether Artus is criticizing them or French society. The notion of restriction, whether in costume or in behavior, is repeated often in the novel. Thus when Artus seems to allude to "natural law [*la regle naturelle*]," his critique seems to expand from that of transgressive dressing to that of any cultural repression of natural drives or states of being. The elaborate ritual of dressing itself is infinitely multiplied: "Ils ne laissent pas de changer ainsi en ce pays-là de jour & de nuit [They never left off changing (their clothes) in this country, either day or night]" (*H* 21). Thus, although the hermaphrodites seem to submit to extreme restrictions, they also escape such limitations by the infinite parodic repetitions of such restrictive behavior.

Artus emphasizes the ornamental aspects of gender distinction and links these aspects to the notion of instability by means of the hermaphrodites' shaky mode of walking, prized as aesthetically superior to a firm step (*H* 27). Thus, even the hermaphrodite's movement is dictated by social norms, in spite of the inconvenience of this mode of propulsion. Utility, and any possible "natural" behavior, is overwhelmed by artificial marks of gender, just as the body of the hermaphrodite is overwhelmed by clothing in the frame narrative.

As if to emphasize this artificiality, Artus creates the world of the hermaphrodites as a tissue of textual references, artistic embellishment, and theatrics. Musicians sing airs based on Petronius's *Satyricon,* and the bedchamber of the next, apparently even more important, hermaphrodite is decorated with scenes of mutable sexuality from Ovid's *Metamorphoses,* that of Caeneus in particular (*H* 30).[12] Within this artificial context, the narrator notices a statue of a man in the middle of the bed, and this statue is or becomes confused with the hermaphrodite himself: "Le visage étoit si blanc, si luisant & d'un rouge si éclatant, qu'on voyoit bien qu'il y avoit plus d'artifice que de nature; ce qui me faisoit aisément croire que ce n'étoit que peinture [The face was so white, so bright, and of a red so striking that one saw clearly that there was more artifice than nature involved; which easily made me believe that this was nothing more than paint (or a painting)]" (*H* 31). Distinctions between real and artificial, fact and fiction, are easily blurred in this realm of indistinct genders. Again, the bed, the room, the clothing—even the surface of the hermaphrodite's skin (or at least the makeup on it)—are described, but no sense of essential identity is apparent.

It is at this point, when the statue is confused with the hermaphrodite by means of the word *idole,* that language becomes an issue in the narrative and is inextricably linked to the basic problems of gender and identity that have been suggested so far:

> En cette ruelle allerent les trois personnes . . . & commencerent à invoquer cette idole par des noms qui ne se peuvent pas bien représenter en notre langue, d'autant que tout le langage & tous les termes des *Hermaphrodites* sont de même que ceux que les Grammairiens appellent du genre commun, & tiennent autant du mâle que de la femelle: toutefois desirant sçavoir quels discours ils tenoient-là; un de leur suite, de qui je m'étois accosté & qui entendoit bien l'*Italien,* me dit . . . (*H* 31)

> [The three people went to this bedside . . . and began to invoke this idol by names which have no equivalent in our language, inasmuch as the entire

language and all of the terms of the *Hermaphrodites* are of that same sort which Grammarians call the "common" gender, and take as much from the male as from the female. Nonetheless, wishing to know what subjects they were discussing, one of their retinue, whom I had approached and who understood Italian, said to me . . .]

The *idole* is designated by various names, none of which can be translated into French. The problem is that the French language does not have a common gender, one that serves as both masculine and feminine. Still, the narrator manages to elicit an approximate translation of the *discours* from someone who understands Italian.[13] This problematic being can be represented only in the most indirect fashion. The arbitrary imposition of signs of identity extends to language itself, which does not have any necessary relation to the thing being observed, and which in fact cannot express that thing. Using *cette idole* as the antecedent in this long sentence, the text designates the hermaphrodite by the pronoun *elle*, thus achieving an oscillation between masculine and feminine. The narrative also uses *ce que* (that which) to indicate the hermaphrodite, thus achieving a sort of neuter: "mais aussi-tôt ce que j'avois tenu pour muet & sans vie, commença à parler [but immediately that which I had held to be mute and without life, began to speak]" (*H* 32). Ambiguous identity is thus mirrored by unstable or vague language.

The palace of the hermaphrodites begins at this point to resemble a series of Chinese boxes. The narrator moves on to another room, richer than the first (*H* 32–33). Obviously, this next hermaphrodite is even more important than the previous one, yet it resembles the other fairly closely (*H* 33). This succession of "important" hermaphrodites becomes nightmarish; all sense of order or hierarchy is destroyed, and no one seems to be in charge, although this second "important" hermaphrodite does go into a council room purportedly to discuss the business of state. This secret room is called "something like" the wardrobe (*H* 34). Although actually a great deal of state business was conducted in the king's dressing room, Artus seems to suggest that the most important business of *this* state *is* the wardrobe itself. Clothing is part of the performative nature of power and of gender; according to Butler, that which many consider essential gender identity is in fact created by signs that are inscribed on the surface of the body over the course of time by repeated actions dictated by social norms.[14] Such are the signs enumerated by Artus.

The problematic nature of signs of gender is linked to the problematic nature of signs in general in the two representative figures of hermaphroditism. After wandering the halls of this palace and admiring the numerous artworks, the narrator comes across statues of the island's heroes, in particular, those of Hermaphroditus and Heliogabalus. These figures seem to represent the two extremes of gender confusion. Heliogabalus is neuter, neither male nor female, an empty cipher. Hermaphroditus is both male and female, and thus a self-contradictory being (at least in the context of social norms). Given that the narrator finds the book of laws next to these statues, and the laws categorize various signs of identity (particularly those related to gender), one could link Heliogabalus to Sextus Empiricus's skeptical aphasia (occurring when the impossibility of distinction and categorization leads to silence; *Outlines*, I, 20, 110–13) and Hermaphroditus to skeptical suspension of judgment (occurring when multiple possibilities are allowed to coexist without any choice being made; *Outlines*, I, 22, 114–15). Thus these figures create a transition to a long discussion of laws and language that dominates the novel.

Social Hypocrisy as an Ideal

Most of the remaining narration concerns this book of laws of conduct and governance of the island, laws that create and confirm the ambiguity of hermaphroditism and that connect gender ambiguity to moral and epistemological confusion. For the most part, Artus links gender ambiguity to religious diversity in the section "Ordonnances sur le fait de la religion" (Ordinances on religious matters). This diversity leads to the virtual annihilation of religion: the rites of Bacchus, Cupid, and Venus constitute the official religion of the realm, and all other religions are banished unless they contribute to sensual pleasures. Any accommodation of other religions is for appearances' sake, and not because of any belief (*H* 43–44). As mentioned before, this is not merely a criticism of Henri III, but of the entire *Politique* faction at court, the moderates who realized that the wars of religion would simply destroy France rather than restore Catholicism as the sole religion.

For the most part, the laws of the hermaphrodites are redefinitions of social norms; for example, "The greatest sensuality will be held throughout this Empire as the greatest sanctity" (*H* 46). Similarly, cowardice is redefined as worthiness; "presumptuous vanity" becomes "a perfect knowledge of oneself." This last quality borders on narcissism, which would probably be an appropriate form of love for a hermaphrodite, who is at once him/herself and an other. Such narcissism is suggested throughout the laws: "Personal desires will be held to be Reason itself throughout this our Empire . . . otherwise, one will be thought to be an enemy to himself" (*H* 46, law 7). The hermaphrodites create a strange mirror world (but one that reflects negatively) of French society. This mirror opposition is achieved by the use of paradox, a turning of language upon itself.

The paradoxical definitions of moral values are echoed by a contradictory presentation of these values; hypocrisy thus becomes the ideal hermaphroditic behavior. In turn, hypocrisy privileges language as the supreme expression of hermaphroditic identity: "We advise all of our subjects, when they encounter those who consider piety important, an event which should be avoided as much as possible, to discourse about matters of faith with great zeal" (*H* 45, law 3). This hypocrisy extends to every aspect of culture; for example, the hermaphrodites should use brave words around genuinely courageous military men (*H* 45, law 3, continued). Thus hypocrisy creates a gap between word and deed (signifier and signified) that becomes almost absolute opposition. Those who speak of bravery are not brave; the words supplement the missing deed, but this supplement also stands in opposition to the actual cowardice of the hermaphrodites. Similarly, words that are considered to be of great "substance" in French culture are shown to be empty in hermaphrodite culture: "Nous voulons & entendons que tous ces mots de conscience, tempérance, repentance, & autres de pareil sujet, soient tenus tant en la substance qu'aux termes, pour choses vaines & frivoles [We wish and intend that all those words of conscience, temperance, repentance, and others of similar meaning, be held as empty and frivolous things, the substance as well as the words themselves]" (*H* 45, law 4). In other words, not only do libertine terms replace chivalric ones in a reversal of cultural norms, but a gap is created between what the laws call *substance* and what they call *termes.* The *substance* is then emptied from these terms, and only the signifying surfaces of the terms remain. This emphasis upon the signifier divorced of any meaning is then linked to the question of appearance and therefore of clothing and toilette, the two elements that dominate the introductory section of the novel:

> Nous réputons la bonne mine & l'apparence en toutes choses que ce soit, beaucoup plus que l'action, d'autant qu'elle cache beaucoup d'effets avec

> moins de peine. C'est pourquoi nous exhortons tous nos sujets, de quelque état, qualité ou condition qu'ils soient, de l'acquérir, autant dissimulée que faire se pourra & de la préferer à toute autre vertu. (*H* 45–46, law 6)
>
> [We respect good looks and appearance at all times, much more than action, since looks get more results with much less difficulty. This is why we encourage our subjects, of whatever class, quality, or condition they may be, to acquire good looks, as artificial as they can possibly be, and to prefer this appearance to any other virtue.]

Not only is appearance valued above action, but this appearance must be cultivated to be as divorced from any "essential" or "natural" being as possible. This cultivation of sign systems devoid of meaning makes the hermaphrodites themselves virtually unreadable. The hermaphrodites not only lack respect for the established symbols of culture, they replace them with their own system of signs, or give new signification to whatever symbols they appropriate; thus the church is more suitable for the "mysteries of Venus" (*H* 48, law 11) than for the mysteries of the Catholic Mass. Entertainment becomes the hermaphrodites' preferred form of worship—understandably so, as entertainment would involve masks and role playing. Singers, dancers, actors, and comics become the ministers of the temple, and the most lascivious poets are the preachers (*H* 51, law 18). Sexuality is thus linked to this role playing, this entertainment, rather than portrayed as some inherently necessary part of society. This role playing is portrayed as bisexual, and therefore most threatening to the social (sexual) hierarchy; the hermaphrodites have mistresses and male lovers (*H* 47, law 11). A person playing both the passive (then considered feminine) and active (masculine) roles annihilates gender hierarchy and puts into doubt these value-ridden designations of passive and active.

If there is no stable or foundational meaning, no one true gender, no one true religion, then the hermaphrodites are protean beings who change to suit their circumstances. Thus not only are they of dual nature, they are beings who can infinitely multiply their roles. They are self-supplementing creatures who have refused to accept the basic premises that buttress French society, and so are free to reinvent themselves constantly. They define themselves by their roles, thus demonstrating a recognition of the performative power of social roles and liberating themselves by this recognition. This liberation can be read as irresponsibility that might lead to social chaos, but this conservative view is belied by the already chaotic conditions created by dogmatic repression of differences in Renaissance France, conditions mentioned at the opening of Artus's narrative.

A further example of the delicate balance between the perceived threat of pluralism caused by the denial of dogmatism and the violent religious extremism that threatened the very existence of France can be seen in the articles of faith of the hermaphrodites:

> Nous ignorons la création, rédemption, justification, & damnation, si ce n'est en bonne mine & en paroles. . . .
>
> Nous ignorons s'il y a aucune temporalité, ou éternité au monde, ni s'il doit avoir un jour quelque fin, de crainte que cela ne nous trouble l'esprit, & nous cause de la frayeur. (*H* 55, I, II)

> [We know nothing of the creation, or of redemption, justification (by faith), and damnation, unless it is all achieved with good looks and clever words. . . .
>
> We do not know if there is any temporality or eternity in the world, nor if there must be an end some day, for fear that this might trouble our spirits and cause us a fright.]

Obviously, the hermaphrodites trivialize numerous religious beliefs, and to some extent trivialize themselves by refusing any form of ethics or ideals (other than parodic forms).

But the force of this parody is undeniable in the face of insistent dogmatic categorization of every aspect of religious life. The proliferation of doctrine, the minuteness of detail expected in every person's understanding of such doctrine, renders religious belief almost absurd—albeit with tragic consequences. One need only compare the hermaphrodites' articles to parts of the deadly serious "Confession de Bordeaux," which Huguenots were forced to repeat publicly if they did not wish to be executed (this following the massacre of Saint Bartholomew's Day). In the case of categorizations of sin, the distinction between mortal and venial, although declared clear by the church, is in effect blurred: "I confess that the sins are distinct, according to the transgression, some mortal, such as the desire for debauchery, others venial, such as the feeling of debauchery which is void of desire and consent."[15] Because the words *feeling* and *desire* are not defined in this context, the difference between these two terms, and thus between the two forms of sin, remains blurred. Furthermore, all of doctrine becomes based on terminology rather than any form of essential belief, and the terms themselves are neither defined nor used in a consistent fashion. Because of this dependence on language, the instability of language undermines doctrine. This form of forced belief, on incredibly detailed questions of doctrine that seem to have no foundation in the experiential world, seems no more rational to the modern eye than the skepticism of the hermaphrodites.[16]

Yet one begins to wonder while reading their laws if the hermaphrodites are so revolutionary after all, or if they are not merely the logical extension of an overly codified society, one in which identity is clearly and repressively defined in every possible detail. Thus the hermaphrodites create "unrules" that negate this codification: "We know nothing of a providence superior to human matters, and believe that everything occurs purely by chance" (*H* 56, 4). In fact, they believe in nothing, and so their articles are articles of unfaith, rather than of faith. They refuse to accept mere faith as a basis for action: "We know nothing of any other life than the present one" (*H* 56, 6). They believe only in the performative, not the pedagogic or foundational, aspect of society.

Marriage also is recognized as a performative, rather than foundational, role, and therefore adultery is not only condoned, but encouraged: "We also wish that that which our opposition calls adultery be in fashion, in honor, and in good repute throughout our Empire" (*H* 59, 6). Even the negative sign used by society to designate this behavior is denied. Similarly, incest is allowed (*H* 61, 11). Echoing Sextus, the hermaphrodites dismantle all the fundamental relations that drive society, but most of all, they attack marriage and the family. The incest taboo is considered by anthropologists to be one of the bases of social interaction, and therefore of social identity, in that it both "distinguishes and binds" families.[17] Without the laws that constitute identity (and all of the hermaphrodites' rules are basically antilaws that undo all current laws and taboos), society disintegrates: "We wish to eliminate all degrees of consanguinity among our Subjects. . . . It is for this reason that we abolish from this moment forward those names of father, mother, brother, sister, and others, and so wish that only those of *Monsieur* and *Madame* be used" (*H* 62, 14). The hermaphrodites are now flatly rejecting the signifiers that create identity, whereas previously they simply parodied such social roles; in this light, it is ironic that they retain the gender distinctions implied by the words *Monsieur* and *Madame*.

This freedom from rigid roles is expressed at every level of signification, for example in the clothing, which is freed from hierarchical constraints:

> Chacun pourra s'habiller à sa fantaisie, pourvu que ce soit bravement, superbement & sans aucune distinction ni considération de sa qualité ou faculté. . . . Aussi tenons-nous pour une regle presque générale parmi nous, que tels accoûtrements honorent plutôt qu'ils ne sont honorés: car en cette Isle l'habit fait le moine, & non pas au contraire. (*H* 79–80, 13, "La police")
>
> [Each one may dress according to his/her whims, provided that this is done elegantly, proudly, and without any distinction of or consideration for rank or privilege. . . . We also hold as an almost general rule among ourselves, that such garb brings honor more than it reflects honor: for on this Island, the clothes make the man, and not the other way around.]

Recognition of the artificial nature of social roles brings on the breakdown of those roles, and of the hierarchy supported by those roles. The dissolution of class hierarchy is accompanied by that of gender, as preference is given to feminine attire for all of the inhabitants of the island (*H* 80, 14). Here again, Artus reveals the artificiality of gender roles by means of the changeable nature of fashion; but he links gender to other social roles—familial, class oriented, and religious. Clothing becomes a means of linking these social roles to more general issues of signification and knowledge, issues that inevitably return to the primacy of language.

Hermaphroditic Heteroglossia

Artus devotes an entire section of his novel to *entregent,* in particular to conversation and etiquette. The language of the hermaphrodites is at once a richly abundant and inventive self-supplement, and a sort of annihilating antisupplement:

> Leurs discours seront le plus souvent de choses controuvées, sans verité, ni sans aucune apparence de raison, & l'ornement de leur langage sera de renier & de blasphémer posément, & avec gravité faire plusieurs imprécations & malédictions, & autres fleurs de notre Réthorique pour soutenir ou pour persuader le mensonge, & lorsqu'ils voudront persuader une chose fausse, ils commenceront par ces mots: La verité est. (*H* 91, 4)
>
> [Their conversations will consist most often of wholly invented matters, without any truth or appearance of reason, and the proper embellishment of their language shall be to abjure (renounce) and blaspheme calmly and to curse and swear with gravity, and other such flowers of Rhetoric used to support or give credence to a lie. Whenever they wish to persuade someone of an utter falsity, they will begin with the words: "The truth is . . ."]

But here, in this reversal of "truth," the reader falls upon a basic paradox: If the basic mode of speech of the hermaphrodites is a lie, then are they telling the truth when they write this law about lying? Such a paradox calls into question the very nature of "truth."

The hermaphrodites use language to oppose what has been accepted as normal society, urging their subjects to lose a good friend rather than a *bon mot* (*H* 92, 7), to mix blasphemy into their conversation (*H* 93, 9), to slander (*médire*, to mispeak) without regard for family, society, or friendship (*H* 93, 10). Language is their means of opposition, their way of rendering social norms absurd by revealing their factitious nature. When face-to-face with the king: "We order our people to say only pleasant things to their Prince" (*H* 95, 13). Yet in his absence, his subjects' language can be quite different indeed: "These above-mentioned Officers will permit all sorts of slanderous sermons and libellous pamphlets against the honor of the Prince and of his State" (*H* 73, 2). Language itself is perpetually reinvented, as there is no fixed relation between signifier and signified:

> Par grace et privilege spécial nous voulons aussi qu'il soit permis à nos Sujets d'inventer les termes, & les mots nécessaires pour la civile conversation, lesquels sont ordinairement à deux ententes: l'une presentant à la lettre ce qu'ils auront envie de dire: l'autre un sens mystique de voluptés, qui ne sera entendu que de leurs semblables. (*H* 94, 12)

> [By special grace and privilege we wish also that our Subjects be permitted to invent the terms and words necessary for civil conversation, which words ordinarily have two senses: one presenting to the letter whatever they wish to say; the other a mystical meaning of sensuality, which will only be understood by those who resemble them (their equals).]

The question remains, if words have two meanings, then what does a hermaphrodite *mean* to say when it uses these words? Foundational meaning is dissolved merely by these dual possibilities. Language breaks down almost entirely through its constant reinvention:

> Nous leur avons permis & permettons d'avoir dès maintenant, & à toujours quelque langue, ou jargon composé à leur fantaisie qu'ils nommeront de quelque nom étrange, comme *Mésapotamique, Pantagruelique*, & autres. Useront aussi de signes au lieu de paroles, afin d'être entendus en leurs pensées plus secrettes, par leurs consçachans, & sans être découverts. (*H* 95, 14)

> [We have permitted and will continue to permit them to have now and forever some language or jargon invented according to their whim (or by

their imagination), to which they will give some strange name like *Mesapotamian*, *Pantagruelian*, or some other such name. They will also use signs instead of words, in order to make even their most secret thoughts understood.]

This dissolution of language, even at the level of gesture, mirrors the dissolution of a society driven by performative repetition of externally imposed roles. By permitting the infinite multiplication of sign systems according to individual whim or imagination, the hermaphrodites recreate not only language but themselves. Heteroglossia becomes a form of self-determination.[18] If identity is revealed only through such signs as costume, language (title or name), and behavior (deportment—*entregent*), then how can it be established that identity is not created by these outward signs? Once this doubt is raised, it cannot simply be dismissed, for any attempt to define a person other than by outward signs leads merely to aphasia. No essence of identity is available to us. Thus Artus, in raising the issue of the relationship between sign systems and identity formation, enters into a revolutionary discourse, even though he disguises such subversion by his use of the supposedly normative form of satire.

Notes

1. For example, see Thomas Laqueur, *Making Sex: The Body and Gender from the Greeks to Freud* (Cambridge: Harvard University Press, 1990); Julia Epstein, "Either/Or—Neither/Both: Sexual Ambiguity and the Ideology of Gender," *Genders* 7 (Spring 1990): 99–142. Ann Rosalind Jones and Peter Stallybrass analyze cultural constructs of the hermaphrodite, including a brief consideration of Artus's novel, in their essay "Fetishizing Gender: Constructing the Hermaphrodite in Renaissance Europe," in *Body Guards: The Cultural Politics of Gender Ambiguity*, ed. Julia Epstein and Kristina Straub (New York: Routledge, 1991), 80–111

2. In this case, Constance Jordan's chapter titled "Sex and Gender" in her book *Renaissance Feminism: Literary Texts and Political Models* (Ithaca, N.Y.: Cornell University Press, 1990), 134–247, is exemplary (especially 136–37).

3. The first edition of this work, published around 1605, contains no information on publisher, place of publication, or date, but rather is inaugurated by an intricate engraving of Henri III as a hermaphrodite, with doggerel verse beneath it. Copies of this original edition are very rare. Many editions of this work were published in the eighteenth century as supplements to Pierre de L'Estoile's *Journal de Henri III*, as was the edition I have used (Paris: La Veuve de Pierre Gandouin, 1744). This is an expanded version of the Duchat edition. All references to the *Isle des hermaphrodites* in this chapter are to this edition (except the doggerel from the frontispiece of the original

edition). Page numbers for references to *Isle des hermaphrodites* appear in the text with the abbreviation *H*; all translations are mine.

4. Richard Popkin, *The History of Skepticism from Erasmus to Spinoza* (Berkeley: University of California Press, 1979).

5. Sextus Empiricus, *Outlines of Pyrrhonism*, trans. R. G. (Cambridge: Harvard University Press, Loeb Classical Library, 1976), book I, chap. 16, 11.178 seq. Page numbers for further references to this work appear in text.

6. Jacques Derrida, *De la grammatologie* (Paris: Seuil, 1967), 203–34.

7. See Laqueur, *Making Sex*, "Destiny Is Anatomy," 25–62; and "New Science, Once Flesh," 63–113.

8. Judith Butler, *Gender Trouble: Feminism and the Subversion of Identity* (New York: Routledge, 1990), 33, 92.

9. The structure and much of the content of this novel also echoes Jean de Léry's *Histoire d'un voyage fait en la terre du Brésil*, ed. Jean-Claude Morisot (Geneva: Droz, 1975), a work that also combines examples of cultural relativism with criticism of Catholicism and of repression of the Huguenots. Although Artus was undoubtedly aware of works that specifically mentioned hermaphrodites, most particularly René Goulaine de Laudonniére's *Histoire notable de la Floride* (Paris: Auvray, 1586) and Theodore de Bry's similar description in *America* (*Brevis narratio eorum quae in Florida americae provinicia Gallis acciderunt . . .* (1591), the most evident textual echoes are of Léry's work. Artus's title echoes that of Columbus's famous letter, *Epistola de insulis nuper inventis*. I explore these sources in the introduction to my forthcoming edition of *Isle des hermaphrodites* (Paris: Champion).

10. See Donna Haraway, "A Cyborg Manifesto: Science, Technology, and Socialist-Feminism in the Late Twentieth Century," in *Simians, Cyborgs, and Women: The Reinvention of Nature* (New York: Routledge, 1991). "A cyborg is a cybernetic organism, a hybrid of machine and organism, a creature of social reality as well as a creature of fiction. Social reality is lived social relations, our most important political construction, a world-changing fiction" (149).

11. The restrictive potential of clothing is expressed in the "Discours de la vieille" in Jean de Meun, *Roman de la Rose*, ed. Daniel Poirion (Paris: Garnier-Flammarion, 1974), 13319–50.

12. Ovid, *Metamorphoses*, book 12, 168–535. Artus confuses Caeneus, who does not return to female form, with both Tiresias (who changes into a woman and back again; book 3, 316–38) and Erysichthon's unnamed daughter, to whom Neptune has given the power to change form at will (book 8, 850–74).

13. This can be read as a reference to the speculation during Henri's reign that he acquired his sexual preferences in Venice (French polemicists liked to think that homosexuality was an Italian speciality), as well as to Henri's love of Latin letters. See Jean Boucher in his treatise *De Iusta Henrici tertii abdicatione e Francorum regno* (*On the just renunciation of Henry the Third by the people of France*) (Lugduni: Ioannem Pillehotte, 1591), 327–43.

14. "The effect of gender [or power] is produced through the stylization of the body. . . . This formulation moves the conception of gender off the ground of a substantial model of identity to one that requires a conception of gender as a constituted *social temporality*." Butler, *Gender Trouble*, 141.

15. Je confesse les pechés estres distincts, selon la transgression, les uns mortels, comme desir de paillarder, les autres veniels, comme l'esmotion à paillardise, sans le desir et consentement. Article 36, cited by Théodore Agrippa d'Aubigné in his *Histoire universelle*, vol. 1, ed. André Thierry (Geneva: Droz, 1981), 134.

16. Even early skeptics and *Politiques* saw the detailed and Inquisitional imposition of this doctrine as cruelly absurd in the face of the ignorance of the average Catholic (let alone in the face of the different beliefs of the Protestants). See Montaigne, "Des Cannibales," in the *Essais*, vol. 1, ed. Pierre Villey (Paris: PUF, 1965), 209.

17. Butler, *Gender Trouble*, 39.

18. This view is echoed by Donna Haraway in her "Cyborg Manifesto": "Cyborg imagery can suggest a way out of the maze of dualisms in which we have explained our bodies and our tools to ourselves. This is a dream not of a common language, but of a powerful infidel heteroglossia" (181). Haraway, like Artus, uses language metonymically to designate all of the sign systems that are used to construct culture.

10 *Anthropometamorphosis*: John Bulwer's Monsters of Cosmetology and the Science of Culture

Mary Baine Campbell

> CHICAGO—A white supremacist, motivated by his hatred for anyone "feeding off Aryan beauty," has confessed to the execution-style murders of a Chicago-area plastic surgeon and a San Francisco hairdresser, officials said yesterday. Jonathan Haynes, 34, will undergo psychological testing to determine his fitness for trial in the murder of Dr. Martin Sullivan, whom he had allegedly gunned down on Friday. Haynes, whose last job was testing mouthwashes in a Bureau of Alcohol, Tobacco and Firearms lab in Maryland, admitted that he had marked Sullivan for death because of the prominence of his advertisement in the phone book, said Andy Knott, a spokesman for the county prosecutor's office. Knott said Haynes also made statements implicating himself in the May 27th, 1987, murder in broad daylight of the San Francisco hairdresser, Frank Ringi, in his salon. Police there are charging Haynes with Ringi's killing. . . . In an appearance Monday in a north suburban Chicago court, Haynes, who refused a lawyer's services, announced, "I condemn fake Aryan cosmetics. I condemn bleached blond hair, tinted blue eyes and fake facial features brought [*sic*] by plastic surgery." "This is the time that we face up to it, and stop feeding off Aryan beauty like a horde of locusts in a field of wheat," he said.
>
> *Boston Globe*, August 11, 1993

> Our English Ladies, who seeme to have borrowed many of their Cosmetical conceits from barbarous Nations, are seldome knowne to be contented with a Face of Gods making.
>
> JOHN BULWER, *Anthropometamorphosis*, 1654

My purpose here is not to explain the story of Jonathan Haynes, quoted above. His moralized morphology is propelled by circumstances far removed from those of John Bulwer, a seventeenth-century London physician and author of several books on sign language and lipreading, based at least in part on his successful experience in teaching the deaf.[1] There is a historical relation between the very different hysterias of the murderer and the doctor, however: the men expressed themselves on the entwined subjects of racial identity and consumer culture at separate points on a line that traces the development of international capitalism. Separated from Bulwer by class as well as by nation and century, Haynes and his actions may look initially odder to us (articulate academics with access to public forums for the expression of our ideas). But some of the structure of Haynes's idea originates in the premises of Bulwer and those for whom he spoke. Both men have an anatomical sense of ethnic identity, and both understand the coexistence of different racial or ethnic physical features as mimetically unstable: one physical type is likely to alter itself in the direction of the other. Neither seems to concentrate on miscegenation as a threat to ethnic identity (though doubtless both fear it), because they are preoccupied with the problem of the "self-made man" (as Bulwer terms it in his opening poem): they fear above all what Haynes calls the "fake," that is the *fait, factus*, fabricated, the culturally produced, the constructed.[2] Both men live in times of rapid technological innovation and development, and in the wake of sudden increases in levels of contact between distant nations and peoples. We will return later to the differences between their ideas, the difference that history makes.

The first of three editions of the many-titled *Anthropometamorphosis* appeared in 1650; its dedicatory letter refers to Bulwer's previous books as "public paroxysms."[3] The label seems at first both appropriate and weird for printed books about gesture, especially one's *own* books. But Bulwer is in fact a paroxysmal writer, and as such a good registrar of crisis. In *Anthropometamorphosis* we find a tantrum marking the crossroads of a number of emergent social and intellectual structures, a text that might serve as magnetic center of several analyses: the histories of fashion, the body, anthropology, wonder-books, monstrosity, abjection, semiosis, plastic surgery, nationalism, commodity capitalism, and subjectivity meet up here, as well as histories of the concepts, central to all of these topics, of "nature" and "culture." It is of serious interest to a student of the history of "culture" that these areas of experience and expressivity

Figure 10.1. Frontispiece to the 1653 edition, *A View of the People of the Whole World.* (By permission of the Houghton Library, Harvard University.)

come together in one text, and that the text in question *is* a paroxysm. As will become obvious, Bulwer's hysterical categorizing offers concrete and literal support to much of Julia Kristeva's psychoanalytic articulation of the structure, personal *and* social, of abjection: "The twisted braid of affects and thoughts I call by such a name does not have, properly speaking, a definable *object*. . . . The abject has only one quality of the object—that of being opposed to *I*."[4] "A deviser of territories, languages, works, the *deject* never stops demarcating his universe, whose fluid confines—for they are constituted by a non-object, the abject—constantly question his solidity and impel him to start afresh."[5] The subtitle alone (of the first edition) can make the point: . . . *Historically Presented, In the mad and cruel Gallantry, Foolish Bravery, ridiculous Beauty, Filthy Finenesse, and loathsome Lovelinesse of most NATIONS, Fashioning and altering their Bodies from the Mould intended by NATURE.* But this book should not be read as a case of personal anxiety, though it is that. Bulwer's strange grab bag of ethnographic shudders seems to have spoken well for some of the rage and bewilderment of its time: he published an expanded, illustrated edition in 1653 and again in 1654, under a significantly different title: *A View of the People of the Whole World; or, A Short Survey of their Policies, Dispositions, Naturall Deportments, Complexions, Ancient and Moderne Customes, Manners, Habits and Fashions.* The personal psyche has been projected here onto the widest possible screen.[6]

Although this title page boasts proudly that the work is "everywhere *adorned*" (with "Philosophical *and* Morall . . . Observations") and that the "Figures are annexed" "[f]or the Readers greater *delight*" (emphases added), it is in fact adornment and its delight—Fashion in its most ordinary modern sense—that focuses the anger of Bulwer's text. The work participates in a discourse ongoing throughout the century and beyond, on both sides of the Channel, in many genres and media, "*le discourse de la Mode*" (as so many French treatises were titled). But the usual pair of polarized terms at the heart of the discourse—substance and ornament would be one version of this pair—does not hold when the matter to be stylized is the human body itself. I came upon this work not in pursuit of fashion, or even of monsters, but searching out precursors of the modern discipline of anthropology. I want to describe it not as it presents itself—at once a wonder-book and a satiric fulmination against "gallantry," an entry in the seventeenth-century European resistance to "newfangleness"—but as part of an answer to the question, Where did we come by the modern notion of "culture" (and what did it look like in its youth)?

The twenty-four chapters of Bulwer's encyclopedic book, each focused on a specific body part, offer us a long, rabid, but usefully syncretic (or hybrid) example of the forces of "Nature" marshaled rhetorically against the inherent monstrosity of "Culture." It does not *assume*, as later writers of the Enlightenment so often would, a virtue in Nature superior to those on parade in the Culture of European cities, it *declares* it, over and over again. Even less like the the later proponents of the Noble Savage (and more like modernist anthropologists), it locates Culture characteristically in the islands and jungles of the lands newly discovered or re-discovered by European commerce and cosmography. A grossly over-simplified summary of *Anthropometamorphosis* would claim that it represents England as Nature; Asia, Africa, and America as Culture; and the recent discovery of Fashion by "our English Gallants" as the corrupting effect on English Nature of its new commerce with foreign Culture(s).

Such a summary would be partly true: in the chapter "Face Moulders, Stigmatizers and Painters," Bulwer explicitly chastises "Our English Ladies, who seeme to have borrowed many of their Cosmetical conceits from barbarous Nations" (260–61). (For a visual comparison, see Figure 10.2, which is an illustration from the appendix.) But no hysterical text is simple. Bulwer's loathing of (and incompletely repressed fancy for) everything but himself (whatever that might be) requires him to castigate as monstrous beings and forms both congenital and "artificial," native and foreign, attractive and repulsive to him and to others. To extrapolate from this "View of the People of the Whole World" a coherent or even stable definition of monstrosity or nature would be beside the point. Instead, we will examine a tempest, and the disastrous path of its associations.

Two general associations we have already made are those (1) between the early European study of foreign cultures and a contemporary, mostly satiric discourse on Fashion and (2) between Fashion and monstrosity—especially monstrosity as conceived in Kristeva's analysis of horror. Abjection and absorption of other cultures must be important functions in a period that saw established the economic importance of *consumer* capitalism; what bourgeois Europe could and would not swallow morally (culturally) in the early days of colonial empire is interestingly non-identical with the geography of its material (and human) consumption. In Bulwer's book we see, most saliently of all for the investigator of early anthropology, the mechanics of abjection applied to European and *British* cultural practices. From the beginning of empire to the end, we find books about British "style" that start with descriptions of the life-ways of its colonies: British mores are Bulwer's moral destination.[7] His xenophobia ranges appropriately far, but it comes home to roost in his

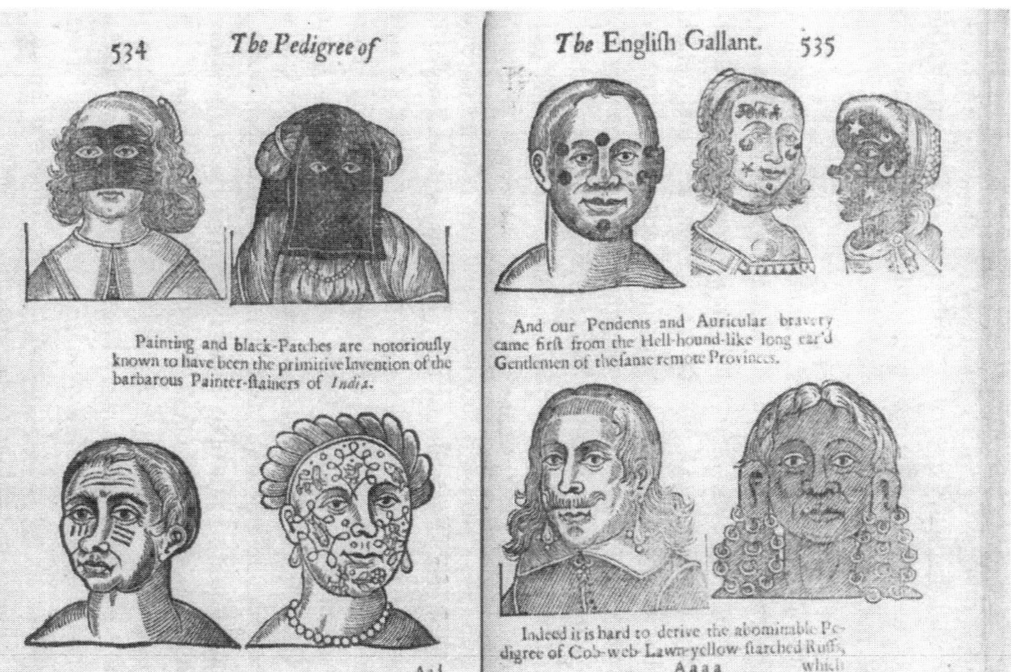

Figure 10.2. "The Pedigree of the English Gallant." (By permission of the Houghton Library, Harvard University.)

closing appendix, "The Pedigree of the English Gallant." "If it be true that the abject simultaneously beseeches and pulverizes the subject, one can understand that it is experienced at the peak of its strength when that subject, weary of fruitless attempts to identify with something on the outside, finds the impossible within."[8]

Bulwer states his aim this way in the dedicatory letter of the first edition: "What I here present you with, is an Enditement framed against most of the Nations under the Sun; whereby they are *arraigned* at the Tribunal of Nature, as guilty of High-treason, in Abasing, Counterfeiting, Defacing and Clipping her coin instampt with her Image and Superscription on the Body of Man" (1650). A Nature that mints coins and presides over law cases is certainly English, but whether its behavior is strictly natural is a question Bulwer avoids. His Nature is whatever he wants her to be, mainly, and he knows her secret aims and wishes intimately: using one's hand as a dish (like Diogenes) is "no way contradictory to the intention of Nature," however, "it is plain, by the full length and position of the Hand . . . that nature never intended the Hand to be as a Fork" (184–85). "For a woman to be shorne, is clearly against the intention of Nature" (58), but Nature "made it lawfull for us [men] to cut it" (59). The true "office of Cosmetickall Physick" is "to conform [the Bodies of Infants] most to the advantage of Nature" (intro., B2r), though all such shapings of skull and frame as are practiced by Russian, Tartar, and Native American "Nurses and Midwives" are "Abasements of that coin instampt" with Nature's image. Obviously, Bulwer's touchstone, in making determinations about Nature's design, is how he and his friends dress, wear their hair, and raise their children. He has company in this attitude, of course, but few confessedly reactionary provincials have composed an ethnological encyclopedia around their intuition of the Natural.

Given Bulwer's self-centered conception of Nature, it is little wonder that his implicit definition of the monstrous overlaps almost completely with the category of "foreign." He could have left it at that—most people do—but in fact he was an intellectual: the semantically functional dichotomy was and is "natural/artificial," not "natural/foreign." The latter pair is merely circumstantial. It *so happens* that foreigners are mostly unnatural and monstrous. Since it sometimes happens that the English ("our English Gallants") are unnatural too, especially fops and women, there must be a metaphysical term transcending geographic location in which to frame the charges brought before Nature's Tribunal. The term of course is *artificial,* though it does not apply to all cases we might imagine: "Every part of the new-born Infants Body is to be formed, and those parts that ought to be concave, must be pressed in; those which should be slender, contrained and repressed; and those which are naturally prominent, rightly drawn out: The Head also is diligently to be made round" (intro., B2r). This manipulation is not artificial, because the result will be a head of the sort Bulwer happens to know is "intended by Nature." So that you will know it too, he details it geometrically in the chapter on "skull-fashions." What *is* artificial is the distinctly un-English (i.e., unnatural) skull-fashion of, for instance, the Russians, "who love a broad forehead, and use Art to make it so" (78). "To vindicate the Regular beauty and honesty of Nature from those Plastique imposters, we say, that a forehead which keeps its natural magnitude is one of the unisons of the face, whose longitude . . . is the third part of the face, and ought to answer the length of the Nose, so that if we compare it to the rest of the face, it ought to have the proportion of a half part to a duple" (81), and so on, and so on.

This and other clear geometries of the natural face make it obvious why Africans of Guinea or Aethiopia must have artificial—that is, monstrous or cultural—faces, for "how can [a flat] Nose beautifie a round Face, such as the Guineans, and they of Caffarain the lower part of Aethiopia are said to have, unlesse wee will imagine such a rotundity, as makes a Concave or hollow Face, with which a Camoise Nose may have some indifferent correspondency. To speak the truth, this Nose being gentilitious and native to an Ape, can never become a Man's face" (1650, 86).[9] (Bulwer is humorously aware that bodily norms are contested; he delights in such ironies as the absurd ethnocentricity of "they of Bolanter," who "have Eares of a Span long, and it is held such a note of gallantry among them, that those that have not their Eares long, they call them Apes" [1654, 145]. It's a crazy mixed-up world.)[10]

To support his category of the "artificial," Bulwer depends heavily on the notion of acquired traits. The usual etiology of monstrous differences from the English norm he assumes to be the gradual pseudo-naturalizing of one or another people's "fashionable elegancie," his most spectacular example, borrowed from Thomas Browne's *Pseudodoxia Epidemica,* being the "Blackness of Negroes," with which the final ethnographic chapter of the first edition ends.[11] (The section is shifted in later editions to the middle of the final chapter.) This is an extreme; often enough Bulwer is perfectly accurate in his perceptions of the "constructedness" of the traits and practices he details—tatooing, for instance, or femininity. His response to these constructions is axiomatic and unmodulated: "Considering these strange attempts made upon the naturall endowments of the Face, one would think that some men felt within themselves an instinct of opposing Nature, . . . whereas they should strive against their own inward, they oppose their outward Nature" (241).[12]

One would certainly think that about "some men," and not only in respect to the care and adornment of the personal person. The passage expands its focus at this point and begins to detail a very long and elaborate topographical and even cosmographical metaphor, adumbrated earlier and supported in later figures: the face, already defined in terms of its most proper longitudes and latitudes, becomes first a natural landscape and then a political territory.[13] Although the lesson seems to be lost on Bulwer (that "men . . . should strive" inside and *not* outside their own proper political borders), it is hard to miss either the avowed or the unconscious dynamics of colonial and imperial expansion in this account of "the little world of beauty in the face" (242). Where "man transported with vaine imaginations . . . findes Hils, he sets himself to make Plains; where Plains, he raseth Hils; in pleasant places he seekes horrid ones, and brings pleasantnesse into places of horrour and shameful obscurity." If the body is the Other (World), Bulwer's allegory tells us the moral price of conquest: "When [Man] thinks he triumphs over his subdued and depraved Body, his own corrupt Nature triumphs over him" (241). This victory of corruption is Satanic, of course, introducing yet another character not to be confused with the self: it is "a strategem of the enemy of our Nature," who it turns out is a "cuning politique Tyrant" sending domestic opposition out of the City (of the self) "to fight with the enemy, to the end that venting his violence and fantasticalnesse abroad, [the Tyrant] may have plenary power to tyrannize at home at his pleasure" (241).[14]

It is in this extended figure that Bulwer defines the matter of his book, the intersection of the cosmos and the cosmetic: for "as the greater World is called Cosmus from the beauty thereof, the inequality of the centre thereof contributing much to the beauty and delightsomenesse of it; so in this Map or little world of beauty in the face, the inequality affords the prospect and delight" (242). The bodies of those "barbarous nations" afford the perfect synecdoche both for the nations, with their competing *cosmoi,* and, in their obviously decorated state, for the antinatural business of Culture per se. The Aethiopian body, generated at first by the "prevarication of Art" (174, quoting Cardanus), both stands for and is a part of the Aethiopian cosmos, "subdued and depraved" but potentially triumphant over the cosmetic styles of England, "our Nature."

Although the book attacks foreign fashions, the true target of its didactic wit is the English Gallant; its tough love is designed as a kind of prophylactic against the "vaine imaginations," "foolish bravery," and "filthy finenesse" discoverable in the "People of the Whole World" here set before us for our undeniable but dangerous delectation. The multiculturalism of seventeenth-century English consumer culture has already begun to break down the sovereign borders of gender identity, apparently, and God alone knows what further dissolutions might stem from this: the end of the human species is a possibility, given that sex change on the part of women and sodomy on the part of men are consequential expressions of the gender inequality at "the centre of" English society. (It is true that Parcelsus offers good information on how to propogate homunculi "without the conjunction of women" [492], but such "non-Adamiticall men" are not strictly speaking human and anyhow the process isn't Natural, or even English—Paracelsus is German.)[15]

Gender is the snarl in Bulwer's argument: he does not want to argue, with Aristotle, that women are technically monstrous in their dissimilarity from the norm (not that he is friendly toward women, but his differentia are ethnic or "national");[16] on the other hand, many of the differences women exhibit seem to be cultural—that is, constructed—ergo monstrous, or at least supported and augmented by cultural means. I have already mentioned the difficulty with maintaining the naturalness of gender differences in hairstyle: if, as Bulwer declares in the chapter on eyes, "true beauty is referred to the successe and goodnesse of utility," then one or the other of the genders does not exhibit true beauty in the trimming of its hair, as the fundamental uses of head hair cannot be different between the sexes. ("The prime end of the Haire of the Head is to defend the skin, the second use is to defend the Braine from injuries from without, or from within"; 50.) I have also alluded to the difficulty of maintaining the dichotomy natural/foreign in the face of that gender whose features and adornments are both English and unmasculine. Shaving the chin must be considered "piacular and monstrous" in men;

"to be seen with a smooth skin like a woman, a shameful metamorphosis" (199). Yet it cannot be denied that in general, "men of the New world . . . have store of milk in their breasts" (319). Are the spontaneous beardlessness of English women and breast milk of Brazilian men natural *and* monstrous at once? What a quandary! Are the English customs that discourage facial hair in women and breast milk in men artificial? But English customs are the very definition of Nature; except for the foppish manners of Gallants, there should be no need to speak of English customs, there should be none to speak of. Sadly, custom must be called in: "to what ends should we either mingle or change the custome, or the sequestering variance of virile nature with feminine, that one sex cannot be known and distinguished from another?" (60). As with the production of Nature-shaped infants, Nature needs a little help from art in realizing some of her intentions. (The "tip of the Ear," for instance, "seems in a manner to be perforated with an invisible hole . . . wherein the Athenians were wont to hang their golden Grass-hoppers." So pierced ears are natural. And yet, "this is no warrant for the monstrous practices of these men . . . who so shamefully load it with Jewels . . . , and use such force of Art to tear and delacerate the most tender particle thereof, stretching it to so prodigious a magnitude"; 156.)

In an unsurprising dodge, women become precisely what Ronald Reagan said they were ten years ago, the guardians and transmitters of culture. Eluding the logical conundrums they generate as phenotypes themselves for his matrix of assumptions about the natural, Bulwer concentrates on them especially as the Nurses and Midwives who introduce so many artificial shapes in the bodies of the infants under their care, or as the dangerously imaginative maternal vessels of infants in their most formative stage. Midwives not only swaddle and deform us as children, snipping septums and foreskins and pressing down protuberant "asses ears," but their interferences instill in us from the start a taste for the altered and the perverse: Gallants are the logical outcome of meddling midwives and nurses, as are the less emphasized ladies of fashion. Bulwer also supports the thesis, recently analyzed by Marie-Hélène Huet, that monsters are produced by the vivid fantasies or perceptual experience of their mothers during pregnancy;[17] such a thesis supports his notion of women as female agents of interruption in the male continuity of natural process.

Women are in some ways represented here as the missing link: ontogenically intermediate as well as intermediatory. Even the normative geometric descriptions of "absolute" women and their body parts produce an effect similar to the static ethnographic writing quoted on every page of Bulwer's book. The slide is easy from a description of a woman's "natural" lips—"somewhat full . . . , coral, imitating Vermilion, a little disjoyn'd, yet so as the teeth are scarce discovered, while she holds her peace or laughs not, unmoved" (132)—to the more fully alien *effictio*, which characteristically reads as if it describes a statue or an engraving rather than a living agent.[18] Women are intermediate between men and the beasts they continually threaten to revert to as well as between Englishmen and foreigners: some men, as Bulwer sternly records, have intercourse with beasts *instead* of women (493). And the figments of their imaginations are intermediate between bodily and Platonic realities: the hairy girl of Pisa was conceived as an effect of "the Picture of St. John the Baptist, painted after the usual manner clothed in Camels haire, whose image hanging in her Chamber the mother had wishtly beheld" (475).

It is not, I think, beside the point to wonder what Bulwer considered his illustrated book's effects were likely to be on the unborn children of its owners' wives. The imagination, and the cultural intelligence that designs and stores conceptions of decor—the cosmetic intelligence—are dangerous shifters in the multiplicitous text of the "greater World." As long as "Images and Superscriptions" can be "instampt" in books and broadsides they can be disseminated in the frighteningly manipulable flesh of our progeny, as well as the less intimate fashions of clothing, adornment, and sexual taste adopted in adulthood by Gallants and Ladies of Fashion. Instead of (or in addition to) "Nature's coin," a considerably increased quantity of commercial coin was circulating in the 1650s between England and places very different from England, the English and the very different people whom and from whom the English bought. Even the innocent commodities of this trade could smuggle in notions of physiological difference dangerous to the national stock: "The shape of Spanishe Stockings sold upon our Exchange, whose shortnesse speaks them to have been made for women, seems to intimate that the women there, have great Legs and very little Feet" (426).

In this formative stage of British use of knowledge about Others, monstrosity remains as important as ever in the popular consciousness. The difference is that it is now seen as transmissible to home—thus

Bulwer's appendix "The Pedigree of the English Gallant." Commodity capitalism and print have disseminated monstrosity widely and provocatively: biological and mechanical reproduction are intimately linked, as is made explicit in Bulwer's use of printing and engraving terms in discussing Nature's minting of the normal.

Culture, in the days preceding the first theorized work of cultural anthropology, Lafitau's *Habits of the American Savages,*[19] seems associated positively with barbarians, women (especially loose women), and "effeminate men"—as of course it still is, in its aspects of the artificial and the unnatural. It has not become a universal category yet by Bulwer's time: it is itself Queer, because the people who carry and transmit it are Queer. Contact with such people is necessary, to reproduce the race and/or grow the economy, but it is also one of the greatest dangers facilitated by the age of print. Bulwer's own book, patched together with chaotic amplitude from countless and diverse prior texts, organized by a blazon of body parts, stuffed with dangerous images of alien cultures and suggestive comparisons, raging in affect and unrestrained by conventions of genre or discipline, is as monstrous as any text "instampt" and engraved in its moment.

Perhaps the most uncanny of Bulwer's monsters is the multicultural female folk-dancing monster introduced in the penultimate chapter ("On Leg and Foot-fashions"), Catherine Mazzina, born in Avignon in 1594,

> of a comely forme, and 27 inches and a Palme over in heighth, but wanting Hips and Legs, and consequently Feet, her Armes were perfectly formed, being longer than her breast and trunke, the lower part of her body did in a manner appeare bifid, emulating the bottom of a Harpe; She spake to purpose, sung, plaid on a Lute, danced with her hands Spanish, Mauritanian, Italian and French dances, in like manner to the sound of Musique she so composed the Gestures of her imperfect body, that they who had seene her afar off, would doubtelessly have said, she had danced with her Feet. And as to the endowments of the mind, there was nothing wanting to her which is granted by Nature to other men. Moreover she was endowed with both Sexes, yet she drew nearer to a woman, and was more vigorous in that Sex, and therefore was rather called a woman than a man. (453)

Catherine is several kinds of hybrid at once, including a representative of mixed notions of monstrosity: although unmoralized, she sounds like a typical broadside monster in physical shape, while at the same time coming under Bulwer's new more "artificial" and cultural paradigm. Her bifid, Harpe-like "lower part" could be the result of her mother's having stared at printed broadsides of monsters—or perhaps of her mother's desire to have a Harpe?[20] The lute playing and dancing of the "comely" Catherine show her a typically feminine and aspiring bourgeoise—a familiar, homely character to Bulwer's readers; but she sounds a little too bright, her knowledge of dancing a little too cosmopolitan, and of course she has a penis. As a hermaphrodite, she is a regular, unsurprising (if still rather risqué) monster—her shock value in the context of Bulwer's previous 452 parasitically ethnographic pages comes from her knowledge of so many cultures and her ability to transmit (translate?) the language of dance from the feet to her hands. In other words, she is a hermaphrodite of *culture* as well as of sex and gender.

Of course she *is* moralized, not explicitly but by the tone of Bulwer's opus generally. Bulwer seems to intend her as the emblem of what is ridiculous in "fashion"—the cosmopolitan quality of her knowledge combines with its uselessness to make her the perfect creature of empty fashion, and her leglessness and consequent footlessness both mark the emptiness of the attainments and punish her for them. Bulwer has elsewhere explained why women are not inherently monstrous, and how we know that: quoting another Italian (the "Marquesse of Malvezzi") he stresses that their differences have a *use*: "They who believe that Woman . . . is not an Errour or a Monster, must confesse she is made for Generation, and if she be made for this end . . . it is necessary she be endued with parts that move unto that end." Nature informs us directly about this telos of womankind, for "so soone as she is represented unto us . . . man doth by Nature hasten to contemplate her for the end to which she was made by Nature" (493). A woman without a "lower part" (without an "end") has taken the sterility of fashion to its literal extreme—as is demonstrated, at least in Bulwer's terms, by her veritably ethnographic knowledge of dances, of foreign body languages.

The discerning reader has already noticed, perhaps, that Catherine Mazzina sounds a bit like Bulwer—a specialist in body languages and gestures, an armchair dilettante of ethnography, a multilingual European with a penis. Both seem avid, hysterical, filled with a weird *jouissance*. Their differences, then, should tell us something about Bulwer: one is a "monster" and the other a potentially monster-genic analyst of monstrosity; one is a dancer and the other a student and teacher of body language; one is a set of texts (by Aldrovandi, Hoffman, and others), the other an author whose texts are all patchworked together from other texts. One is an Italian born in France who performs African dances, the other an Englishman from England who writes in English.[21] One is a "woman," and the other is a "man." It's a good bet Catherine wouldn't score very well on the "intended by nature" test, despite her comeliness, her vigor, her intelligence, and her penis. She seems easily read as the precise shape of Bulwer's nightmare self, doomed to live out as subject the role of all those abjected objects in the twenty-four "Scenes" of his ethnoballetic encyclopedia.

Michel-Rolph Trouillot's recent essay "Anthropology and the Savage Slot" reminds his fellow anthropologists that, "like all academic disciplines, [anthropology] inherited a field of significance that preceded its formalization." He is interested in the construction of the phantasm "savage," rather than in the "monster" that preoccupies Huet, and insists, "Anthropology did not create the savage. Rather, the savage was the raison d'être of anthropology."[22] His essay complicates the by now received truth that "the savage or the primitive was the alter ego the West constructed for itself" by pointing out that "this Other was a Janus, of whom the savage was only the second face. The first face was the West itself, but the West fancifully constructed as a utopian projection."[23] I think a reading of Bulwer's *Anthropometamorphosis* might complicate that complication further. The "first face" need not only be the paradisal utopia of Montaigne or the orderly one of More, it could also be the simply normal utopia of home—or rather home reimagined *as* "normal" (Dorothy's Kansas). And the second face need not only be "the savage," constitutively distant. Monsters can live next door, especially if monstrosity is construed as meaning altered ("Transform'd"), ab-normal.[24]

The concept of the savage, then, was not the *only* "raison d'être of anthropology." Bulwer's book composes passages of what Trouillot calls "paraethnography" into a satirical treatise on cosmetics, and points it at local as well as exotic targets, homegrown deviations from a bodily standard imagined as "natural," if rarely encountered. The "self-made man"—that is, the monster/fashion plate—seems to have been another slot that "preceded the formalization of anthropology." Anthropology has always had antiquarian and folklore studies as (paradoxically) marginal poor relations—middle-class European and later "Western" study of the peasantry and the working classes has always seemed parallel to the study of cultures geographicly exotic. Early sociology concerned itself with "deviants" and the working class as well. In Bulwer we can observe all these abjections unified under the rubric of the "artificial" and a hysterical near admission that one can barely escape the rubric oneself. Between the postfeudal social mobility that permits and even requires men and women to "make themselves" and the circulation of exotic imagery that encourages them to make themselves strange, it is hard to imagine how poor Nature will communicate her intentions to an increasingly imperial and self-conscious Europe.

Manners, customs, and *fashions* are the early modern terms that covered the terrain roughly equivalent to the *culture* of modern anthropology. Clothes and dances, jewelry and body language, erotic self-presentation and carriage were observed at home and abroad, by the fashion conscious and the protoanthropologists both. This makes sense, and seems obvious. But it also seems somewhat neglected as a way of more deeply imagining "the larger thematic field"[25] on which anthropology set up its tents. The "discourse de la Mode," with its demonic women, fops, and social climbers, its innovations and superficialities, its abandonment of all that is sturdy, deep, and "natural" about the suddenly self-conscious culture of Europeans at home, is closely tied to the sudden appearance of a (distant) *mirror* in the sixteenth century.[26] Michael Taussig is talking about that self-consciousness in "The Report to the Academy," which opens *Mimesis and Alterity*:

> Now the strange thing about this silly if not desperate place between the real and the really made-up is that it appears to be where most of us spend most of our time as epistemically correct, socially created, and occasionally creative beings. We dissimulate. We act and have to act as if mischief were not afoot in the kingdom of the real and that all around the ground lay firm. That is what the public secret, the facticity of the social fact, being a social being, is all about. . . . Try to imagine what would happen if we didn't in daily practice thus conspire to actively forget what Saussure called "the arbitrariness of the sign"? Or try the opposite experiment. Try to imagine living in a world whose signs were "natural."[27]

Bulwer seems to have felt himself, as many did, confronted with a choice between these two experiments, and wishing earnestly he could "return" to some world before the idea of natural signs had to be considered a thought experiment. He has Taussig's *jouissance* but not his serenity, so his book is silly if not desperate. Still, try to imagine "the unstoppable merging of the object of perception with the body of the perceiver"[28] from the point of view of someone who had never heard of genes, whose country had just been through a civil war, and whose civilization had recently undergone the discoveries of such image cornucopias as print, America, engraving, and the microscope. The idea that the social fact was "factitious" and that the customs preserving gender identity were malleable might well make someone anxious, especially someone atop the gender hierarchy; the prevalence of alien or fictional representations might seem to threaten (or excite) all who perceived them with reproductive chaos. Bulwer sees in fashion a bone-deep penetration of the body politic, a self-consciousness that could give his people fatal vertigo. The work of nature is hard to preserve in an age of mechanical reproduction. I would disagree then with Huet about what the "monster" is a sign of—it is not of the fact that we can never be sure of paternity, but perhaps that we can never be sure of any kind of identity, at least not through the means of a stable visual signifier.[29]

Jonathan Haynes, killer of plastic surgeons and hairdressers in the name of preserving visible ("natural") Aryan identity, is supported in his hysterical ideation by the survival in our culture of a sense of one's own ethnic identity as dependent on visual signs, and also the sense of alteration (fashion, culture) as perverse. He does not seem to be bothered, as Bulwer was, by Euro-American appropriation of African, Hispanic, and Amerindian fashions and gestures, however—his is not an ontological problem. Nor does he mind alteration except *insofar* as it seems to appropriate "Aryan" features (no longer identical with the ideal proportions and dimensions outlined in manic detail all over Bulwer's text, but then, Bulwer had never heard of "Aryans"). Haynes expresses a feeling, common among those descendants of Europe who never benefited much from the European hegemony getting under way in Bulwer's time, that the Other must want to be Me. Why? Because my relatives took everything She had, including her fashions and her genes, and She wants it back.

Notes

1. Besides the work under discussion here, Bulwer's published works (which earned him the epithet "Chirosoph") include *Chirologia; or, The Natural Language of*

the Hand (London, 1644), *Philocophus; or, The Deafe and Dumbe Man's Friend* (London, 1648), and *Pathomyotomia, or a Dissection of the significative Muscles of the Affections of the Minde* (London, 1649). *Chirologia* and its companion treatise, *Chironomia*, have been published in a modern diplomatic edition by James W. Cleary (Carbondale: Southern Illinois University Press, 1974). The *Dictionary of National Biography* notes the oddness of Bulwer's failure, given his interests, to invent a sign language for the deaf, and also points out that his "discovery of methods for communicating knowledge to the deaf and dumb" preceded John Wallis's more celebrated 1662 presentation of his deaf pupil to the Royal Society by at least fourteen years. Work in this area had been done previous to Bulwer's in Spain (and reported in England) by two Benedictine monks, Pedro Ponce and Juan Paulo Bonet; I wonder what inspiration the Spanish and English took from the habit of African slaves, who, transported in mixed language groups to keep them from communicating, learned the European languages of the slave traders and sailors by lipreading. Such a possible source would at least fit nicely with the patterns of appropriation and consumption betrayed in Bulwer's *Anthropometamorphosis.*

2. The penultimate couplet of the opening poem in the first edition, "The Full intent of the Frontispiece unfolded; Or, A through-description of the National Gallant": "Thus *capa peia* is that *Gallant great, / Horrid, Transformed self-made Man,* Compleat" (1650, A4v). (Compare Edward Brathwaite's conduct book, "The English Gentleman," in *Times Treasury; or, Academy for Gentry* [London, 1652].)

3. For the most part, I will be quoting from Bulwer's expanded edition of 1654. Where there is reason to cite from the first edition (1650), I will point out that I am doing so. The 1653 edition, which I have looked at in the Houghton Library at Harvard, has considerably more front matter (including the wonderful allegorical frontispiece shown here in Figure 10.1) than does the microfilm of the 1654 version, but it is not widely available. Page numbers for all references appear in text.

4. Julia Kristeva, *Powers of Horror: An Essay on Abjection,* trans. Leon S. Roudiez (New York: Columbia University Press, 1982), 1.

5. Ibid., 67. See especially chap. 4, "From Filth to Defilement," which attempts to find "correspondences" between the abjection of individual subjects and the collective abjection of the symbolic systems they inhabit and maintain.

6. According to Oldys's *British Librarian* (London, 1738), the new title was "seemingly added by the Printer to advance the universal reading of the Author" (365). For an extended reading of the kind of gaze (and its growing popularity) implied in such a title—"A View of the People of the Whole World"—see Mary Louise Pratt, *Imperial Eyes: Travel Writing and Transculturation* (London: Routledge, 1992).

7. At the other end of the story, see for instance Dick Hebdige's *Subculture: The Meaning of Style* (London: Methuen, 1979).

8. Kristeva, *Powers of Horror*, 5.

9. I have quoted from the first edition here; in the expanded 1654 edition the passage appears on pp. 130–31, except for the last sentence, which has been moved to an earlier location on p. 128. It is noteworthy that some of the most excrutiating sentences and passages about African physiologies in the 1650 edition are moved or broken up in the later editions.

10. Bulwer fears the unlike likeness of apes as well as of foreigners, and makes a

point of their threatening nearness to us in his introduction, where he anticipates Darwin, or rather Lamarck: "In discourse I have heard to fall, somewhat in earnest, from the mouth of a Philosopher . . . That man was a meer artificiall creature, and was at first but a kind of Ape or Baboon, who through his industry (by degrees) in time had improved his Figure and his Reason up to the perfection of man" (B3r).

11. For Browne's (much less xenophobic) treatment of "blackness," see Thomas Browne, *Pseudodoxia Epidemica*, ed. Geoffrey Keynes, in *The Works of Sir Thomas Browne*, vol. 2 (Chicago: University of Chicago Press, 1964), bk. 6, chaps. 10–12.

12. The introduction here of an interior to the monstrous helps inaugurate another long history, the history of abnormal psychology, which is to say psychology. That is not my chief interest, but it is worth noting that this one late text of monstrosity intersects the early modern histories of both anthropology and psychology.

13. "Through frustrations and prohibitions, this [maternal] authority shapes the body into a *territory* having areas, orifices, points and lines, surfaces and hollows, where the archaic power of mastery and neglect, of the differentiation of proper-clean and improper-dirty, possible and impossible, is impressed and exerted. . . . Maternal authority is the trustee of that mapping of the self's clean and proper body." Kristeva, *Powers of Horror*, 72. In Kristeva's description of abjection (that which creates the symbolic forms of the monstrous, the sacred, the Other), especially in its public forms (e.g., religious ritual), the threat posed by the maternal is "that of being swamped by the dual relationship, thereby risking the loss not of a part (castration) but of the totality of [one's] living being. The function of these religious rituals is to ward off the subject's fear of his very own identity sinking irretrievably into the mother" (64). It is easy to see the mapping and itemizing proclivities in Bulwer's text as, in part, magical hedges against such loss, and would help to explain his frequent reference to "Woman" as "that impotent Sexe"—an otherwise somewhat surprising epithet in a work that emphasizes "that Sexe's" power to create human (and monstrous) shapes.

14. The "tyrant" of Bulwer's metaphor sounds more like Cromwell than Charles, though many signs point to Bulwer's being a Puritan or even a Dissenter. He is scrupulously unpolitical in his writings, but he is so learned and Latinate a man that it is hard to explain his absence from the alumni rolls of Oxford and Cambridge. He may have been educated in Holland. I have been unable to determine whether he was a member of the College of Physicians.

15. Bulwer's discomfort with male asexual reproduction would seem to challenge Marie-Hélène Huet's claim that "what made monstrosity monstrous was that it served as a public reminder that, short of relying on visible resemblance, paternity could never be proven." *Monstrous Imagination* (Cambridge: Harvard University Press, 1993), 33–34. I think she is partly right, but that monstrosity involves several different categories of identity and their interrelations: a child created without the assistance, however theoretically passive, of a female partner, though it might stand as unusually clear evidence of paternity, would not stand as evidence of female submission to male sexual domination—would not then be a sign of the difference (only conceivable hierarchically) between male and female.

16. See Aristotle's *Generation of Animals*, trans. A. L. Peck (Cambridge: Harvard University Press, 1963): "The female is as it were a deformed male" (2.3.175); "The first

beginning of this deviation [from the generic type] is when a female is formed instead of a male" (4.3.401). Quoted in ibid., 3, 93.

17. Huet, *Monstrous Imagination.*

18. Here, for instance, are the Giachas: "The Giachas or Agagi of the Ethiopian Countreys beyond Congo, have a custome to turn their Eyelids backwards towards the Forehead and round about; so that their skin being all black, and in that blacknesse shewing the white of their Eyes, it is a very dreadfull, and divilish sight to behold; for they thereby cast upon the beholders a most dreadfull astonishing aspect" (93). That the slide to the generic barbarian, male and/or female, is not blocked by gender seems partly due to the sense of gender's disappearance into monstrously blurred "variance" in those distant landscapes and facescapes. Female gender was close to no gender.

19. Joseph Lafitau, Fr., *Moeurs des sauvages amériquaines* (Paris, 1724).

20. The relation of female desire to monstrosity was a long-lived one (not yet deceased): Huet quotes Pietro Pomponazzi: "If a pregnant woman greatly desires a chickpea, she will deliver a child bearing the image of a chickpea. That is how Cicero's family got its name" (*De naturalium effectum admirandorum causis* [Basel, 1556]). More than 150 years later, James Blondel sees the need to satirize those who believe that "the mere Longing for *Muscles* [mussels] is sufficient to *transubstantiate* the true and original Head of the Child into a *Shell-Fish*" (*The Power of the Mother's Imagination over the Foetus* [London, 1729]). See Huet, *Monstrous Imagination*, 16–14 and (for Blondel's pamphlet war) 64–67.

21. Bulwer includes at least one other European monster who is not living in the "right" country: "Scaliger remembers a certaine little Spaniard covered with white haires, which he reports to have been brought out of India, or to have been borne of Indian parents in Spaine" (475).

22. Michel-Rolph Trouillot, "Anthropology and the Savage Slot: The Poetics and Politics of Otherness," in *Recapturing Anthropology: Working in the Present*, ed. Richard G. Fox (Santa Fe, N.M.: Academic Research Press, 1991), 18, 40.

23. Ibid., 28.

24. Medieval monsters were mostly imagined as species, and species on the world's margins. By the seventeenth century, however, they had become local, even intimate: Pepys's servant James Paris, in his manuscript history of monsters (c. 1680) begins literally at home, with the delivery of a monster in his childhood home to a friend of his mother's, an inveterate reader of illustrated "Almanacks": "This Accident was Kept very Secret, and the Child being a Monster and not having been Cristened was wrapped in a Clean Linnen Cloth and put in a littel woodden Box and Buried very Privately, in a part of our Garden which I Caled my Garden. . . . A few Dayes After being Buisy in my little Garden, I Discovered a little Box, in which I found this Little Mounster, which I Buried Again" (*Prodigies and Monstrous Births of Dwarfs, Sleepers, Giants, Strong Men, Hermaphrodites, Numerous Births and Extreme Old Age etc.* [British Library, MS Sloane 5246], quoted in Dudley Wilson, *Signs and Portents: Monstrous Births from the Middle Ages to the Enlightenment* [London: Routledge, 1993], 94).

25. Trouillot, "Anthropology and the Savage Slot."

26. It might be worth noting that the modern mirror itself was a Renaissance invention, or rather arrived in Italy from Asia during the Renaissance.

27. Michael Taussig, *Mimesis and Alterity: A Particular History of the Senses* (New York: Routledge, 1993), xvii–xviii.

28. Ibid., 25.

29. See, of course, Marjorie Garber's "Spare Parts: The Surgical Construction of Gender," in *The Lesbian and Gay Studies Reader*, ed. Henry Abelove, Michele Aina Barale, and David M. Halperin (New York: Routledge, 1993), 321–36, a discussion of the twentieth-century discourse of the "transsexual" that resonates everywhere with Bulwer's terror (and joy) in the face of the "self-made man."

IV Monstrous History

11 Vampire Culture

Frank Grady

In his 1982 essay "The Dialectic of Fear," Franco Moretti makes a persuasive case for reading the vampire of Bram Stoker's *Dracula* as a metaphor for capital.[1] According to Moretti, the novel operates on one level as a parable about the dangers of monopoly capitalism, constituted by Stoker as an external threat in the monstrous, predatory, acquisitive, and above all utterly foreign figure of the count, "a rational entrepreneur who invests his gold to expand his dominion: to conquer the City of London."[2] Opposing Dracula in the name of individualism and economic liberty, then, are a small band of valiant Britons (aided by the lore of Van Helsing and the financial resources of the American Quincey P. Morris) who struggle to use their considerable economic power to do good, and thus to engineer the "purification" of capital used for a moral purpose. In so doing, Moretti charges, they reveal their complicity with "the great ideological lie of Victorian capitalism, a capitalism which is ashamed of itself and which hides factories and stations beneath cumbrous Gothic superstructures; which prolongs and extols aristocratic models of life; which exalts the holiness of the family as the latter begins secretly to break up"[3]

In the century since Stoker's novel was published, the monopoly capitalism of the Victorian era has evolved into what Fredric Jameson, following Ernest Mandel, calls "late" capitalism (or "multinational" or "commodity" capitalism), "the purest form of capital yet to have emerged, a prodigious expansion of capital into hitherto uncommodified areas."[4] The relentless march of commodification has not spared the realm of the supernatural, or the figure of the vampire: one count graces breakfast cereal boxes, while on television the telltale tooth marks help make the case for Reese's Peanut Butter Cups and another vampire appears on a PBS children's show—teaching them to count, no less! Vampirism has also been assimilated into the current American fascination with identity politics and ethnic self-definition: in the made-for-TV movie *Blood Ties* (1991), members of the vampire enclave in Santa Barbara refer to themselves euphemistically throughout as "Carpathian-Americans" (who just happen to have some unusual cultural traditions). Even Dracula himself has been domesticated, reimagined as a figure of romance rather than horror: in Francis Ford Coppola's 1992 film version of *Dracula*, the vampire—portrayed as the victim of a dogmatic and unfeeling clerisy—ultimately dies redeemed and released by a purifying love rediscovered (rather nonsensically) across the centuries.

Nowhere has the vampire been more vigorously rehabilitated, or with more popular success, than in Anne Rice's *Vampire Chronicles*, a series inaugurated in 1976 with *Interview with the Vampire* and continuing to date through *The Vampire Lestat* (1985), *The Queen of the Damned* (1988), *The Tale of the Body Thief* (1992), and *Memnoch the Devil* (1995). Coppola's redemptive view of Dracula pales next to Rice's, whose vampires are romantic, aristocratic, elegant, and erudite aesthetes, predators who are always erotic and occasionally ethical (Lestat and some of his companions occasionally boast of feeding only on murderers), and in many ways deeply fascinated with humanity, despite being forever excluded from it. In fact, as the following analysis will show, Rice's vampires are the immortal custodians of Western culture, that realm of aesthetic endeavor that capitalism has always imagined as the repository of its conscience, "the site where a disinterested concern for formal beauty and emotional authenticity could be protected from the relentless commodifications of consumer capitalism."[5] Her vampires are, ultimately, humanists.

> In its terrible excitement it should make a widespread reputation and much money for you.
>
> LETTER FROM CHARLOTTE STOKER TO SON BRAM, 1897[6]

To call Rice's vampires humanists is not to say that they are not interested in or surrounded by wealth. They are awash in it, in fact, and over time their centuries-old investments have matured and produced incalculable interest. Most of Rice's cast plow the money back into art and real estate and luxurious furnishings and airplanes and limousines, in addition to the traditonal black velvet capes. They are vampires for the

1980s, surely: Lestat's first move when he rises from the earth in 1984 New Orleans (where he had been performing the vampiric equivalent of hibernation for a half century) is to find himself a lawyer who helps procure him a birth certificate, driver's license, and social security card, and who gets him access to the "old wealth" waiting in "coded accounts in the immortal Bank of London and the Rothschild Bank."[7] That these institutions are described as "immortal"—a word elsewhere reserved for the vampires themselves ("I am the Vampire Lestat. I'm immortal. More or less," read the opening lines of *The Vampire Lestat*)—demonstrates the intimate connection between Rice's vampires and wealth.[8] The association is certainly evident in *Dracula*, where the count's castle is littered with coins and jeweled ornaments (66), but there the process of accumulation is almost magical; the gold is gathered from those places in the forest where fairy lights mark buried treasure, as Dracula explains (33). In Rice's novels the possession of wealth is more natural, or rather naturalized; whereas the initial accumulation comes from the plunder of human victims, over time the money is thoroughly laundered by institutions and intermediaries that direct it into the antiseptic "coded accounts." If, like Dracula, Lestat must seek out his own Jonathan Harker to assist in the initial transactions, we should note that he is put in possession of a great hoard in 1780s Paris by his maker vampire Magnus (who immediately immolates himself, though presumably not out of guilt over his own cupidity). Lestat is already once removed from the process of accumulation when he sets out to find a sufficiently greedy lawyer who will help him administer his "inheritance" and transform illegitimate gains into legitimate wealth.[9]

Moretti quotes *Dracula*'s Mina Harker on the uses to which such wealth might be put: watching her allies work puts her in mind of "the wonderful power of money! What can it not do when it is properly applied; and what might it do when basely used" (376). In Moretti's interpretation this distinction is ultimately a false one, part of the "great ideological lie" that the novel seeks to obscure. Given this indictment, it might seem naive for me to claim that what distinguishes Rice's vampires from Stoker's is what the former spend their money on. But in accordance with what Jameson has identified as "the logic of late capitalism," that is precisely what I wish to argue.

Though Rice's vampires "tend to be a rather materialistic lot," as one of their critics charges in *The Queen of the Damned*,[10] they are also as a rule generous to their human relatives and favorites, and prodigal tippers. But mostly they use their wealth to maintain an elegant and elevated style of living that is based not on conspicuous consumption—indeed, the last thing a vampire (with the exception of Lestat) wants to be is conspicuous—or on the ascetic Protestant ethic that Moretti attributes to Dracula,[11] but on an adherence to aesthetic principles as the surest bulwark against an uncertain (if unending) world. As Lestat says, "We live in a world of accidents finally, in which only aesthetic principles have a consistency of which we can be sure" (*QD* 6), and it is in pursuit of those principles that Rice's vampires spend their time, energy, and fabulous riches. They are, as noted above, aesthetes, and their dwellings—with the exception of the usually unadorned crypts—reflect not only taste and style but a sense of mission, as if to be a vampire is to be a curator of culture. "Kingdoms rise and fall," reflects Lestat. "Just don't burn the paintings in the Louvre, that's all" (*VL* 273).

Thus Rice fills her texts with vampire dwellings that are virtual museums: Maharet's compound in Sonoma filled with Mayan, Hittite, and Etruscan art, as well as six thousand years of genealogical records (*QD* 140); Armand's Night Island, the home of the vampire coven at the end of *The Queen of the Damned*, where they admire artworks by Matisse, Monet, Picasso, Giotto, Gericault, Morandi, and Piero della Francesca while listening to Bach and Vivaldi (*QD* 462, 466); and most impressively the various homes of Marius, the most refined of the vampires. His eighteenth-century Aegean hideaway is a literal museum, full of Grecian urns and Oriental statues, Persian carpets, stuffed beasts and birds, giant murals, an enormous room housing a menagerie and aviary and conservatory, an immense library filled with manuscripts and books and newspapers and globes and busts and fossils, and an eighteenth-century salon, with rosewood paneling, framed mirrors, painted chests, porcelain clocks, and upholstered chairs (*VL* 373–75).

What this aesthetic eclecticism represents—what it accomplishes in *The Vampire Chronicles*—is, I would argue, a purification of capital similar to the process Moretti sees at work in *Dracula*. In our era, however, this purification depends not on the identification and subsequent expulsion of a monstrous representative of "misused" capital, but on an identification between the previously discrete realms of commerce and culture. Capital is purified not by its separation from but by its association with the aesthetic and cultural realm represented by this vampiric connoisseurship, or alternately, by "the dissolution of an autonomous sphere of culture" and its absorption into the social realm.[12] Vampirism is the device that enables this fusion, specifically through the immortality it brings. Adjusting to immortality is the chief preoccupation of Lestat and his cohorts—more of a preoccupation, I would argue, than the drinking of blood, the necessity for which declines as Rice's vampires become truly old. Rice's apologetics for the figure of the vampire now come into focus: the older and wiser her vampires become, the less parasitic and more aesthetic grow their tastes and needs, and the more important they seem to the preservation of art and music and literature.[13]

Their immortality makes possible a certain gothicism of taste and habits, and here I mean gothicism in the architectural sense, as it applies to a cathedral that combines several generations of styles without descending to aesthetic incoherence. One would be tempted to call this vampiric habit consciously postmodern in its eclecticism, were it not so resolutely focused on high-culture texts and artifacts and the experience of the high points of Western history.[14] Rice's vampires form a small elite group whose *curricula vitae* are literally a syllabus of Western civilization: there's Marius, the historian from Augustan Rome who as a young vampire walked in the library at Alexandria (libraries are a recurrent setting in the novels), later became a painter in Quattrocento Venice in the company of "Giambono, Uccello, the Vivarini and the Bellini" (*VL* 293), and still later directed films in early-twentieth-century Hollywood; Khayman, one of the most ancient of vampires, whose presence in ancient Miletus, Athens, and Troy now subjects him to the fascinated inquiries of the youngest member of the coven; Armand, a collector of paintings who, thanks to Lestat's influence, managed the Theatre des Vampires in eighteenth- and nineteenth-century Paris; and of course Lestat himself, son of a marquis in prerevolutionary France who embarks on the grand tour with his mother Gabrielle (also now a vampire) to visit the monuments and museums and cathedrals of the West and Asia Minor and Egypt, before becoming a plantation owner in nineteenth-century Louisiana and a rock star in 1980s San Francisco.

That Rice's vampires are essentially an aristocratic group is confirmed repeatedly throughout the *Chronicles.* Marius assures Lestat that they were both "chosen for immortality for the very same reason . . . that we were nonpareils of our blond and blue-eyed race, that we were taller and more finely made than other men" (*VL* 384). They are Aryans, unlike "the big ape of vampires, the hirsute Slav Count Dracula," as Lestat later calls him during a brief survey of nineteenth-century vampire fiction (*VL* 500). Marius will later wonder, in the presence of a dozen immortals "from the newborn to the most ancient," "was nobody ugly ever given immortality?" (*QD* 277–78). And one narrative movement of the *Chronicles* is a relentless elimination of those who fail to measure up to these high vampire standards, from the ragged revenants of the secretive Paris coven in *The Vampire Lestat* to the semiliterate rogue vampires of *The Queen of the Damned*—Baby Jenks and the Fang Gang, whose greatest mistake may be their propensity to mock the habits of big-city vampires who wear three-piece suits and listen to classical music.

Although the foray into the world of rock music with which *The Vampire Lestat* begins might seem to play toward more popular interests than the usual elite culture of the vampires, Lestat is nevertheless a living (or rather, undead) example of this gothicism in both style and substance. Within days of his awakening into the twentieth century we find him riding around New Orleans on "a big black Harley-Davidson motorcycle," dressed in black leather but paradoxically listening to Bach's "Art of the Fugue" on a Sony Walkman, indulging both his modern and his eighteenth-century tastes (*VL* 6; it's not surprising that Lestat will later refer to himself as "the James Bond of vampires" [*QD* 7], given that, like Bond, he is very deft at both product placement and the fulfillment of adolescent male fantasies of appetite and power). Even Lestat's English is explained as a function of the diverse influences he has come under in two hundred years: "everybody from Shakespeare through Mark Twain to H. Rider Haggard" has influenced him, and he talks, he says, like a cross between an eighteenth-century Mississippi flatboatmen and Sam Spade (*VL* 4). But we are to understand that he has also discussed Diderot and Voltaire and Rousseau (*VL* 46) and read Cicero, Ovid, and Lucretius (*VL* 382), like any gentleman of the Enlightenment.

Rice's vampires, Lestat especially, are on a grand tour through history, from *The Spectator* (where Lestat's acting on the Paris stage receives notice in the 1780s) to MTV (where his rock videos play incessantly in the 1980s). They both appreciate and in a literal way embody the syncretism that characterizes the late twentieth century, in which "the old was not being routinely replaced by the new anymore."

> In the art and entertainment worlds all prior centuries were being recycled. Musicians performed Mozart as well as jazz and rock music; people went to see Shakespeare one night and a new French film the next....
> In the bookstores Renaissance poetry sold side by side with the novels of Dickens and Hemmingway. Sex manuals lay on the same tables as the Egyptian book of the Dead. (*VL* 8–9)

What for Lestat is a brave new world is from a more critical perspective a postmodern world in which music and literature are thoroughly commodified, though for Rice and her vampires that commodification is largely unproblematic. To characterize it, as Lestat does, as a guarantor of equal access proving that "the old aristocratic sensuality now belonged to everybody" (*VL* 8) is to subscribe to the "great ideological lie" of late capitalism, which holds that the traditional boundary between the incompatible realms of "dead" capital and "living" art can be dismantled without significant disturbance to either field. But, as we shall see, this position cannot be maintained without a victim, a scapegoat who can be made to bear the weight of the contradiction involved in simultaneously affirming and exposing the traditional belletristic humanism of Rice's vampires.

> Lestat is smack-dab in the middle of it now for me. He's reinventing himself all the time, just like Madonna.
>
> ANNE RICE, interview, 1993[15]

Rice's fanciful vampires exist at the boundary and represent, as I have argued, this formerly secret marriage of capital and culture. Their monstrous nature, however elegantly manifested, derives from their blurring of those previously sacred boundaries. For Rice, however, this is all once again relatively unproblematic so far; after all, according to her mythology vampires have for thousands of years easily assimilated themselves into human society and history. We have always accepted this monstrous figure—or rather, we have traditionally found it easy to ignore, allegedly because the vampires have always insisted on absolute secrecy among themselves, and have always forbidden particularly the writing down of any vampiric secrets. The truth, I would argue—and Lestat's later actions prove the point—is that the status of the vampire as imagined by Rice has always been an open secret, tacitly acknowledged and tacitly ignored.[16] In the context of the fiction, Lestat is able to attribute his easy assimilation to the "rational eighteenth-century habit of mind" (*VL* 125) and to the human preference for the "natural explanation":

> And this is a lesson about mortal peace of mind I never forgot. Even if a ghost is ripping a house to pieces, throwing tin pans all over, pouring water on pillows, making clocks chime at all hours, mortals will accept almost any "natural explanation" offered, no matter how absurd, rather than the obvious supernatural one, for what is going on. (*VL* 254)

Beyond this relatively benign poltergeist, on the level of the allegory of capital, this comfortable coexistence can be seen as the product of ideology rather than nature, and it consists of our means "neglecting (or of dismissing as peripheral) that relentless transformation of art works into commodities, within the dominant forms of capitalist society."[17] What these different levels of willful ignorance have in common—what unites mortal preference, neglect, dismissal—is what we might call the fiction of secrecy, the collective capacity to deny that what is palpably true can possibly be real, whether it is the existence of vampires (in the fiction) or the commodification of art (in the world).[18]

It is just this fiction that Lestat challenges by becoming the enormously popular and seductive "Monsieur le Rock Star" known as the Vampire Lestat, and by writing his "autobiography" (Rice's conceit for *The Vampire Lestat*). He threatens to reveal everything about the vampires' existence, to tell all, and thus implicitly to expose the inner workings of this monstrous marriage between the aesthetic and the economic. It is no surprise that he chooses rock music as his vehicle, as one of the major factors working for the success of his enterprise is money—vast sums of it, buying the best equipment, hiring the best producers, luring "the best French directors for the rock video films" (*VL* 14). Money is no object to Lestat, and in the thoroughly corporate world of popular music it can buy success, although Lestat the aesthete will ultimately attribute that success to his own "vision" and his compelling vampire nature.[19] We have seen, however, what it means to be a vampire now.

Of course, many of the vampires that are not part of Lestat's charmed circle of immortal friends object to this idea, this scandalous revelation of their parasitic nature and the illusions about the world that their secrecy presumably makes possible. They threaten Lestat and decry his ambitions and promise to derail his plans. But these skulking vampires are villains from Lestat's perspective, and from Rice's—which puts her in something of a bind at the end of *The Vampire Lestat.* She clearly cannot sacrifice her romantic hero, the "James Bond of vampires," but neither can she depict contemporary capitalist society as fundamentally reformed by his revelations in a novel that, despite its supernatural premises, nevertheless strives to ground itself firmly in the historical world of the 1980s, the world of MTV and limousines and the Pacific Coast Highway. Rice's historical realism, if I may be allowed to call it that, seems to foreclose the possibility of a utopian solution, and Lestat's music seems to promise anything but a spurious harmony.

But in fact it is a different kind of verisimilitude that creates Rice's true difficulty in *The Vampire Lestat,* for what Lestat reveals about vampires and their nature has virtually no effect on his human audience, which refuses to believe that his act is anything but art. And this is the most scandalous (if most truthful) possibility, and the real premise of *The Vampire Chronicles*: that in the 1980s the monstrous might appear *not* to be monstrous, that the most profound revelations might be met with the most perfect indifference—that we might know the truth and prefer to remain enslaved, or at least complicit in its suppression. This indifference is perfectly consonant with the excesses of postmodernism as described by Jameson, which "no longer scandalize anyone and are not only received with the greatest complacency but have themselves become institutionalized and are at one with the official or public culture of Western society."[20] Thus Lestat's desire to start a "great and glorious war" with humanity by forcing humankind to confront the truth of the existence of vampires is doomed to failure—"real revelation and disaster" (*VL* 18) are proscribed not by the world's aversion to violence and vampirism (the stuff of the videos, after all, and the autobiography) but by its prior complicity in their creation.

This is not, however, the sort of message one regularly finds encoded in a popular horror novel. To conclude here would be to make *The Vampire Lestat* into an oppositional text in its own right, offering the sort of insight that could contribute to the fashioning of a utopian solution for its readers, if not its characters. It has exposed a contradiction—and now it must endeavor to cover it back up.

—PLAYBOY: You're clearly not in sympathy with Catharine MacKinnon or Andrea Dworkin, who have proposed recent antipornography legislation.

—RICE: I think they're absolute fools.

Playboy interview, 1993

Rice's solution to this difficulty is a masterstroke of displacement, a perverse and brilliant move given the tradition in which she is working. She creates a figure that will seem monstrous to the monsters and completely displaces the anxiety generated by Lestat's threatened revelations onto Akasha, the eldest of the vampires, in *The Queen of the Damned.* Lestat and his immortal allies, "from the newly born to the most ancient," rally together to defeat the Queen of the Damned, turning her into the *Vampire Chronicles'* Dracula—a monstrous figure opposed by a band of stout and committed humanists who just happen to be vampires themselves, united—as they eventually claim—in the name of preserving the "Human Family" from the one true predator. Even the narration of *The Queen of the Damned,* with its multiplicity of narrators (as opposed to the single voice of *The Vampire Lestat*) moves closer to *Dracula*'s heterogeneous formal style, as the narrative turns from embracing the monster to expelling it. In the movement from *Lestat* to *Queen*—indeed, beginning with *Interview with the Vampire*—Rice enacts the "triple rhythm" that Christopher Craft has identified as an essential formal scheme in such gothic novels as *Frankenstein, Dracula,* and *Dr. Jekyll and Mr. Hyde.* "Each of these texts," Craft writes, "first invites or admits a monster, then entertains and is entertained by monstrosity for some extended duration, until in its closing pages it expels or repudiates the monster and all the disruption that he/she/it brings."[21] Rice, who has expressed her desire to be remembered as working in "darkness" and "romance" along with Hawthorne, Poe, the Brontës, and Mary Shelley,[22] has evidently grasped the formal strategies of the tradition, although she extends the process over three volumes.

Of course, Rice does not expel exactly the same monster she invites in; the lingering embrace of Lestat is balanced not by her repudiation of him—indeed, he returns to star in two more volumes—but by the destruction of Akasha. Why this change? The answer is best sought through another question: Why Akasha?

Awakened from a centuries-long sleep by Lestat's videos, Akasha finds the modern world awash in all those things the more urbane vampires overlook: hunger, poverty, war, disease. Attempting to educate Lestat, who is utterly smitten by his Queen, she ferries him to one poor miserable ghetto after another, to scenes that, after several hundred pages of civilized vampire comfort, are quite arresting.

> She spoke slowly, close to my ear. "Shall I recite the poetry of names?" she asked. "Calcutta, if you wish, or Ethiopia; or the streets of Bombay; these

> poor souls could be the peasants of Sri Lanka; of Pakistan; of Nicaragua, of El Salvador. It does not matter what it is; it matters how much there is of it; that all around the oases of your shining Western cities it exists; it is three-fourths of the world! Open your ears, my darling." (*QD* 302)

Claiming that art does not matter, that history does not matter (*QD* 368), deriding the "idiot foolishness on which the complacency of the rich has always been based" (*QD* 442), Akasha embarks on an ambitious and appalling program of social engineering to alleviate the situation. Her solution is to kill off ninety-nine of every one hundred males in the world, and thus to put an end to the patriarchal hierarchy that has for so long promoted and glorified war and violence. Women, who are by their nature not attracted to violence, will then remake the world into a pacifist Eden. "Women are women!" she tells Lestat.

> Can you conceive of war made by women? Truly, answer me. Can you? Can you conceive of bands of roving women intent only on destruction? Or rape? Such a thing is preposterous. . . . The possibility of peace on earth has always existed, and there have always been people who could realize it, and preserve it, and those people are women. If one takes away the men. (*QD* 371)

And this she begins to do, in scenes of orgiastic carnage set in Sri Lanka, the Aegean, Nepal, Haiti; she is aided at first by an infatuated Lestat, whom she holds up to the female survivors as the essence of despicable masculinity: "Aggressive, full of hate and recklessness, and endlessly eloquent excuses for violence" (*QD* 369).

Thus for Rice the greatest threat to the monstrous status quo and its humanist aesthetic turns out to be a monstrous, hyperbolic feminism, reduced to (unintentional) parody in Akasha's essentialist, separatist dogma.[23] Though the other vampires show an occasional modicum of troubled ambivalence[24]—Lestat at one point acknowledging that Akasha was "absolutely right and absolutely wrong" (*QD* 367), and Marius later charitably admitting that the world is not yet perfect—it is clear once Akasha embarks on her crusade that she must be destroyed.

Throughout the *Queen of the Damned* the abstract nature of Akasha's "militantly feminist principles"[25] is contrasted with the maternal wisdom and experience of Maharet, her enemy of nearly six thousand years and the only vampire who has "never slept, never gone silent, never been released by madness" (*QD* 267), the "true immortal." She evinces a "deep, soft femininity" as opposed to Akasha's imperious, strident demeanor, and plays the Good Mother to Akasha's Bad.[26] And—lo and behold—Maharet is *literally* a mother, having borne a daughter just before her transformation into a vampire in ancient Egypt. Her preoccupation over the ensuing millennia—ultimately, her raison d'être—has been maintaining the records of this daughter's descendants, traced through the maternal line, and promoting the growth and good fortune of what she calls the Great Family.

The Great Family has become, of course, the literal embodiment of the human race, as Maharet explains to her cohorts.

> No people, no race, no country does not contain some of the Great Family. The Great Family is Arab, Jew, Anglo, African; it is Indian; it is Mongolian; it is Japanese and Chinese. In sum, the Great Family is the human family. (*QD* 428)

"This is what is threatened now," realizes Marius (*QD* 429)—this utopian projection of all races and nations harmonized is what the remaining immortals have come together to protect from Akasha's depredations. The boldness of the transformation Rice works here astonishes: in the virtual blink of an eye, her vampires go from disinterested aesthetes to merciful saviors of humanity (and, in the conclusion, back again). Akasha's one field of relevance, her alleged concern for human social welfare as administered through the family in general and motherhood in particular (she does not discourage the women who witness her deeds from regarding her as the Virgin Mary), is discovered to have been preemptively colonized by Rice's postmodern vampires. *The Vampire Lestat* begins with Lestat claiming that "the poverty and filth that had been common in the big cities of the earth since time immemorial were almost completely washed away" (*VL* 8), and although Akasha proves him definitively and incontrovertibly wrong in the *Queen of the Damned*, it simply doesn't matter. Lestat's cohorts turn out to have already invested in sympathy and charity, with an option on maternity—although they have oddly neglected to mention it before now. The late capitalism of Rice's immortals is defined by the commodification not only of art, but also of benevolence.

With Akasha's defeat comes the return of the status quo ante—the same horrifying and "secret" marriage of metaphors, the vampire as parasitic capitalist and the vampire as preserver, arbiter, and (perversely) creator of aesthetic culture. At the end of *The Queen of the Damned*, the coven has moved to Miami. There Daniel listens to Bach, Armand and Khayman play chess, and Marius reads the newspaper in the elegant surroundings of Night Island, a combination mansion and shopping mall financed and built by the vampire Armand, whose capital came from robbing drug smugglers off the Florida coast and recovering lost or stolen masterpieces. On one side of a steel door sits the vampires' villa, richly appointed as always, a realm of elevated if not disinterested aestheticism; on the other lies a thriving entertainment complex of shops, restaurants, and cinemas, a consumer's paradise, a world of commerce. The door may be locked, but it opens to a key—Lestat has one—and thus the membrane between worlds is represented as completely permeable. But then—and this I take to be the meaning of *The Vampire Chronicles* to date—we already knew that.[27]

Notes

1. Franco Moretti, "The Dialectic of Fear," *New Left Review* 136 (1982): 68. The essay is reprinted in Moretti's *Signs Taken for Wonders*, trans. Susan Fischer et al. (London: Verso, 1983). Moretti's insight is based in part on Marx's use of the term *vampire* to refer to the noxious economic activity of capitalism: "Capital is dead labour which, vampire-like, lives only by sucking living labour, and lives the more, the more labour it sucks" (quoted by Moretti, 73). Marx's metaphor itself is a venerable one: the first recorded use of the word in English, in 1679, is quickly followed in 1688 by its metaphorical application to "the Vampires of the Publick, the Riflers of the Kingdom," merchants who export currency. See Katharina M. Wilson, "The History of the Word 'Vampire,'" *Journal of the History of Ideas* 46 (1985): 580–81.

2. Moretti, "The Dialectic of Fear," 68.

3. Ibid., 75.

4. Fredric Jameson, *Postmodernism; or, The Cultural Logic of Late Capitalism* (Durham, N.C.: Duke University Press, 1991), 36; he is citing Ernest Mandel's *Late Capitalism* (London: Verso, 1978).

5. Lee Patterson (paraphrasing Raymond Williams), "Literary History," in *Critical Terms for Literary Study*, ed. Frank Lentricchia and Thomas McLaughlin (Chicago: University of Chicago Press, 1990), 258. Williams himself writes, "We can then see more clearly the ideological function of the specializing abstractions of 'art' and 'the aesthetic.' . . . 'Art' is a kind of production which has to be seen as separate from the dominant bourgeois productive norm: the making of commodities. It has then, in fantasy, to be separated from 'production' altogether; described by the new term 'creation'; distinguished from its own material processes; distinguished, finally, from other products of its own kind or closely related kinds—'art' from 'non-art'; 'literature' from 'para-literature' or 'popular literature'; 'culture' from 'mass culture.'

The narrowing abstraction is then so powerful that, in its name, we find ways of neglecting (or of dismissing as peripheral) that relentless transformation of art works into commodities, within the dominant forms of capitalist society." *Marxism and Literature* (Oxford: Oxford University Press, 1977), 153. On the irony of Rice's characters adopting this position in a popular novel I will have more to say below. It is no coincidence, I would argue, that the birth of this aesthetic realm and Lestat's transformation from mortal man into vampire occur in roughly the same era, the late eighteenth century.

6. This passage from a letter from Charlotte Stoker to her son Bram, on the publication of *Dracula* in 1897, is quoted in Maurice Hindle's introduction to Stoker's *Dracula* (New York: Penguin, 1993), vii. Page numbers in text references to this work refer to this edition.

7. Anne Rice, *The Vampire Lestat* (New York: Ballantine, 1985), 7. Page numbers for further references to this work appear in text and notes with the abbreviation *VL*.

8. Later Lestat will tell his mother Gabrielle—by this point herself a vampire—"Those banks have lived as long as vampires already. They will always be there" (*VL* 353).

9. Rice almost never shows her chief vampires robbing their victims; when such an event does occur, the economic motive is usually somehow displaced—as when the newly made Gabrielle steals the clothes of a young male victim in order to disguise her gender (*VL* 170–71).

10. Anne Rice, *The Queen of the Damned* (New York: Ballantine, 1989), 174. Page numbers for further references to this work appear in text and notes with the abbreviation *QD*. The charge is leveled by David Talbot, leader of the Talamasca, a centuries-old organization dedicated to the study of supernatural phenomena—which ironically operates out of an elegantly appointed, luxuriously furnished Elizabethan manor house outside London. Perhaps not surprisingly, it is Talbot's fate at the end of *The Tale of the Body Thief* to become one of Lestat's vampire children.

11. Moretti, "The Dialectic of Fear," 73.

12. This dissolution, says Jameson, is better imagined as an explosion: "a prodigious expansion of culture throughout the social realm, to the point at which everything in our social life—from economic value and state power to practices and to the very practice of the psyche itself—can be said to have become 'cultural' in some original and yet untheorized sense." *Postmodernism*, 48.

13. The connections among vampirism, death, and literacy are made early in *The Vampire Lestat.* The novel's first Paris scene takes place in the cemetery of les Innocents, "with its old vaults and stinking open graves," where the illiterate Lestat finds a scribe to whom he can dictate a letter to his mother.

In Lestat's first encounter with his maker Magnus, vampirism is specifically allied with literacy itself. In the dreamlike swoon brought on by Magnus's bite, the illiterate Lestat revisits a scene from his youth endowed with a new power: "And I was sitting in the monastery library and I was twelve years old and the monk said to me, 'A great scholar,' and I opened all the books and I could read everything, Latin, Greek, French. The illuminated letters were indescribably beautiful" (*VL* 82). A few months later, the vampire Lestat realizes suddenly that he has actually acquired literacy, by a kind of osmosis: "One night in March, I realized as Roget read my mother's letter to me that

I could read as well as he could. I had learned from a thousand sources how to read without even trying" (*VL* 127).

14. Dracula, too, turns out to have been a defender of the West, as he says twice—once to Jonathan Harker and once to Mina Harker when he seeks to vampirize her: "Whilst they played wits against me—against me who commanded nations, and intrigued for them, and fought for them, hundreds of years before they were born—I was countermining them" (370). For centuries, Dracula had declared to Harker, his people guarded the Turkish frontier and represented Christian Europe's last line of defense against Islamic invasion, a claim that tends to collapse Harker's notion of the boundary between East and West. The count delivers an extensive dissertation on his family's (and his own) exploits in these wars in chapter 3, concluding with the declaration, "Ah, young sir, the Szekelys—and the Dracula as their heart's blood, their brains, and their swords—can boast a record that mushroom growths like the Hapsburgs and Romanoffs can never reach" (43). This hubris is never explicitly challenged in the novel. Once again—or, with respect to Rice, once before—the vampire has articulated his immanence to the very Western civilization he is perceived as threatening. For a brief account of the political theme in *Dracula*, see Richard Wasson, "The Politics of *Dracula*," *English Literature in Transition* 9 (1966): 24–27.

15. Anne Rice, quoted in Cynthia Robins, "Queen of the Night: Why Anne Rice has Her Teeth in America's Neck," *San Francisco Examiner Image Magazine* (October 31, 1993), 15.

16. Rice claims that "the Chronicles are about how all of us feel about being outsiders. How we feel that we're really outsiders in a world where everybody else understands something that we don't." "*Playboy* Interview: Anne Rice," *Playboy* (March 1993), 64. The idea of an "open secret" is the subtext of this remark. Rhonda Rockwell has suggested to me that the novels' homoeroticism, often coyly characterized as androgyny by Rice herself, also falls into this category. See also note 18 below.

In a sense, the "open secret" concept of vampirism derives from the first complete English vampire story, Polidori's "The Vampyre; A Tale," published in 1819. There the protagonist, Aubrey, discovers that Lord Ruthven is a vampire when he watches Ruthven die in Greece and then sees him reappear on the London social circuit months later. But Ruthven with his dying breath had gotten Aubrey to swear to keep the fact of his death a secret for a year and a day, and, bound by his oath (which Ruthven takes pains to remind him of), Aubrey cannot prevent Ruthven from paying court to and ultimately proposing marriage to Aubrey's sister. Aubrey dies insane, driven mad by his secret, and Miss Aubrey becomes the vampire's latest victim.

17. Williams, *Marxism and Literature*, 154.

18. See Louis Althusser's remark from *Reading Capital* that "what classical political economy does not see, is not what it does not see, it is *what it sees*"; (quoted in Michael Sprinker, *Imaginary Relations: Aesthetics and Ideology in the Theory of Historical Materialism* (London: Verso, 1987), 275. For an exegesis of the ideological power of the "open secret" that tries to go beyond Althusser and Machery, see D. A. Miller, *The Novel and the Police* (Berkeley: University of California Press, 1988), especially chap. 6, "Secret Subjects, Open Secrets."

19. Although Rice herself claims that "rock music is perhaps the only universally influential art form to rise from the proletariat" (in Katherine Ramsland, *The*

Vampire Companion: The Official Guide to Anne Rice's The Vampire Chronicles [New York: Ballantine, 1993], 26), the music of *VL* seems as much the product of high production values as of any aesthetic power; Lestat himself repeatedly dismisses the lyrics as "puerile" (*VL* 537). But elsewhere Rice seems cagier about the state of popular music nowadays: "MTV has taken Madonna and Michael into the living room. The astonishing thing is that they have taken all of this counterculture imagery and made it mainstream" (quoted in Robins, "Queen of the Night," 15). Perhaps we can say that Lestat's efforts are simply well timed, and quote Jameson again: "What has happened is that aesthetic production today has become integrated into commodity production generally: the frantic economic urgency of producing fresh waves of ever more novel-seeming goods (from clothing to airplanes), at ever greater rates of turnover, now assigns an increasingly essential structural function and position to aesthetic innovation and experimentation." *Postmodernism*, 4–5.

20. Jameson, *Postmodernism*, 4.

21. Christopher Craft, "'Kiss Me with Those Red Lips': Gender and Inversion in Bram Stoker's *Dracula*," *Representations* 8 (1984): 107. The parallel between Rice's series and Shelley's novel is particularly apt, because *Frankenstein* introduces us to a monster (and Lestat is made to seem monstrous by the narrator of *Interview with the Vampire*), lets the now articulate monster tell his own story (as in the "autobiographical" *VL*), then proceeds to expel the monster (as in *QD*).

22. Robins, "Queen of the Night," 12.

23. For a different and more detailed analysis of Akasha's (and Rice's) feminism considered along the preoedipal/oedipal axis, see Devon Hodges and Janice Doane, "Undoing Feminism in Anne Rice's Vampire Chronicles," in *Modernity and Mass Culture*, ed. James Naremore and Patrick Brantlinger (Bloomington: Indiana University Press, 1991), 158–75. I have not dealt with the issue of the sexuality of Rice's vampires at all here; this essay is a good place to start on that topic.

24. This ambivalence mirrors that in Rice's own self-acknowledged "feminism," evident in those moments in her *Playboy* interview (!) where she moves from dismissing Catharine MacKinnon and Andrea Dworkin as "absolute fools" (56) to acknowledging that there has never been a time "when women have been so vulnerable to rape" (56) and calling for the fullest extent of legal protection: "You cannot tell women that the price of equality is that they might get raped" (58).

25. The phrase, used without irony, is Katharine Ramsland's, from *The Vampire Companion*, 4. This $30 volume, published by Ballantine (which also publishes the mass-market paperback editions of Rice's novels), is a strange cross between *The Tolkien Companion* (and other guides to fictional universes) and E. D. Hirsch's *Dictionary of Cultural Literacy*: a thousand-plus-entry glossary offering "an insightful exploration, appreciation, and interpretation of all the characters and events, names and places, symbols and themes" in the *Chronicles*, as the dust jacket claims, "written with the full cooperation of Anne Rice." Dedicated to establishing the philosophical and psychological seriousness of Rice's novels, Ramsland—who is also Rice's biographer—peppers the *Companion* with entries on abandonment, the absurd, conformity, dominance/submission, evil, free will, guilt, inversion, nihilism, passivity, transvaluation, and victim psychology, and discusses the symbolic resonance of horses, gates, dogs, oceans, rats, stairways, towers, windows, wine, and wolves, to

name a few. (The importance of the symbol to romantic aesthetic theory ought to be noted here; Ramsland subscribes to the same brand of aesthetics as do Rice's vampires.) Occasionally Ramsland's vehemence gets the better of her; thus, in the entry on Nietzsche (whose name appears nowhere in the *Chronicles*), we read, "Although Rice claims never to have read Nietzsche, the parallels between his ideas and her works are too strong to ignore. And Rice did attend school when existentialism was a pervasive influence on college campuses, so she was exposed—at least in a cursory way—to Nietzsche's ideas" (291).

26. Rice's women characters are all somewhat stereotypical. Lestat's mother, Gabrielle, is an earlier example of this problem (and of Rice's disingenuousness about her vampires' sexuality). When first made immortal, Gabrielle tries to dress and act like a man, and when this effort fails (despite her attempts to cut it, her long hair grows back overnight to the length it was when she was made a vampire—gender essentialism *de la coiffure*), she is slowly edged offstage to go and seek out "natural beauty"—the romantic sublime—which interests her far more than the monuments and cathedrals that fascinate Lestat. She disappears for two hundred pages in *The Vampire Lestat*, and is significantly absent for Marius's long account of his creation and his discovery of the original vampires, Akasha and Enkil.

27. Neither Rice's novels nor Rice herself is immune to the kind of commodification Rice represents within the novels' pages: both she and the Lestat fan club were initially horrified to discover that the bankable but bland Tom Cruise had been cast as Lestat in the 1994 film version of *Interview with the Vampire*, based on Rice's screenplay. After previewing the film, however, Rice changed her tune (perhaps, as one critic suggested, after someone explained the phrase "percentage of gross" to her), taking out two-page advertisements in *Daily Variety* and the *New York Times* to praise the film and Cruise's "courageous" performance, and later, in December 1994, buying more ad space to respond to the film's detractors. The film grossed more than $100 million, though that did not stop Warner Bros. from including a two-minute "Message from Anne Rice" in the videocassette version. In this message, Rice first describes *Interview* as a film "that I love with all my heart" before moving to an unabashed plug for *Memnoch the Devil*, which "could be the last book I ever write with [Lestat]." She concludes by reminding us, somewhat urgently, that the story is "not just about vampires—it's really about us" (Warner Home Video, 1994). I could not agree more.

12 The Alien and Alienated as Unquiet Dead in the Sagas of the Icelanders

William Sayers

In the medieval Icelandic culture of the supernatural, one who recrossed the boundary from death to life was called *aptrgangr* (revenant) or *draugr,* derived from the Indo-European root *dhreugh* (harm, deceive). In the *draugr,* spirit is not breathed into matter so much as material corporeality is retained by the restless spirit. The collected evidence, literary and folkloric, medieval and later, gives a consistent picture of physically active dead beings who bear the earth of the grave or the sodden clothing of death at sea. Not only are their bodies uncorrupted, but in the cases of the physically most active and temperamentally most malevolent, they are larger, heavier, and, above all, stronger than in life, the faces darker and the eyes more terrifying. Our chief early sources for conceptions of the unquiet dead are the family sagas. In this chapter, I examine the purposes to which literary deployment of the *draugr* motif is put in the immediate context of three principal sagas. First, a general sketch, on the basis of cognate material, will give an understanding of the purported nature of the dead who cross life's *limen,* and a ground against which individual revenant figures will later be seen to act.

The Nature of the Dead

Although contact with the earth of the burial site seems to be the source of the swelling and dark color of the *draugar,* these dead have no overt affinity with fertility, as is often the case in agrarian societies in more temperate climates. As in many traditional societies, the Norse dead are thought privy to knowledge not accessible to the living, although in our sources from the Christian era this notion is independent of more formally organized theological conception. Thus Óðinn resuscitated a seeress in order to learn the future of gods and men (*Vǫluspá*); Guðriðr's husband Þorsteinn returns from the dead in the Vinland sagas to predict her future and that of her illustrious descendants in Iceland (*Eiríks saga rauða*, chap. 6; *Grœnlendinga saga*, chap. 6).[1] Perhaps to facilitate and control such mediation, commemorative stones for the dead were often located on boundaries between cultivated fields and the wilderness. As for the emotional tonality of death, heroes are sometimes seen rejoicing inside their lighted howes or mountainsides (e.g., Gunnarr in *Njáls saga*, chap. 78) and the heroic dead join Óðinn in Valhǫll to fight all day and feast all night. The less attractive cold realm of Hel seems, however, to have been the lot of the common dead. The dead are not necessarily ill disposed toward the living. In *Eyrbyggja saga* (chaps. 54ff.) men drowned at sea and farmworkers who succumbed to illness—in both cases for supernatural, possibly magically induced, reasons—return among the living as an envious social nuisance without being actively harmful. The focus in this study, however, will stay with revenants both active and malevolent.

The dead resemble the living in valuing their rest and their property, so that breaking into a grave mound for treasure often results in physical combat in the grave with the deceased (*Harðar saga*, chap. 15). Given that the grave dweller is activated by the intrusion, death seems a latent state from which corpses could be provoked by the living or drawn back by spiritual contagion if they were themselves a *draugr*'s victim. In examples to be considered below, a more important stimulus to such interaction lies in the spiritual disposition of the *draugr* before death, a sense of incomplete disengagement from life's affairs that is reflected in the arrested organic processes in the grave. Consonant with other dichotomies of early medieval life in the North, *draugar* favor the cold and dark of the long autumn and winter nights for their haunting. They seem tied to the geographic areas of their burial sites and former lives, and in their often stagewise return from distant graves to their communities, they kill livestock and shepherds, then household servants, and often end by riding the rooftrees of the farmhouses, a metonym of human culture in the North, terrorizing the residents and seemingly intent on bringing down the buildings. In general, their crossing of the boundary back into life is accompanied by only elemental human functioning, that is, recognition of human interests and artifacts, which they seek to destroy, but no use of weapons or tools. Predatory and destructive only, they are not consumers of life's bounty. The conflict of the dead with the living is, however, conspecific. Although the *draugar* may display affinities with the trolls and other malevolent emanations of the natural world, their appearance is human, their actions partake of the human world, and on occasion they are capable of speech. But material destruction is more common than conversation, wrestling more usual than rhetoric, although variance from this pattern could be turned to great stylistic effect. Sorcerers and the uncanny make up a special subset of revenants. Like some archaic warriors found in the early, ancestral chapters of the sagas, they are capable of shape-shifting after death. Sea mammals, perhaps because of their amphibious and thus dual nature, are a preferred form (Þórveig in *Kormáks saga,* chap. 18).

The intense corporeality of the *draugr* has consequences not only for his actions but also for his disablement. Typically, a corpse was removed through a temporarily breached wall in the house, to prevent easy reentry, and interred at some distance from the cultivated area around the farmhouse, often under a cairn, to prevent resurgence (*Heiðarvíga saga,* chap. 9; *Eyrbyggja saga,* chap. 34). More aggressive and less honorable solutions were practiced on the socially inferior or otherwise marginalized. In cases where future revenant activity might be suspected from the outset—for example, sorcerers who had been put to death—the bodies might be sunk at sea (*Laxdœla saga,* chap. 37) or burned and the ashes scattered on the seashore or at sea (*Laxdœla saga,* chap. 24; *Eyrbyggja saga,* chap. 63). The objective was to deconstruct the dead physically, to eliminate the vehicle for a renascent spirit. Another impediment was dismemberment, typically the severing of the head from the body (*Flóamanna saga,* chap. 13). Decapitation was a physical remedy; in one instance (treated below), legally evicting the revenants was a social remedy. These two approaches are combined in scenes that have been under-evaluated, such as those in which the *draugr*'s head is cut off and placed at his buttocks.

Áns saga bogsveigis, although drawn from the "romances of antiquity" (*fornaldarsǫgur*), in its coarse explicitness provides a clue to the interpretation of the social neutralization of the *draugr*: "He hewed his head off and straightened him out and pushed his nose into the cleft [of his buttocks], that he might not come back as a revenant [literally, not walk (as) dead]."[2] Other works describe this action as putting the head between the thighs (*Bárðar saga*, chap. 20; compare *Grettis saga*, chaps. 18, 35, and the similar humiliating position forced on prisoners as a cruel practical joke in *Fljótsdœla saga*, chap. 13). To interpret this method of forestalling revenant activity, we must consider the specific nature of medieval Norse acts of public shaming. These included the erection of a *níðstǫng* (pole of defamation), which might carry the spitted body of a mare or a horse's head or the carving of men engaged in sodomy; and the circulation of scurrilous verses, or simply coarse defamatory statements, about an individual's passive homosexual activity with men, trolls, and animals or of a face befouled with excrement as a result of coprophagy. It is the circumstances of this last condition that were created in the position of the *draugr*'s severed head. Brought under the social control of the loss of honor, it was hoped that the *draugr* would shun human company.

The *draugr* episodes in the family sagas reflect popular conceptions of the state of death that have been turned to narrative purpose, either to establish parameters for heroic activity by populating and defining the world the hero conquers or, more ambitiously, to carry thematic concerns. The family sagas are composed according to unstated but consistent criteria that determine the relevance of narrative matter, which might, broadly speaking, be characterized as affecting public policy and social agency, family and factional feud, and individual status and power. As an assertively historical genre that presupposes a comprehensible (if perhaps dated) ethos and provides sufficient narrative and relational detail to authorize audience speculation on psychological states and processes but seldom explicitly illuminates the interior of characters, the family sagas are selective in their use of supernatural effects such as revenants. It is in realistic environments that the circumscribed and generally believable actions of the *draugar* occur. Their corporeality also contributes to credibility, creating a monstrousness not irremediably foreign, although implacably inimical to human life.

Three *Draugr* Biographies

The early chapters of *Laxdœla saga* are dominated by the story of Óláfr Hǫskuldsson, or Óláfr *pái*, "the Peacock," as he came to be called. He is the son of a prominent Icelander and an apparently mute slave girl who proves to be the daughter of an Irish king. Óláfr's youthful years are an effort toward legitimation, first of his aristocratic Irish ancestry, and second of his status in Iceland. Earlier, the saga introduced Víga-Hrappr (Killer-Hrappr), who is characterized as Scottish on his father's side, with his mother's family coming from the Norse communities of the Hebrides, where he had been raised. Strong, overbearing, and intractable, he had fled to Iceland on the heels of his refusal to pay compensation for his misdeeds, but there he had alienated his neighbors by his extortionate behavior. When Hrappr senses that death is approaching, he asks to be buried upright under the floor of the main room of the house, in order to keep an eye on his property. The saga continues:

> And difficult as he had been to deal with during his life, he was now very much worse after death, for his corpse would not rest in its grave; people say that he murdered most of his servants in his hauntings after death, and caused grievous harm to most of his neighbours. The farm at Hrappstead had to be abandoned and Vigdis, Hrapp's widow, went west to her brother Thorstein Black the Wise, who looked after her and her property.[3]

In an effort to put a stop to the haunting, the local chieftain, Óláfr's father, Hǫskuldr, had Hrappr's corpse disinterred and moved to a site far from paths and pastures. This provided some alleviation, but when Hrappr's son Sumarliði took over the family farm, he went mad and soon died. The *draugr* does not draw the line at family members, seemingly denying the inheritance right of his son. Later, when another farmer, Þorsteinn, attempts to resettle Hrappr's farmstead, he is drowned at sea, after seeing a huge seal with human eyes circling the ship. The important consequence of this accident is that a falsified account of the sequence in which men, women, and children perished in the accident later leads to contention over land claims; Hrappstead remains derelict.

Óláfr's social eminence leads to his ambition to take over the rich lands of Hrappstead. He acquires the property at a bargain price and erects a fine house; at the same time, he has unprecedented success both as a stock raiser and as a mediator in others' disputes. When a cowherd asks for other work because of physical attacks by the long-dead Hrappr in the cow barn, Óláfr undertakes to provide a remedy. In the ensuing confrontation, Óláfr thrusts at Hrappr with a fine spear he had been given by the Norwegian king on his trip of self-authentication to Norway and Ireland, but the *draugr* snaps off its point and sinks into the ground. The next day, Óláfr has Hrappr exhumed and finds the corpse undecayed. A pyre is built, the corpse burned, and the ashes scattered at sea, and Hrappr's haunting comes to an end. Ineffectual against Hrappr in combat in the revenant's nocturnal environment, Óláfr is successful against the quiescent *draugr* only in the light of day.

Self-imposed exile or flight from Norway by many of the original settlers and a substantial Celtic slave component in the households of settlers coming to Iceland from Ireland and the Western Isles seem to have marked Icelandic ethnogenesis with an ambivalence toward objects and often persons of Norwegian and Celtic provenance. Despite their prestige, they are not always adequate to the rigors of Icelandic circumstances. In the Hrappr incident this xenophobic doubt is symbolized both in Hrappr's origins and in the gift spear that ineffectually breaks off, although it serves as a provisional deterrent.

But Óláfr's essentially mechanical solution to death's predations on life is not replicated in the larger pattern of events in the saga. The career of the half-Irish Óláfr, for all its material and social success, is marked by instances of indecision, as if his talent as a conciliator in others' affairs leads him to temporize and mediate rather than act swiftly and forthrightly in his own (e.g., failure to oppose his daughter's ill-advised marriage, the consequences of his fosterage of Bolli). Óláfr is also unconscious of the reasons for his success, which has supernatural origins. He has a superb ox, Harri, whose appearance and behavior would have alerted a more astute man to its paranormal character. When the ox shows signs of age, Óláfr has it slaughtered, but is then visited in a dream by a supernatural woman, whose affinities seem to lie with the *landvættir* (land spirits) and who claims to be Harri's mother. Her "Icelandic" favor had assured Óláfr of his good fortune and may even have contributed to his successful elimination of Hrappr. The woman threatens vengeance on Óláfr, saying she will cause the death of his favorite son. These events are the dark preface to the triangle drama of Kjartan Óláfsson, Guðrún, and Bolli that occupies the central portion of the saga. Although the episode of the *draugr* Hrappr seems successfully resolved, like most incidents in the family sagas it is not truly self-contained. Some of its byproducts and residue persist, like the carryover from life into *draugr* status. We may provisionally identify this as a spiritual contagion resulting from interaction with the unquiet dead, and look for its presence and effect in other sagas. From a typological perspective, the dream appearance of Harri's mother and her ominous forecast will also have parallels, as will the motif of the exceptional ox.

Eyrbyggja saga is one of the richest family sagas in terms of deployment of supernatural motifs, although this in itself does not bear directly on theme or guarantee ethnographic accuracy for the period depicted in the work. For example, the rivalry between two "wise women," Geirríðr and Katla, for the attentions of a young man, Gunnlaugr, has psychological credibility but is situated in larger ambient social circumstances, the male economic and political world around the female magical and sexual one. This also gives the creator of the saga occasion to show the physical effects of nightmares—the young man being ridden like the *draugar* ride the ridgepoles—sensory illusions, supernaturally protective clothing, and other sorcerers' paraphernalia. A later complex of incidents revolves around Þórgunna, a matron of Norse-Irish extraction, much like Hrappr with his Scottish ties (chaps. 50ff.). Although a practitioner of Celtic Christianity at a time when Iceland had only recently adopted the new faith, she too gives the impression of interest in young men and skill in magic, the latter a characteristic elsewhere attributed to Hebrideans. When the usually reserved Þórgunna interprets meteorological portents to indicate that her death is near, she makes bequests to the church at Skálholt and leaves instructions that she be taken there for burial. But her rich bedclothes, which had been envied by Þúriðr, the mistress of the household where she had taken up residence, are to be destroyed. In the narrative economy and logic of the *saga,* such injunctions are worthy of mention only if disregarded, and so it happens that the housewife appropriates a portion of the deceased's finery. This lies at the origin of a series of supernatural events called the Fróðá Marvels, after the farmstead. The revenant motif is prominent, and its effects on the community are highlighted; a more personalized *draugr* manifestation follows later in the saga (see below).

In comparison with Hrappr, Þórgunna shows a somewhat different aspect of life after death. True to form, the packhorse charged with transporting the body to Skálholt repeatedly throws off its burden. Yet when the burial party seeks shelter at night and is refused food at a farmhouse, Þórgunna rises naked from the dead to enter the kitchen and prepare and silently serve the needed meal. Here social criticism is being delivered and social order restored; Þórgunna disappears when the farmer sees his error and makes a formal offer of hospitality and help. The farmhouse is purified with holy water and the corpse safely delivered to the church.

Back at Fróðá, however, no corrective has been introduced, as Þúriðr is still in possession of the proscribed bedclothes. Like Óláfr's failure to understand the source of his material and social good fortune, Þúriðr's acquisitiveness represents a dysfunctional relationship with the supernatural, and responsibility for the negative effects that are soon manifest ultimately lies with an individual. The household stock of dried fish is consumed by a supernatural seallike creature; another seal's head rises from the floor of the main room and persistently eyes the bedclothes; a farmhand dies and returns as a conventional *draugr,* killing others and adding them to his following; other innocent persons drown at sea or die of disease within the household, then return in disconcerting but essentially pacific fashion to resume their places around the central fire. But these revenants, with their nostalgia for communal life, are open to the arguments of law, and Snorri the Priest (or Chieftain), whose complex portrait as an astute and wily politician is successively filled in by many of the episodes of the saga, is able to rid the household of the haunters by leveling against them a charge of trespass and harassment of the living. He then burns the offending bedclothes to preclude further nefarious activity. Christian rites of exorcism are introduced, but in reality have only a complementary effect to the clearing of the house through this native Icelandic legal ploy. But societal balance is not restored before eighteen of the thirty servants have died and another five fled. As in *Laxdœla saga,* the economic dimension of revenant activity is made explicit.

The Fróðá Marvels are bracketed by events in the life, death, and return of another important figure in *Eyrbyggja saga,* Þórólfr, called *bægifótr* (lame foot) as a result of a dueling injury that occurs early in the tale, when he questionably acquires his first property. Þórgunna's story then casts a retrospective light on earlier recounted events in Þórólfr's life, setting up audience expectations for his possible role in death. Þórólfr, a former Viking and thus having experience from abroad, shares personality characteristics with Hrappr—he is domineering and unjust—but his role in the complex narrative is substantially greater (chaps. 8ff.). As Hrappr stood in contrast to the socially responsible Óláfr *pái,* Þórólfr has a son, Arnkell, cut from very different cloth. Arnkell attempts mediation in situations where he is repeatedly matched against Snorri, but Þórólfr continues to fuel contention over landholding, and his character worsens with age (chaps. 30ff.). Thwarted in his effort to advance his economic interests by changing sides, Þórólfr returns to his farmstead one night, settles himself in his high seat without eating, and in the course of the night dies, apparently imploding with anger and frustration. Consistent with the saga's efforts to provide heathen "color," the removal of Þórólfr from the house is described in detail: the corpse is not handled until the eyes are well closed; a back wall is broken down, later to be rebuilt, so that the deceased will not find his way back into the house; the body is hauled by sledge with great difficulty (a hint of increasing weight) high into a valley, where it is buried and covered with stones.

Not unexpectedly, Þórólfr does not loosen his grip on the living easily, again "changing sides." The conventional hauntings begin: stock and shepherds are maddened and killed; the *draugr* works his way down the valley to the farmhouse, adding victims to his revenant troop. His malice seems particularly directed toward his widow, perhaps best seen as the mistress of his former household (compare Glámr, below), but not toward his son Arnkell. The latter, responsibly but in limited fashion, solves the immediate problem by disinterring his father's still uncorrupted body and moving it with even greater effort—the oxen going mad, breaking their traces and plunging into the sea—to a promontory where it is buried and sequestered behind a high wall of stone. Þórólfr haunts no more during the life of Arnkell. Out of filial duty, we assume, Arnkell does not apply the ultimate remedy to the *draugr* of decapitation and scabrous dishonor.

The local feud continues to simmer, abetted by gossip and public opinion siding with either Arnkell or Snorri. When Arnkell is eventually killed, his father's haunting resumes, causing one farm after another to be abandoned (chaps. 63ff.). Þórólfr is taken from the grave a second time, larger and darker than ever, and even proves resistant to the flames of the pyre ordered by Þóroddr Þorbrandsson. Eventually, the body is burned, and the ashes are scattered in the sea. The spiritual toxin that permitted one *draugr* to enlist others is still at work, however. An injured cow that against better judgment had been spared from slaughter licks stones to which Þórólfr's ashes have adhered. The cow is then served by a mystery bull whose dapple-gray hide suggests supernatural affiliation, and has a calf. Despite its preternaturally rapid growth and strength, the calf, called Glæsir, is treated like a pet. Heedless of an old woman's repeated warnings, the animal's master, Þóroddr the *draugr*-burner, is eventually gored and dies. The bull disappears into a swamp, like a *draugr* sinking back into the earth. Thus another good man, guilty only of oversight and prevarication, is caught in an initially innocuous chain of cause and effect, then is finally lost through his own error of judgment. In the sagas this pattern of the trivial proving critical is often repeated in the human actions that spark and sustain feud. As in the juxtaposition of Hrappr and the ox Harri's mother, the *draugr*'s potential for malice can be coeffective with other supernatural forces if both go unattended. If the dead are not effectively dealt with and relations with the supernatural are mismanaged, disaster is compounded. *Eyrbyggja saga* displays the most elaborate intertwining of the *draugr* and related motifs, such as supernatural animals, into the general story line. Their association with the dynamics of feud and overall saga trajectory is neither central nor casual, but even slim otherworldly strands draw together in the inevitable, culminating open conflicts.

In the "person" of Glámr, *Grettis saga Ásmundarson* offers the most celebrated instance of a *draugr*; this superior status is borne out by his use of speech and prophecy. As the saga is largely a series of episodes bearing on the life and destiny of the outlaw hero, the revenant is less insidiously woven into the narrative than in the above cases, but rather comments on it. Nonetheless, Glámr is not an unnuanced character, and the account of his haunting and meeting with Grettir is both graphic and detailed (chaps. 33ff.). Before the roving Grettir appears on the scene, the farmer Þórhallr's land is plagued by evil spirits (*meinivættir*), and he has difficulty in keeping shepherds. An acquaintance recommends he engage Glámr, a Swede from Sylgsdalir in Sweden, only recently arrived in Iceland. Glámr is big and strong, with a strange air, harsh voice, gray eyes, and wolf-gray hair. Irascible and unsociable, he is instinctively disliked by the mistress of the household. He also exhibits a strong distaste for Christian ritual, such as the pre-Christmas fast and church attendance, in this perhaps reflecting some awareness on the part of the saga's creator of Sweden's relatively late conversion from paganism. At the same time, Glámr says he is not afraid of phantoms. The farmwife's prediction of the ill that will befall those who eat on a fast day is borne out when Glámr is found dead high in a valley marked by a violent struggle. As a revenant, Glámr is not self-generated, as Hrappr and Þórólfr seem to be, but is part of a chain of malign supernatural activity. Glámr's corpse displays all the signs of future *draugr* status: darkened, swollen, stinking (a new feature, perhaps in contrast to the perfumed corpses of saints), difficult to displace toward the community down in the valley. It proves impossible to bring Glámr to church burial, and the body changes location at night until finally buried under a pile of stones. The expected hauntings begin, resulting in terror, madness, and damage to farm buildings. Eventually, a farmhand and a girl are killed, although not transformed into revenants. In fact, the saga makes explicit their safe burial under Christian aegis, suggestive of the growing strength of the new faith, although again Christian exorcism is not yet fully adequate to counter the native Icelandic preternatural.

The scene is then set for the appearance of Grettir, who at this stage in his life is still looking for challenges that can be exploited in his self-realization and quest for glory. His encounter with Glámr is prompted by ambition more than by the responsibility noted in the cases of the chieftains Óláfr and Arnkell. To set the stage for the confrontation with Glámr, this saga makes explicit comment on *draugar* when Grettir is advised by his host, "From evil beings like Glam only evil can be gained, and it is always better to deal with human beings than with monsters of his kind."[4] Eventually Grettir takes up a position in the partially ruined farmhouse to wait for the nightly depredations. In the theme of the hall as social and cultural microcosm, the aesthetic effects of growing menace, and the description of the natural features of moon and scudding clouds, the scene compares well with Grendel's attack on Heorot in *Beowulf*, and genetic ties between the two have been proposed. In the present context, these features and the detail of the cataclysmic struggle must be passed over in favor of Glámr's speech after Grettir has succeeded in thrusting him out through the symbolically significant doorway and pinning him to the ground. The clouds part to reveal the moon and Glámr's eyes, the only thing, Grettir reveals in an admission of interior state rare in the saga, that ever frightened him. The eyes may represent the possession of knowledge from the other side. Grettir is momentarily powerless, and Glámr says:

> You have been very determined to meet me, Grettir, but it will hardly surprise you if you do not get much luck from me. I will tell you this: you have acquired by now only half of the strength and vigour which you were destined to get if you had not met me. I cannot take away from you what you already have, but I can see to it that you will never be stronger than you are now, and yet you are strong enough, as many will find to their cost.

> Up until now your deeds have brought you fame, but from now on outlawry and slaughter will come your way, and most of your acts will bring you ill luck and misfortune. You will be made an outlaw and forced to live by yourself. I also lay this curse on you: you will always see before you these eyes of mine, and they will make your solitude unbearable, and this shall drag you to your death.[5]

Glámr's biographical speech is dense with rhetorical effects that complement the wheel of fortune motif of ascent toward strength, glory, and community, and inevitable descent into powerlessness, outlawry, and solitude. From the abstractions of strength and glory to the concrete particular of demonic eyes, the heroic is whittled down to the timorous. The free public and intralegal life of renown for great deeds will yield to a private life of personal memory, solitude, and fear of the dark. This might be characterized as knowledge from the *draugr* perspective, from the "other side," of man's inevitable social, physical, and spiritual decline, but it is more rewarding to identify an authorial voice here, with the revenant serving as ventriloquist's dummy, making this an existentialist statement on the vagaries of human destiny and on the consequences, ultimately and most tellingly psychological, of outlawry. The medieval Icelandic sentence to "solitary" was not confinement in the locked center of society but exile to its contingent natural periphery, where man was marooned in an unknowable and thus constantly threatening world: extralegal man condemned to be "one who lies out" (*útlagr*) beyond the community, its epistemic and legal frameworks, and human fellowship and language.

But without pausing to reflect on this prophetic statement and its potential for anagnorisis, Grettir recovers his strength and presence of mind. He draws his single-bladed sword and cuts off the *draugr*'s head, which he places between its thighs, the revenant's faculty of speech having augmented the honor-related stake for both parties. The corpse is then burned for good measure, and the ashes buried in a sack far from places frequented by animals or men. Glámr's speech comes at a watershed in Grettir's life. But like the technician disposing of nuclear waste, Grettir, although his reputation is at its zenith, seems to have been infected by Glámr, even if not forced through death to the ranks of the revenants. The remainder of the saga fulfills Glámr's prophecy, despite some good deeds on Grettir's part; although his moral stature increases, his luck declines. In what follows his humor is darker, his temper shorter, and his sensitivity to insult more promptly triggers retaliation. Our knowledge of his underlying fear of darkness and the effects of solitude privileges us to see such actions as aggressive defensiveness. After Grettir had faced up to Glámr, we may wonder how anything could further inspire fear in him, fear of the dark being so groundless and trivial in a saga hero as to seem an instance of black humor. But Glámr's faculty of speech and his momentary control of discourse, the advantage of his greater evil, is geared to performative utterances, and what he says of necessity becomes the new reality. However incongruous, it is fully effective. Glámr's speech overdetermines Grettir's future.

In many respects, Glámr is Grettir's alter ego—in physical appearance, temperament, fierce independence, and self-confidence—and this perspective may assist in deheroicizing Grettir for analysis. Perhaps this correspondence is to suggest that Glámr can more readily read Grettir's destiny. In volunteering preferential knowledge, the revenant has taken a step from death and nature toward Grettir, who meets him halfway, his life before and after the meeting consisting of significant steps, some unwilled, from society toward nature. But, in my judgment, we miss the author's intentions if we see in Grettir's defeat of Glámr the successful suppression of the societally less positive features of his own personality. Although some of Grettir's subsequent actions are more nearly altruistic than previously (e.g., helping people get to church, but himself unable to complete the church-sponsored ordeal), his psyche has darkened as did the *draugr*'s body. The author is charting not so much the evolution of a man's personality as the realization of his fate. Despite Grettir's growth in awareness, after Glámr's rhetorically competent and effortless dismissal of the myth of self-sufficiency the hero is incapable of affecting the greater lines of force that shape his future. Glámr's speech can also be read as an invalidation of the old heroic ethos of the Viking age. Statements or events to similar effect occur at comparable moments, usually after midpoint and the conversion of Iceland, in several other sagas.

Narrative Ends and Ideology

The *draugr* episodes in *Laxdœla saga, Eyrbyggja saga,* and *Grettis saga* clearly share common assumptions concerning the nature and behavior of revenants, particularly that psychological imbalance, especially as evidenced in ethical behavior, will leave anger and malice in the existence beyond life. In the vindictiveness of the active dead, their sense of unfinished business and maintenance of blood feuding past life's limit, there is an almost juridical conception of incomplete process. To reverse this perspective, the reappearance of revenants among the living is less in violation of natural law, as some kind of continuing semiconscious, "hibernating" existence seems assumed, than a violation of social and territorial law, a transgression and trespassing. In these three realizations of the unquiet dead, *Laxdœla saga* offers the simplest deployment, almost a type-scene; the success of the goodwilled but less than fully decisive and astute Óláfr is overshadowed by the later loss of his son Kjartan. In terms of the supernatural, we are solidly in the pagan period of postsettlement Iceland, with its *landvættir* and *fylgjur* (fetches). In *Eyrbyggja saga,* the relations of Þórólfr, alive and dead, with his son Arnkell and with the other chieftain, Snorri, and his later emanation in the bull Glæsir, link the outmoded ethos of the Viking period—transformed into territorial acquisitiveness in Iceland—with factional and family feud and contention over economic resources. The supernatural effects serve largely aesthetic ends, grim as they are, enriching the plotline rather than addressing more abstract concerns. Still, the interaction of pre-Christian magic and concepts of the dead with Celtic and Norse Christianity emerges in the saga as a distinct although not fully resolved narrative strand and ideological issue. In *Grettis saga,* the *draugr* episode, despite the high craftsmanship apparent in the description of the struggle and in Glámr's speech, is from a compositional point of view indistinguishable from many others (hero seeks out and defeats monstrous adversary). Yet, written from the perspective of the fourteenth century, it is also a more pointed commentary on the worldview of the family sagas than the others, if with this shorthand we mean the question of the social career and personal destiny of the ambiguous insider/outside, hero/outlaw.

Before exploring the revenant episodes on the level of ideology rather than of character and plot, it is instructive to note briefly the deployment of the motif in other literary forms, the "contemporary sagas" that deal with events of the thirteenth century (whereas the family sagas, composed then and later, treat of those of roughly 950 to 1100) and the "sagas of olden days" (*fornaldarsǫgur*) or mytho-heroic romances, which might superficially be characterized as escapist in that they look neither to the difficult present nor to its immediately preceding idealized past. In the romances, the revenant motif is simply another means to illustrate heroic self-realization, and the land of the dead is just another exotic country. Typical for the romance's lack of interest in the functioning of society, these are not true revenants who leave the grave to haunt and destabilize the community, but jealous howe-dwellers (*haugbúi*) waked from their sleep by the questing and acquisitive hero or heroine (*Hervarar saga ok Heiðreks*, chap. 13, motifs carried into the Latin medium of Saxo Grammaticus's *Gesta danorum*, 11.3ff.). In the romance, the movement is not of monster toward community but of hero toward the monstrous, and may have affinities with early conceptions of initiation. From this perspective, the family saga *draugr* appears as a dark pastiche of the romance hero, his quest taking him from death into life. As the undead of romance carry no ideological charge, the hero's task is simple physical dominance and disposal. Christian means may also be applied, more directly and efficaciously than in the family sagas, which depict a historical period in which the new faith was taking first root and demonic forces were still robust.

The contemporary sagas that go under the collective name of *Sturlunga saga* are written in a mode of heightened realism in which one need not look beyond life itself to find its antithetical properties. There is horror enough in humanly severed hands and feet, disfigurement and castration. Tellingly, the single instance of the living dead in the contemporary corpus is in recensions of a saga devoted to the bishop Guðmundr Árason in which the revenant is a woman with a seal's head (e.g., *Guðmundar biskups saga hin elzta*, chaps. 34ff.). She has no role in contention or other plot; her exorcism is merely Christian wonder-working, little different than the romance hero's brisk eradication of monsters. It is because of her sins—guilt rather than anger or frustration—that the dead woman cannot rest in peace. The family sagas, on the other hand, are set, if not written, in a pre-Christian world or the immediate postconversion period, by which time the conception of personal sin as productive of interiorized guilt seems not to have penetrated deeply into either the literary or individual consciousness.

I turn now to the *draugr* motif as it shapes four interrelated problem areas in the fictional world of the family sagas, before offering summary comment on its resonance with the political, economic, social, and cultural conditions of the Age of the Sturlungs, the period of composition. These are ethnogenesis, Christianity, ethics and the economy, and chronology and causality.[6] The corpus of family sagas and, more pointedly, *Landnámabók* (The book of settlements) reflect a very conscious

Icelandic concern with ethnogenesis, and with the recognition and maintenance of distinct identity. The statement of original settlers fleeing oppressive rule in Norway, a frequent feature of introductory chapters of sagas, is just as often matched by a later account of a prominent Icelander being received at a Norwegian court like visiting aristocracy. The Celtic lands, from which many Norse and Norse-Celtic land-takers were drawn along with their Celtic slaves, is viewed with a similar ambiguity, *Landnámabók* offering examples of "good" slaves acculturating quickly in the new country, "bad" slaves being exterminated after mutiny. It is within this framework that we must consider the rather explicit "foreign" origins of the *draugar*: Víga-Hrappr, Norse in culture but part Celtic by blood and raised in the Western Isles; Hallbjǫrn Kotkelsson in the same saga, who combines Hebridean origins and life as a sorcerer with *draugr* malevolence; the more ambiguous Þórgunna; Glámr, from Sweden, a country that otherwise often supplies berserks to the saga world; Þórólfr, a former Viking who would seem to have plied his freebooting in the Western Sea, different from later Icelanders who seek martial fame abroad chiefly under the aegis of aristocratic or royal authority and patronage. The importance attached to lineage in the family sagas assured that these geographic origins were kept in mind by the original audience. The point the sagas are making, although the equation is never explicit, is essentially defensive and slightly xenophobic. Once past the settlement period, aliens fit less successfully into normative Icelandic life. This, plus certain personality preconditions, results in their often going frustrated and unfulfilled to their deaths, making them prime material to be reactivated as revenants. There is a similar tendency to locate future *draugar* among the less wellborn elements of society. From the viewpoint of ethnic awareness it is as if the transgressive element that is common to all societies were here being neutralized by being led back into a foreign or base ground. In the family sagas the indigenous social ills of the thirteenth century seem recast in a xenophobic mode in which the uncanny and suspect Scot and Swede are the obverse of the royal Norwegian patron and host: they are foreign and the outcomes of their contributions are disruptive. The former recalls the ambiguous Celtic component in the settlement of the island; the latter stands for both the expulsive royal power of the ninth century and the seductive coercion of Norwegian rule of the thirteenth. Both are predicated on landholding and territorial control. But why should the Celtic origins still be a matter of concern three hundred years after the settlement of Iceland, that is, in the thirteenth century, when the genre of family saga was solidly established? Conceptions of time and causality provide a partial answer, offered below.

The Christian-*draugr* interaction is not fully realized in the sagas, in the sense that the issue remains largely on the level of narrative detail from which the public may draw its own conclusions, although steered by such credible mouthpieces of orthodoxy as the mistress of the house in *Grettis saga* and the statement that Glámr was more "evil" than other revenants. Some native conceptions of the supernatural were fitted *en bloc* into the Christian thought-world and into the sagas in the viewing of revenants, dream women, trolls, and others from Outside as demonic or demonically inspired creatures. The Christian view of demonology was that demons sought to entrap those who still believed in them by seeming to intrude in their interests in earthly affairs. Thus the old supernatural, still active, could have malign effects even though a new remedy was available. And the material body, the *draugr*'s vehicle, was quintessentially the Devil's target. The larger Christian spiritual force field of the sagas, in which both *draugar* and feud were encompassed, eventually imposed resolution, although not before considerable suffering and loss had taken place.

In terms of normative ethics, the future *draugar* were on the margin even in life, either through extortionate treatment of political and economic rivals (just barely within social conventions and just outside legal ones) or in their preferred antisocial existence as loners. These qualities are greatly enhanced in death. Ignoring the boundary between death and life as set in natural law, *draugr* predation on the community also ignores the laws of property and social hierarchy and violates the norms of reciprocity by being one-sided and wholly destructive. At home in the exclusionary conceptual Útgarðr (Outer World) of giants and trolls, the *draugr* is symbolically beyond the law; no kinsmen can be pressed for compensation for his misdeeds. This leads to the perhaps unlikely consideration of ghosts, monsters, and the economy. It is clear that whatever their ideological charge and entertainment value in the family sagas, the *draugar* meet the criteria of saga subject matter by virtue of their relevance to economics. The corporeality of the *draugar* translates into concrete material loss: servants and family maddened or killed, stock slaughtered, buildings destroyed. Repeatedly, we learn that farms were abandoned because of the harassment and losses. Although Iceland was the last discrete European geographic area to be populated, within sixty years of the initial settlement all the arable land had been claimed in the resource-scarce, volcanic, subarctic island. Subject to the chieftains and powerful free landholders, the tenant farmers, women, servants, the aged, and the young must have made up large contingents on individual farms and were not economically competent on their own. Thus we must judge an effective *draugr* haunting to constitute a substantial net loss to the rural economy, which generated surpluses in only a few areas and was from the outset dependent on foreign imports. *Draugr* activity did not cause wealth to circulate in the community, but cut it off at its source.

Diachronic linkages in the sagas, such as curses, prophecies, dreams, portents, and ominous detail, create the impression of an implacable unfolding of events in which saga characters entertain the enabling fiction of freedom of action, but a freedom conditioned by individual personality and by the common honor-driven ethos, with its fatalistic component. In one sense, prolepsis is inherent in the very concept of the *draugr*: those alienated from society in life reemerge in the narrative, returning from death to plague the living. Often these developments must have been anticipated by the saga public on the basis of the few explicitly stated personality traits. Taken together, revenants, prophecies, threats, and the like may seem to weigh heavily against the realism claimed for the family saga genre, but it should be recalled that Icelandic society did believe in such glimpses of the future (witness the popularity of dream interpretation books down through the centuries). Saga art differs from life in that predictions are almost inevitably realized with dire consequences as part of the narrative economy. As the saga (despite intertextuality) is a non-self-reflective genre, with little in the way of explicit authorial statement, foreshadowing is turned into event, is narrativized in type-scenes, and often requires the involvement of an interpreter or listener in addition to the person most critically implicated. Later, the multiple warp threads of plot are recrossed by the weft of events happening in real time as they were earlier described in compressed discourse. The frequent use of prolepsis suggests that Icelandic authors were acutely aware of historical evolution and of the changes their society had undergone since the settlement, and that they saw both continuity and change as determined by forces greater than the individual, so that in accounts of personal destinies they made outcomes inevitable through the "reinforcement" of foresight, just as they must, in hindsight, have seen how their own individual fields of action had shrunk and altered with similar inevitability by the troubled thirteenth century.

As genre, the family saga may have roots in early Icelandic historiography based on continental Latin models or in native Norse storytelling tradition, or a combination of these in interplay with other still-unquantified factors, but it is also the spiritual product of the troubled Age of the Sturlungs that saw Iceland turn and be turned toward Norway and Europe in new and materially consequential ways. Iceland would submit to Norwegian rule between 1262 and 1264 as the lesser of several evils. The establishment of the Icelandic church and the practice of tithing, the institutional interests of the Norwegian church, the concentration of political and economic power in a handful of powerful families, their factional disputes and the Norwegian monarchy's exploitation of them to further its own ends, greater strains on the now fully appropriated natural and agricultural resources, perhaps accompanied by climactic deterioration and volcanic activity—these and other developments put Iceland of the thirteenth century under a degree of stress that is far from the ethical tension that accompanied the feuding in an earlier, in the sagas doubtless consciously gilded, age.

If we consider the raid made on Sauðafell, the household of Sturla Sighvatsson, by Þórðr Þorvaldsson in *Íslendinga saga* (chap. 71), a principal component of *Sturlunga saga*, and its victimization of women, children, elderly, and clerics, we see a scene comparable to the dead Glámr's raid on Þórhallr's farm. The attention in both accounts to the material detail of the farmhouse itself is striking. The scenes of humiliation and mutilation, even assassination, that are grisly commonplaces in lives of farmers and others in the contemporary sagas, are as if the spirit of the *draugr* had been ingested by a whole society. With such violence resident within the community, these literary works had no need to call in supernatural revenants for additional effects of horror. Under these circumstances, the individual free farmer, who functions as the ethical, economic, and political unit of agency in the family sagas, was swept up into, or aside by, social and political forces beyond his control. So terrorized, he was driven from the free political process like the farmer families from their *draugr*-haunted valleys. Gruesome and destructive, the *draugr* in his materiality is still not far removed from the everyday reality of rural

Icelandic existence. His corporeality makes him an immediate and effective reification of grasping, extralegal self-interest. In one sense he seems more truly Icelandic in death than in life, foreign origins having been offset by time spent in the Icelandic earth. One might then suggest that the *draugar,* with their rapacious reclamation of land and their strength drawn from the soil, are an encoding of the destabilizing, larger-than-individual-life, antisocial territorial expropriations of the later Age of the Sturlungs, which return to the saga world as the revenant returns to life, so that through the figure of analepsis the golden past is intermittently haunted by its gray future. The *draugr* is a true *monstrum,* a portent of future events.

In its generic definition and social dynamics the Icelandic saga is permeable to nonnormative, morally indefensible forces that find expression in land seizure, the seduction of dependent women, petty vengeance prompted by envy, sexual and honor-related defamation for political purposes, killing on a whim, the prosecution of feud through the choice of significant but not always morally involved victims. Yet the family saga, unlike the contemporary saga, admits this subject matter in order to identify it, make it finite, containable, and ultimately susceptible to neutralization. Similarly, the virulence of the *draugr* is suffered and absorbed, but the family sagas present this as a process of inoculation from which the community is eventually to emerge more resistant. From this perspective the foreign origins of this supernatural menace in the sagas can be read as equivalent to the often negative effects of Norwegian favor taken back to Iceland. The historian may judge that their real-life counterparts were weakness in the Icelandic legal and socioeconomic structures. Maintenance of a supposed earlier societal balance, the family sagas suggest, would have precluded their grim epilogue in the dark dynamics of the Age of the Sturlungs.

The symbolic relationship to the real political and material conditions of the age of composition that is inscribed in the clearly ideological texts of the family sagas reveals ambiguous relations with the Norwegian throne at three historical stages: harsh rule encourages the self-reliant to emigrate from Norway to Iceland; later, Icelanders are generously recognized at aristocratic Norwegian courts, but this may be only a prelude to further problems back in Iceland; finally, a renewal of expansionist royal policy brings the Icelandic people and their land under Norwegian rule. But against this rise-and-fall paradigm is seen a teleological imperative in the spread of Christianity, the linear, not cyclic ("revenant"), dimension of human history. Grettir's career, as summarized by the prescient Glámr, personalizes and capsulizes these larger developments in early Icelandic history, with its climb from an early self-fulfilling heroic age to the vigor and renown of manhood, then decline (his sentence of outlawry equivalent to the breakdown of Icelandic law), and finally the solitude of individual powerlessness. Just as Grettir's life was of darker temper and increasingly circumscribed action but informed by greater consciousness and conscience, Iceland grew in moral awareness after the conversion even if the *draugr*-like recurrence of feud showed it little better able to live by the new moral code. Then, after the civic disruption of the first half of the thirteenth century, submission to Norwegian hegemony realized another of the xenophobic fears of the past, but also, paradoxically, brought Christian Iceland into the greater European community. The family saga foresees the social forces that the thirteenth century will unleash, but, as a literary genre devoted to societal models of the past, it imposes resolution and closure and lays its *draugar,* in a centripetal movement that leaves at tale's end a functioning world, not the simple heroic world of the pagan past, but a sadder, wiser, potentially more compassionate world under the new Christian faith.

Notes

1. The family sagas are cited by chapter from the standard Íslenzk fornrit series (Reykjavík: Híð íslenzka fornritafélag, 1933-). The romances are gathered in *Fornaldarsögur Norðurlanda,* 4 vols., ed. Guðni Jónsson (Reykjavík: Íslendingasagnaútgáfan, 1950) and the contemporary sagas are published as *Sturlunga saga,* 2 vols., ed. Jón Jóhannesson, Magnús Finnbogason, and Kristján Eldjárn (Reykjavík: Sturlunguútgáfan, 1946).

2. Han hjó af honum hǫfuðit ok dró hann út ok stakk nefinu i klof honum, at hann gengi eigi dauðr (chap. 5).

3. *Laxdæla Saga,* trans. Magnus Magnusson and Hermann Pálsson (Harmondsworth: Penguin, 1969), chap. 17. The Norse original reads: "En svá illr sem hann var viðreignar, þá er hann lifði, þá jók nú miklu við, er hann var dauðr, því at hann gekk mjǫk aptr. Svá segja menn, at hann deyddi flest hjón sín í aptrgǫngunni; hann gerði mikinn ómaka þeim flestum, er í nánd bjuggu; var eyydr bœrinn á Hrappsstǫðum. Vigdís, kona Hrapps, rézk vestr til Þorsteins surts, bróður síns; tók hann við henni ok fé hennar."

4. *Grettir's Saga,* trans. Denton Fox and Hermann Pálsson (Toronto: University of Toronto Press, 1974), chap. 34. The original reads: "Illt mun af illum hljóta, þar sem Glámr er; er ok miklu betra at fásk við mennska menn en við óvættir slíkar."

5. Ibid., chap. 35. The original reads: "Mikit kapp hefir þú á lagit, Grettir,' sagði hann, 'at finna mik, en þat mun eigi undarligt þykkja, þó at þú hljótir ekki mikit happ af mér. En þat má ek segja þér, at þú hefir nú fengit helming afls þess ok þroska, er þér var ætlaðr, ef þú hefðir mik ekki fundit; nú fæ ek þat afl eigi at þér tekit, er þú hefir áðr hreppt, en því má ek ráða, at þú verðr aldri sterkari en nú ertu, ok ertu þó nógo sterkr, ok at því mun mǫrgum verða. Þú hefir frægr orðit hér til af verkum þínum, en heðan af munu falla til þín sekðir ok vígaferli, en flest ǫll verk þín snúask þér til ógæfu ok hamingjuleysis. Þú munt verða útlægr gǫrr ok hljóta jafnan úti at búa einn samt. Þá legg ek þat á við þik, at þessi augu sé þér jafnan fyrir sjónum, sem ek ber eptir, ok mun þér erfitt þykkja einum at vera, ok þat mun þér til dauða draga.'"

6. One might also pursue the matter of the *draugar,* sexuality, and gender. None of the revenants displays any gender dislocation in death, but on the other hand there is no explicit reference to active sexual drive. Given that women's status before the law displayed the same incapacitation as outlaws' beyond the law, and that the *draugar,* in rather different ways, were transgressive encroachers on life, one might question whether there was, not affinity, but some situational correspondence between women and revenants. The question, however, seems too hypothetical to pursue on the slim body of evidence. But either woman's nurturing *cultural* function within the household or her *natural* function in the regenerative cycle, or a combination of both, seems to alert Þórhallr's wife in *Grettis saga* to the peculiarities and latent menace of Glámr before his death and earns him her dislike (compare Þórólfr's persecution of his widow in *Eyrbyggja*).

13 Unthinking the Monster: Twelfth-Century Responses to Saracen Alterity

Michael Uebel

A History of Unthought

A system of thought . . . is founded on a series of acts of partition whose ambiguity, here as elsewhere, is to open up the terrain of their possible transgression at the very moment when they mark off a limit. To discover the complete horizon of a society's symbolic values, it is also necessary to map out its transgressions, its deviants.

MARCEL DÉTIENNE, *Dionysos Slain*, 1979[1]

Every system of thought traces, as if along a Möbius strip, its own system of unthought, and in the process unfolds a history of alterity that reveals how the other, "at once interior and foreign," has been provisionally unthought, exteriorized, and "shut away (in order to reduce its otherness)."[2] Though "shut away," the other is absolutely integral to the selfsame, a necessary parable (Gr. *parabole*, juxtaposition, comparison, from *paraballein*, to set beside), as Michel Foucault suggests, of the self: "The unthought (whatever name we give it) is not lodged in man like a shrivelled-up nature or a stratified history; it is, in relation to man, the Other: the Other that is not only a brother, but a twin, born, not of man, nor in man, but beside him and at the same time, in an identical newness, in an unavoidable duality."[3] Both exterior and indispensable, this "obscure space" of the unthought has, according to Foucault, only "accompanied man, mutely and uninterruptedly, since the nineteenth century."[4] Yet the terms of Foucault's own description of the unthought open up the tantalizing possibility that indeed "man and the unthought are, at the archaeological level, contemporaries,"[5] and that therefore local histories might be written to describe unthought *before* the nineteenth century. Histories of unthought would commence, then, not with the advent of the human sciences and their discovery of the unconscious, but with specific discursive moments, when otherness as an ever-changing category is read as historically grounded. Histories of unthought cannot, therefore, provide a transcendental totalizing foundation for historical inquiry, but only local insights into types of discourse and the cultural contexts in which they are embedded. These histories map above all sites of violence—the irruption and disruption of unthought[6]—in order to reveal the proximate, sometimes unlivable, duality of other and self that inaugurates and defines subjectivity, identification, community.

To sketch such local histories of unthought, where unthought demarcates or corresponds to some uninhabitable domain of alterity, one must make a strategic assertion: imagining otherness necessarily involves constructing the borderlands, the boundary spaces, that contain—in the double sense, to enclose and to include—what is antithetical to the self. These limit regions are characterized by two intersecting paradoxes that will guide our preliminary inquiry of the contradictions inherent in imagining monstrous otherness as a form of twelfth-century unthought. These are the paradoxes of the proximate construction of otherness and of the spatiality of boundary lines themselves. The first paradox holds that alterity is never radical, because the terms of any binarism interdepend, interanimate—"but to differing degrees," Jonathan Dollimore crucially reminds us, for "in one kind of interdependence the one term presupposes the other for its meaning; in another more radical kind of interdependence the absolutely other is somehow integral to the selfsame. In the latter, *absence or exclusion simultaneously becomes a presence*."[7] The second paradox arises from the boundary line's double status as both marker of separation and line of commonality. Because borders mediate and, to follow Michel de Certeau, are "created by contacts, the points of differentiation between two bodies are also their common points. Conjunction and disjunction are inseparable in them."[8] Boundaries simultaneously partition reality, by separating continua into discrete entities, and serve as lines of contiguity that generate a proverbial gray area. Flickering between contact and avoidance, interaction and interdiction, border lines are thus spaces "in between," gaps or middle places symbolizing exchange and encounter, facilitating translation and mutation. Sites of potential contestation, they are the areas wherein identity and sovereignty are negotiated, imaginatively and discursively, in relation to the necessary other.

Monsters, as discursive demarcations of unthought, are to be treated not exclusively as the others of the defining group or self, but also as boundary phenomena, anomalous hybrids that constantly make and unmake the boundaries separating interiority from exteriority, historical world from fictional otherworld, meaning from nonsense. Because they blur categorical distinctions with their heterogeneity and mobility, monsters are especially symbolic of displaced, hence threatening, matter. Aversion to the ambiguity of such boundary phenomena falls under the famous category of "pollution behavior," a "reaction which condemns any object or idea likely to confuse or contradict cherished classifications."[9] Monsters, by inhabiting the gap between exclusive zones of intellectual or social meaning, deliver a threat to the zones' integrity, or, more precisely, to the assumption that such zones can be delimited in the first place. In other words, monsters expose classificatory boundaries as fragile by always threatening to dissolve the border between other and same, nature and culture, exteriority and interiority.

It is therefore understandable why monsters are at home in the belief structures of myth. They are mythic creatures in the precise Lévi-Straussian sense: as figures of liminality or in-betweenness, monsters, like the structures of myth circumscribing them, are at the same time charged with the insoluble task of resolving real social contradictions and with the function of inventing symbolic solutions to imaginary contradictions. In this sense, histories of unthought are thus concerned with the historical reasons for what is socially marginal or liminal becoming symbolically central. At the level of cultural formation and social reality, the monster is rejected, "shut away," and made safe, while at the same time it plays freely in the very realm in which it is exiled and enclosed—the shared imaginary of the normal, dominant culture. The repudiation through which official cultural identity emerges is at the same time a production in the imaginary of the defining limits of subjectivity. The dominant subject, writes Judith Butler, "is constituted through the force of exclusion and abjection, one which produces a constitutive outside to the subject, an abjected outside, which is, after all, 'inside' the subject as its own founding repudiation."[10] Thus unthought, or unthinking, involves the double process of repudiation and production, distancing and proximation. Unthought reminds us that monsters always already dwell in the imaginary, but do so in the special sense that Kristeva attaches to the experience of abjection: "I experience abjection only if an Other has settled in place and stead of what will be 'me.' Not at all an Other with whom I identify and incorporate, but an Other who precedes and possesses me, and through such possession causes me to be. A possession previous to my advent: a being-there of the symbolic."[11]

While a history of unthought maintains that the other as abject is socially constructed, it relies upon theories of abjection like Kristeva's to explain subjective identity and anxiety. To understand, for example, monsters and Saracens in the Middle Ages as figures of abjection who constitute in the cultural imaginary the limits of Christian identity, we must see these figures as boundary phenomena inseparable from their place at the territorial edge and inside the symbolic structure. When twelfth-century writers push the monster to the edge, force it to discursive thresholds, collective identity emerges, but it does so only under the constant threat of the monster it created. The monster becomes joined to the "human," constituting its limits and haunting those borders as the persistent possibility of their transgression and unmaking. Transgressions of territory, obfuscations of origin, mutations of history, and violations of family, ritual, sex, and gender norms by Saracen monstrosity are, we will see, transcoded into the monster-body terms of pollution, dismemberment, and excrement. Producing a cultural identity over and against the Muslim monster, twelfth-century historians constructed a set of limits that were imperiled by the act of exclusion itself.

Historia and the Threat of Islam

And all the werewolves who exist in the darkness of history . . . keep alive that fear without which there can be no rule.
MAX HORKHEIMER and THEODOR ADORNO, "The Importance of the Body," 1972[12]

In 1190, as Roger of Howden recorded in his chronicle, Richard I stopped at Messina on his way to the Holy Land to visit a certain Cistercian abbot named Joachim, who was earning a reputation as a wise prophet, a gifted interpreter of the Book of Revelation.[13] Richard and his retinue of churchmen "took great delight" in hearing a detailed, animated description of the seven-headed dragon of Antichrist waiting to devour the faithful, the offspring of the Holy Church. The seven heads, Joachim of Fiore explained, represented the seven persecutors of the Church, five of whom have passed, one of whom is, and one of whom will be. Among those who have passed was Muhammad, and "the one who is" was none other than Richard's nemesis Saladin, over whom the prophet predicted Richard's eventual victory. Though the bishops attending Richard would dispute Joachim's general interpretation of Revelation, and even Roger himself would implicitly question it by following it in his chronicle with two different, more standard, interpretations, one aspect would remain clear—the prophetic association of Muslims with the monstrous instruments of Antichrist.

In the West, Islam, taken to be the culmination of all heresies,[14] was seen as a sign of apocalypse, a foreshadowing of Antichrist, as early as the polemical writings of the Cordovan martyrs Eulogius and Paul Alvarus (ca. 854).[15] Joachim had in a sense only revived the coherent vision of Islam developed by the early Cordovan martyrs, who had imaginatively constructed the other in the shape of the known by placing it in the framework of Christian apocalypse. Explaining the threat of Islam in terms of the fulfillment of biblical prophecy epitomized a type of analogical thinking—recognizing oneself in the other, as in a mirror—that dominated Western conceptions of otherness.[16] Islam, construed as the perverse supplement of Christianity, became Latin Europe's perfect antithesis, and as such an essential part or limit of its identity. From the late seventh until the late seventeenth century, Islam in one of its forms—Arab, Ottoman, or Spanish and North African—seriously challenged the existence of Christianity. According to R. W. Southern, Islam epitomized alterity in the Middle Ages. "The existence of Islam," he argues, "was the most far-reaching problem in medieval Christendom," a danger that was "unpredictable and immeasurable."[17] This "problem" was essentially one concerning the integrity and preservation of apparently inviolable boundaries. It was the problem of unthought: How can identity be configured as both effective limit and collapsable boundary? Like the monstrous race of Cynocephali (dog-headed men) with whom they were often identified, Saracens and their religion symbolized the blurring of ideal boundaries, such as those separating rational man from animal or civilized man from barbarian.[18] Boundaries thus became contested spaces, areas betwixt and between, where relations had to be determined: What was the relation of the historical trajectory of Islam to Christian *historia*? Of Muhammad to Christ? Of the Koran to the Bible? Of the Muslim afterlife to the Christian heaven? Indeed, the indeterminacy Latins perceived in Islam was felt to have terrible consequences: the Saracens, "with all the appearance of a swarm of bees, but with a heavy hand, came fast out of Babylon and Africa into Sicily; they devastated everything and all around," wrote Erchimbert, a monk at Monte Cassino in the late eleventh century.[19] The image of irrupting, swarming Saracens figures an other without place, a shifting, mobile threat to the limits of Christendom. The nomadic other is especially repellent, for it symbolizes the perpetual difficulty of asserting difference and distance.

Such border anxiety in crusade literature often takes the form of an obsession with preserving the purity and fixity of origins. The reports of Pope Urban II's speech launching the Crusade at the Council of Clermont on 27 November 1095 univocally proclaim and crucially dramatize the importance of recovering the Holy Lands. Whatever other reasons, ideologically speaking, impelled restoring the Holy Lands to Christian rule—the rescue of the Eastern Church, the alleviation of internal strife, the exercise of a new awareness of Christian Empire and of holy war—the recovery of origins remained the primary motivation for crusade. Lamentations 5:2 echoed throughout the long history of conflict with Islam: "Hereditas nostra versa est ad alienos, domus nostrae ad extraneos [Our inheritance has been turned over to strangers, our home to foreigners]." In his account of Urban's speech, Robert the Monk associates the earthly place of Jerusalem with rightful Christian inheritance of the heavenly Jerusalem: "Enter upon the road to the Holy Sepulchre; wrest that land from the wicked race, and subject it to yourselves. That land, which as the Scripture says 'floweth with milk and honey,' was given by God into the possession of the children of Israel. Jerusalem is the navel of the world; the land is fruitful above others, like another paradise of delights [Iherusalem umbilicus est terrarum . . . quasi alter Paradisus deliciarum]."[20] The universal identification of Jerusalem as *umbilicus terrarum* makes concrete the importance of the place of origin in the rejection of Muslim appropriations. In his description of Jerusalem as paradise and fountain, Guibert of Nogent provides another, more embellished, account of Urban's plea to recover the place of Christian inception:

> Let us suppose, for the moment, that Christ was not dead and buried in Jerusalem, and had never lived any length of time there. Surely, if all this were lacking, this fact alone ought still to arouse you to go to the aid of the land and city—the fact that "Out of Zion shall go forth the law and the

> word of the Lord from Jerusalem!" If all that there is of Christian preaching has flowed from the fountain of Jerusalem, its streams, whithersoever spread out over the whole world, encircle the hearts of the Catholic multitude, that they may consider wisely what they owe such a well-watered fountain. If rivers return to the place whence they have issued only to flow forth again, according to the saying of Solomon, it ought to seem glorious to you to be able to apply a new cleansing [*repurgium*] to this place, whence it is certain that you received the cleansing of baptism [*baptismatis purgamentum*] and the witness of your faith.[21]

Islam, it was maintained, obstructs and clouds the clear doctrinal origins of Christianity, preventing at the source the dissemination of salvific dogma. The crusades represent, then, a series of new beginnings—cleansings—that are simultaneously returns to origin.

Thus at stake in these representative accounts of crusade propaganda is the proper source, order, and movement of providential history, the achievement of a Christian telos. Islam threatens the preservation and renewal of sacred history by setting up an alternative, deviant history. For twelfth-century historians such as Otto of Freising, the theological interpretation of history rested upon *translatio imperii* (transference of empire), the placement of "the Roman Empire at the end of a succession of ancient empires as a providential preparation for the age of Christ, in the course of history as well as in the geography of salvation."[22] The predestination of the Roman Empire guaranteed, through the crucial role it played in unifying mankind, that all men would be receptive to the dispensation of grace. The universality of Empire figures the universality of the Christian world order. Thus Otto of Freising, as propagandist of the Holy Roman Empire, saw in the vision of Daniel the transference of empire from the Romans to the Greeks to the Franks to the Lombards and finally to the Germans.[23]

The existence of Islam jeopardized the translation, and hence the universality, of Christian empire. Another transference became thinkable: the westward movement of civilization might be halted in a return to its Oriental source. Holy Empire might be replaced at the end of history by the rising Islamic empire. The survival of Christian Empire became a matter of preserving its place and time in the composition of history, a matter of maintaining its geographic and historical source, so compactly symbolized in the image of *umbilicus terrae*. This emphasis on the convergence of place and time in the representation of history was reflected in twelfth-century formulations of *mundus* (world) and *saeculum* (century, age).[24] Representing history depended upon establishing relations of *mundus* and *saeculum*, for example, plotting the movement of civilization from East to West.[25] In *De arca Noe morali*, Hugh of St. Victor writes that, in order to represent the complexity of history, "loca simul et tempora, ubi et quando gestae sunt, considerare oportet [one ought to consider time as well as place, where as well as when events happened]."[26] The threat of Islam as a perversion of history, a turning away from the providential order of place and time, was a recurrent theme in the histories and polemical writings of the twelfth century. Gerald of Wales, for example, writing on *tempestate Saraceni* (the furious rise of the Saracens) in *De principis instructione*, linked place and time in an argument concerning Muslim carnality fueled by the devil's plot (*arte diabolica*) for a hot climate. Gerald describes the Arabs' having been seduced by the false magical arts of Muhammad, led into corruption by this false prophet's (*pseudopropheta*) lax laws and by the effects of regional climate (*calore regionis urgente et ad hoc impellante*).[27] Geography vigorously determined the kind of history that Islam would generate.[28]

Signifying absolute alterity, the threatening place of Islam on the margins of Western history—*mundus* and *saeculum*—confounded the imperial ambitions of Christianity. In a letter to Saladin in 1188, Frederick I Barbarosa was surprised and incensed by the Saracen leader's ignorance of Roman history's securing the rights of Christians to the Holy Lands:

> However, now since you have profaned the Holy Land, which we rule by the empire of the eternal king, in protection of the inhabitants of Judea, Samaria, and Palestine, our imperial responsibility demands that we combat with due punishment the presumption and culpable audacity of such great wickedness.... For we scarcely believe that this is unknown to you, these recent events from the writings of the ancients and from the old histories of our own time. Do you pretend not to know about both Ethiopias, Mauratania, Persia, Syria, Parthia, where Marcus Crassus our ruler met his premature death, Judea, Samaria on the sea, Arabia, Chaldea, and Egypt itself, where, for shame, Antony, a Roman citizen, a man endowed with the marks of virtue, though not extending to the excellence of temperance, which otherwise was proper for a soldier sent out on such high missions, was with little sense a slave for the love of Cleopatra?[29]

The letter continues in this vein, enumerating next the nations and races subject to the sway of Roman empire and *historia*, forces that, if Frederick wished, could be effectively marshaled against Saladin. Frederick presents a Roman imperial history—including the place of Emperor Marcus Crassus's untimely death and a moral tale censuring Antony's imprudent love of Cleopatra—inescapably bound to the fate of Christian crusade. In emphasizing Saladin's ignorance of Roman history and imperial right as garnered "ex scripturis veterum et ex antiquis historiis nostri temporis [from the writings of the ancients and from the old histories of our own time]," Frederick dramatizes the Saracens' position outside proper history. From a place that at once threatens and stabilizes Roman rule, the marginal alternative that Saracen imperial history represents in effect authorizes Christian imperial history, calls it into being, demanding that the crusade narrative be retold, reaffirmed. Yet efforts to fix—in both senses, to set in place and to repair—such bounded narratives are immensely difficult and persistently subject to failure.

Islam, as several modern historians have pointed out, was rarely understood on its own terms, but grasped in its relation to Christianity. That is to say, Islam was cast in terms of an ideological image "whose function was not so much to represent Islam in itself as to represent it for the medieval Christian."[30] Over and against Saracen monstrosity, the Latin West defined itself internally. Community and solidarity were the essential results of the ideological work of facing hostility from without and shaping discourses to address the challenges of opposition. Norman Daniel, in his study of crusade propaganda, has argued convincingly that the churchmen composing such polemics were consciously writing *for* their coreligionists rather than *against* the Muslims. The ideological significance of anti-Muslim propaganda resided in the fact that it "both sprang out of and served to fortify the sense of Christian solidarity." A desire for uniformity in the form of religious orthodoxy was perceived "to be a precondition of . . . solidarity. To establish that a whole religion, *lex*, was in every respect the reverse or denial of European society was immensely helpful in creating a mental as well as a physical frontier."[31] But if imagining the Muslim other as the inverse, or alter ego, of the Christian self generated necessary mental and physical frontiers, then it also produced, as a result of such lines of division, spaces or zones wherein identities were (re)formed through negotiation, interaction, and engagement. The cultural formations taking place at the frontier are the results of a doubly specular process rather than of entrenchment, as Daniel seems to imply. That is, while it is certainly true that Latin Christendom constructed Islam as its mirror reflection—reversed as such images are—it is equally true, and culturally significant, that in the process Christendom also revealed *itself* to be "a play of projections, doublings, idealizations, and rejections of a complex, shifting otherness."[32] Thus to emphasize Western solidarity and totality in the face of the other is somewhat misleading. It obscures the potentially unstable dialectics and ideological play generating and constituting cultural opposition. By shifting the emphasis from the terms of the binary—Christian/Saracen—to the tensions structuring it, we can understand the fashioning of twelfth-century identity in terms of both "Christian solidarity" and the "play of projections" or differences opening up the obscure space of unthought. This seems crucial to underscore because such a shift necessarily calls into question the imperviousness of the frontiers delimiting identity.

Despite obvious risk, the boundaries separating Latin Europe from its others were consistently crossed, reflected across. A sustained Christian missionary impulse, gaining great momentum in the thirteenth century, has led one historian to label that period "the century of reason and hope,"[33] an era of philosophical contemplation of cultural otherness and a time of theological optimism in the unity of differences. Occupying the center stage in this so-called period of reason and hope was the social enactment of a long literary tradition of Byzantine and Spanish anti-Muslim polemics in dialogue form[34]—namely, the famous debate of William of Rubroek with the Buddhists and Muslims at Karakorum, 30 May 1254. Of course, translation across cultural divides had already been the optimistic concern of Peter the Venerable, who expressed his wish in the *prologus* to the *Liber contra sectam sive haeresim Saracenorum* that his book be translated into Arabic, "just as the abominable error could come across [*transmigrare*] to the knowledge of the Latins." "The Latin work," he continues, "when translated into that strange language [*peregrinam linguam*], may possibly profit some others whom the Lord will wish to acquire life by the grace of God."[35] In any case, the historical forces bringing together and encouraging or requiring exchange between Latins and their others were not limited to the desire for conversion. Other arenas of cultural exchange and translation included commerce; fields of learning such as astronomy, navigation, medicine, and philosophy; literature and literary forms; and court culture.[36] But whatever the modality, crossing the boundaries between cultures meant necessarily identifying with others, acknowledging, in the very process of cultural growth and community formation, the degree to which the other is constituent of the selfsame.

Corpus Christianus

Non est sacrilegis locorum differentia; non est personarum respectus.

[To the sacrilegious, there is no distinction of place and no respect for persons.]
WILLIAM OF TYRE, *Historia rerum in partibus transmarinis gestarum*[37]

Islam, a threat to the origins and univocality of Christian history, functioned in the twelfth-century imaginary as a sign of deviation or perversion—in short, as a sign of monstrosity. Virtually no responses, learned or literary, to Muhammad and his religion failed to evoke this. Indeed, the primary cluster of images reflecting the ways Islam was imaginatively fashioned conveys the complex threat to subjective wholeness that monstrosity alone poses: attributions to Muslims of limitless enjoyment and unarrestable desire,[38] of sexual deviation,[39] of powers of seduction,[40] of madness,[41] of disorder,[42] and of idolatry.[43] Crusade histories are left inscribed with the traces of this fear of an anomalous other who represents a rootless, discontinuous, corrupting subjectivity. What ultimately binds together these characteristics is an anxiety over the stability and placement of the actual boundaries marking differences between the two cultures.

Alan of Lille begins the fourth book of *Contra paganos* with a rather grandiloquent overview of his subject matter:

> Now let us turn our writing against the disciples of Muhammad. Muhammad's monstrous life, more monstrous sect, and most monstrous end [*finis*: limit] is manifestly found in his deeds. He, inspired by the evil spirit, founded an abominable sect, one suitable for fleshly indulgences, not disagreeable to pleasures of the flesh; and therefore these carnal men, allured by his sect, and humiliated by the errors of various precepts, have died and continue to die miserably; the people call them with the usual appellation Saracens or pagans.[44]

In the concatenation "monstrous life, more monstrous sect, most monstrous end"—the last part most certainly a reference to the Western myth of Muhammad having been devoured by pigs (or dogs, according to Alan)[45]—are condensed the energies of polemical biography and theological controversy. The religion of Muhammad is marked above all by its willful "error" (L. *errare*, to wander from a place, to deviate from a course), by its monstrous transgression of the norms and bounds of Christianity. In this connection, *monstruosissimus finis* can be construed as "most monstrous border, boundary, or limit." In the Christian imaginary the limits of Islam were coextensive with the extremes of everything monstrous. Islam began where Christianity imagined itself leaving off.

For Peter the Venerable, who commissioned the first translation of the Koran into Latin in 1143 and wrote the first systematic refutation of Islamic doctrine in the Latin language, Islam was a monstrous hybrid of everything antithetical to Christian belief. In a letter to Bernard of Clairvaux, Peter legitimates his project of translation by evoking patristic example: "Hoc ego de hoc precipuo errore errorum de hac fece universarum heresum, in quam omnium diabolicarum sectarum quae ab ipso Salvatoris adventu ortae sunt reliquiae confluxerunt, facere volui [I wanted to (follow patristic example) concerning that foremost error of errors, concerning the dregs (waste) of the entire heresy, into which the remnants of all the diabolical sects have flown together, whose source is the very coming of the Saviour]."[46] As the depository of all Christian heresies, a kind of cloacal stream of dissidence, Islam, through its cultural marginality and hybridity, became a measure of Christianity's symbolic stability and purity.

In the prologue to *Liber contra sectam*, Peter asks a series of rhetorical questions that more precisely define the nature of Islam's threat: "Et quae unquam o lector heresis adeo aecclesiae Dei nocuit? Quis unquam error adeo rem publicam Christianum vexavit? Quis in tantum terminos eius rescidet? Quis tant massa perditorum numerum infernalem adauxit? [And what heresy yet, reader, has so injured the Church of God? Which error yet has so vexed the Christian republic? What has broken down its boundaries by so much? What has increased the number of the damned by such a quantity of lost ones?][47] The urgent, penultimate question, "What has broken down its boundaries by so much?" points not only to the extent of Muslim irruptions into the Christian republic but to the specific anxiety attending such violations. If its boundaries are permeable, its extremities unstable, then how will Christianity preserve its foundational center?

Peter, who, like many of the theologians for whom he wrote, could not finally decide whether Muslims were heretics or pagans,[48] perceived in Islam a nefarious mixture of Christian, heretical, and pagan doctrines.

Muhammad, he argued, had indiscriminately fashioned a monster out of the religions that preceded him: "et sic undique monstruosus, ut ille ait, 'humano capiti cervicem equinam, et plumas' avium [Mahumet] copulat.[49] . . . Dehinc processu temporis et erroris, in regem ab eis quod concupierat, sublimatus est. Sic bona malis permiscens, vera falsis confundens, erroris semina sevit, et suo partim tempore, partim et maxime post suum tempus segetem nefariam igne aeterno concremandum produxit [and thus utterly monstrously, as he says, 'he (that is, Muhammad) joined to the human head a horse's neck and the feathers of birds.' . . . Hence in the progress of time and error, he was elevated by them to the kingship which he desired very much. Thus mixing good things with evil things, mixing truth with falsity, he sowed the seed of error, and in part in his own time, in part especially after his time, he produced a devilish crop to be burned in eternal fire]."[50] The image of the "devilish crop" (*nefariam segetem*), growing up from the seeds of error planted in a mixture of good and evil, truth and falsity, figured an otherness without *and* a danger within. Composed of elements of the exterior and interior, the hybrid with its sealed fate served as a figure for menacing alterity and perhaps as a warning to more local forces of impurity and dissidence.[51]

No other set of images better dramatizes Western anxiety over the convergence of the exterior and interior than the images of corporal dismemberment universally used by propagandists of the first crusade. Originating in a late-eleventh-/early-twelfth-century letter allegedly sent by Alexius I Comnenus to Count Robert of Flanders, these images, deployed to evoke repulsion and desire for vengeance among the Latins, found their way into several accounts of Urban's harangue at Clermont.[52] In his appeal for aid against the advancing infidels, Emperor Alexius details some gruesome violations of religious, sexual, and ethnic prohibitions:

> For they circumcise Christian boys and youths over the baptismal fonts of Christian [churches] and spill the blood of circumcision right into the baptismal fonts and compel them to urinate over them, afterward leading them violently around the church and forcing them to blaspheme the name of the Holy Trinity. Those who are unwilling they torture in various ways and finally murder. When they capture noble women and their daughters, they abuse them sexually in turns, like animals [*ut animalia*]. Some, while they are wickedly defiling the maidens, place the mothers facing, forcing them to sing evil and lewd songs while they work their evil.[53]

Repugnant to a society especially dependent upon taboos and hierarchies, Saracen atrocities in the Holy Land were assaults against the fabric of Western identity. Saracens, "haec impiissima gens [this most impious people]," have polluted and destroyed (*contaminant et destruunt*) the inviolable lines separating the sacred from the profane.[54] These violations of sacred space, metaphors for infidel intrusion into the Holy Land, are expressed in terms of bodily violations, encoded as monstrous acts opening up a vulnerable Christian body. As anomalous hybrids of anti-Christian vice, who spill the circumcision blood of innocent Christian boys like Jews in the popular anti-Semitic literatures and who copulate *ut animalia*, Saracens embody a shifting, intrusive menace to the sanctity of the Christian *corpus*. In the polemical and propagandistic literature such threats assume many ideological representations—as the threatening possibility of dismemberment, of rape and sodomization,[55] of invasion by vast numbers,[56] of unholy profanation[57]—but these representations function together in a "discursive chain"[58] to convey the danger posed to the boundaries and limits defining Christianity as a religion apart from and superior to its others.[59] Indeed, representations of intrusion and dismemberment, like images of monstrosity, make for such excellent propaganda because they function within a broad field of signification. Such representations, operating metonymically within a set of related images and metaphorically in a system of analogies, serve as a symbolic matrix through which anti-Muslim writers filtered ideas of community and identity. Transgressions of sexuality, territory, family, and ritual are transcoded into the terms of body dismemberment.

Christian accounts of corporeal integrity and purity were inevitably expressed in terms of the body as a site, a topography of licit and illicit areas.[60] Indeed, the renunciation of the natural body in Judeo-Christian thought only served to reaffirm its ideological centrality. Thus an elaborate system of analogies developed between the physical body and the political or collective body.[61] The body often served to map political and religious hierarchies. Humbert of Moyenmoutier's *Adversus simoniacos* (1057), for example, conflates the individual and collective body in order to illustrate the famous tripartite scheme of societal organization and to emphasize the subordination of the masses to ecclesiastical and secular powers.[62] In Humbert's treatise the Church is represented as the eyes, the lay nobility as the chest and arms, and the masses as the lower limbs and extremities.[63] The body was the principal paradigm through which the sacral community was imagined. Fulcher of Chartres begins the *Historia Hierosolymitana* with a commentary on the transgressions of Pope Urban's rival Guibert, the archbishop of Ravenna, that compares the integrity of the Church and the peace of Europe to a strong, wholesome body.[64] And in the *Policraticus* (1159), John of Salisbury maps the body politic onto the organic body: "The state [*res publica*]," he writes, "is a body [*corpus quoddam*]"; he then proceeds, in the manner of Humbert, to detail the correlation of political rank with bodily location.[65] Given this set of relations figuring the security of hierarchical organizations, it is not surprising, then, that anxieties concerning religious identity and political integrity should be distributed across bodily landscapes. Somatic symbols constitute the ultimate network through which different levels and domains of social classification and psychic reality are transcoded.

Robert the Monk and Guibert of Nogent, in their versions of Urban's exhortation at Clermont, are the most graphic about the kind of threat Islam posed to what William of Tyre had confidently called "an inviolable faith."[66] The race of Saracens, writes Robert,

> has either entirely destroyed the churches of God or appropriated them for the rites of its own religion. They destroy the altars, after having defiled them with their uncleanness. They circumcise the Christians, and the blood of the circumcision they either spread upon the altars or pour into the vases of the baptismal font. When they wish to torture men by a base death, they perforate their navels, and dragging forth the extremity of the intestines, bind it to a stake; then with flogging they lead the victim around until, the viscera having gushed forth, the victim falls prostrate upon the ground. Others they bind to a post and pierce with arrows; others they compel to extend their necks and then, attacking them with naked swords, attempt to cut through the neck with a single blow. What shall I say of the abominable rape of the women, which to speak of is worse than to be silent? The kingdom of the Greeks is now dismembered by them and deprived of territory so vast in extent that it cannot be traversed in a march of two months.[67]

To these bodily violations, Guibert adds a description of Saracen cruelties suffered by pilgrims to the Holy Land:

> What shall we say of those who took up the journey without anything more than trust in their barren poverty, since they seemed to have nothing except their bodies to lose? They not only demanded money of them, which is not an unendurable punishment, but also examined the callouses

> of their heels, cutting them open and folding the skin back, lest, per chance, they had sewed something there. Their unspeakable cruelty was carried on even to the point of giving them scammony to drink until they vomited, or even burst their bowels, because they thought the wretches had swallowed gold or silver; or, horrible to say, they split their bowels open with a sword and, spreading out the folds of the intestines, with horrible mutilation disclose whatever nature holds there in secret.[68]

At work in these two passages of anti-Muslim propaganda is a cluster of anxieties, at once imperial, religious, sexual, economic, and epistemological. Robert the Monk most overtly establishes an analogy between the limits of imperial geography and the boundaries of the human body. For him the images of cutting and penetration figure Christian territorial losses as the result of Muslim invasion. The Eastern Church and the Holy Land have been cut off from the Christian world by the effects of Saracen "dismemberment" and infiltration. Robert multiplies detailed images of torture to the (male) Christian body not merely for dramatic effect or lasting impression upon the memory of his readers but to convey something of the ways Saracens both imagine and enjoy unmaking the boundaries that define what is holy.[69] The Saracens reduce the body to its utter materiality, stripping it of any religious signification and opening it up to the flux and chaos of the merely physical. Saracens make the Christian body into an object of manipulation and observation, converting the Christian from the position of subject to the status of object of knowledge. Images of Christian bodies penetrated with weapons and with mastering gazes reveal the imposition of the epistemological dichotomy of subject and object onto hierarchical relations of race, gender, nationality, and religion. Thus in Guibert's vision of Saracen torture, the body's boundaries are manipulated for the ultimate purpose of examination. Whereas in Robert's account the Saracens' motives—defilement and destruction—are radically anti-Christian, in Guibert's they assume an almost scientific tenor—dissection and investigation. Here the Christian body is the object not only of inventive cruelties but of probing gazes that turn the body into a place where something—money or shit—is hidden. Turned inside out, the body reveals "whatever nature held there in secret," and in the process is demystified. The intestines here represent the last covering of a secret, a kind of veil for truth conceived materially. Articulating one of the dominant tropes of Western metaphysics—truth lies hidden in a veil—Guibert's anti-Muslim text ends up highlighting one of the imagined differences between Christians and Saracens: the difference between spiritual pursuits, investment in the transcendent future, and carnal appetites, investment in the material present.

In both descriptions of tortures in the Holy Land, the Christian body in pain is objectified, turned into a thing whose boundaries preventing undifferentiated contact with the external world are annihilated by the Saracens. United by the appropriation of a metaphor, these writers deploy images of anatomical mutilation to symbolize mutilated subjectivities, identities whose borders have been unmade. These corporeal boundaries, however, may be all that the Saracens can dismantle. Guibert's remark that the pilgrims seem to have *only* their bodies to lose challenges the idea of total appropriation. That is, it seems the Muslims can penetrate and interrogate only the body; they cannot penetrate the transcendental mysteries and meanings of Christian faith. Thus Saracen materiality or carnality is set against Christian renunciation, as in the moment when the pilgrims' calluses, the physical signs of their piety, are misrecognized as concealments of their supposed riches. The Saracen attempt to lock Christians in their objectified bodies fails at the precise moment when these bodies assume the discursive aspect of piety and martyrdom.

Crumbling Differences: Monsters and Ideology

If, as Guibert of Nogent's treatment of Saracen alterity suggests, boundaries between self and other in the twelfth century could be drawn with some measure of confidence, in the security of marked differences, such confidence only concealed deep cultural anxieties and the perennial need for boundary markers. There was, as we have observed, profound desire to demarcate the spaces of non-Christian others, who were defined, to paraphrase William of Tyre, by their very disrespect of place and physical limitation. As the success of the crusades became more doubtful, as the symbolic significance of *bellum justissimum* in the cultural imaginary increased, canon legislation worked extensively to keep Christians apart from Muslims and Jews. Church authorities in the eleventh and twelfth centuries, for instance, aggressively condemned miscegenation, construed as sexual relations between a Latin Christian and a non-Christian, non-European partner.[70] The Council of Nablus (1120) enacted harsh penalties against Latin men in the Holy Land who consorted sexually with Muslim women.[71] In Gratian's *Decretum* (1140), Christians were strictly forbidden to receive service in Muslim households and were excommunicated for living in them. And the Fourth Lateran Council (1215) codified laws, already enforced locally, that forbade Muslims and Jews to hold any position of public authority and required that they wear distinctive clothing. To draw definite limits around the Christian corpus, in order to exteriorize and to unthink the territory others were imagined to inhabit, became a preoccupation of twelfth-century historians and churchmen who thought about their own place and role in history. Cultural identity rested upon preserving the closure of history (time and event) and the integrity of place (space and boundary), indelibly marking them as exclusive and exclusionary categories.

The histories of the first crusade emphasize this necessary conflation of time and space by representing the abjected monster as perpetually troubling the border lines of sacred history and holy land. Yet it is the monstrous other who generates a double understanding of identities formation by residing neither on the outside nor on the inside, but "where the most intimate interiority coincides with the exterior and becomes threatening, provoking horror and anxiety."[72] Monsters structure the boundaries of cultural space by marking a cultural break, reminding one of the limits of a culture's self-definition and of the consequences of transgression. Indeed, monsters are warnings (L. *monere*)[73] that, as spatial objects and their temporal representation, in a sense predict their own arrival,[74] the arrival of a thing at once unthought and actively menacing. In moral terms, for instance, monsters signify the condition into which an individual might degenerate, the result of the interior becoming as horrible as what was imagined to be exterior. In this the monster forces a double understanding of identities formation: identity emerges through exclusionary means, over and against the monster who is posited as radically other; yet the monster, residing in interstitiality, also leads back to, and comes to inhabit, the intimate place of identity.

"The point where the monster emerges," writes Mladen Dolar, "is always immediately seized by an overwhelming amount of meaning. . . . it has immediate social and ideological connotations. The monster can stand for everything that our culture has to repress." But this projection of what is repressed or disavowed onto the monstrous does not alone account for the monster's meaning. The monster, Dolar continues, "is always at stake in ideology—ideology perhaps basically consists of a social attempt to integrate the [monster], to make it bearable, to assign it a place."[75] The discursive site assigned to the monster is thus not merely the inevitable point at which the repressed returns, but rather its ultimate inscription in a zone of unthought, a space where ideological struggles around identity never cease. When the monster becomes integrated into the symbolic domain, the discursive dimension of the monster blurs the line between interiority and exteriority.

This blurring of the distinction between internal and external, the division upon which identity is predicated, is manifest at those moments in the crusade histories when Christians are discovered, with shock and revulsion, to share with Saracens many of their most monstrous traits. In their *historiae* of the first crusade, for example, Fulcher of Chartres and Raymond d'Aguilers describe, in terms as horror-filled as those reserved for Saracen atrocities, the opening up of graves and the burning and disemboweling of Saracens by crusaders greedy for loot.[76] Fulcher and Raymond, along with other historians, also document the horrors of Christian cannibalism, a sign of beastliness universally imputed to the Saracen other.[77] Images of cannibalism, disinterment, and corporal mutilation circulate here as displacements of an interior radical alterity that is consistently disavowed. Moreover, these images function as signs of Christian monstrosity prior to their practical explanation or moral justification—that is, to being explicable by greed, hunger, poetic justice, retaliation, or propaganda. The image monstrosity generates is one of the abject having become proximate. The despised monster crosses over the border of subjectivity because discursive practice refuses to name it as utterly different. For a moment, differences between the other and the same are suspended; for a moment, the monster seems to escape the prison of unthought.

Yet the monster's inscription in a unique network of symbolic domains in the twelfth century—psychic structures, historical order, topography, and the human body—confined it to its dialectical function in the self/other opposition. The Saracen disrupted the Christian's universe *and* produced its limits. The Saracen not merely oscillated between these two possibilities, but, in the shape of the monster, bridged the gap between them. The empty ideological space between Islam and Christianity that the monster Saracen catastrophically came to fill became the site of unthought, where a horror of sameness replaced a horror of difference.

Notes

For their helpful comments and suggestions, I would like to thank Debra Morris, Vance Smith, Nick Frankel, and Dug Duggan.

1. Marcel Détienne, *Dionysos Slain*, trans. M. Mueller and L. Mueller (Baltimore: Johns Hopkins University Press, 1979), ix.

2. Michel Foucault, *The Order of Things: An Archaeology of the Human Sciences* (New York: Vintage, 1970), xxiv.

3. Ibid., 326.

4. Ibid., 326–27.

5. Ibid., 326.

6. As a boundary phenomenon, that which the normal figures as part of its exterior—as contrary, *contra naturam*, monstrous, or "queer"—inevitably becomes the silent victim of intolerance, abjection, and violence. Such an insistence upon queerness, upon the social logic of otherness, writes Michael Warner, "has the effect of pointing out a wide field of normalization . . . as the site of violence." "Introduction," in *Fear of a Queer Planet: Queer Politics and Social Theory* (Minneapolis: University of Minnesota Press, 1993), xxvi.

7. Jonathan Dollimore, *Sexual Dissidence: Augustine to Wilde/Freud to Foucault* (Oxford: Clarendon, 1991), 229; emphasis added. Or, as Dollimore puts it in a trenchant aphorism, "To be against (opposed to) is also to be against (close up, in proximity to) or, in other words, up against" (229).

8. Michel de Certeau, "Spatial Stories," in *The Practice of Everyday Life*, trans. Steven Rendall (Berkeley: University of California Press, 1984), 127.

9. Mary Douglas, *Purity and Danger* (New York: Praeger, 1966), 36. Much attention has been focused on the cultural and psychological significance of strong aversions to ambiguity; see, for example, Julia Kristeva, *Powers of Horror: An Essay on Abjection*, trans. Leon S. Roudiez (New York: Columbia University Press, 1982); Peter Stallybrass and Allon White, *The Politics and Poetics of Transgression* (Ithaca, N.Y.: Cornell University Press, 1986); Iris Marion Young, *Justice and the Politics of Difference* (Princeton, N.J.: Princeton University Press, 1990), chap. 5; and Eviatar Zerubavel, *The Fine Line: Making Distinctions in Everyday Life* (Chicago: University of Chicago Press, 1991), chaps. 3–4.

10. Judith Butler, *Bodies That Matter: On the Discursive Limits of "Sex"* (New York: Routledge, 1993), 3.

11. Kristeva, *Powers of Horror*, 10.

12. Max Horkheimer and Theodor W. Adorno, "The Importance of the Body," in *Dialectic of Enlightenment*, trans. John Cumming (New York: Herder & Herder, 1972), 234.

13. Roger of Hoveden, *The Annals of Roger of Hoveden*, trans. Henry T. Riley (London: Bohn, 1853), 2:177–87.

14. The idea that Islam was a kind of false Christianity, a deviation from orthodoxy rather than a separate religion in its own right, was influential among even the most informed churchmen and historians, such as Peter the Venerable, William of Malmesbury, Thomas Aquinas, and Ricoldo of Montecroce.

15. The date cited is that of Alvarus's *Indiculus Luminosus.* The works of the Cordovan martyrs are collected in *Patrologiæ cursus completus: Series latina,* ed. J.-P. Migne (Paris: Migne, 1844–91) (hereafter *PL*), 115:705–870. The *Indiculus Luminosus,* containing Alvarus's interpretation of the Book of Daniel in terms of the rise of Islam as the fourth and final kingdom, is in *PL* 121:397–566.

16. In my view, the central theme of Norman Daniel's seminal study *Islam and the West: The Making of an Image* (Edinburgh: Edinburgh University Press, 1960) is the way that Islam as an autonomous religion was displaced by its representation within a limited range of vocabulary and imagery. Islam was domesticated by strictly analogical understanding—Muslims, it was maintained, worship a false trinity of idols, and Muhammad was an apostate Roman cardinal.

17. R. W. Southern, *Western Views of Islam in the Middle Ages* (Cambridge: Harvard University Press, 1962), 3, 4. See also Edward Said's discussion of Islam as "a lasting trauma" (59) for medieval Europe. *Orientalism* (New York: Vintage, 1979), 58–72.

18. One of my favorite examples is the famous Borgia *mappa mundi* that pictures in northern Africa a cynocephalic king of the Saracens seated on a throne and holding court for two subjects as monstrous in appearance as himself. The rubric reads: "Abichinibel rex est Sarracenus Ethipicus; cum populo suo habens faciem caninam, et in cedent omnes nudi propter solis calorem [King Abichinibel is an Ethiopian Saracen among his subjects who have dog faces, and all go about naked on account of the sun's heat]." Vicomte de Santarém, *Essai sur l'histoire de la cosmographie et de la cartographie pendant le Moyen-Age,* 3 vols., ed. Martim de Albuquerque (Lisbon: Administração do Porto de Lisboa, 1989), 294. The conflation of Saracens and dogs occurs frequently in the French *chansons de geste,* where the Muslims are frequently portrayed as barking like dogs when they rush into battle. See C. Meredith Jones, "The Conventional Saracen of the Songs of Geste," *Speculum* 17 (1942): 205. The identification of cynocephalics with Muslim "Turks" extends of course beyond the Latin polemical tradition. In fact, the polemical tradition gained its force from popular folktales and romances. David Gordon White, in his outstanding book *The Myths of the Dog-Man* (Chicago: University of Chicago Press, 1991), 61–62, mentions the Slavic folk identification of Turks with dog-headed man-eaters.

19. *Heremberti Epitome Chronologica,* ed. Lodovico Antonio Muratori, 5:18–21; trans. in Norman Daniel, *The Arabs and Mediaeval Europe* (London: Longman, 1975), 56.

20. Robert the Monk, *Historia Hierosolymitana,* cap. 2 in *Recueil des historiens des croisades* (hereafter *RHC*), 16 vols. (Paris: Academie des Inscriptians et Belles Lettres, 1841–1906), vol. 3 of *Historiens Occidentaux* (hereafter *HO*), 729.

21. Guibert of Nogent, *Historia quae dicitur Gesta Dei per Francos,* lib. 2 in *RHC,* vol. 4 of *HO,* 138. This English translation, from August C. Krey, *The First Crusade: The Accounts of Eye-Witnesses and Participants* (Gloucester, Mass.: Peter Smith, 1958), 38, has been modified.

22. M.-D. Chenu, *Nature, Man, and Society in the Twelfth Century: Essays on New Theological Perspectives in the Latin West,* ed. and trans. Jerome Taylor and Lester K. Little (Chicago: University of Chicago Press, 1968), 185.

23. Otto of Freising, *Chronica sive historia de duabus civitatibus,* ed. Roger Wilmans (Leipzig: Hiersemann, 1925), in *Monumenta Germaniae Historica,* ed. Georg Heinrich

Pertz (Hannover: Hiersemann, 1868), 20:116–301. In English, *The Two Cities: A Chronicle of Universal History to the Year 1146 A.D.*, ed. Austin P. Evans and Charles Knapp, trans. Charles Christopher Mierow (New York: Octagon, 1966), 94.

24. See Chenu, *Nature, Man, and Society*, 170, 186–87.

25. Hugh of St. Victor, *De vanitate mundi*, iv in *PL* 176:720.

26. Hugh of St. Victor, *De arca Noe morali*, iv.9 in *PL* 176:667.

27. Gerald of Wales, *De principis instructione*, dist. 1, in *Geraldus Cambrensis de principis instructione liber*, Rolls Series 21 (London, 1891), 70.

28. See also William of Malmesbury, *De gestis regum*, ed. William Stubbs, Rolls Series 90, 2:393ff. Climate theory was used to explain the bestiality of Orientals living in the hot regions. See Jacques de Vitry, *Libri duo, quorum prior orientalis, sive Hierosolymitanae: alter, occidentalis historiae nomine inscribitur* (Douay, 1597), vol. 1, cap. 6, 25–26.

29. Gerald of Wales, *De principis*, dist. 3, 268. The letter is also included in the histories of Benedict of Peterborough, Roger of Howden, Ralph of Diceto, and Ralph of Coggeshale, and in the *Itinerarium regis Ricardi.*

30. Said, *Orientalism*, 60.

31. Norman Daniel, "Crusade Propaganda," in *The Impact of the Crusades on Europe*, ed. Harry W. Hazard and Norman P. Zacour (Madison: University of Wisconsin Press, 1989), 77. W. Montgomery Watt subscribes to the same view of Islam's effect on Latin Europe, saying that Islam "provoked Europe into forming a new image of itself." *The Influence of Islam on Medieval Europe* (Edinburgh: Edinburgh University Press, 1982), 84. For a good discussion of the historical formation of Europe, see Denys Hay, *Europe: The Emergence of an Idea* (Edinburgh: Edinburgh University Press, 1968).

32. James Clifford, "On *Orientalism*," in *The Predicament of Culture* (Cambridge: Harvard University Press, 1988), 272.

33. See Southern, *Western Views of Islam*, 34–66.

34. The work of Adèl-Théodore Khoury is indispensable: *Les théologiens byzantins et l'Islam: textes et auteurs (VIIIe–XIIIe s.)* (Paris: Beatrice-Nauwelaerts, 1969); *Apolegetique byzantine contre l'Islam (8–13 s.)* (Altenberge: Verlag für Christlich-Islamisches Schriftum, 1982); *Polemique byzantine contre l'Islam (8–13 s.)* (Leiden: E. J. Brill, 1972). See also Paul Khoury, *Matériaux pour servir à l'étude de la controverse théologique Islamo-chrétienne de langue arabe du VIIIe au XIIe siècle* (Altenberge: Telos-Verlag, 1989), who argues that "l'activité théologique est, par structure, une activité de dialogue" (4). See also Jean-Marie Gaudeul, *Encounters and Clashes: Islam and Christianity in History*, 2 vols. (Rome: Pontificio Instituto di Studi Arabi e Islamici, 1984), who argues that the history of Islamo-Christian relations is one of failed dialogue. On the centrality of the dialogue form in Western polemics against Islam, see M.-Th. d'Alverny, "La connaissance de l'Islam en Occident du IXe au milieu du XIIe siècle," *Settimane di studio del Centro italiano di studi sull'alto medioevo* 12 (1965): 577–602.

35. Peter the Venerable, *Liber contra sectam sive haeresim Saracenorum*, D 180vs; quoted in James Kritzeck, *Peter the Venerable and Islam* (Princeton, N.J.: Princeton University Press, 1964), 229.

36. Three discussions of the cultural effects of contact with the Muslim other are

found in Vladimir P. Goss, ed., *The Meeting of Two Worlds: Cultural Exchange between East and West during the Period of the Crusades* (Kalamazoo, Mich.: Medieval Institute, 1986); María Rosa Menocal, *The Arabic Role in Medieval Literary History: A Forgotten Heritage* (Philadelphia: University of Pennsylvania Press, 1987); and Dorothee Metlitzki, *The Matter of Araby in Medieval England* (New Haven, Conn.: Yale University Press, 1987).

37. William of Tyre, *Historia rerum in partibus transmarinis gestarum*, 1.15 in *RHC*, vol. 1, pt. 1 of *HO*, 41; translation mine.

38. Saracens were defined in terms of desire and enjoyment. What frustrated Western writers most was the ease with which their desires were satisfied: The Saracens, writes Guibert of Nogent, "have ruled over the Christians at their pleasure, and have gladly frequented the sloughs of all baseness for the satisfaction of their lusts, and in all this have had no obstacle." *Historia quae dicitur Gesta Dei per Francos*, in Krey, *The First Crusade*, 38. Casting Muslims in terms of their limitless desire must have had some value as an explanation for their successes. Theirs was a desire that knew no psychological or spatial limits. Humbert of Romans, for instance, claims to have seen with his own eyes "the holy chapel, in which the Muslims who were on their way to the Lord Frederick [II] quartered themselves; and it was said as certain [*pro certo*] that they lay there at night with women before the crucifix." *Opusculum tripartitum*, 1.7, in *Appendix ad fasciculum rerum expetendarum et fugiendarum sive tomus secundus*, ed. Edward Brown (London, 1690), translated in Daniel, *Islam and the West*, 110.

39. Manifestations of boundless desire included adultery, polygamy, concubinage, and sodomy (in the full range of practices covered by this term—in short, sexual acts *contra naturam*). These were said to be practiced openly and encouraged under Muslim law. Ramón Martí, for instance, described Muhammad's law as "immunda, nociva, et mala" and focused his treatise "De seta Machometi" on Muslim sexual practices defined repeatedly in these terms: "contra legem naturalem," "contra preceptum Dei," "contra bonum prolis," and "contra rei publice utilitatem." See Josep Hernando I Delgado, "Le 'De Seta Machometi' du Cod. 46 d'Osma, œuvre de Raymond Martin (Ramón Martí)," in *Islam et chrétiens du Midi (XIIe–XIVe s.)*, ed. Edouard Privat (Toulouse: Cahiers de Fanjeaux, 1983), 353–54. Rather than multiply references to Muslim sexual deviation and excess here, I refer the reader to Norman Daniel's fine overview of the subject in *Islam and the West*, especially his chapter titled "The Place of Self-Indulgence in the Attack on Islam," 135–61.

40. Desire, enjoyment, and deviation powerfully combined in the image of Islam as the religion of seduction. The crusades were in many senses projects to recover land that had been seduced away from Christian holds. Thus William of Tyre begins his *Historia* with an account of how Muhammad, with his "doctrina pestilens," "Orientalium regiones et maxime Arabium seduxerat" (*Historia rerum in partibus transmarinis gestarum*, 1.1 in *RHC*, vol. 1 of *HO*, 9). Or Cardinal Rodrigo Ximénez (1170?–1247), archbishop of Toledo, who described Muhammad as the seducer of Spain. See his *Historia Arabum*, 1.1, in *Historia Saracenica qua res gestae Muslimorum inde a Muhammede Arabe . . . Arabice olim exarata a Georgio Elmacino, etc.*, ed. Thomas Erpenius (van Erpe) (Leiden, 1625). Jacques de Vitry also figures Muhammad as the aggressor in the *Historia Hierosolimitana abbreviata* (ca. 1221), where the rubric

to his biography of Muhammad reads, "Vita Machometi, qualiter seduxit terram sanctam, sive ecclesiam orientalem" (Paris, B. nat., lat. 6244A; cited in Daniel, *Islam and the West*, 348 n. 2). And St. Thomas Aquinas lays bare the role that desire and the attractiveness of enjoyment played in Muhammad's victories: "He seduced the people by promises of carnal pleasure to which the concupiscence of the flesh goads us. His teaching also contained precepts that were in conformity with his promises, and he gave free rein to carnal pleasure. In all this, as is not unexpected, he was obeyed by carnal men." *Summa contra Gentiles*, 1.6; translated in James Waltz, "Muhammad and the Muslims in St. Thomas Aquinas," *The Muslim World* 66 (1976): 83.

41. Images of madness pervade anti-Muslim polemical writing. The antithesis of Western medieval ideologies that endorse rationality and order, madness, from the first moments of crusade, was adduced as an explanation of the Saracen threat—paradoxically, the religion and its practices could be explained only in terms of the unexplainable. The annotator of the autograph manuscript of Peter the Venerable's corpus of translations and treatises (the Toletano-Cluniac corpus, MS Arsenal 1162) applies the epithet *insanus* (madman) to Muhammad; the annotator's view is consistent with both Jewish attitudes toward Muhammad (as *m'shugga* [mad], based on Hosea 9:7, "the prophet [man of the spirit] is mad") and a long Western tradition that conflated Muhammad's epilepsy with madness and demonic possession (on this, see Daniel, *Islam and the West*, 27–32).

42. Images of Muslim disorder center on the confused form of the Koran; there was an obvious relation, so the argument went, between Muhammad's madness and the self-contradictory, repetitive, and irrational nature of the Koran. Western readers, fortunate to have access to Robert of Ketton's 1143 translation, found the text wholly inconsistent with reason and repellent to logic. In discussions of the Koran, we come very close to the kinds of ideological constructions of the other that impute to it notions of flux, ambivalence, and mixture. To Daniel's thorough discussion of the image of the Koran in *Islam and the West*, 57–67, I would add two interesting sources: a treatise on Saracens titled "Mores Sarracenorum et leges quas Mahumeth observare constitute prophetando sarracenis" (London, British Library, Cotton Faustina, A. 7, ff. 150v–156v), which takes up the "problem" of the Koran and its form at 155v; and Thomas Aquinas's comments on the monstrous construction of the Koran in *Summa contra Gentiles*, 1.6.

43. On the ideology of idolatry and its central role in the imagination and fabrication of the other in the Middle Ages, see Michael Camille, *The Gothic Idol: Ideology and Image-Making in Medieval Art* (New York: Cambridge University Press, 1989).

44. *Liber quartus contra paganos, Opinio paganorum qui dicunt Christum conceptum fuisse de flatu Dei*, ed. M.-Th. d'Alverny in "Alain de Lille et l'Islam. Le 'Contra Paganos,'" in *Islam et chrétiens du Midi (XIIe-XIVe s.)* 331–32; translation mine. For the full text of Alan's tract, see *De fide catholica contra hæreticos sui temporis*, *PL* 210:305–430.

45. References to the prophet's scandalous death are common in the polemical writings. Most often Muhammad was believed to have been devoured by pigs rather than dogs. See Gerald of Wales's *De principis instructione*, 68. Gerald's view represents those of Guibert of Nogent, Ranulph Higden, and Matthew Paris. Alan appears

to have inherited the view of a ninth-century Spanish legend of Muhammad; see M.-Th. d'Alverny, "Alain de Lille et l'Islam," 320–21.

46. Peter the Venerable, *Epistola ad Bernardum Claraevallis*, A 4rs, ed. James Kritzeck, in Kritzeck, *Peter the Venerable and Islam*, 213.

47. Peter the Venerable, *Liber contra sectam sive haeresim Saracenorum*, D 179vs, in Kritzeck, *Peter the Venerable and Islam*, 225.

48. See Peter's argument, which ends with an invitation to his readers to decide the question for themselves, in *Liber contram sectam*, D 179vd–180rs, in Kritzeck, *Peter the Venerable and Islam*, 226–27.

49. Horace, *Ars poetica* 1.1–2.

50. Peter the Venerable, *Summa totius haeresis Saracenorum*, A 2vs, in Kritzeck, *Peter the Venerable and Islam*, 208.

51. Crusade propaganda and anti-Muslim polemic functioned primarily, if not exclusively, ideologically to unify Christian Europe, to create, in Benedict Anderson's formula, "a religious community" free from disrupting internal forces such as heretics and unbelievers. On community and nation as ideological structures, the products of imagination, see Benedict Anderson, *Imagined Communities: Reflections on the Origin and Spread of Nationalism* (London: Verso, 1983).

52. The letter, almost unanimously taken by modern historians to be a Western forgery circulated before the first crusade, survives in at least three manuscripts of the early twelfth century. Incorporated into the histories of Robert the Monk, Guibert of Nogent, and William of Tyre, the letter was an important document in determining the trajectory of thought regarding Muslim alterity and violation of Christian sanctity. For a discussion of the letter's authenticity and origin, see Einar Joranson, "The Problem of the Spurious Letter of Emperor Alexius to the Count of Flanders," *American Historical Review* 55 (1950): 811–32. The Latin text is in Heinrich Hagenmeyer, ed., *Die Kreuzzugbriefe aus den Jahren 1088–1100: Eine Quellensammalung zur Geschichte des Ersten Kreuzzugs* (Innsbruck: Wagner, 1901), 130–36; a fine English translation by John Boswell appears in the appendix to his *Christianity, Social Tolerance, and Homosexuality* (Chicago: University of Chicago Press, 1980), 367–69.

53. Hagenmeyer, *Die Kreuzzugbriefe*, 131; Boswell, *Christianity, Social Tolerance*, 367.

54. Hagenmeyer, *Die Kreuzzugbriefe*, 133, 132.

55. Representations of Saracen sexual violence are stock features of crusade literature. The "Spurious Letter of Alexius Comnenus to Count Robert of Flanders" accuses the Saracens of sodomizing their victims and having already killed "sub hoc nefario peccato" a Christian bishop; ibid., 132. Albert of Aachen describes the Saracens as ravishing nuns and other women during the first crusade and raping Armenian women at 'Arqa (see his *Historia Hierosolymitana*, in *RHC*, vol. 4 of *HO*, 288, 358). Raymond d'Aguilers charges that the Muslims hold out the incentive of easy opportunities for rape in order to incite their troops. See *Le "Liber" de Raymond d'Aguilers*, ed. John Hugh Hill and Laurita L. Hill (Paris: P. Geuthner, 1969), 155.

56. The vast numbers of Muslims and their victories over Christians were to twelfth-century historians both puzzling and threatening. William of Malmesbury, for instance, attributes to Urban the lamentation that the enemies of Christendom inhabit two-thirds of the world, Asia and Africa, and have been oppressing the Chris-

tians in the remaining one-third for three hundred years in Spain and the Baleares (see his *De gestis regum*, 2:393–98). William, in his *Commentary on Lamentations*, sees the expansion of Islam as a result of God's judgment on impious Christians (see Oxford, Bodleian 868, f. 34v). As another link in the "discursive chain," polygamy among the Muslims was often adduced as the source of their vast numbers. In a manuscript of Matthew Paris's *Chronica maiora* (Cambridge, Corpus Christi College 26, f. 87), there is an illustration of Muhammad holding two scrolls in the center margin. One of them reads "Poligamus este. Scriptum est enim crescite et multiplicamini [Be polygamous, for it is written increase and be multiplied]."

57. Images of profanation such as the ones I have cited were perhaps the most dominant group of images in anti-Muslim polemic. Like images of monstrosity and boundary breaking, such images were applicable to a wide range of Muslim beliefs and practices. The images conveyed notions of pollution, disorder, and fluidity. The crusades became a cleansing of the Holy Land; see Fidenzio of Padua, *Fidentii . . . liber de recuperatione Terrae Sanctae*, xvi, in vol. 2 of *Biblioteca Bio-bibliografica della Terra Santa e dell'oriente Francescano*, 5 vols., ed. P. Girolamo Golubovich (Quaracchi, 1905).

58. This term is used by Stuart Hall to characterize the mechanics of ideology. Ideologies operate in "discursive chains" wherein "ideological representations connote—summon—one another." "Signification, Representation, Ideology: Althusser and the Post-Structuralist Debates," *Critical Studies in Mass Communication* 2 (1985): 104–5.

59. A fine example of this emphasis on the blurring and breaking of the limits that define Christianity is William of Tyre's account of Urban's crusade speech, where he catalogs Saracen violations in the Holy Land. See *Historia rerum in partibus transmarinis gestarum*, 1.15 in *RHC*, vol. 1, pt. 1 of *HO*, 39–42.

60. See Peter Brown's excellent book, *The Body and Society: Men, Women, and Sexual Renunciation in Early Christianity* (New York: Columbia University Press, 1988), for sources of medieval ideas on the body and its structure as a system of boundaries.

61. Indeed, Ernaldus of Bonneval wrote in his commentary on the first chapter of Genesis that cosmic unity derived from God's ordered arrangement of natural things, distributed like the members of a great body (*quasi magni corporis membra*). See the prologus of *De operibus sex dierum* (*PL* 189:1515–16). On the place of the body and the body as place in the symbolic representation of social experience, see Mary Douglas, *Natural Symbols: Explorations in Cosmology* (New York: Pantheon, 1970).

62. On the tripartite functional organization of medieval society—the holy, the warring, and the working—which Georges Dumézil traced to its origins in Indo-European culture, see Georges Duby, *Les trois ordres ou l'imaginaire du féodalisme* (Paris: Gallimard, 1978); and Jacques Le Goff, "Les trois fonctions indo-européennes, l'historien et l'Europe féodale," *Annales E.S.C.* 34 (1979): 1187–1215.

63. Humbert of Moyenmoutier, *Adverus simoniacos*, *PL* 143: 1005ff. There is a discussion and translation in André Vauchez, "Les laïcs dans l'Eglise à l'époque féodale," *Notre Histoire* 32 (1987): 35.

64. See Fulcher of Chartres, *Historia Hierosolymitana*, in *RHC*, vol. 4 of *HO*, 326.

65. John of Salisbury, *Policraticus*, 5.2, ed. C. C. J. Webb (Oxford, 1909); in English by John Dickinson, *The Statesman's Book of John of Salisbury: Being the Fourth, Fifth,*

and Sixth Books, and Selections from the Seventh and Eighth Books, of the Policraticus (New York: Knopf, 1927).

66. William of Tyre, *Historia rerum in partibus transmarinis gestarum*, 1.15 in *RHC*, vol. 1, pt. 1 of *HO*, 41; English translation in *A History of Deeds Done beyond the Sea* 1:90.

67. Robert the Monk, *Historia Hierosolymitana*, cap. 1 in *RHC*, vol. 3 of *HO*, 727–28; English translation in Dana C. Munro, *Urban and the Crusaders* (Philadelphia, 1895), 5–6.

68. Guibert of Nogent, *Historia quae dicitur Gesta Dei per Francos*, lib. 2 in *RHC*, vol. 4 of *HO*, 140; English translation in Krey, *The First Crusade*, 40.

69. It should be clear that my account of alterity in the twelfth century aims at complicating the prevalent idea that such terrifying descriptions of the Saracens were strictly (and merely) emotional *excitatoria*. Thus statements like this one in a recent essay by James Muldoon have a very limited place in a history of the ideology of difference in the Middle Ages: "The purpose of describing the non-European in terrifying or grotesque terms was to appeal to the emotions—not the minds—of readers or hearers." "The Nature of the Infidel: The Anthropology of the Canon Lawyers," in *Discovering New Worlds: Essays on Medieval Exploration and Imagination*, ed. Scott D. Westrem (New York: Garland, 1991), 116.

70. See Burchard of Worms, *Decretum* 9.30, in *PL* 140:830; and Ivo of Chartres, *Decretum* 8.204, in *PL* 161:626.

71. The Council of Nablus—not a church council in the ordinary sense but rather a *parlement* (see Prawer)—decreed that a Christian man guilty of miscegenation with a Saracen woman was to be castrated and the woman's nose was to be cut off. See *Sacrorum conciliorum nova et amplissima collectio*, ed. Giovanni Domenico Mansi, 60 vols. (Paris: Hubert Welter, 1901–27), 21:264. On the Council of Nablus, see Joshua Prawer, *Crusader Institutions* (Oxford: Clarendon, 1980), 15–17; and Hans Eberhard Mayer, "The Concordat of Nablus," *Journal of Ecclesiastical History* 33 (1982): 531–43.

72. Mladen Dolar, "'I Shall Be with You on Your Wedding Night': Lacan and the Uncanny," *October* 58 (1991): 6.

73. Good discussions of medieval etymology for *monstrum* are found in John Block Friedman, *The Monstrous Races in Medieval Art and Thought* (Cambridge: Harvard University Press, 1981), 108–30; and Claude Lecouteux, *Les monstres dans la littérature allemande du Moyen Age: Contribution à l'étude du merveilleux médiéval*, 3 vols. (Göppingen: Kümmerle, 1982), 2–3.

74. See Louis Marin, "Frontiers of Utopia: Past and Present," *Critical Inquiry* 19 (Spring 1993): 399–400.

75. Dolar, "'I Shall Be with You,'" 19.

76. See Fulcher of Chartres, *Historia Hierosolymitana*, lib. 1, cap. 28, and lib. 2, cap. in *RHC*, vol. 3 of *HO*, 359, 390; and Raymond d'Aguilers, *Historia Francorum qui ceperunt Iherusalem*, cap. 8, vol. 3 of *HO*, 249.

77. See Fulcher, *Historia*, cap. 24, 352; Raymond, *Historia*, cap. 14, 271; also, the *Gesta Francorum Iherusalem expugnantium*, in *RHC*, vol. 3 of *HO*, 498. For more Christian anthropophagy, see the chronicle of Ademar of Chabannes and the popular early-fourteenth-century poem *Richard Coer de Lyon*. The imputing of cannibalism

to Saracens and especially to the Mongols—to the Oriental other—was universal. See, for example, "The Tartar Relation" (*Historia Tartarorum*), a largely ethnographic description of the Mongols written down in 1247 by a certain C. de Bridia upon the occasion of Plano Carpini's return to Europe, in R. A. Skelton, Thomas E. Marston, and George D. Painter, *The Vinland Map and the Tartar Relation* (New Haven, Conn.: Yale University Press, 1965), 97. Or, concerning the taste of Mongols for pickled human flesh in the Egerton manuscript version of Mandeville: *The Buke of John Maundeuill. being the Travels of John Mandeville, Knight 1322–56. A Hitherto Unpublished English Version from the Unique Copy (Egerton Ms. 1982) in the British Museum . . . together with the French Text, Notes, and an Introduction*, ed. George F. Warner (London: Roxburghe Club, 1889), 123. For a recent overview of Western myths of Mongol cannibalism, see Gregory G. Guzman, "Reports of Mongol Cannibalism in the Thirteenth-Century Latin Sources: Oriental Fact or Western Fiction?" in *Discovering New Worlds: Essays on Medieval Exploration and Imagination*, ed. Scott D. Westrem (New York: Garland, 1991), 31–68.

14 Dinosaurs-R-Us: The (Un)Natural History of *Jurassic Park*

John O'Neill

> Kids are our real audience.
>
> JURASSIC PARK

Americans love big things, including themselves. They even love things bigger than themselves, like America. Recently, Americans have demonstrated an extraordinary affection for carnivores larger than themselves—returning the earlier efforts by King Kong and other aliens such as ET to love Americans. Even when Americans love tiny creatures like Mickey Mouse what they love is their espousal of the cardinal American virtues of hardworking, asexual aggression tirelessly practiced by the little guys in totally controlled, aseptic environments such as that they have come to worship at Disneyland.[1] The Disney complex contains both a psychic and technocultural apparatus through which Americans have totally erased nature and its aboriginal peoples, including the real history of their own domestication. The continuing fascination of the Disney complex depends upon its ability to reanimate itself through displacement either into the remote future, as in *Star Trek*, or into the remote past, as in *Jurassic Park* (*JP*).[2]

In America, however, all fun is serious fun. Having lost its (un)natural opponent in Communism, American capitalism is now challenged by the globalization of capitalist greed, which gobbles up anything that tries to hide behind national barriers. Unless it can prove itself to be equally rapacious, American capitalism will be destroyed by its global predators, or else American capitalism must colonize outer space in compensation for its threatened terrestrial dominion. Here the miscegenation of science and fiction has for years colonized our intergalactic imagination with reruns of the history of rebarbarism of humankind and its recivilization by American technoculture and asexual intelligence. These experiments with the satellization of American culture, when combined with their terrestrial counterpart in Disneyland, provide us with a framework for siting *JP*.

Jurassic Park is science fiction because science is a mode of fiction. Genetic engineering in particular represents the ideal/practical cross-fertilization of science, engineering, and commercialism that has characterized American capitalism. In the context of the exhaustion of First World industrialism, *Jurassic Park* renews the cultural myth of the self-made "man." Because in late capitalism there can be no question of linking science fiction to the political fiction that gave birth to early modern capitalism, *Jurassic Park* is limited to a biofiction produced "offshore." Yet I think it can be shown to have a definite political and historical message. Although ostensibly a creation story with a modern science fiction event at its center, *Jurassic Park* is actually a repetition of the biblical story of "man's" inability to repeat the Divine creative act. This time the agents are Science and Commerce, or Knowledge and Greed, and what is violated by their monstrous desire to clone Nature is fuzzy logic, or the law that any total system must generate chaos. Thus the narrative events of *Jurassic Park* reenact the conflict between apparent omnipotence (the combination of scientific knowledge and evil) and a limited creation whose fuzzy logic guarantees the long-run survival of humanity despite its reckless attraction to omnipotence. Although Jurassic Park is an offshore techno-Eden, it is a thoroughly American transplant operation designed to be reimported into the American heartland and from there sold to the rest of the world. This scheme, however, involves not just a return to good old Yankee commercialism; it is also an attempt to reconnect the United States to itself as the original landscape of humankind, that is, the giant heartland of free-ranging predatory monsters in that glorious evolutionary moment before all this became extinct (except for whales, which still fascinate us for some such reason). *Jurassic Park* therefore is thoroughly revisionist natural history (to which even Stephen Jay Gould succumbs, as we shall see later). It rewrites paleontology in the name of a technology (simulation) whose capacity for remaking history is entirely reduced to the American history of making profits at the box office. *Jurassic Park*'s success, so far from surprising us, is understandable if we consider the current failure of nerve in U.S. industrial history. By the same token, it reasserts Yankee cultural imperialism by replacing the Bible story, with the difference that the Book of Genesis becomes the Book of Genetic Engineering, in which forms are "naturalized" as dinosaurs whose animation is nevertheless entirely due to a combination of computerization, engineering, and theater crafts that is the pride of old-order industrialism. The failure of the biotech phantasy at the heart of *JP* is the beginning of American wisdom. It represents the limits of the United States as an old-order industrial culture trying to civilize itself at the movies, where myths have no more substance than popcorn.

The more the United States experiences crisis in an alien world, the more it needs to know that aliens—from Communists to ET—are at heart Americans. It is the ideological task of science fiction to confirm this political fiction by projecting the American image into remote past/future time. Here animalized or miscegenated androids are released from cybernetic slavery by a more ethical U.S. technoculture and its wise use of friendly fire. The infantilization of science as kids' culture is also a prime contributor to the consumerized pedagogy that dominates the United States. By the same token, docile consumerism increases the production anxiety of Americans and in turn feeds their fascination with science fiction in which the awkward creature succeeds against overwhelming odds. Of course, kids' science is just as hopelessly unsuited to the world of global information and competitive schooling as it is nicely congruent with the ideology of fun as education. Here the media portrayal of the omnipotent computer—solving crime, ignorance, disease, and disaster—represents a prime cargo-cult function inasmuch as its myth of fingertip control erases the real unpredictability of fortune between the players in the world of hard- and software production. Here, as elsewhere, the "regular" computer culture is fed by its nerds, nuts, loners, and whizzes, whose productive anxiety underwrites the carefree consumers of computer toys.

The productive crisis of U.S. industry is replayed in the procreative struggle between Dr. Alan Grant and Dr. Ellie Sattler, set against the creative enterprise of *JP*. Here science seems able to accomplish what sexuality seems ready to abandon. Setting aside what is culturally obnoxious about American children, Lexis and Tim are from a "broken family," and whereas Ellie appears able to combine feminist strokes with a desire for family, she nevertheless needs some miracle or other to convert Alan to familism. Drs. Sattler and Grant also represent the exhaustion of intelligence unable to recombine with the adventure of *JP*'s spirited capitalism. They can be bought for a song but lack the vision to sell themselves at a price high enough to provide for the future of the past they so love. Ellie and Alan are a couple in love with their dead babies. Even this love has to be sparked by John Hammond's mad enterprise of amusing the world's children with animals whose asexuality is essential to their controlled simulation, which is in turn the key to the controlled amusement provided by *JP*.

There is, however, a disciplinary aspect to all consumer culture that begins with its panoptical capture in store videos, mall police, and the dressage involved in crowd control at large spectacles, where again multiple television eyes instantly replay the crowd's orderly amusement.[3] *JP*'s visitor center is, then, the heart of the controlled tour of the wild it unlends to sell to its visitors, who will circulate through Dino-park locked in wild jeeps that tamely ride a computerized monorail. Each next visitor can learn from watching the previous car how to behave, just as airline passengers watch themselves going through airline safety procedures in preparation for their phantasy of flight. Real passengers don't get high, they just fly! Real children, then, don't go wild except in the safety of *JP*. Thus the disciplinary culture of amusement produces a self-imposed order that simulates family, neighborhood, and friendship as its commercial by-products. The American Way of Life can be discovered along a monorail in place of the less secure adventure of America's wagon trail.

JP, of course, can amuse children only through a highly controlled regression to "their" level of aggression, destruction, and death—short of omnipotent reversals by adults who after all do love them. All the events of *JP*—and hence all its surprises—are bound to this structure of order and chaos, heightened by the potential failure of the computer system that produces the story that produces the book that produces the film that reproduces the ultimate lesson about monsters, that is, that machines are more reliable than machines that turn into animals or human beings. In turn, this lesson contains the larger lesson that machines cannot deliver the American Way of Life—however much Americans might desire such delivery in order to escape from the family production of American values.[4]

In *JP* we enter the past through the flying machine that is most symbolic of U.S. imperialism—the helicopter/heliraptor. This technobird has already taught the world's peasants to equate the sun with death rather than life while offering life to its wounded and the refugees it rescues from its own death spray—so celebrated in *Miss Saigon.* A similar reversal of past/present and of life/death is repeated in *JP*'s visitor center, where one can live the reversal of today and yesterday, inside and outside, fiction and reality in endless simulation of animate/inanimate beings. Here the distant and exotic past is brought into the familiar TV/computer control tower. This universalizes American culture by projecting it into the past and future in a benign colonization or evolutionary history on behalf of the future amusement of American kids and their families. Natural history is reduced to cultural history through the machinery of its theme park, already developed for Disneyland, where all artifacts monstrously double as commodities.[5]

The real monster in *JP* is not found among its technobeasts; rather, it is John Hammond, whose project is to capture the imagination of the world's children:

> You know, Jurassic Park's really made for children. The children of the world really love dinosaurs, and the children are going to delight—just *delight*—in this place. Their little faces will shine with the joy of finally seeing these wonderful animals.[6]

Hammond's apparently benign project of re-creating the world's largest pets for the world's greatest kids is not redeemed by his cancellation of its rapacious clones. He risks the destruction of Ellie and Alan's family line as well as the potentially new line of adoption for Lexis and Tim. Without a family, Lexis and Tim are little monsters who risk losing their chance of reentering the family by so confirming Alan's distaste for children that even Ellie's combination of feminist independence and maternal desire is helpless to win him over. Of course, both Alan and Ellie have to be seduced away from their dead love of paleo-pets for the kids to be removed from the endangered species list. What is monstrous about Hammond is that he believes that *Jurassic Park* can combine science, law, and commerce at the point where each is fused by its own greed with an inexhaustible prospect of profit and power. To this end, Hammond risks collapsing the natural history of birth and death into a single catastrophe. By playing grandfather to the park and to its visitors, Hammond usurps the missing family and its uncertain reconstitution through Ellie and Alan.

The complete Americanization of America, however, requires the continuous commercial reinspiration of the exhausted American family. At home, this is achieved through placing children very close to the navel of the TV, from where they can watch for themselves the natural events of the primal family acted out by talking animals whose own history of destruction and near extinction—except for being saved on TV—constitutes their immediate bond with children who are survivors of their own endangered species. Away from home, kids are commercially conscripted to the game of carnivorous visits to the Big M—the rapacious eating machine they cannot control[7]—where in exchange for endangering the family-species they can buy *JP* dino-trinkets. Thus the overall spectacle in *JP* is one where children must escape from baby-eating monsters who entertain them while they eat and drink from the sacramental store (the Big M) through which they become Jurassic Park communicants. In short, the spectacle is one of America as a commercial zoo in which all the events and processes of animal and human interaction are managed in the name of the postbiblical phantasy of a totally fabricated environment and at unimaginable profit, as the management system totally administers every element of *Jurassic Park*—the novel, the film, the children's books, toys, and so on—that are the real bite on children.

In *JP*, America can celebrate its emptiness as depth—its paleo-heartland has become the homeland of the world; largest mobiles and their companion giants, McDonald's and Coca-Cola. Here, we see the origin of the new American family—Dr. Grant, Lex, and Tim nestled in a commercial treetop in a world nicely balanced between their own carnivorous nature, watched over by McDonald's (MAC-ah-DON-ah-DULLS), and the friendly vegetarian brachiosaurus ("you say it like this BRACK-ee-oh-SOR-us"), whose counterpart is Coca-Cola (a leaf drink) (COK-ah-COL-ah). In this paleo-Eden kids can learn pidgin English and pidgin mathematics. What is four stories tall and weighs as much as a herd of elephants? How much does a herd of elephants weigh? One might as well ask, if Dinosaurs-R-Us, why aren't lizards, crocodiles, mice, worms, and fleas us? But I suppose that's the sort of question that only eggheads ask. Of course, there is an answer—but it's nerdy. Let's get back to the paleo-parking lot and the greening of the American family in the Age of Abortion.

Dinomania?

In view of the box-office reception of *JP*, one might sympathize with the desire of penniless paleontologists to be welcomed into the Disneyland complex—a fate no worse than that of those dignified curators who have permitted the marketization of the museum into a shop complex. But it is curious to see a natural historian of the stature of Stephen Jay Gould leap from his pedestal to side with the kids' concept of paleontology. Like many contemporary adults, Gould is as anxious to prove that he was once a kid—a "dinosaur nut"—as he is to claim minority status with nerds, misfits, and his sole friend, who was christened "dino" while he himself bore the stigma of "fossil face."[8] Despite this unnatural history, Gould and his friend persevered to become dinomaniacs, albeit with a more graceful reception in the university. Yet Gould still seeks to justify himself with the kids. This time he is better armed—or so he thinks—to answer "the most pressing question of the Nineties: Why are children so fascinated with dinosaurs?"

Gould begins by disavowing any unconscious motive—which he equates with Jungian archetypes—rather than the more relevant Freudian mechanism of ambivalence because a psychologist friend of his explained to him that something can't be both *scary* and *safe*! Having set aside psychoanalysis (the science of such contradictions), Gould is free to explore the historical question; that is, why weren't fossil kids from his generation able to see *Jurassic Park* like today's kids? He toys with two possible answers—one flattering to teachers of paleontology, but lacking conviction, and the other more likely but courting the extinction of the very discipline as a science sacrificed to a commercial fiction, painstakingly engaged in the animation of relics that hitherto moved only nerd paleontologists:

> When I was a child, ornithopods laid their eggs and then walked away forever. Today, these same creatures are the very models of maternal, caring politically correct dinosaurs. They watch over their nests, care for their young, form cooperative herds, and bear such lovely peaceful names as *Maiasauria*, the earth lizard (in contrast with such earlier monickers as *Pachycephalosaurus*, the thick bonehead). Even their extinction now appears in a much more interesting light. They succumbed to vaguely speculative types of "climatic change" in my youth; now we have firm evidence for extraterrestrial impact as the trigger for their final removal.[9]

Gould knows that the evil genius in kids' culture is commerce, but he lets it slip through his fingers because he insists upon the natural historian's fascination with a moment of origin—a fascination that whether he likes it or not is explained in Freudian psychoanalysis and merely toyed with in *JP*. Gould succumbs to his fascination with the simulation techniques in *JP*—while vainly trying to set its abuse of the DNA record straight, because he is curiously open to the populist argument that scientists can be wrong about their own business, especially when claiming that something can't be done that good old American know-how (technology) eventually gets done. Although Crichton's novel makes the necessary genuflection to a form of scientific nonpossibility through its reliance upon snippets of chaos theory (the impossibility of the perfectly controlled system), Gould is seduced by the movie and its "postmodern" re-creation of his pet loves as a mixed bunch of politically correct, corporate, and feminist predators. Whatever its faults, *JP* is redeemed by the "technical wizardry" that went into the animation of Gould's childhood dinosaurs, awakening in him something akin to religious awe:

> How cruel, how perverse, that we invest the most awesome expertise (and millions of bucks) in the dinosaurs, sparing no knowledge or expense to render every detail, every possible nuance, in the most realistic way. I have nothing but praise for the thought and care, the months and years that went into each dinosaur model, the pushing of computer generation to a new world of utility, the concern for rendering every detail with consummate care, even the tiny bits that few will see and the little sounds that fewer will hear. I think of medieval sculptors who lavished all their skills upon invisible statues on the parapets, for God's view is best (internal satisfaction based on personal excellence in modern translation).[10]

Gould's translation of technomania into moral excellence is, of course, potentially insane. Are we to admire the forging in the pistol that blows off our head? Should we admire the skill in making techno-gargoyles for a culture that by Gould's own standards is "Neanderthal"? Can we lament, as Gould does, the perversion of otherwise good technology—or good paleontology—if we do not blame the prince, the government grantor, the entrepreneur or the filmmaker on the ground that these "folks" merely challenge us to be "up-front" about our own values? Can Gould really believe that Crichton and Spielberg feel as sold out as himself by selling out themselves? Gould's lament ends with a plea for cultural death with dignity—please don't put our museum in an amusement park—please don't extract "more dollars per fanny" from our educational institutions. Still proclaiming the "cerebral and entirely conceptual" origins of his fascination with origins, Gould's lament remains mired in his unconscious protest against capitalist anality and the "prick" of personal advantage that will one day remove the past from all human memory. Hadn't we better call for Dr. Freud?

The inverted elitism of Gould's nerdy childhood renders him insensitive to the fate of the children he considers so marvelously served by *JP*'s monsters. In reality, the pedagogical issues that worry him in the commercial miscegenation of the museum and the amusement park are raised right in the American home and school. Here pedagogy has been reduced to dinagogy in what is known as children's educational television. The central feature is that the historical family—the truly endangered species—is naturalized by assigning the role of the missing parent to animal figures with whom children can share the anxiety of extinction. Although parents appear tolerant of the politically correct animalized indoctrination that dehistoricizes and disenchants the child's imagination, their rage at *Barney and Friends* represents the dark side of their embrace of defamilization. As can be seen from revised Barney songs such as those presented below, it aggravates their fear that the techno-baby-sitter may have seduced their babies with unconditional love:

A Barney-Basher's Songbook[11]

The Original (sung to the tune of "This Old Man")
I love you
You love me
We're a happy family
With a great big hug
and a kiss from me to you
Won't you say you love me too?

Revisionism
I hate you
You hate me
Let's go out and kill Barney
Then a shot rang out
and Barney hit the floor
No more purple dinosaur.

Same-Sex Alternative
I love you
You love me
Homosexuality
People think that we're just friends
But we're really lesbians.

Family Values
I hate you
You hate me
We're a dysfunctional family
Then a shot rang out
and Barney hit the floor
No more purple dinosaur.

What the Barney bashers fear is that their fossil kids may demand more family time, reversing history and progress. Here, of course, it is the dino-parents who have been betrayed by the double-bind message of dependence/autonomy in current family ideology. Thus the flight into *JP* obeys not only the prophecy of chaos theory but is also driven to its own nativity scene—*the extrafamilial egg*—regenerated by a combination of science and commerce, witnessed by a family that needs its own recombination miracle:

> "Why do these volunteers have to bring their kids, anyway?" Alan asked.
> Ellie didn't answer. She knew how Alan felt about kids. For some reason, he just didn't like them. . . . Ellie loved Alan. But he could be so annoying—especially when it came to kids. She wondered if he would ever change. If not, could they have a future together?[12]

All of the events of *JP* work toward Alan's evolution from an alien scientist into a treetop family Tarzan whose change of heart will permit Ellie to reorient her independent womanhood and its displaced affection for dino-pets into marriage, kids, and career. In other words, the kids are the endangered species not because they might be eaten by dinosaurs but because without the family there is no game of hatch as hatch can—unless, of course, they get bit parts in a movie about the extrafamilial egg:

> In the back of the helicopter, Alan sat with Lex and Tim. Ellie smiled at him. She never thought he'd be so comfortable with kids. He'd changed in the past couple of days. But then, she thought, they all had. They had made it out alive—they were survivors.[13]

JP's dino-family is in any case programmed for its evolution into the two-career, two-child family inasmuch as dino-babies appear to have been set in the pattern of single-season maturity—requiring minimal parental care—giving them a decided evolutionary advantage over slow-loving families.[14] Of course, dino-baby will not have had time to incubate a brain, but this can be offset by the gift of a computer and continuous consumer programming.

Genesis in Jurassic Park

The death of God involves a double murder. It is not only that sons must kill the father and steal his knowledge for the gift of science. Daughters, too, must murder, silencing the womb, floating life in a petri dish, gift of the biosciences. The emancipation of the human family from the biology of the Bible is the last stage of Prometheanism. The death of the father waits in the psyche and in language for the death of the mother achieved in the biosciences.

To celebrate their future the new foundlings must attend the spectacle of the past's reanimation—the new Easter of the dino-egg fertilized by the marriage of science and commerce. *JP* is the Bethlehem of bioscientism and a renewed biorevolution.[15] Here all children are summoned to witness the rebirth of the struggle for life and the survival of the computerized fit. Here is proclaimed the end of mammalian humanity powerless against brutes and terrified into divinity. The good news of geneticism is that only the computerized intelligence capable of practicing DNA eugenics upon itself can master the biblical chaos.

The potential infertility of Ellie and Alan's relationship is doubly increased by the contemporary loss of family authority and by the substitute authority of the procreativity of the biosciences. Here the death wish of the American family is fed by the life wish of the sciences that promise to underwrite individualism and consumerism. In a future where science can make babies, we shall no longer need to subordinate enjoying ourselves to (re)producing ourselves. Here the only risk to consumer sovereignty is the usual one of the restriction of brands/clones in favor of efficiency and profitability—in short, the risk that our own person may not sell well and be removed from the DNA strip. However, the positive fancy in bio-shopping should also be addressed if we are to understand the perennial attraction of the amusement park as a Garden of Eden in which we get to make all the animals—even if they and ourselves are only toy animals. In short, there is in the *JP* story an infantile fantasy of bypassing the primal scene of reproduction through a combination of lab, computer, and art skills that the superkid can master, renewing human history as a game run by and for children.

In *JP* the primal scene is transposed to the scene of primeval birth—the splitting of dino-egg witnessed by the paleo-family, Ellie, Alan, Lexis, and Tim. Here the children are attendants to a wildlife birth that is entirely induced by the unnatural history of *JP* geneticism and its crazy scheme of superovulation. Worse still, the embryo is confused with an egg to be found in the supermarket or at Toys R USA. More like a gumball than an egg, dinovum is, however, the perfectly atomic origin of the individual conceived without social relations. Thus the extrafamilial egg fulfills the phantasy of an aboriginal choice of life. The price of the choice is the interchangeability of the raw material of humanity, bringing DNA into the same market where human labor stills struggles with the gap between the sovereignty of consumption and the servitude of production. Here history repeats itself. Just as labor was discovered to be "inefficient" (it built the Cathedral of Chartres, the Taj Mahal, and the Stradivarius, as well as the great roads, bridges, and ships of the world), so human sexuality is now discovered to lack quality control and even to be fraught with sterility. Thus the unconscious fear of loss of control drives the expansion of control into our very DNA. The birth of biotechnology promises a second genesis to which we will owe the re-creation of ourselves and our food chain—all in the name of better living. It is therefore imperative to maximize the spectacle of *in vitro* fertilization, surrogate pregnancy, and transplantation, as well as the new animal and plant genetics that will complete the industrialization of nature through the capture of its information codes. No one notices that soon as many people will be required to launch a baby as are now required to launch a satellite!

Yet beneath the fantasy of the new geneticism, we may sense old-order questions. Who am I? Why am I? What am I to do? My parents are not my parents—they are DNA shoppers; my mother was not my mother—her mother was to help her out; my sex is not my sex—it is the sex picked for those who bought me. I am the child of the end of the family. Henceforth I shall be ruled by conjugal convenience rather than the family romance. Henceforth I shall not need to think myself but rather to keep up with the fashions in the biomarket, in the market schools, and in the marketplace.[16] Henceforth I am both the omnipotent child and the impotent child. The genetic primal scene requires no self-discovery beyond a bare look into the microscope. No life stories emerge beyond the history of one's biorepairs. The end of childhood.

Here, then, we have a marvelous superimposition of nature and culture in which everything that is monstrous in the contemporary history of the family is projected through film, reducing prime time to primal time—despite Gould's distaste for such unnatural arguments. We currently celebrate the death of *Deosaurus* in the hope that it may be reversed through the birth of Dino-saurus conceived by computerized eggheads with commerce and amusement for a dream-start to an infinity of profit. Suffer little children, then, to enter the kingdom of consumerism, where adults are less wise than their own children and deserve to die from the virus of obsolescence they have unleashed upon everything that money can buy. If obsolescence kills future time in order to bring childhood closer to adulthood, the paleo-renaissance kills past time in order to bring adulthood even closer to childhood. This double strategy of time collapse and the consequent erasure of intergenerationality is necessary in order to subject history to empty time and thereby to reduce the history of mind to the instant recovery of factoids. For this temporal strategy to succeed, it is also necessary that the content of human history be reduced to its simulacra so that the events of history are entirely consumed by their replay. This in turn permits the complete externalization of culture and history, so that our experience can be set forward and backward at will.

The new geneticism completes the end of patriarchy. Sperm banking and quality control will dominate sperm production, rendering obsolete the current ideologies of dephallicization and feminism because they have no control over the biomaterial selection of life. The advent of the biogenetic identity card, however, raises once again the question of the relations between power and desire. Once desire is merely the exhausted image of an obsolete species, power solidifies without fear that we shall refuse to imprint upon it. Love finally becomes an illness without any trace of divinity, knowledge is severed from information, and memory is exhausted by retrieval systems. No law opposes this because there is no longer any subject of knowledge, no longer any subject of desire, no transgression. The law will have been entirely absorbed by the ownership of the means of communication. It cannot be opposed by its clones because each is the same and each incapable of forming relations of opposition.

Mything in Jurassic Park

However unfortunate the biblical creation may have been, it has left us with the project of wanting offspring without either labor pains or the painful labor that is the price of the civility that clothes our original shame. To switch from the first creation story to the second creation story, however, we have not only to drop God the Father—a currently unfashionable self-image, in any case—but we have also to drop even the modified heterosexuality practiced by the Holy Family. The current exhaustion of the family does not lie in its present practices so much as in the expectation of its future members that they may be able to take out *in vitro* contracts on themselves, thereby bypassing the punishments of the biblical family. While they wait for their own second coming in the laboratory of the future, their old-order sexuality, which had toyed with old-order promiscuity-cum-contraception, now migrates into video and telephone sex on credit. Thus pornography simulates sex that is everywhere and nowhere, promising to revive marriages without reinventing the family.

The limit of the biosciences is not provided by our humanism because our humanism, when combined with our science, has no limits. Of course, there is still a gap between the capacity of our contemporary science and biotechnology to realize our ultimate self-conquest, for we mean to undo the creation myth and remake it in the image of ourselves making ourselves. This is the second-generation Prometheanism underlying all robotic culture and the ultimate aim of our bioculture. But the paradox of a wholly scientific creation is that it re-creates a myth of parthogenesis as the counterpart to a degendered science whether promoted by old-order males or new-order females. The parthogenetic myth in turn has origins in Aristotelian embryology, which also plays a part in monster theory.[17]

According to Aristotle, and later Freud, children should be *like* their fathers—that is, creative. But they cannot *be* their fathers because their fathers are not procreative. So children must also be like their mothers, that is, little monsters, reminders of sexual difference and aberrant nature. Just as females deviate from the male form, so human and animal form may also degenerate into forms that resemble but significantly differ from the species norm. The source of such monstrous deviations was also believed to lie in the maternal imagination—as the phantasy of bypassing paternity through parthogenesis. Thus the struggle over resemblance results in the male counterstrategy of cloning, which decides the issue of generation once and for all as a work of male imagination. The true child is a work of science fiction, which as such directly fascinates every child with the dream of its own birth. The struggle over generation, however, renders the family the ultimate monster, because without scientific control it continues to produce offspring that do not resemble their parents. But the society that controls birth must produce families that resemble one another—otherwise the reduction of law to science remains incomplete. This is the ultimate goal of biopolitics. Meantime, the transition to the biostate is eased through the sacrifice of body parts yielded by children and youth to compensate for the imperfections of our biotechnology until such time as it no longer requires to be fed by desire and transgression, for once we can make children, we should be able to make them trouble-free to themselves as well as to ourselves.

The technosaurs in *JP* are really a combination of alchemy, art, science, and humanism rather than the wild miscreants of a godless science. In any case, *JP* is no better as work of fiction than its monsters, given that its ambition is to breed itself in thousands of commercial fetishes spun off from the film-of-the-book-of-the-film. *JP* is a work of postmodern alchemy, that is, a blend of science-fiction-commerce that refuses to be grounded anywhere else than at the box office. Of course, *JP* spawns interpretation—even on the part of its creator, Spielberg, who considered it unfit for his own children while cashing in on every other family's lack of such censorial authority. Evidently, *JP* was more scary to make than it is to see—just as it is more boring to watch than to interpret. What makes *JP* boring is that it is not constructed around any romantic conflict between art and science—despite its superficial spiel on the inability of technology to dominate nature completely. There is no nature in *JP*—any more than there is any science, philosophy, or poetry. *JP* is a theme park from which nature has been totally erased through the commercial colonization of an island for an adventure in risk capitalism. The only nature in *JP* is human nature—lifted in by helicopter, bringing with it the viruses of commerce, law, greed, power, and self-deception, which flourish under the culture of Yankee imperialism so long as it does not lose its nerve.

The rise and fall of imperial greed is a cycle wholly internal to human history—and does not represent any ability of Nature to reject Culture, returning us from time to time to sanity. Yankee culture knows no bounds to its pragmatism, and its pragmatism encounters no moral limit other than its own failure of nerve. Our culture does not let Nature speak to us—any more than it allows our science to correct our humanism or our humanism to delimit our science. In short, the biototalitarianism of the new science totters upon the sublime of our disappearance as a species in favor of a program or chip whose animation ends in our death.

In *JP* the drama of nature's silence unfolds around an egg—the last universe to be conquered by science and commerce, which are in turn the inseparable counterparts of the struggle between good and evil. Nevertheless, this eggo-maniacal project involves a family history inasmuch as the dead family of Lexis and Tim also needs a restart through its visit to Jurassic Park.

A creation myth is either individual, like Pygmalion, or collective, like that in the Bible.[18] Of the two, the individual myth is the most monstrous, because it denies its origin in the collective myth. *JP* is on the whole a biblical myth, whatever the aspirations of Crichton and Spielberg. In the first place, *JP* aims to produce order—Jurassic Park—where before there was chaos—the end of the age of dinosaurs. Second, *JP* is the story of a willful (re)creation out of nothing (eggs frozen in time). Third, it involves a reproductive act with global significance for the Age of Abortion. Fourth, the first asexual creation story is embedded in a second sexual creation story involving the struggle between good and evil. Finally, the story relegitimates the original economy of divine, human, and animal relations.

In *Jurassic Park* we encounter the mythic interface between the history of the family and the familization of history that accounts for the unaccountable box-office success of *JP*—given that it is otherwise a monster made from a not very popular book and a not very scary movie whose by-products are not very exciting fetishes. To get beyond this, we have to fashion an unconscious for Spielberg that he (and certainly Crichton) may not deserve—who knows? So what fixates us in *JP*? It is the eye of the dinosaur—which looks into us, looking at it with its teeth. In these "terrifying" moments the audience's desire for incorporation by the monster shifts from the collective scene to the other scene (*die andere Schauplatz*) of individual incorporation—the desire to be eaten by the mother/father body. In *JP* the dino-eye triangulates the unwilling father, the desiring mother, and the terrible-terrified children—turning the elders into children and the children into elders, collapsing the generations, turning life into death and death into life. The eye of the dinosaur is the eye of the awful child who needs to be conceived in the unconscious desire of its parents killing their love, tearing them apart. The fear of the family is its founding romance: Spielberg rightly protects his children from his incestuous creation.

Notes

1. Arthur Asa Berger, "Of Mice and Men: An Introduction to Mouseology or, Anal Eroticisms and Disney," *Journal of Homosexuality* 21 (1991): 155–65.

2. Throughout this essay, the *Jurassic Park* or *JP* to which I refer is a composite entity constructed from the novel by Michael Crichton, *Jurassic Park* (New York: Ballantine, 1990); *Jurassic Park: The Junior Novelisation*, adapted by Gail Herman from a screenplay by Michael Crichton and David Koepp, based on the novel by Michael Crichton (London: Red Fox, 1993); and the 1993 Spielberg film *Jurassic Park*, the events of which are closer to the junior novel than to the original text—a difference that does not matter.

3. Clifford D. Shearing and Phillip C. Stenning, "From the Panopticon to Disney World: The Development of Discipline," in *Perspectives in Criminal Law*, ed. Anthony N. Doob and Edward L. Greenspan (Toronto: Canada Law Book, 1984), 335–49.

4. John O'Neill, *Plato's Cave: Desire, Power and the Specular Functions of the Media* (Norwood, N.J.: Ablex, 1991).

5. Louis Marin, "Utopic Degeneration: Disneyland," in *Utopics: The Semiological Play of Textual Spaces* (Atlantic Highlands, N.J.: Humanities Press, 1990), 239–58.

6. Crichton, *Jurassic Park*, 199.

7. John O'Neill, "*McTopia*: Eating Time," in *Utopias and the Millennium*, ed. Krishan Kumar and Stephen Bann (London: Reaktion, 1993).

8. Stephen Jay Gould, "Dinomania," *New York Review of Books*, August 12, 1993, 51–56.

9. Ibid., 51.

10. Ibid., 54.

11. *Globe and Mail*, October 6, 1993.

12. Herman, *Jurassic Park*, 4–6.

13. Ibid., 87.

14. Claudia Barreto et al., "Evidence of the Growth Plate and the Growth of Long Bones in Juvenile Dinosaurs," *Science* 262 (December 24, 1993): 2020–23.

15. John O'Neill, *Five Bodies: The Human Shape of Modern Society* (Ithaca, N.Y.: Cornell University Press, 1985).

16. John O'Neill, *The Missing Child in Liberal Theory* (Toronto: University of Toronto Press, 1994).

17. Marie-Hélène Huet, "Monstrous Imagination: Progeny as Art in French Classicism," *Critical Inquiry* 17 (Summer 1991): 718–37.

18. Jean-Jacques Lecercle, *Frankenstein: Mythe et philosophie* (Paris: Presses Universitaires de France, 1988).

Contributors

Mary Baine Campbell is associate professor of English at Brandeis University. She is the author of *The Witness and the Other World: Exotic European Travel Writing, 400–1600* (1988) and a collection of poems, *The World, the Flesh, and Angels* (1989). She is currently finishing another collection of poems, as well as a book on related developments in prose fiction, science, and an emerging anthropology in early modern Europe.

David L. Clark teaches in the Department of English at McMaster University, where he is also codirector of Plurality and Altérité: Discourses and Practices, an interdisciplinary research group. He is coeditor of and contributor to two volumes: *Intersections: Nineteenth-Century Philosophy and Contemporary Theory* and *New Romanticisms: Theory and Critical Practice.* He has also contributed essays to numerous other volumes. He has guest edited two issues of *Recherches sémiotiques/Semiotic Inquiry*: "Language, History, and the Romance of Fact" and (with Caroline Bayard) "Reading Baudrillard Now."

Jeffrey Jerome Cohen is assistant professor of English and associate director of the Program in Human Sciences at George Washington University. He has published articles on gender theory and the cultural construction of monstrousness. His project in progress is titled *Sex, Monsters, and the Middle Ages.*

Frank Grady is assistant professor of English at the University of Missouri-St. Louis, where he teaches, among other things, Old and Middle English literature. He has published essays on Langland, Gower, Chaucer, and *The Travels of Sir John Mandeville.*

David A. Hedrich Hirsch is assistant professor of English at the University of Illinois, Urbana-Champaign. His essay in this volume is part of a work in progress that interrogates the tensions between social fraternity and bourgeois family values in nineteenth- and twentieth-century literature and politics.

Lawrence D. Kritzman is the Ted and Helen Geisel Third Century Professor of the Humanities and professor of French and comparative literature at Dartmouth. His most recent books are *The Rhetoric of Sexuality and the Literature of the French Renaissance* and *Auschwitz and After: Race, Culture and the Jewish Question in France.* He is completing books on politics and French intellectuals and on history and memory.

Kathleen Perry Long teaches French in the Department of Romance Studies at Cornell University. She has published articles on baroque poetry and a book on metamorphosis in Renaissance lyric; she is currently preparing an edition of Thomas Artus's novel *L'Isle des hermaphrodites, nouvellement descouverte,* as well as a book-length study of hermaphrodites as cultural icon in the late sixteenth century.

Stephen Pender is a graduate student at the University of Toronto.

Allison Pingree is preceptor of expository writing at Harvard University. Her research focuses on constructions of personal identity in American literature and culture. She is completing a manuscript on "figures of replication": characters, gestures, images, and language in late-nineteenth- and early-twentieth-century American fiction that critique dominant cultural values not through direct opposition, but through extreme embodiments or literalizations of those values. Her essay on another pair of conjoined twins, "The 'Exception That Proves the Rule': Daisy and Violet Hilton, the 'New Woman' and the Bonds of Marriage," appears in *Freakery: Cultural Spectacles of the Extraordinary Body.*

Anne Lake Prescott teaches in the Department of English at Barnard College, Columbia University.

John O'Neill is distinguished research professor of sociology at York University, Toronto, and a fellow of the Royal Society of Canada. He is the author of *Five Bodies*, *The Communicative Body*, *Critical Conventions*, and *The Poverty of Postmodernism*.

William Sayers completed graduate studies at the University of Toronto and the University of California, Berkeley, and has taught there as well as at Princeton University and other universities in Canada and the United States. His research interests include Old Norse-Icelandic, Irish, and Anglo-Norman languages and literatures, and intercultural contacts in the North Sea area.

Michael Uebel teaches in the Department of English at the University of Virginia. He is currently at work on a study of conceptions of otherness in early medieval utopic narrative. He is the coeditor of a volume of essays titled *Race and the Subject of Masculinities* and is currently editing, with D. Vance Smith, a collection of essays on medieval culture and forms of exchange.

Ruth Waterhouse gained her B.A. and M.A. degrees at the University of New England, and her Ph.D. at Macquarie University. She has taught an eclectic range of subjects, including Old English and literary discourse and children's literature. She has been involved in undergraduate courses, honors courses, and postgraduate courses. She has now retired.

Index